PROJECTIVE ECOLOGIES

Chris Reed & Nina-Marie Lister

**Harvard University
Graduate School of Design**

www.gsd.harvard.edu

www.actar.com

for Edan, Etta, J. Lukas, Jasper, Noah, Rhys, and Silas

Contents

Ecologies, Plural and Projective

Charles Waldheim

The *Projective Ecologies* project, as proposed by Chris Reed and Nina-Marie Lister in this publication, is the culmination of a multi-year research initiative at the Harvard Graduate School of Design and the GSD's Department of Landscape Architecture that aspires to articulate the contemporary role and status of ecology across the design and planning disciplines. Building on the *Ecological Urbanism* initiative at the School, *Projective Ecologies* asks timely questions regarding the deployment of "ecological" as an adjectival modifier to urbanism. While these inquiries are relevant for the range of disciplines represented at the GSD, they are particularly pressing for landscape architecture. In the discourse around landscape urbanism and ecological urbanism, critical questions persist as to the role of ecology in relation to design. Which ecologies are invoked in those formulations, by whom, and toward what ends? *Projective Ecologies* addresses these varied readings and describes the plural and projective potentials of the biological model for contemporary design culture.

In his essay in this volume, Christopher Hight claims that ecology is among the most important epistemological frameworks of our age. Hight's assertion is based on the fact that ecology has transcended its origins as a natural science to encompass a diverse range of meanings across the natural and social sciences, history and the humanities, design and the arts. From its origins as a proto-disciplinary branch of biology in the nineteenth century, ecology developed into a modern science in the twentieth century and increasingly toward a multidisciplinary intellectual framework in the first decades of the twenty-first century. This disciplinary promiscuity is not without its problems, intellectually and practically. The slippage of ecology from natural science to cultural lens remains the source of quite a bit of confusion and limits communication within and across the disciplines of landscape architecture, urban design, and planning. *Projective Ecologies* sheds significant light on those diverse disciplinary valences and mobilizes the production of knowledge and projection of space through various ecological understandings.

The publication does so in three ways. First, the essays and projects collected here begin by unapologetically defining ecologies in the plural. Second, the publication advocates for the projective potentials of the ecological framework by illustrating fluency across a spectrum of disciplinary formulations. Finally, the projects, drawings, and diagrams included here articulate a robust representational paradigm for the ecological in contemporary design culture.

Following Henri Lefebvre, we can postulate that the effects of urbanization are effectively planetary in scope. If so, what are the implications for thinking about the relation between ecology and urbanization? The theoretical frameworks, analytical tools, and projective practices of the urban arts have been developed on a presupposed distinction between the urban and the ecological. For much of their history, each of these terms has been conceived in opposition to the other. The origins of urbanism in architectural culture and a preoccupation with the architectonic form of the city have contributed to this collective blind spot. The classical definition of ecology as the description of species in relation to their environments, absent human agency, is equally problematic. Taken together, the cumulative effect of describing ecology as outside the city, and the urban as external to ecology, continues to have a profound impact on our thinking across the urban arts. *Projective Ecologies* questions those old oppositions in favor of multiple readings of ecology understood simultaneously as model, metaphor, and medium.

The *Projective Ecologies* initiative begins with the enduring understanding of ecology as offering a model of the natural world. This most fundamental definition is evident in the work of Richard Forman, Eugene Odum, and others referenced in this volume. Reed and Lister invoke a point of tangency between the production of scientific models (through testing and falsification) and the symmetrical activity of design (through model making and matching). While the historical chasm between the habits of mind and methods in the sciences and design persists, *Projective Ecologies* articulates a plausible relation between ecology as a model of the world and the agency of design in the shaping of that world. In addition to its status as model, ecology has come to be an equally effective metaphor for a range of intellectual and disciplinary pursuits. References in this volume to the work of Gregory Bateson, Giorgio Agamben, and Félix Guattari, to name but a few, illustrate the fecundity of ecological thinking. This metaphorical understanding of ecology has been particularly significant for its subsequent absorption into the discourse around design. While landscape architecture and urban planning have historically tended to view ecology as a kind of applied natural science, architecture and the arts have received ecology as a metaphor imported from the social sciences, the humanities, and philosophy. The *Projective Ecologies* project aspires to articulate and integrate those diverse disciplinary antecedents within the discourses of design. It does so by invoking a third reading of ecology as medium. *Projective Ecologies* proposes a synthetic understanding of ecology as a medium of thought, exchange, and representation. Reed and Lister invite readers to embrace the breadth of that medium and to project an equally broad range of alternative and better futures through design.

PROJECTIVE
ECOLOGIES

Chris Reed & Nina-Marie Lister

"Oekologie is the comprehensive science of the relationship of the organism to the environment."
Ernst Haeckel, *Generelle Morphologie der Organismen* (1866)

"We are not outside the ecology for which we plan—we are always and inevitably a part of it. Herein lies the charm and terror of ecology."
Gregory Bateson, *Steps to an Ecology of Mind* (1972)

"Ecology must stop being associated with the image of a small nature-loving minority or with qualified specialists. Ecology in my sense questions the whole of subjectivity."
Félix Guattari, *The Three Ecologies* (1989)

Ecological Thinking, Design Practices

Chris Reed and Nina-Marie Lister

The past two decades have witnessed a resurgence of ecological ideas and ecological thinking in discussions of urbanism, society, culture, and design. In science, the field of ecology has moved from classical determinism and a reductionist Newtonian concern with stability, certainty, and order in favor of more contemporary understandings of dynamic systemic change and the related phenomena of adaptability, resilience, and flexibility. Increasingly these concepts of ecological thought are found useful as heuristics for decision-making generally and as models or metaphors for cultural production broadly, and for the design arts in particular. This places landscape architecture in a unique disciplinary and practical space, equally informed by ecological knowledge as an applied science, as a construct for managing change, and, within the context of sustainability—as a conceptual model of cultural production or design.

But ecology is not simply a project of the natural sciences. Many researchers, theorists, and social commentators have used ecology as an overarching idea or metaphor for a set of conditions and relationships with political, economic, and social implications—or even redefined the term "ecology" to include these realms as broader context. Félix Guattari, writing in *The Three Ecologies,* for instance, argued that ecology is as much bound up in issues of social and economic power, demographics, and political struggles and engagement as it is operating in relationship to environmental forces. Reyner Banham, in a new architectural and urban history text for Los Angeles in 1971, outlined a combination of "geography, climate, economics, demography, mechanics, and culture"—made evident only via movement on the city's characteristic roads and freeways—that constitutes four organizational "ecologies" for metropolitan Los Angeles (Surfurbia, The Foothills, The Plains of Id, and Autopia).[1] Kazys Varnelis referred to the "networked ecologies" of Los Angeles as "a series of codependent systems of environmental mitigation, land-use organization, communication, and service delivery."[2] Ecologists themselves have for some time now addressed the implications of an emerging scientific discourse: Canadian ecologist C.S. Holling, writing about new ecological research and models in 1970, spoke as much of the planning and management implications of this new line of thinking as he did about the science behind it, while Eugene Odum drew direct connections to energy and economics in his 1977 paper "The Emergence of Ecology as a New Integrative Discipline."

These expanded ideas and definitions of ecology are the starting point for this book. *Projective Ecologies* takes stock of the diversity of contemporary ecological research and theory—embracing Guattari's broader definition of ecology as at once environmental, social, and existential—and speculates on potential paths forward for design practices. Where are ecological thinking and theory now? What do current trajectories of research suggest for future practice? How can advances in ecological research and modeling, social theory, and digital visualization inform, with greater rigor, more robust design thinking and practice?

Here the modifier *projective* is both important and suggestive: with it, we recognize the constructed nature of ecologists' models for the physical and dynamic aspects of the natural world, as well as the limits of science in separating the observer from phenomena observed. Steward Pickett commented at the Critical Ecologies symposium (organized by Chris Reed at the Harvard Graduate School of Design in Spring 2010) that, in fact, all that ecologists have to work with are their conceptual models of ecosystems, as only rarely can they test ideas on and in the ecosystem itself. The term *projective* thus embraces the creative and speculative ambitions of representation—the drawings and often heuristic models that scientists, designers, and others use to help demonstrate and explain ideas. In many cases, it is through this work of modeling, whether writing or drawing, that ecological ideas have continued to emerge and are clarified.[3]

Projective Ecologies, then, is an explicit recognition of a plurality of ecological theories and applied research underpinning contemporary understandings of cultural and natural living systems. It spans a broad spectrum from philosophy and the humanities to the social and biological sciences. Landscape ecology, human ecology, urban ecology, applied ecology, evolutionary ecology, restoration ecology, deep ecology, the ecology of place, and the unified theory of ecology (also called neutral theory of ecology) are but a few of the specialized areas of ecologically oriented research that have emerged over the past decades and continue to inform our thinking about the various interrelationships between plants, animals, and the physical, biological, cultural, and experiential world in which we live. In this regard, this collective body of work is a recognition of a growing alignment between these ideas and contemporary theories about the complex, unpredictable, and emergent nature of the world—a world increasingly recognized as a hybrid of culture *and* nature, where old dualisms are being supplanted by transdisciplinary thinking, uneasy synergies, complex networks, and surprising collaborations.

This alignment is manifest in a range of scientific inquiries about human adaptation and evolution. It is demonstrated in the work of notable evolutionary biologists and ecologists such as Lynn Margulis, E.O. Wilson, and Niles Eldredge, and social and physical anthropologists such as Jane Goodall, Margaret Mead, and Richard Wrangham; in the characteristics of emergence documented through the mid-to-late twentieth century by systems theorists Ludwig von Bertalanffy, Arthur Koestler, Buckminster Fuller, Gregory Bateson, Stafford Beer, Stuart Kauffman, Russell Ackoff, and Donella Meadows; in the breakthrough work of physicists Ilya Prigogine and Murray Gell-Mann; in the popular science writing of Steven Johnson, Robert Lewin, Daniel Botkin, and Fritjof Capra; in the behavior of dynamic networks as in the work of Albert-László Barabási and Kathleen Carley; and finally, in investigations of complex adaptive systems—among and between a broad range of disciplines.

The translation of these ideas into practice, while still nascent, has been similarly widespread across the disciplines. Evidence of the growing acceptance of a complex, adaptive systems paradigm can be seen in business (from management theory to social entrepreneurialism and network organization), education (collective learning), engineering (from systems design to asynchronous computing applications), and cultural production (digital media design, etc.). In addition, a growing number of transdisciplinary think tanks and institutes are dedicated to the study of complex systems, emergence, and uncertainty, including notable organizations such as the Santa Fe Institute for the study of complexity, Harvard's Wyss Institute for Biologically Inspired Engineering, the Sustainability Institute, and the Center for Complex Network Research in the United States; and the International Institute for Applied Systems Analysis in Austria, and the Max Planck Institute for Dynamics of Complex Technical Systems in Germany.

These institutes and the inquiries and speculations they foster point toward an enrichment of ecological thinking in the last part of the twentieth century and into the twenty-first. The result is a collective representation of the different but parallel modes of research and vehicles for communication that are pushing these ideas forward. In this frame, then, the project of revolutionizing critical thinking in ecological research and design practices can be understood to be as much a project of the humanities and social sciences as it is one of the natural sciences, and as much an instigation of new theory as it is of new applications and practices. New transdisciplinary theories such as post-normal science (e.g., Funtowicz and Ravetz 1994), the unified theory of ecology (e.g., Hubbell 2001) and learning organizational theory (e.g., Senge 1990, 2000) are evidence of the move past discipline-centered reductionism and toward integrative theories that operationalize synergistic modes of thinking and practice.

In carrying forward this discourse, *Projective Ecologies* is a collection of original essays and selected reprints of pivotal works by a range of both prominent and emerging voices from a number of ecologically related disciplines, including ecological sciences, governance, art and design theory, architecture, and landscape architecture. Collectively, the texts present advances in parallel fields that have integrated and advanced research on complex adaptive systems and the consequent implications for the applied design arts. They also capture new thinking about design and the informants to design in an era that has, to a large extent, accepted the ideas of complexity and adaptability and integrated these into its attendant practices. The essays are accompanied by a series of archival, prototypical, and contemporary images and drawings that have been specifically curated to explore the implications of ecological models for design. These are arranged in broad categories that both reflect and reinterpret central ideas within complex adaptive systems theory. But we are as interested in the various reverberative effects—the unforeseen associations, the surprising synergies and speculations—that the multi-scalar combinations of the pull-out drawings (and their loose relationships to the essays) may prompt as we are in the underlying structures we use to organize them.

The first few essays lay the critical foundations for the book. Our own essay outlines three "Parallel Genealogies" that inform this work, though the lenses of the natural sciences, humanities, and design arts. James Corner's 1997 "Ecology and Landscape as Agents of Creativity" is a seminal piece that persuasively connects emerging theories and explicitly argues for broader creative and imaginative agendas embedded in ideas of nature, ecology, and landscape. Christopher Hight then theorizes this work in his essay "Designing Ecologies," tying the *Projective Ecologies* work to the Landscape Urbanism movement and to the broader project of landscape that reemerged in the late twentieth century in design. Reprints of C.S. Holling and M.A. Goldberg's "Ecology and Planning" from 1971 and of selections from Wenche E. Dramstad, James D. Olson, and Richard T.T. Forman's 1996 *Landscape Ecology Principles in Landscape Architecture and Land-Use Planning* provide historical context and remind us that ecologists have been exploring the implications of complex adaptive system theory on the planning and design fields for several decades. While the latter book may be well known by designers (having been cited by Stan Allen in his 1999 work *Points + Lines: Diagrams and Projects for the City*), the former text is less familiar in this context and only recently started to serve as a touchstone in theory courses.

The next three essays explore contemporary understandings of nature and environment and the hybridity that is now routinely used to describe our intertwined condition. Selections from Daniel Botkin's seminal work *Discordant Harmonies* speak to the ways in which humans can no longer distance themselves from the environment—that we all interact in a biosphere that pulses and changes through the multiple effects of human and non-human actions and events. This 1990 publication was critical in tracing evolving views and understandings of nature and—more important—bringing them to a popular audience. Erle Ellis's essay, "A Taxonomy of the Human Biosphere," rewrites the classic world maps of ecotones to include new categorizations that recognize the profound influence of humans on the natural world (through agriculture, resource extraction, urbanization, etc.). Jane Wolff's contribution, "Cultural Landscapes and Dynamic Ecologies: Lessons from New Orleans," extends her interest in making legible the lives of cities that lie at the intersections of a powerful fluvial environment and human intention.

The following three essays tie complex adaptive ecologies directly to the project of design and the city. Robert E. Cook's essay "Do Landscapes Learn? Ecology's 'New Paradigm' and Design in Landscape Architecture" from 1999 is a reprint of a lecture he delivered to numerous design schools in the late 1990s, essentially outlining the possibilities of using the new model of ecology as both mechanism and metaphor for design practices in landscape architecture. Peter Del Tredici's text, "The Flora of the Future," frames a new way of thinking about the unique ecological communities that have established themselves in cities and their natural habitat remnants—non-native communities that are nevertheless very much adapted to the new circumstances and conditions of these urbanized (and urbanizing) places. David Fletcher's reprinted essay from 2008, "Flood Control Freakologies," describes the freakish ecologies that have emerged in the accidental overlap of urban and infrastructure systems in the channel of the Los Angeles River—conditions that marry the highly altered and engineered circumstance of the river with nascent environmental and social ecologies, which, when considered together, offer new ways of thinking about the designed and engineered city.

Finally, the last three essays point forward, offering departure points as the project of complex adaptive systems and design is updated, reformulated, superseded. Frances Westley and Katharine McGowan provide insights from the social sciences on the ways in which "messiness"—nonlinear, experimental, and sometimes chaotic processes of iteration, discovery, and feedback—can advance problem-solving and collaborative initiatives in multiple realms, including governance, business, and design. Sean Lally's essay on energy identifies new territory for exploration in which the performative aspects of design are pushed to modulate microclimates and energy flows and thereby create new logics for design—as well as new vocabularies about atmospheres, gradients, intensities, and washes that can supplant ecologically derived categories of thinking. Sanford Kwinter speculates further, broadening the context for our expanded understandings of ecology to plumb the anthropologic realms. With reference to theories developed by Jakob von Uexküll and Richard Wrangham, Kwinter opens up new worlds for discovery and testing that include human physiology, human and animal ethology, and social-environmental relations.

But these are mere beginnings. The bigger project initiated by this volume is to better and more critically understand both the *context for* and *implications of* the various relationships that have developed between ecological and design thinking. In this way, *Projective Ecologies* casts a critical eye on the history of ecological design thinking and practice while looking ahead to speculate on new opportunities for design. Indeed, the long-term goal is inspire our readers—designers, ecologists, and others—to turn the page and move forward: to present new frameworks for thinking, new synergies and cross-fertilizations among disciplines, and new ways of designing within a dynamic living world.

Notes

1_ Reyner Banham, *Los Angeles: The Architecture of Four Ecologies* (Berkeley, CA: University of California Press, 2001).

2_ Kazys Varnelis, *The Infrastructural City: Networked Ecologies in Los Angeles* (Barcelona, New York: Actar and Columbia University Graduate School of Architecture, Planning, and Preservation, 2008), 15.

3_ James Corner has long made the argument that drawing and representation are as much constructive and projective acts as they are indicative of an idea already formed. See especially "Eidetic Operations and New Landscapes" in James Corner, ed., *Recovering Landscape: Essays in Contemporary Landscape Architecture* (New York: Princeton Architectural Press, 1999).

Parallel Genealogies

Chris Reed and Nina-Marie Lister

The processes of which ecology and creativity speak are fundamental to the work of landscape architecture. Whether biological or imaginative, evolutionary or metaphorical, such processes are active, dynamic, and complex, each tending toward the increased differentiation, freedom, and richness of a diversely interacting whole. There is no end, no grand scheme for these agents of change, just a cumulative directionality toward further becoming. It is in this productive and active sense that ecology and creativity speak not of fixed and rigid realities but of movement, passage, genesis, and autonomy, of *propulsive life unfolding in time.*
James Corner, "Ecology and Landscape as Agents of Creativity" (1997) [1]

Ecology is, by definition, a transdisciplinary science focused on the relationship between living organisms and their environments. A relatively new science, its modern roots emerged in the early twentieth century with the work of Frederic Clements and Henry Gleason, American botanists who studied the interactions between plant communities, and Sir Arthur Tansley, a British botanist and zoologist whose research on the interactions between plant and animal communities and the environment led him to coin the term "ecosystem" in 1935.[2] The interdisciplinary work of these pioneers prompted the development of models of ecological succession that dominated plant biology during the early twentieth century and became the basis for the new integrated science of plants, animals, and the environment eventually known as ecosystem ecology.

    The implications of this developing work were not limited to the natural sciences; in fact, popularization of these emerging world views was manifest in more widely read writings in the humanities and reverberated in other fields as well, including large-scale project management, governance, and planning. Complex adaptive systems thinking made its way into the design arts as landscape was being rediscovered as both model and medium for design, and the environmental movement was becoming mainstream.

    Today "ecology" has been co-opted to refer to almost any set of generalized ideas about environment or process, rendering the term essentially meaningless. To recover a critical sense of ecology as a specific set of ideas—at once environmental, social, and mental (as Félix Guattari would argue)—that can continue to inform design thinking and practice, we start by identifying three important and parallel genealogies of ecology over the past three decades: in the natural sciences, the humanities, and design.

As a young science, and one focused on various aspects of living systems at different scales, modern ecology has been characterized by a schism between divergent approaches adopted by two major subfields. While ecosystem ecology began in earnest in the last three decades to include a complex systems perspective, population ecology remained largely fixed in a conventional scientific approach using reductionist modes of inquiry and experimentation as developed throughout the last century.[3] Both subfields, however, share three main areas of investigation that are designed to answer questions of "what," "how," and "why": structural ecology (concerned with description, classification, and natural history), functional ecology, and evolutionary ecology.

The origins of ecosystem ecology are found in the mid-1950s with the work of brothers Eugene and Howard T. Odum, zoologists by training who published the first English-language textbook in ecology, *The Fundamentals of Ecology* (1953). Yet ecology was not considered a valid science until the late 1960s, concomitant with a rise in modern environmentalism brought on by growing public concerns over air and water pollution, population growth, resource depletion, and the health risks of persistent chemicals brought to light by Rachel Carson in 1962 in her iconic work, *Silent Spring*. With the field's subsequent acceptance into the fold of mainstream science, the volume of published ecological research increased significantly, in large part due to the acceleration of applied field research made possible by dedicated funding for the study of environmental and resource management problems. Given that the majority of ecological research was established in an era of growing environmental concern and awareness, ecology has been closely linked to environmentalism—in both the media and by scientists themselves—and therefore to normative science akin to medicine, in that the work is goal-oriented toward some improvement in health or well-being.

With the dual rise of ecosystem ecology (concerned with large spatial and temporal scales, made possible by new observational technologies using remote sensing and geographic information systems to map and model complex data) and applied field ecology (oriented to solving urgent environmental problems, from biodiversity loss to resource depletion), there has been a steady paradigm

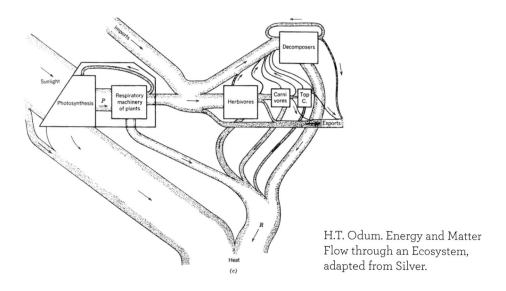

H.T. Odum. Energy and Matter Flow through an Ecosystem, adapted from Silver.

shift in ecology as a discipline over the last quarter century. As scientific re-search and published evidence on whole ecosystem function mounts, ecological thinking across the scales of inquiry and application has moved toward a more organic model of open-endedness, flexibility, resilience, and adaptation and away from a mechanistic model of stability and control. In other words, ecosystems are now understood to be open systems that behave in ways that are self-orga-nizing and that are to some extent unpredictable. In effect, change is built into living systems; they are characterized in part by uncertainty and dynamism.

Throughout most of the twentieth century, high-school biology courses were taught to the early models of (linear) ecological succession; that is, that ecosystems gradually and steadily succeed into stable climax states from which they don't routinely move unless disturbed by a force external to that system. An old-growth forest is one of the classic examples usually given, in which the forest matures and then remains in that state permanently, such that any disturbance is considered an aberration. Yet large-scale longitudinal research in ecosystem ecology has clearly shown that change is not only built into these systems but in some cases ecosystems are dependent on change for growth and renewal.[4] For example, fire-dependent forests contain tree species that require the extreme heat of fire to release and disperse seeds and facilitate forest renewal—and sometimes, a shift in the complement of species. All ecosystems are constantly evolving, often in ways that are discontinuous and uneven. While some ecosystem states are perceived by us to be stable, this is not strict stability in a mathematical sense; this is simply our human, time-limited perception of stasis. The work of Canadian ecologist C.S. "Buzz" Holling pioneered this concept in terms of resource management. He referred to ecosystems as "shifting steady-state mosaics," implying that stability is patchy and scale-dependent, and is neither a constant nor a phenomenon that defines a whole system at any one point in time or space.[5]

Much recent work in applied ecology has been about trying to understand those ecosystem states that we perceive as stable, and thereby useful to us, such that we want to encourage apparent stability. This perspective has profound implications from the humanities to management applications to design, as it rests on the recognition that humans are not outsiders to the ecosystem—rather, we are participants in its unfolding. This perspective also fundamentally challenges the Western Judeo-Christian ideology that humans are the dominant species and therefore have a responsibility (even a moral obligation) to manage or control other species and resources.

Of course humans are designers as well. We shape the ecosystems in which we live, sometimes profoundly and irrevocably. This reality means that there is a pressing need for a more sophisticated understanding, derived through empirical research, of the current state(s) in which an ecosystem appears to be stable. This knowledge is critical to our ability to manage resources sustainably, which means having sufficient knowledge about a given ecosystem so that it can be guided (using specific design or management interventions) back to some recognizable, desirable, and resilient state after a sudden or surprising change. Much of the applied ecological research into dynamic ecosystems has been focused on wilderness ecosystems and large natural landscapes being managed for resource extraction, such as boreal and temperate forest ecosystems, the tundra, and tropical rainforest ecosystems. The collapse of the Canadian cod fishery in the 1990s has also been studied in this context.[6]

Some of the classic examples of normal (yet often catastrophic) ecosystem change include forest fires, pest outbreaks, and significant storm events.

These events are taking on a new relevance today as the frequency and magnitude of storms has been observed to be increasing—a change attributed to climate disruption. When major storm events happen (particularly in densely populated or urbanizing regions), they can trigger a series of changes in species distribution, nutrient regimes, and resource availability, which can effectively push an ecosystem into a new state—one that might ultimately be inhospitable for certain species, populations, resources, or people. Given the uncertainty inherent to ecosystems in a complex systems paradigm, coupled with the uncertainty around climate disruption, it is likely necessary to change the way we design and manage interventions in our ecosystems. The challenge of the paradigm shift toward complex systems thinking is to realize that we cannot manage whole ecosystems; rather, we can manage *ourselves* and our activities.[7] This realization will have profound implications for the way we design.

The recognition that we ought to shift from managing ecosystems from a principally economic perspective to managing human actions *within* ecosystems is not new. Evidence of a concerted shift in management approaches began in the late 1980s, shortly after Yellowstone National Park was ravaged by a series of forest fires that could be neither controlled nor contained using conventional methods. At the time of the fires (which burned more than one-third of the park), the National Parks Service management approach still included a general fire suppression policy. Although park managers had begun to allow small controlled burns in some national parks since the 1970s, there was no widespread abandonment of fire suppression as an ecological management strategy until after the Yellowstone fires had threatened one of America's most iconic wilderness landscapes. Forest ecologists have argued that it was the legacy of this policy and a century of fire suppression in the parks that essentially created the ecological conditions that triggered the Yellowstone burns at an uncontrollable scale and intensity. Contemporary management practice is to allow smaller, natural fires to burn more frequently—and in some cases, to prescribe and set small-scale controlled burns, even in urban areas. For example, prescribed burns take place annually in the Oak Savannah of Toronto's High Park, a culturally and ecologically significant ecosystem. Whether wild or urban, certain ecosystems are now recognized as adapted to and dependent on fire to renew, evolve, and change.

An urban example of the paradigm shift in ecology and related management approaches and design interventions can be seen in how our response to floods has changed over the past quarter century, as specifically reflected in a gradual transition from flood *control* to flood *management*.

At least a decade before the devastation of Hurricane Katrina in 1995, ecologists and hydrologists were warning that the U.S. Army Corps of Engineers' approach to flood control was effectively pushing the lower Mississippi basin toward a catastrophic threshold for change and potential collapse. Through a long-term policy of flood suppression, diking and damming, coupled with the removal of coastal wetlands and intensive settlement of the floodplains, the natural flood-adaptation mechanisms of the basin were impaired. The devastation of the hurricane in 2005 was catastrophic indeed, not only for the resources and the economy of the region but for the lives of many of its most vulnerable citizens. This particularly poignant example makes clear that traditional top-down or command-and-control engineering strategies based on a reductionist approach to living systems do not work. There is a growing recognition that what is needed are more flexible, adaptive approaches to managing human activities and designing within the systems that sustain us—and this is the overarching implication of the paradigm shift in ecology that is upon us. What designers make of this implication has much to do with how change and dynamism are understood and interpreted in the humanities and within cultural production.

Humanities

While scientists were making their preliminary findings known through scientific journals and other discipline-specific media, a number of researchers in the humanities set themselves to exploring what might be the social and cultural implications of this emerging research. These works, intended for audiences from a multiplicity of disciplines, took on this impulse to tie humans to nature and deal with what it means to be inextricably part of this world around us, this thing that had for so long been beyond humans—out there, "the other," nature.

Daniel Botkin was one of the first science writers to bring new ideas about ecosystem behavior to the humanities and the popular press, to establish a bridge between the natural sciences and the humanities—and between academic research and the mainstream press. His seminal 1990 work *Discordant Harmonies: A New Ecology for the Twenty-first Century* (excerpted in this volume) brought new ideas about ecology to a broader audience. Through engaging stories about moose on an island in the Great Lakes or elephants in Kenya's vast landscape or old forests in New Jersey, Botkin illustrated how models of ecological stability were being overturned by evidence on the ground; that management practices that favored strict definition of landscape environments (interiors distinct from exteriors) and human control were proving fatal to the same populations that these practices were put in place to protect; and how the idealized climax forest was, in fact, closely dependent on—and changed over—time.

Botkin's tracing of a succession of concepts about ecology and environment (via the metaphors of divine order, organic comrade, the great machine) illustrates these ideas' cultural roots while simultaneously exposing their shortcomings, in favor of an all-embracing yet situational model of the dynamic biosphere. Here humans are fully enmeshed in the forces and dynamics that influence climate and life on the planet, yet the conditions that we may encounter on the ground are fleeting and momentary—caught up in cycles and dynamics that are ever-changing and somewhat just out of reach. Botkin argues that our management practices (planning, policy, governance, and day-to-day activities) must adapt themselves to this new scientific understanding of the world—that principles of order, control, and limits will eventually doom the very things we want to protect. Such a direct connection between scientific inquiry, cultural ideas, and management and planning practices harkens back to Holling's 1970 essay, reprinted in this volume, on ecology and planning that seeded new interest in nonscientific audiences—including designers and planners—in the dynamism of the natural environment.

But even as humanists and journalists were dealing with these new models of connectivity and embeddedness, a number of scholars took on the task of wondering aloud whether this was all there was—if, in Carolyn Merchant's terms, nature (which includes notions of the other, or something still beyond the reach of humans) was indeed dead.[8] These authors proposed the idea that, even if we are physically and biologically tied to the natural world—and even if our actions have distinct impacts on and sometimes lasting reverberations within the world around us—there is still something unknowable and uncontrollable that is simply beyond the human capacity to comprehend. Whether this is a characteristic or animal trait, or an idea about the wild, wildness, or the wilderness, this essence was important for these authors to define and maintain as something that exists but is elusive—that occurs regardless of human presence or intervention.

Robert Pogue Harrison, in his 1993 work *Forests: Shadow of Civilization*, documents many civilizations' attempts to both negotiate natural forces around them and conceptualize that society's relationship to the natural world. Drawing on the principles of the Italian drawing technique called *chiaroscuro* (among other cultural and literary references), through which a foreground element (a lone tree, for example) emerges visually from the background (a forest) via a series of light and dark marks that are developed in relationship (and in physical proximity), Pogue Harrison argues that it is only in dynamic relationship with the physical world that each is made evident. In other words, the apparent contrast between humans and nature can be delineated only by a set of devices that are common to them—an inherent recognition that we can talk about the nature world or ecology only via a set of models that are intrinsically human.

Neil Evernden's *The Social Creation of Nature* (1992) is foremost among these works, which include Gary Snyder's collection of stories, *The Practice of the Wild* (1990); Max Oelschlager's *The Idea of Wilderness* (1993); and William Cronon's edited collection *Uncommon Ground: Rethinking the Human Place in Nature* (1995). Evernden traces societal (and philosophical) relationships between various world civilizations and the natural world, arguing that the simple act of naming ("Nature") was a first step in removing the physical world (as well its demons and uncontrollable characteristics) from the human world—an act of domestication that allowed humans to both sever and control it. He argues for *qualities*, as opposed to nameable things, that might describe that which exists beyond human control: "Wildness is not 'ours'—indeed, it is the one thing that can *never* be ours. It is self-willed, independent, and indifferent to our dictates and judgments. An entity with the quality of wildness is its own, and no other's."[9] Evernden's entreaty to set the world (nature) free in order to save it— to simply let nature do its thing—could only be heard within a scientific context that had recently dismissed stasis and control in favor of dynamism and open-endedness in natural systems.

Sanford Kwinter extends these speculations in the architectural world in his 2008 essay "Wildness (Prolegomena to a New Urbanism)." Here Kwinter references a vicious attack on a jogger in Central Park, Viet Cong tactics in America's war with Vietnam, and the research of the Santa Fe Institute as examples that somehow deal with entities that are uncontrolled or uncontrollable: "The 'wild' is the logic of animal societies (packs, flocks, and swarms), of the immixings and inadvertencies of the natural world (storms, quakes, abundance, extinction), and of complex adaptive systems in general, even those of an entirely artificial kind."[10] Kwinter calls for a redefinition of the design project and the broader project of urbanism in ways that exhibit or sustain essential characteristics of messiness, indirectness, openness, and indeterminacy: "to approximate these *ecological* forces and structures, to tap, approximate, borrow, and transform morphogenetic processes from all aspects of wild nature, to invent *artificial* means of creating living artificial environments."[11] Kwinter has brought to a specifically architectural readership the same quest that others in the humanities had proposed in the preceding decade—but this time expressed in specifically architectural language.

In a similar shift in thinking related to the anthropology of food, Michael Pollan's work ingeniously breaks down distinctions that have persisted between the natural world and humans, and between environmental and industrial systems. In *Second Nature,* Pollan postulates that new ideas about human-nature interactions—alternatives to traditional attitudes of complete dominion over nature or total acquiescence to it—must be formulated to better deal with the environment's inherently unstable nature. In *The Botany of Desire,* Pollan twists our preconceptions of human agency alone being responsible for certain evolutions or selections of plants (e.g., apples, tulips, marijuana, potatoes), in fact ascribing human characteristics of desire and domestication to the cultivated plants, and further reinforcing the breakdown of distinctions between the actions and artifacts of humans and those of the natural world. Pollan extends the complexities about relationships between various altered ecologies and industrial production networks in *The Omnivore's Dilemma,* tracing the history of scientific modifications to crops and their ties to contemporary large-scale food production and distribution networks, and their various impacts on the environment and human and ecological health. Here Pollan focuses on the larger interconnected webs that arise from and structure behaviors in the world (at multiples scales)—webs that are as much political and economic as ecological and scientific.

Design Thinking and Practices _____

In design practices, contemporary ideas of ecology and planning can be traced to the work of Ian McHarg in the late 1960s and early 1970s, in which analysis and assessment of natural resources (geology, soils, water, habitat, etc.) could inform the best places and ways to develop land for social occupation.[12] McHarg's methodology gave quantitative value to resources and systems long ignored in the formulation of development plans, and his approach was popularized by municipal and regional planners across the United States and eventually in other places around the world. With hindsight, the methodology can easily be criticized for its claims of objectivity, and for its objectification of landscape components as things simply to be mapped and quantified. But McHarg's practice opened up planning thought to the idea of the interconnectedness between cities, suburbs, and the natural world: design *with* nature. McHarg's position leading one of the world's foremost schools of landscape architecture and the emerging discipline of regional planning at the University of Pennsylvania is significant. He quickly became an authority in the academic world of design and planning, and his ecologically based work—that helped determine environmentally informed development strategies—was widely supported by environmentalists, planners, and the development community, and changed the way the design professions regarded natural systems.

But even as McHarg's methodology was taking hold, newer ideas about ecology were emerging. Some of these were based in part on new observational and analytical techniques available to derive and record data from large-scale ecosystems. Richard Forman's research is a key example of a new direction in applied ecology that rose to prominence along with the availability of LandSat imagery and computer-aided geographic information systems analysis during the 1980s and early 1990s. Notably, Forman's work was undertaken at

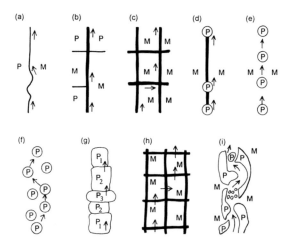

Richard T.T. Forman. Movement among Non-Adjacent Elements.

Harvard University in the Graduate School of Design, where he developed new understandings of and new terminologies for ecological systems, described as matrices, webs, and networks, for instance, and characterized by adjacencies, overlaps, and juxtapositions.[13] This work recognized the dynamic, living nature of ecological systems—not just the physical elements McHarg was mapping, but how the material of the physical world supports the movement and exchange of ecological matter (water, seeds, wildlife). Holling was a contemporary of Forman, and his work was also important at this juncture. A pioneer of the notion of resilience and its implications for adaptive management practices, Holling suggested the importance of his work for decision-making, but did not himself work with designers, aligning instead with large-scale resource management more typical of the northern landscapes in which he was working.

Still others pushed these ideas further. Indeed, as noted earlier, the field was shifting away from an understanding of systems that attempt to achieve a predictable equilibrium or steady-state condition to systems typically in states of change, adapting to subtle or dramatic changes in inputs, resources, and climate. Adaptation, appropriation, and flexibility became understood as the hallmarks of "successful" systems, and it is now widely accepted (if not fully understood) that it is through an ecosystem's ability to respond to changing environmental conditions that persistence is possible.[14]

Concurrently, a number of design practices were engaging ecological processes—and sometimes open-endedness—in their design works. Richard Haag at the Bloedel Reserve in Washington State both hyper-amplified woodland decay and composition in the Moss Garden and framed out groundwater fluctuation—a phenomenon that extended far beyond the garden or the reserve—in the beautifully simple and abstract Hedge Garden. Both gardens were firmly rooted in landscape traditions—English or naturalistic gardens for the former, French Beaux-Arts and formalist Modern gardens for the latter—but gave new presence to those forces and dynamics that are beyond the control of the designer, and whose informants and implications reach to scales of influence much larger than the space of the particular project.

Richard Haag Associates. Groundwater Garden at Bloedel Reserve, Bainbridge Island, Washington.

The work of George Hargreaves and Hargreaves Associates, and the projects of the so-called earth artists that greatly informed that work (Robert Smithson's 1969 *Asphalt Rundown,* 1970 *Partially Buried Woodshed,* and 1970 *Spiral Jetty;* Michael Heizer's 1969 *Double Negative*; and works by Nancy Holt, James Turrell, Walter de Maria, etc.), extended this trajectory of design research. Candlestick Point Park on San Francisco Bay was among the early works of that firm that deliberately engaged open-ended environmental processes, and it did so more explicitly than Haag's work. Here, the Bay edge of the project was armored where a taut green lawn touched the water, but this plane of grass gave way along its edges to an extension of the rocky intertidal zone of the Bay—physically and spatially bringing the waters of the Bay (and its various offerings of floating logs, condoms, animal skeletons, plastic bottles, and waste) into the space of the park. While Haag's Hedge Garden was an inward-focused, carefully framed space with a simple plane of water that would register environmental cycles, Hargreaves's 1985–1993 Candlestick project radically inverted this relationship, throwing open the space of the public park or garden and subjecting it to the larger forces of the Bay.

Hargreaves Associates. Intertidal Zone at Candlestick Point Park, San Francisco.

These experiments and speculations were not isolated. Michael Van Valkenburgh's 1988 Ice Walls at Radcliffe College examined the freezing, thawing, and visual/temporal effects of water in its multiple states; here, simple chain-link fences served as the scaffold for allowing the physical properties of one of the essential media of landscape and human life to shift and change state in relationship to ambient heat and light. Rem Koolhaas/OMA's proposal for the Parc de la Villette included a linear forest conceived as a temporal garden that allowed the growth tendencies of two contrasting tree species to play off each other and create ever-changing vegetal and spatial effects. The early work of Michel Desvigne and Christine Dalnoky set out strategies in which growth, succession, and careful editing of newly planted urban or industrial forests could be seen to reintroduce environmental dynamics into sites and projects that had erased—or at least significantly dampened—ecological effects. Desvigne's work is especially significant in that it does not deny the human hand; these projects are carefully curated over time to allow for both ecological succession and human occupation. In this sensibility, Desvigne has effectively, if implicitly, embraced a dynamic systems perspective founded on the notions of "both/and" rather than the customary preoccupation with a binary worldview based on "either/or" interpretations of reality.

The shift in ecological thinking and research, and its counterparts in process-oriented design experiments, opened new worlds for critical discourse in design and urbanism: Stan Allen identified the new ecology along with engineering systems as important examples of "material practices" that focused

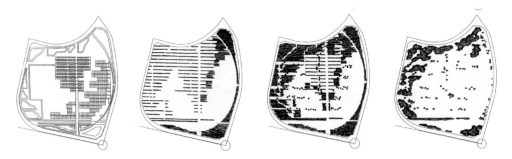

Michel Desvigne Paysagistes. Landscape Succession over Thirty Years, Thomas Plant, Guyancourt, France.

not so much on "what things look like" but more on "what they can do."[15] Allen's explicit reference to work of landscape ecologist Forman—marrying the operative and performative aspects of dynamic ecologies with emerging design theory—moved the discussion of complex adaptive systems out of the domain of environmentalism and landscape alone and into the center of design discourse and theory.

Allen's continuing work in collaboration with James Corner and this essay's coauthor, ecologist and planner Nina-Marie Lister, on Toronto's Downsview Park Competition of the mid-/late 1990s imagined the setting up of physical scaffolds that would sponsor the propagation of emergent ecologies, natural systems that would be seeded initially and evolve with an increasing level of complexity and adaptability over time. The Downsview competition brief was itself significant in that it required entries to account for long-term timeframes and make explicit some comfort with irreducible uncertainty in terms of project evolution.[16] And although the OMA scheme won the day, proposals by the Corner-Allen and Bernard Tschumi teams have resonated within ongoing design discussion and teaching.

Since this time, a number of design practices have taken up these ideas, while others have adopted analogs of responsive systems to inform design thinking. Adaptive building systems or elements—fenestration systems that automatically respond to changing light levels, keeping building interiors cooler—are now widespread, promulgated by designers and architects such as Chuck Hoberman, Foster and Partners, and others. Ecological cyborgs, which hybridize infrastructural function and ecological responsiveness by diverting waste resources from industrial operations, are on the drawing tables of cross-disciplinary design practices like Stoss. Longer-term management and curatorial strategies for large-scale open space, infrastructure, and urban projects now allow for feedback loops and multiple possible outcomes (if/then scenarios, especially in work by Field Operations and others). Even the structure of multidisciplinary design teams and academic alliances has been affected. Ecologists such as Steward Pickett and Richard Forman have long-standing relationships with design thinkers and design schools, while others such as Steven Handel and Stephen Apfelbaum have aligned themselves with design practice through applied ecological research.

New modeling programs and visualization techniques offer one path forward for exploration and experimentation. Flow modeling, scripting, and processing software in particular provide time-based platforms for representing and programming change and evolution. Applied research into the relationship of energy and atmosphere suggest other promising avenues for investigation.

But few designers have yet ventured beyond the metaphors and mechanics supplied by these two-decades-old models to design effectively for adaptation to change, or to incorporate learned feedback into the designs, or to work in trans-disciplinary modes of practice that open new apertures for the exploration of new systems, synergies, and wholly collaborative work. This is the project ahead: *Projective Ecologies* charts a course leading the sciences, humanities, and design culture toward a more rigorous, robust, and relevant engagement across the domains of ecology and design—one to be fully explored in the coming years.

Notes

1_ James Corner, "Ecology and Landscape as Agents of Creativity," in George F. Thompson and Frederick R. Steiner, eds., *Ecological Design and Planning* (New York: John Wiley and Sons, 1997). Corner was among the first to speak of the potential agency of ecology for design thinking and practices. This essay, in a sense, represents the development of this trajectory in Corner's research and teachings at the University of Pennsylvania throughout the 1990s, when Chris Reed was his student and research assistant there. In 1999, Corner began to embed these ideas into his emerging design practice, explicitly for the first time in the Downsview Park Design Competition in Toronto, on which he collaborated with Nina-Marie Lister. Corner's embrace of indeterminacy, flux, and emergence of ecological processes within design practice have their roots in this work and the collaborations that resulted from it.

2_ Frank B. Golley, *A History of the Ecosystem Concept in Ecology: More Than the Sum of the Parts* (New Haven: Yale University Press, 1993), citing Arthur Tansley (1935).

3_ See N-M. Lister, "Biodiversity: Bridging Science and Values," in D. Waltner-Toews, J.J. Kay, and N-M. Lister (eds.) *The Ecosystem Approach: Complexity, Uncertainty, and Managing for Sustainability* (New York: Columbia University Press, 2008), and N-M. Lister, "A Systems Approach to Biodiversity Conservation Planning," *Environmental Monitoring and Assessment* 49 (2/3), 1998: 123–155.

4_ See, for example, one of the earliest of its kind, the Hubbard-Brooks Study by F. H. Bormann and G.E. Likens, *Patterns and Process in a Forested Ecosystem* (Berlin: Springer-Verlag, 1979).

5_ C.S. Holling, "Cross-Scale Morphology, Geometry and Dynamics of Ecosystems,"

Ecological Monographs 62(4), 1992: 447–502. See also C. S. Holling, "The Resilience of Terrestrial Ecosystems: Local Surprise and Global Change," in W.C. Clark and R.E. Munn, eds., *Sustainable Development of the Biosphere* (Cambridge: Cambridge University Press, 1986), 292–320.

6_ Dean Bavington, *Managed Annihilation: An Unnatural History of the Newfoundland Cod Collapse* (Vancouver: UBC Press, 2010).

7_ This paradigm shift and attendant approaches for management and design of decision-making processes within complex socio-ecological systems has been explored by Lance Gunderson, C. S. Holling, and Stephen Light, eds., in *Barriers and Bridges to the Renewal of Regional Ecosystems* (New York: Columbia University Press, 1995); described by Lance Gunderson and C.S. Holling, eds., in *Panarchy: Understanding Transformations in Human and Natural Systems* (Washington, D.C.: Island Press, 2002); and elaborated by Waltner-Toews, Kay, and Lister, eds., in *The Ecosystem Approach.* Further research and publications are noted at http://www.resalliance.org/.

8_ Carolyn Merchant, *The Death of Nature: Women, Ecology, and the Scientific Revolution* (San Francisco: Harper Collins, 1980).

9_ Neil Evernden, *The Social Creation of Nature* (Baltimore: Johns Hopkins University Press, 1992), 120.

10_ Sanford Kwinter, "Prolegomena to a New Urbanism," in *Far from Equilibrium: Essays on Technology and Design Culture* (Barcelona: Actar, 2008), 187.

11_ Ibid., 191.

12_ See Ian McHarg, *Design With Nature* (New York: John Wiley and Sons, 1967/1992).

13_ See numerous publications by Richard T.T. Forman, including *Land Mosaics: The Ecology of Landscape and Regions* (Cambridge: Cambridge University Press, 1995).

14_ Among the many essays that address this shift are Robert E. Cook, "Do Landscapes Learn? Ecology's 'New Paradigm' and Design in Landscape Architecture," Inaugural Ian L. McHarg Lecture, University of Pennsylvania, March 22, 1999, published in *Environmentalism in Landscape Architecture,* Dumbarton Oaks Colloquium Series in the History of Landscape Architecture 22 (Washington, D.C.: Dumbarton Oaks, 2000), and reprinted in this volume, and Nina-Marie Lister, "Sustainable Large Parks: Ecological Design or Designer Ecology?" in Julia Czerniak and George Hargreaves, eds., *Large Parks* (New York: Princeton Architectural Press, 2007).

15_ Stan Allen, "Infrastructural Urbanism," *Points + Lines: Diagrams and Projects for the City* (New York: Princeton Architectural Press, 1999), 52–53.

16_ See the full presentation of the scheme by Field Operations/Stan Allen + James Corner in Julia Czerniak, ed., *CASE: Downsview Park Toronto* (Munich and Cambridge, MA: Prestel and Harvard University Graduate School of Design, 2001). For a discussion of the competition brief and the idea of scaffolding, see Kristina Hill's essay "Urban Ecologies: Biodiversity and Urban Design" in the same volume.

Ecology and Landscape
as Agents of Creativity

James Corner

Published 1997

Unchanged within to see all changed without,
Is a blank lot and hard to bear, no doubt.
Samuel Taylor Coleridge[1]

The existence of which we are most assured and which we know best is
unquestionably our own, for of every other object we have notions which may
be considered external and superficial, whereas, of ourselves, our perception is
internal and profound.
What, then, do we find?
Henri Bergson[2]

The processes of which ecology and creativity speak are fundamental to the work
of landscape architecture. Whether biological or imaginative, evolutionary or
metaphorical, such processes are active, dynamic, and complex, each tending toward the
increased differentiation, freedom, and richness of a diversely interacting whole. There
is no end, no grand scheme for these agents of change, just a cumulative directionality
toward further becoming. It is in this productive and active sense that ecology and
creativity speak not of fixed and rigid realities but of movement, passage, genesis, and
autonomy, of *propulsive life unfolding in time.*

It is odd, then, that while ecology and creativity have each received increasing
attention over the years, there remains ambiguity over their content and relationship
toward one another, especially with respect to their agency in the evolving of life and
consciousness. It is striking, for example, that the possibilities for a vibrant exchange
between ecology, creativity, and the design of landscape have barely been recognized
beyond mechanical and prescriptive methods. Moreover, landscape architecture's appropriation of ecology and creativity—and the manner in which they are understood
and used—has rarely led to the production of work that is equal in effect and magnitude to the transformative phenomena these topics represent. Contemporary landscape
architecture has drawn more from objectivist and instrumental models of ecology (the
emotional rhetoric of some environmentalists notwithstanding), while design creativity
has all too frequently been reduced to dimensions of environmental problem solving
(know-how) and aesthetic appearance (scenery). This lack of inventiveness is both surprising and difficult for many landscape architects, especially those who originally entered the field believing that ecology and artistic creativity might *together* help develop
new and alternative forms of landscape. This failing points to a relationship between

ecology, creativity, and landscape that is either incongruous and impossible to reconcile or (and more likely) to a potential relationship that has not yet been developed—a potential that might inform more meaningful and imaginative cultural practices than the merely ameliorative, compensatory, aesthetic, or commodity oriented.

My concern in this essay is to outline the grounds that are necessary for this potential to appear. I argue that ecology, creativity, and landscape architecture must be considered in terms other or greater than those of visual appearance, resource value, habitat structure, or instrumentality. Instead, these somewhat restrictive traditional views might be complemented by an understanding of how ecology, creativity, and landscape architecture are metaphorical and ideological representations; they are cultural images, or *ideas*. Far from being inactive, however, these ideas have profound agency in the world, effecting change in a variety of material, ideological, and experiential ways. These cultural ideas and practices interact with the nonhuman world in such a way as simultaneously to derive *from* while being constitutive *of* nature, human dwelling, and the modes of relationship therein. What is important and significant here is how ecology and landscape architectural design might invent alternative forms of *relationship* between people, place, and cosmos. Thus, the landscape architectural project becomes more about the invention of new forms and programs than the merely corrective measures of restoration.

If one were to conceive of landscape architecture as an active agent in the play of evolutionary intervention, how would one have to construe ecology and creativity in design practice? In what ways would they have to be appropriated for landscape architecture to function as a significant evolutionary agent—one that might develop greater diversity and reciprocity between the cultural world and unmediated Nature? Of what would such a creative ecology consist?

The Ecological Idea

Ecology has assumed a heightened level of significance in social and intellectual affairs during the past few decades. This emergence is due, in large part, to an increased awareness of local and global environmental decline, a view that continues to be shaped through vivid media coverage and well-organized ecological activism.[3] The lesson of ecology has been to show how all life upon the planet is so deeply bound into dynamic, complex, and indeterminate networks of relationships that to speak of nature as a linear mechanism, as if it were a great machine that can be either intrinsically or extrinsically controlled and repaired, is simply erroneous and reductive. The ecological view, with its emphasis on temporal, interactive processes, has been further reinforced by new scientific findings of nonlinearity, complexity, and chaos dynamics. While ecology speaks of a "harmony of nature," writes ecologist Daniel Botkin, it is a harmony that is at the same time "discordant, created from the simultaneous movements of many tones, the combination of many processes flowing at the same time along various scales, leading not to a simple melody but to a symphony at some times harsh and at some times pleasing."[4]

While the full measure of these and other emerging views of ecology remains to be realized, the idea of ecology has diversified to such a point that it can no longer be used with unambiguous clarity. Today, one may observe that "ecology" is appropriated as much by corporate and media industries as by environmentalists, land-artists, or politicians. Although ecology has generally been understood as providing a scientific account of natural processes and their interrelationships, the fact that it also both describes and constructs various ideological positions to be taken with regard to nature points to a greater significance. Ecology is never ideologically (or imaginatively) neutral, despite claims of its objectivity. It is not without values, images, and effects. Instead, ecology is a social construction, one that can initiate, inform, and lend legitimacy to particular viewpoints (from "green politics" to nationalism to feminism, for example). Ecology constructs particular "ideas" in the imagination of its advocates; it conjures up particular ways of seeing and relating to Nature—views that range from the extremely rational to the most mystical and religious.

It is, therefore, necessary to distinguish two "natures": The first, "nature," refers to the *concept* of nature, the cultural construction that enables a people to speak of and understand the natural world, and that is so bound into ecological language; the second, "Nature," refers to the amorphous and unmediated flux that is the "actual" cosmos, that which always escapes or exceeds human understanding.

The development of the ecological idea of nature in the cultural imagination—how one conceives of, relates to, and intervenes in Nature—is a radically different kind of reflection than what is found in current instrumentalist (or problem solving) approaches toward ecology in landscape architectural design and planning, wherein "ecology," "nature," "landscape," and "environment" form the primary foci of attention, considered as separate from and external to culture. By "culture," I refer to more than just the behavioral and statistical characteristics of a human group (something that human ecology claims to describe), and invoke instead the image of an unfolding and multivariate artifact, a dynamic entity constructed from the vocabularies, attitudes, customs, beliefs, social forms, and material characteristics of a particular society. Culture is a thick and active archaeology, akin to a deep field that is capable of further moral, intellectual, and social cultivation. Thus, people can only ever *know* what they have made (their language, representations, and artifacts). "Because for thousands of years we have been looking at the world with moral, aesthetic, and religious claims," writes Nietzsche, "with blind inclination, passion, or fear, and have indulged ourselves in the bad habits of illogical thought, this world has gradually *become* so strangely colorful, frightful, profound, soulful; it has acquired color but we have been the painters: the human intellect allowed appearance to appear, and projected its mistaken conceptions onto things."[5] For Nietzsche, the cultural world (like nature) is the result of an accumulation of "errors and fantasies," an accrual that is nothing less than "a treasure: for the *value* of our humanity rests upon it."[6] It is this dynamic, representational, and "erring" characteristic of culture, then, that descriptive and instrumentalist ecology fails to recognize, although it is itself a constituent part and product of the cultural milieu (and is, therefore, just as fictional). In other words, many landscape architects and planners who are advocates of ecological views often fail to understand how the metaphorical characteristics of ecology inform and construct particular realities. Moreover, the sheer diversity of ways in which different social groups represent, speak of, experience, and relate to Nature embodies a richness—a treasure of fictions—that a strictly scientistic ecology (ironically) cannot embrace—nor even acknowledge—its own image within that richness.

The Ambiguities of Ecology within Landscape Architecture

Ecology has been particularly influential in landscape architecture and planning, especially since the publication of Aldo Leopold's *A Sand County Almanac* (1949), Rachel Carson's *Silent Spring* (1962), and Ian McHarg's *Design with Nature* (1969). Earlier American naturalists such as George Perkins Marsh, Henry David Thoreau, Ralph Waldo Emerson, John Muir, and, later, Lawrence Henderson had no doubt partly influenced some late-nineteenth- and early-twentieth-century landscape architects—most notably Frederick Law Olmsted, Charles Eliot, Jens Jensen, and Warren Manning. The cumulative result over the past century, but especially since the original Earth Day, has been the establishment of ecology as a central part of landscape architectural education and practice.

Whereas ecology has changed and enriched the field of landscape architecture substantially, it has also displaced some of landscape architecture's more traditional aspects and prompted a somewhat ambiguous and estranged disciplinary identity (the oft-asked question: "Is it art or science?"). A number of schools of landscape architecture, for example, now teach little visual art, design theory, or history, focusing instead upon natural science, environmental management, and techniques of ecological restoration. Although these aspects of landscape study are important, one cannot help but feel a concern for the loss of foundational traditions, especially landscape architecture's agency as a representational and productive art, as a *cultural* project. The subsequent polarization of art from science, planning from design, theory from practice, and the lack of critical reflection within "ecological design" circles are further symptoms of this forgetfulness. While the countertendency to privilege design and form at the exclusion of ecological ideas has proven to be retrogressive and productive of environments more like entertainment landscapes than significant places for dwelling, the appropriation of ecology within landscape architecture has yet to precipitate inventive and animistic forms of creativity. This failure is evidenced most embarrassingly in the prosaic and often trivial nature of much contemporary built work, whether it claims to be "ecological" in its design or not.

Moreover, it is ironic that the lively and spontaneous morphogenesis characteristics of evolutionary creation—the active life processes of which ecology speaks—are rarely paralleled in the modern landscape architect's limited capacity to transfigure and transmute. This lack of imaginative depth and actual agency is compounded by often uncritical, reductive, and sometimes even exclusionary views of what is considered to be "natural." For example, the popular conception of ecological design as reconstructing "native" environments is not only founded upon illusory and contradictory ideas about a noncultural "nature," but also displays a remarkably nonecological intolerance of alternative viewpoints and processes of transmutation (terms such as *foreign* and *exotic* betray an exclusivity and privileging of the *natives*).

Given the increased marginalization of contemporary landscape architecture, it would seem promising for landscape architects to look to ecology less for techniques of description and prescription (and even less for its apparent legitimizing of images of "naturalness") and more for its ideational, representational, and material implications with respect to cultural process and evolutionary transformation. After all, as social ecologist John Clark argues, "The flowering of the human spirit and personality is a continuation of natural evolution. Liberation of the human imagination from the deadening effects of mechanization and commodification is one of the most pressing ecological issues."[8] It is ironic that the emancipation of human creativity through the imaginative appropriation of ecological ideas and metaphors has been largely neglected by contemporary landscape architects (and especially those who wave the flag of ecology), even though the deeper traditions of landscape architecture are founded upon such existential objectives. The garden, for example, was historically developed as a place of both connectivity *and* differentiation between people and the world of Nature. Here, the exchange that occurs through cultivation (of food, body, spirit, and physical and psychological relationship) literally unites and distinguishes human life and Nature. The persistent archetype of the garden portends an ecological consciousness that is simultaneously useful and symbolic, one that is rooted not in an external world of nature but with a particular culture's mode of *relating* to Nature. The same power of relationship is encoded not only in the construction of physical places, but also in maps, images, and other place-forming texts.

The difficulty for many landscape architects today lies in a forgetfulness of (and perhaps, too, a skepticism toward) the power that symbolic representation can have in forging cultural relationships, both between one another and between one and Nature. This loss of traditional focus is compounded, in part, by the privileging of a scientistic ecology (utilized in highly rationalized descriptive and prescriptive ways) over phenomenological forms of ecological consciousness (which are all too often wrongly belittled by scientistic ecologists as having naïve or trivial goals with respect to the massive technoeconomic scale of the ecological "crisis"). The popular notion that subjectivity, poetry, and art are welcome in the private domains of the gallery or the library, but are no match for the power of "rational" instrumentality in "solving" the real problems of the world is to understand these problems in terms that are somehow *external* to the world of symbolic communication and cultural values.[9] This use of ecology as a rational instrument in landscape architectural design and planning not only externalizes the "problem," but also promotes human domination over the nonhuman world—a world that is either rendered mute and inert or deified as a privileged domain over culture. This continual emphasis upon rational prowess—often at the exclusion of phenomenological wonderment, doubt, and humility—also fails to recognize the very minor degree to which the combined landscape architectural constructions around the world have affected the global environment, especially when compared to the scale of industrialization, deforestation, and toxic waste. In contrast, the impact that gardens, parks, and public spaces (and also maps, images, and words) have had on the formation of cultural and existential values has historically proven to be immeasurable. Landscape architecture's focus of concern simply can never be that of the external environment alone but must always entail profoundly cultural interests and ideas.

Clearly, the point remains that, although ecology has surfaced in modern landscape architectural discourse (as in public life in general), a culturally animate ecology—one that is distinct from a purely "scientistic" ecology—has yet to emerge. That such an urgent development might derive from, and contribute to, more animistic types of creativity than current frames of instrumentalism would allow points to a necessary dialogue between scientific and artistic worlds. Such an emphasis asks that ecology inform and embrace those poetic activities that create meaningful relationships between people, place, and earth. An eco-imaginative landscape/architecture would be creative insofar as it reveals, liberates, enriches, and diversifies both biological and cultural life. How, then, might the ecological idea precipitate imaginative and "world-enlarging" forms of creative endeavor? In turn, how might landscape architectural creativity (informed through its representational traditions) enrich and inform the ecological idea in the imagination and material practices of a people?

Modernity and Environment

Prior to any further discussion of the above themes, it might be helpful to outline some of the central characteristics of modernity (the Western cultural paradigm that stems from development during the late sixteenth century). To discuss the significance of ecology and creativity outside this context is to overlook their relationship within a larger cultural sphere. Of particular importance is an appreciation for how an all-pervasive belief in human "progress" underlies much of what is troublesome in our current age.

The widespread faith in the capacity of technology to make a more perfect world in the future first arose during the sixteenth and seventeenth centuries, when new advances in science (from Copernicus, Galileo, and Descartes, to Newton and Bacon) and the rise of capitalist market economies inspired many Enlightenment intellectuals to assume that people could master nature. With progressive optimism, it was believed that all disease and poverty could be eradicated while material standards of living could be improved. The many successes of modern science during the past 300 years (especially in medicine and communications) have continued to foster the expectation that further advances in technology will continue to solve all of humankind's problems. That this same science has also led to the development of "darker" technologies, such as nuclear weaponry and the production of toxic waste, has proven to be increasingly troubling. Similarly, more apparently benign experiments such as Biosphere II, in

Arizona, point to a future in which people might live in their own self-manufactured environments, in which the threats (and marvels) of nature are not allowed to intrude (or appear)—except, of course and inevitably, by accident.

Clearly, it is fair to observe that advances in technology and productivity have not led to an equivalent growth in either moral or ecological consciousness.[10] A corresponding decline of the sacred and the spiritual has only compounded the deterioration of ethical measures in society, especially in terms of establishing the limits for technological inventiveness. This detachment of cultural value from the autonomous, free-wheeling development of a limitless technology is exacerbated by the rise of global, market-based economies, which are governed solely by the capitalist maxims of profit and gain, often at the expense of other people, nations, or life-forms. In turn, the rise of a hierarchical and bureaucratic society—with dominant groups limiting the freedoms of others—has led to radical inequalities, cultural estrangements, and gross reductions in both the cultural and natural spheres. The subsequent loss of alterity and difference portends an increasingly homogeneous and impoverished life-world—one that might have the busy appearance of pluralism, but only as media image and rarely as a co-presence of radically "other" realms. In sum, the belief in human progress and mastery over Nature, for all of its good intentions and successes, has at the same time promoted an often brutally mechanistic, materialistic, and impersonal world, a domain in which the potential creativity of both Nature and culture is diminished to dull equations of utility, production, commodity, and consumption.

The fallacies of progressivist and objectivist practices are sustained in large measure by another primary characteristic of the modern paradigm: The tendency to construct binary oppositions, as in the polarization of the human and social world from the natural world.[11] This dualism parallels the dichotomy between subject and object, wherein concepts such as "environment" are conceived as things that are external to humankind. The severing of reality into opposites is again an outcome of Enlightenment (particularly Cartesian) thinking, in which the objective and subjective worlds were absolutely distinguished and separated, and the incommensurability between the artists' "sensibility" and the scientists' "rationality" first arose. The tensions within contemporary landscape architecture between the rational, analytical, and objective "planners" (who put such great emphasis upon a linear process of data accumulation, logical determinism, and large-scale engineering) and the emotional, intuitive, mystical "artists" (who put such great emphasis on subjectivity, emotive experience, and aesthetic appearance) is but one fallacious outcome of this larger, dualistic paradigm.[12]

Although it may be characterized as a "gentle" profession, landscape architecture remains caught within the technoeconomic, progressivist, and dualistic characteristics of modernity. While moderate landscape architecture's contribution to resource management, scenic preservation, zoological and commercial theme park design, and corporate image building has certainly lessened the damage done to the environment, its tendency to conceive and present the landscape as an object—whether aesthetically, ecologically, or instrumentally—has, at the same time, led to further *devaluation* of the environment in cultural terms (the landscape now qualified as resource, as commodity, as compensation, or as system). If landscape architecture is to concern itself with the "ecological crisis" and other difficulties of human life upon the earth, then it must recognize expeditiously how the root cause of environmental and spiritual decline is buried in the complex foundations of modern culture, particularly its political-economic practices, its social institutions, and the psychology and intolerance of much of its citizenry.

Conservationist/Resourcist and Restorative Ecology

From within this modern cultural paradigm, two dominant streams of ecological practices of landscape architecture have emerged: One conservationist/resourcist, which espouses the view that further ecological information and knowledge will enable progressive kinds of management and control of ecosystems; and the other restorative, which espouses the view that ecological knowledge may be used to "heal" and reconstruct "natural systems."

In the conservationist/resourcist view of ecology, the landscape is composed of various resources that have particular value to people—such as forestry production, mining, agriculture, built development, recreation, and tourism. Scenery, too, is considered a resource, as are "heritage areas" and tracts of "wilderness," which are valued as a resource for "future human generations." Through the quantification of economic, ecological, and social values, strategies of landscape conservation are developed as "balances" between human needs and natural life. Ecological concepts provide the landscape manager and planner with rational (and apparently value-neutral) criteria for evaluating the "fit" between proposed land uses and environmental systems. The most popular technique for such evaluation of land is called suitability analysis, developed by McHarg at the University of Pennsylvania during the 1960s. This ecological method allows for the quantification of the various parts that make up a particular ecosystem (or at least those parts that are susceptible to being quantified and mapped); measures the impact for various scenarios of development; and recommends the most appropriate, least disruptive land use.[13] The result is a systematic and rational accounting framework—a resource value matrix—for planning and managing development ("growth").

In his book *Nature's Economy*, Donald Worster recognizes that scientific ecology is used by the conservationist/planner solely to enable a "more careful management of… resources, to preserve the biotic capital while maximizing the income."[14] In criticizing this view, environmentalist author Neil Evernden argues that the use of ecology in resourcist planning is simply the means by which people may achieve "the maximum utilization of the earth as raw material in the support of one species… [even though] environmentalism has typically been a revolt against the presumption that this is indeed a suitable goal."[15] For all its good intentions, a major consequence of the resourcist project is the inevitable reduction of other life-forms and processes of Nature's creation to objectified factors of utility—a devaluation that is often compounded by (and, also, constitutive of) an emotional detachment, or distance, between people and the earth. "In reducing the living world to ingredients that could be easily measured and graphed," observes Worster, "the ecologist was also in danger of removing all the residual emotional impediments to unrestrained development."[16] "To describe a tree as an oxygen-producing device or bog as a filtering agent is [a violence] that is debasing to being itself,"[17] writes Evernden. Both Worster and Evernden conclude that resourcist views of ecology effectively neutralize the wonders of creation; that the objectivist, instrumental manner of manipulating the world leads only to the domestication of all that is genuinely wild, self-determining, and free. "In combating exploitation, [resourcist] environmentalists have [merely] tutored the developer in the art of careful exploitation," Evernden notes.[18] Through such practices, ecology simply promotes an analytic and detached instrumentality, one that facilitates an apparently "harmless" human control over an objectified and inert natural "reserve." In other words, progressivist ecology merely conditions a particular way of seeing that effectively severs the subject from the object. It is this culturally perpetuated relationship to landscape, this continual objectification, that prohibits a more empathetic reciprocity between people and the world. While Evernden's remarks may upset professional land-planners whose practices are founded upon objective, ameliorative, and "rational" means, he points directly to the root source of continued environmental decline: *The will to manage and control something that is "out there," not within.*

The second approach toward ecology in landscape architecture is the restorative. Here, the emphasis is on the acquisition of technical knowledge and skill with respect to the physical reconstruction of landscapes or, at a larger scale, regional ecosystems.

The belief is that the refinement of more ecologically sensitive techniques of land development will minimize damage to local and regional habitats. Ecology is employed by the restorationist to provide a scientific account of natural cycles and flows of energy, thereby explaining the network of interdependencies that comprise a particular ecosystem. Furthermore, ecology provides the restorationist with a palette of native and successional plant materials and planting patterns, allowing for the re-creation of a precultural, "naturalistic" landscape aesthetic. There is little room for cultural, social, and programmatic innovation in restorative work; the primary focus of attention is the natural world and the techniques necessary to recreate it (token gestures toward local heritage notwithstanding). Of course, as restoration is essentially an ideological project—derived from a particular cultural idea of "nature"—it can never escape its inherent cultural status. Unfortunately, restorationists are often as uncritical of this inescapable metaphoricity as they are unaware of the ease with which romantic ideals of "nativeness" can degenerate into exclusionary and "purist" nationalistic attitudes (as most extremely evidenced in fascist Germany in the 1930s and 1940s).[19]

So despising of modern cultural life are some restorationists that a radically ecocentric ideology has emerged in one extreme wing of the environmentalist circle. Although the ecocentric impulse is rarely as fierce in landscape architecture as it can be in some environmental groups, there remains a strong sentiment that urbanity, art, and cultural life in general are grossly inferior to the life of unmediated Nature, a Nature that finds its finest, most creative expression in evolutionary history and wilderness areas (blind though these groups often are to the fact that such views of "untouched nature" are themselves cultural images). Modern dualism and hierarchy (this time, Nature over culture) are not overcome in the ecocentric model, but simply reinforced. It is a model (or an "ethic") that is seriously flawed in its often mystical, antirational, and romantic views of nature—views that privilege ideas of harmony, mutuality, interconnectedness, and stability, while overlooking equally natural phenomena such as competition, exclusion, exploitation, disease, and species extinction.

In both conservationist/resourcist and restorative/ecocentric practices, ecology remains entrenched within the same modern paradigm that many argue is the structural cause of environmental and social decline. Whereas one position utilizes ecology to facilitate further control over the human environment, the other uses it to provide rhetorical force to emotional feelings about the primacy of Nature and the errors of anthropocentricity. In both cases, only the symptoms of ecological distress are dealt with, while causal cultural foundations—the social structures that underlie dualism, alienation, domination, and estrangement—are ignored and unchanged, if not actually upheld. In their dualistic objectifying of the world, both ecological resourcism and restoration are ameliorative at best, and facilitating of exploitation and exclusionism at worst. Unwittingly, landscape architecture, like the multifaceted environmental movement generally, merely replicates and sustains the shortcomings of modernity. Whether the locus of environmental concern be nature or culture, the problem is the belief in a controlling instrumentality and a failure to recognize bioecological constructions as cultural "errors and fantasies"—as treasured fictions that have profound agency in the unfolding of life-worlds.

Radical Ecology

In response to the apparent failing of conventional frames of ecology and environmentalism, other, more radical ecological positions have emerged in recent years.[20] They are radical because their work focuses not on Nature but on the sphere of culture. They are also critical of progressivist ecology and its largely technocratic "solutions" to environmental "problems," believing them to be piecemeal approaches toward the manifestations—rather than the foundational social causes—of ecological distress. Philosophical critiques of anthropocentrism, biocentrism, rationalism, objectivism, patriarchism, dualism, hierarchy, moral rights, and ethics form a ground of the debate, with groups such as the "deep ecologists," the "ecofeminists," and the "social ecologists" at odds with one another over foundational principles. That these debates have occurred infrequently in landscape architectural discourse is profoundly unfortunate, as it will only be through a more sophisticated understanding of ecology— one that transcends its status as a descriptive and analytical natural science and recognizes its metaphoricity as a cultural construction—that ecology's significance for a more creative and meaningful landscape architecture might be realized.

Of the various radical ecologies, the one that appears to be of particular interest for landscape architecture is social ecology.[21] This approach targets the technoeconomic aspects of the modern cultural paradigm and is especially critical of social practices of domination, commodification, and instrumentality. In the development of a "new liberatory project," social ecologists believe that the greatest potential for cultural reformation lies within the power of human imagination and creativity, although they insist as well on the parallel development of alternative social structures (political, institutional, ideological, ethical, and habitual) to those that sustain the modern paradigm.[22]

While social ecology seeks an "ethics of complementarity"—structured through a nonhierarchical politics of freedom, mutualism, and self-determination—its advocates are simultaneously aware of the difficulties of trying to promote change in cultural life without resorting to enforcement or dualism. Instead, some social ecologists believe that political, economic, and institutional change may best be effected less through instrumental means than through the reinvigoration of the cultural imagination. They call for a new kind of social "vision," a "new animism" in which human societies would see the world with new eyes—with wonderment, respect, and reverence. In social ecology, the ecological idea transcends its strictly scientific characteristics and assumes social, psychological, poetic, and imaginative dimensions.

In shying away from solitary or mystical subjectivity, however, social ecology seeks to construct a dialectical synthesis between rational thought, spontaneous imagination, and spiritual development—a dialogue that social ecologist Clark describes as "a more profound inquiry into the nature of our embodiedness—as thinking, feeling humans, and as thinking, feeling earth. [Social ecology] directs us in the dialectic of being in its many dimensions. To the erotics of reason. To the logic of the passions. To the politics of the imagination."[23] Moreover, social ecologists see their project as having an evolutionary and moral imperative. They believe that humanity has developed evolutionarily as "nature rendered self-conscious," as nature reflecting upon itself. It is, therefore, an ecological and moral responsibility for human creativity to, as Coleridge so beautifully wrote, "body forth the form of things unknown";[24] to promote a diversity of evolutionary pathways; and to foster an aesthetic appreciation and sense of responsibility toward the fecundity of Natural and cultural evolution. "Evolution" here refers to a propulsive fecundity that is life itself, predicated upon spontaneity, chance, self-determination, and a directionality toward the "actualization of potential."[25] For social ecologists, people must function as "moral agents," creatively intervening in the unfolding of evolution and the increasing of diversity, freedom, and self-reflexivity.[26]

The irony of this moral imperative is hauntingly rational, for, as Erazim Kohak writes: "If there is no God, then everything is not a creation, lovingly created and endowed with purpose and value by its creator. It can only be a cosmic accident, dead matter propelled by blind force, ordered by efficient causality. In such a context, a moral subject, living his life in terms of value and purpose, would indeed be an anomaly."[27] Kohak shows how civilization is simultaneously of Nature and yet radically different from it. It is within the space of this anomalous dialectic that further discussion of ecology and creativity as active agents in the unfolding of evolutionary time must lie, and from within which more critical and active practices of landscape architecture may emerge.

Human beings, by virtue of their ability to construct a reality through verbal and visual language, are radically different from the wild and indifferent flux that is nature, and different cultures at different times have, of course, related to the same "reality" in significantly dissimilar ways. Cultural "worlds" are composed of linguistic and imagistic structures; they are as much fictional as they are factual, as much symbolic as they are useful. As Nietzche recognized: To a world that is *not* our idea, the laws of numbers [and concepts] are completely inapplicable: they are valid in the human world."[28] The only nature that is real for us is constituted through the field of language. Without language there would be no place, only primal habitat; no dwelling, only subsistence. Moreover, not only does language ground and orient a culture, but it also facilitates moral reflection upon human existence and the existence of others.

The capacity of the human mind to comprehend and reflect upon the comprehensibility of the cosmos was "the most significant fact" of any for Aristotle, and this correspondence underlay the Greek formulation of the word *logos*, which referred to the "natural" symmetry of mind and Nature and to the forging of that relation through language.[29] Of course, the word *ecology* carries with it the union of *oikos* with *logos*, which allows it to be loosely translated as the "relations of home." In tracing this etymology, Robert Pogue Harrison writes: "The word ecology names far more than the science that studies ecosystems; it names the universal manner of being in the world…. *We dwell not in nature but in the relation to nature. We do not inhabit the earth but inhabit the excess of the earth*"[30] (emphasis added). This relation— or network of relations—is something that people make; it is an excess (of which landscape architecture is a part) within which a culture dwells. As such, human dwelling is always an estranged construction, one that can be destructive and parasitic as it can be reciprocal and symbiotic. This view is echoed by Charles Bergman's claim: "Extinction… may always have been with us, but endangered species are a modern invention, a uniquely modern contribution to science and culture. They are one of the unhappy consequences of the way we have come to know animals, the dark side of our relation with nature."[31] Consequently, "even though it is the demise of early forests that elicit our concern," writes Evernden, "we must bear in mind that as culture-dwellers we do not so much live in forests of trees as much as in forests of words. And the source of the blight that afflicts the earth's forests must be sought in the word forests—that is, in the world we articulate, and which confirms us as agents of that earthly malaise."[32]

The realization that nature and culture are constructions, woven together as a network of relationships, has led some to argue that any development of social behavior belongs to a critical revitalization of the powers of signification—to the poetics of world making and transfiguration. Clark, for example, writes of the need to "delve more deeply into those inseparable dimensions of body and mind that dualism has so fatefully divided. As we explore such realities as thought, idea, image, sign, symbol, signifier, and language on the one hand, and feeling, emotion, disposition, instinct, passion, and desire on the other, the interconnection between the two realms will become increasingly apparent."[33] Evidently, the locus of such an enterprise is the liminal space between signifier and signified, mind and matter, intellect and antibody.

People are caught, then, in this place between recognizing themselves as part of Nature and being separate from it. This double sense arises through the acknowledging of "otherness," or the copresence of what is not of culture and what will always exceed cultural definition. This is the wild in its most autonomous and unmediated form. As a radical "other," the wild is unrepresentable, unnameable; and although it can never be captured as a presence, it is at the same time not exactly nothing. The poet Wallace Stevens perhaps best captures this sense in the last few lines of "The Snow Man":

> For the listener, who listens in the snow,
> And, nothing himself, beholds
> Nothing that is not there and the nothing that is.[34]

The nonabsent absence of the "other" escapes being seen or said, and yet it remains the original source of all saying, the first inspiration. All people have likely experienced this at one time or another, especially as young children staring with wonder at the world, or, perhaps, during times of hallucination or of religious and holy encounter.[35] Such "happenings," in turn, precipitate wonder, reflection, language, and ideas, enabling reality to "appear" (partially) and be shared among members of a community. With time, the surrounding of this (partial) reality with words and concepts attributes an everyday status to things, a familiarity.

The difficulty arises when the wonderful original disappears behind an excessively habitual, meaningless language—one in which the signifier has thickened to a "crust," denying the fullness of what is signified to present itself fully as other. Such paralysis occurs when the habits and conventions of cultural signification become so prosaic, so hardened, so total as absolute presence, that one can simple no longer see the self-contained mystery and potential of beings and things in themselves. Banished, also, is the unruly wildness and freedom of the nonhuman other—of what is, in fact, the very source of evolutionary life and human creativity. One need only consider how the engineering of the gene—that last bastion of nonhuman, indeterminate, and wild freedom—is close to being fully mapped, colonized, and manipulated. Our modern-day "wilderness areas" are no refuge either, as they, too, have been charted, mapped, photographed, painted, managed, and "set aside" as a cultural resource. All of creation is apparently becoming less wild and more domesticated, possessed, inert, and drained of all that prompts wonderment and reflection. Habitual modes of knowing and speaking, when hardened and blinkered, simply exclude the otherness that is internal to things, denying them the possibility of becoming, of further emerging and fulfilling their po-tential. The contemporary denial of others is of consequence for both biological evolu-tion as well as for the development of human consciousness and moral reflectivity.[36]

In evolutionary terms, the calcification of life occurs when transmutation slows or ceases, when life stops. In linguistic and cultural terms, this atrophy translates to the deadening of poetic metaphor, to the failure to recognize that metaphor and image are not secondary representations of a deeper, external truth, but are constitutive of a cultural reality and ever capable of inventing truth. This atrophy of the imagination has arisen in large part because of the predominance of empiricist and objective logic, inherited from the promotion of rationality during the Enlightenment. Here, one simply cannot see beyond "X is equal to what is." Creative development both in Natural evolution and the human imagination, however, entails the realization of potential—the bringing forth of latent and previously unknown events and meanings. In the creative process of becoming, "X is equal to what is and what is not (yet)." The revitalization of wonderment and poetic value in human relations with Nature is, therefore, dependent on the ability to strip away the crust of habit and convention that prohibits fresh sight and relationship. One must get behind the veneer of language in order to discover aspects of the unknown within what is already familiar. Such transfiguration is a process of finding and then founding *alternative* worlds. I can think of no greater raison d'être for the landscape architectural project.

In describing the capacity of human thought, George Steiner writes that "ours is the ability, the need, to gainsay or 'unsay' the world, to imagine it and speak it otherwise."[37] Through the *disappearance* of the distinct and separate form of things there is enabled the *appearance* of a radically new form of experience and knowing.

One must first shed the conventional view that language merely describes an external, detached reality, and realize instead that both the signified field and the things signified are combined inextricably in mutually constitutive processes of ever-becoming. Nature as an autonomous, free, irreducible, and animate "other" must be enable to engage with, and have presence for, people, thereby continually challenging human concepts and ways of knowing. As Merleau-Ponty outlines: "It is essential for the thing and the world to present themselves as 'open,' to project us to beyond their predetermined manifestations and constantly to promise us other things to see."[38] This view may entail as much terror and fear as it does harmony and mutuality (which, of course, was the idea of the Sublime in landscape and art during the eighteenth century, and which underlay Otto's ideas of the Holy in the twentieth century). Current attempts to control Nature, to leave it alone, or to conflate it with culture fail to recognize the inevitable anomalous dialectic of human existence.

The emancipation of both nature and the human imagination depends, therefore, first on the capacity to "unsay" the world and, second, on the ability to image it differently so that wonder might be brought into appearance. This transformation and enrichment of meaning belongs to the poetic—to the capacity of the visionary to change vocabularies and break convention so that hidden potentials are made actual. As Joel Kovel recognizes: "We cannot collapse the human and Natural worlds one onto the other, except as a wishful illusion. We have only the choice as to how Nature is to be signified: As an inert other, or as [the poet William] Blake fully expressed, an entity transfigured with spirit."[39] Culture evolves through metaphor and the release of more edifying relationships between things. Poetic transfiguration enables an unfolding of things previously unforeseen, raising people to a perception of the wonderful and the infinite. The aim is one of ever-increasing wholeness, richness, and fullness of differentiation and subjectivity.

The idea that the poetic language of images and likenesses can expand—both imaginatively and literally—the internal structures of the world underlies the writings of the chemist-turned-poet Gaston Bachelard, who believed that poetic image could be "a synthesizing force for human existence."[40] In warning against the studying of matter as an object (as in the scientific experiment), Bachelard insisted instead on the development of a deeply sensual knowledge of the world, derived from how one lives or experiences it. He spoke, also, of the "reverberancy" with which poetic images resonate with human feelings and imagination, describing their constitutive power in forging renewed relations between things. Through his description of "poetic reverie," Bachelard's work shows how the joining of substances with adjectives can derive from matter a spirit—a truth. Hence, one might speak of "humid fire," "milky water," or "night as nocturnal matter."

Bewilderment, Wonder, and Indetermination

These ideas about imaginative renewal through fresh and resonant association were particularly well understood by the Surrealists. Artists such as Breton, Miro, Magritte, Tanguy, and Ernst sought to find correspondences between Natural life and human life through the workings of the psyche and the imagination.[41] In Max Ernst's work, sun, sky, universe, earth, vegetable, animal, serpent, mineral, and human are woven together in ways that are both familiar and radically new. They are uncanny in that their oddness, their strange and bewildering quality, prompts both wonder and imaginative recognition—they evoke *relationship*. The Cartesian dualities of people and Nature, matter and thought, subject and object, male and female, are conflated into fantastic worlds of mutuality, paradox, and difference. In describing certain poetic procedures such as "overpainting," "frottage," and "lop-lop," Ernst insisted upon the "bewitching" of reason, taste, and objectivity. In fact, one of the key procedures in Surrealist transformation was "the exploitation of the fortuitous meeting of two distant realities on an inappropriate plane... or, to use a shorter term, *the cultivation of a systematic bewildering*."[42]

Bewilderment is simply a prerequisite for another form of seeing; it is an unsettled appearance that allows for the double presence of human and other. That the poet or the artist are the seers and makers of such works derives from the traditions of *mimesis* and *poesis*, activities that entail the actualization of potential, the bringing forth of something previously unknown, or even nonexistent. The development of techniques of collage and montage simply represents the deep (natural?) human desire to realize new enlightened visions—new connections and possibilities for relationship between things.[43] Furthermore, the parallels between the vocabularies of ecology and collage are striking—terms such as *indeterminacy, inclusivity, overlay, rupture, simultaneity, stochastic event, instability, association, collusion,* and other morphological processes speak of an ever-renewing "unity through diversity." Similarities between ecology and creative transmutation are indicative of an alternate kind of landscape architecture, one in which calcified conventions about how people live and relate to land, nature, and place are challenged and the multivariate wonders of life are once again released through invention.

These forms of ecological creativity would appear to follow from Henry Bergson's remark in *Creative Evolution* that "the role of life is to inject some *interdetermination* into matter."[44] Bergson speaks of the infinite creativity of biological and imaginative *life*. In his refusal to reduce nature to a physical, "knowable" object, he describes a need to liberate life so that its fullest potentials may come into appearance. Bergson's is a creative evolution of indeterminate unfolding, a process in which "matter is the deposit of life, the static residues of action done, choices made in the past. Living memory is the past felt in the actualities of realities, of change."[45] Such an interrelational view directs us toward more "heterotopic" kinds of activity in space than singular, "utopic" acts. Whereas heterotopia's ad hoc inclusivity and open-endedness portends a disturbing and bewildering prospect, it also systematically denies singularity, totality, determinacy, and hierarchy. As a "structured heterogeneity," such a complex field is neither chaotic nor ordered, but free and organic. Thus, a true ecological landscape architecture might be less about the construction of finished and completed works, and more about the design of "processes," "strategies," "agencies," and "scaffoldings"—catalytic frameworks that might enable a diversity of relationships to create, emerge, network, interconnect, and differentiate.[46]

The aim for the design of these strategic grounds would not be to celebrate differentiation and pluralism in a representational way, but rather to construct enabling relationships between the freedoms of life (in terms of unpredictability, contingency, and change) in the presence of formal coherency and structural/material precision. This double aim underlies—in part—the works of Rem Koolhaas and is particularly well exemplified in his unbuilt proposal for the Parc de la Villette, Paris, in which the delineation and "equipping" of a "strategic field" with "social instruments" was planned to optimize physical, spatial, and material identity while allowing for an almost infinite range of programmatic events, combinations, improvisations, differentiations, and adjacencies.[47] As Sanford Kwinter describes: "All of Koolhaas's recent work is *evolved*—rather than designed—within the hypermodern event-space of complex, sensitive, dynamical indeterminacy and change… [The design principles display] a very clear orientation toward evolutionary, time-based processes, dynamic geometric *structurations*—not structures per se, but forms that follow and fill the wake of concrete yet unpredeterminable events… This is because, instead of designing artificial environments, [Koolhaas] deploys richly imbricated systems of interacting elements that set in motion rather artificial ecologies that, in turn, take on a genuine self-organizing life of their own."[48] The resultant "image" of such designs may not be one that is currently thought to be ecological in appearance (which, as I have argued, remains fallaciously bound up with the ideas of untouched and native "nature"), but its strategic organicism—its deployment as an active agent, a metabolic urbanism—aspires to nothing less than the injection of indetermination, diversification, and freedom into both the social and Natural worlds—values that are surely central to any ecological, moral, and poetic notions about evolutionary and creative life. Other projects by Koolhaas, such as Yokohama Harbor, further demonstrate the oneiric lyricism of programmatic strategies that remain open-ended and promote new life forms and sets of events.

Coda

My purpose in this essay is to present a number of theoretical bases that might allow for a more animate appropriation of ecology in landscape architectural practice. These bases have little to do with the object-centered advocacy of Nature ("environment") or culture ("art") and point instead toward the highly interactive processes in relationships that are *life* itself—life as both a specific and autonomous system of networks, forces, combinations, unfoldings, events, and transformations. What is important in this view is how creative practices of ecology and landscape architecture construct—or, more precisely, *enable*—alternative forms of relationship and hybridization between people, place, material, and Earth. Echoing evolutionary principles, these enabling strategies function less as instruments and ameliorants and more as agents, as processes, as active imbroglios and ever-emerging networks of potential. Obviously, I am speaking here of a landscape architecture that has yet to appear fully, one that is less preoccupied with ameliorative, stylistic, or pictorial concerns and more actively engaged with imaginative, enabling, and diversifying practices—*practices of the wild*.[49]

How may the pulsing flow and flux of wild life, its autonomous status as "other," and its reflective and moral sense to be channeled, liberated, and expressed through an ecology and landscape of creative agents? The answers, I believe, lie within the powers of both Natural and cultural agencies in the evolving of landscapes that precipitate (and are caught within) the processes of indetermination and diversification; landscapes that engage, enable, diversify, trick, and emancipate, and elude—put simply, landscapes that function as actants, as continual transformations and encounters that actively resist closure and representation.[50]

Notes
This chapter originally appeared in George Thompson and Frederick Steiner, eds., *Ecological Design and Planning* (New York: John Wiley and Sons, 1997).

1_ Coleridge 1845, p. 223.
2_ Bergson 1944, p. 3.
3_ Wilson 1992.
4_ Botkin 1990, p. 25.
5_ Nietzsche 1984, pp. 23–24.
6_ Ibid., p. 24
7_ The relationship between biological, evolutionary processes and the human imagination is discussed beautifully in Cobb 1977. Creativity and evolution is also implicit in Bergson 1944.
8_ Clark 1993, p. 351.
9_ Corner 1991, pp. 125–131.
10_Habermas 1983; Goin 1996.
11_Although the tendency to speak of a duality between nature and culture has persisted throughout modernity, the truth of this belief has been challenged by Latour 1993, who argues that the social and natural worlds are inextricably interrelated.
12_Corner 1990.
13_McHarg 1969.
14_Worster 1979, p. 315.
15_Evernden 1993, p. 22.
16_Worster 1979, p. 304.
17_Evernden 1993, p. 23.
18_Ibid., p. 23.
19_Groening and Wolschke-Buhlman 1992 and 1994; Sorvig 1994; and MacKenzie 1987.
20_Zimmerman et al. 1993; Merchant 1992; Oelschlaeger 1991, pp. 281–319.
21_Zimmerman et al. 1993, pp. 345–437.
22_Bookchin 1993 and 1991.
23_Clark 1993, p. 352.
24_Coleridge 1845. Quoted in Cobb 1977, p. 15.
25_Bookchin 1990, pp. 12–48.
26_For more on the idea of agency, see Haraway 1991, Latour 1993, and Rose 1994.
27_Kohak 1984, p. 5.
28_Nietzsche 1984, p. 27.
29_Biehl 1993, p. 375.
30_Harrison 1992, p. 201.
31_Bergman 1990, pp. 1–2.
32_Evernden 1993, pp. 145–146.

33_Clark 1993, p. 352.

34_Stevens 1981, p. 10.

35_Evernden 1992, pp. 107–124; Cobb 1977, p. 30; Taylor 1990; and Vanderbilt 1993.

36_Evernden 1992, pp. 116–124; Oelschlaeger 1991, pp. 320–353; and Bergman 1990.

37_Steiner 1984, p. 398.

38_Merleau-Ponty 1962, p. 384.

39_Kovel 1993, pp. 413–414.

40_Bachelard 1987, p. 107.

41_The importance of the psyche for how people relate to Nature is discussed most profoundly in Jung 1973. Of particular relevance is Jung's discussion of "synchronicity," which, like Bachelard's ideas of "reverberation," describes correspondence between Natural life and human life, especially as apprehended in the unconscious imagination.

42_Spies 1991, p. 43.

43_Corner 1992, pp. 265–275.

44_Bergson, 1944, p. 139.

45_Ibid., p. xiv.

46_Haraway 1991, Latour 1993, Rose 1994.

47_Koolhaas and Mau 1995, pp. 894–939; Lucan 1991, pp. 86–95.

48_Kwinter 1993, pp. 84–85.

49_Snyder 1990.

50_Corner 1996.

References

Bachelard, Gaston. 1987. *On Poetic Imagination and Reverie*. Rev. ed. Translated by Collette Gaudin. Dallas: Spring Publications.

Bergman, Charles. 1990. *Wild Echoes*. New York: McGraw-Hill.

Bergson, Henri. 1944. *Creative Evolution*. Translated by Arthur Mitchell. New York: Modern Library.

Biehl, Janet. 1993. "Dialectics in the Ethics of Social Ecology." Pp. 374–389 in *Environmental Philosophy*, ed. Michael Zimmerman, et al. Englewood Cliffs, NJ: Prentice Hall.

Bookchin, Murray. 1990. *The Philosophy of Social Ecology*. Montreal: Black Rose Books.

—1991. *The Ecology of Freedom*. Rev. ed. Montreal: Black Rose Books.

—1993. "What Is Social Ecology?" Pp. 354–373 in *Environmental Philosophy*, ed. Michael Zimmerman, et al. Englewood Cliffs, NJ: Prentice Hall.

Botkin, Daniel. 1990. *Discordant Harmonies: A New Ecology for the Twenty-First Century*. Oxford: Oxford University Press.

Carson, Rachel. 1962. *Silent Spring*. Boston: Houghton Mifflin.

Clark, John. 1993. "Social Ecology Introduction." Pp. 345–353 in *Environmental Philosophy*, ed. Michael Zimmerman, et al. Englewood Cliffs, NJ: Prentice Hall.

Cobb, Edith. 1977. *The Ecology of the Imagination in Childhood*. New York: Columbia University Press.

Coleridge, Samuel Taylor. 1845. *The Works of Samuel Taylor Coleridge, Prose and Verse*. Philadelphia: Thomas Cowperthwait.

Collingwood, R.G. 1960. *The Idea of Nature*. London: Oxford University Press.

Corner, James. 1990. "A Discourse on Theory I: Sounding the Depths—Origins, Theory, and Representation." *Landscape Journal* 9(2): 60–78.

—1991. "A Discourse on Theory II: Three Tyrannies of Contemporary Theory and the Alternative of Hermeneutics." *Landscape Journal* 10(2): 115–133.

—1992. "Representation and Landscape: Drawing and Making in the Landscape Medium." *Word and Image* 8(3): 243–275.

—1996. "Aqueous Agents: The (Re)Presentation of Water in the Work of George Hargreaves." *Process Architecture* 128: 46–61.

Evernden, Neil. 1992. *The Social Creation of Nature*. Baltimore: Johns Hopkins University Press.

—1993. *The Natural Alien: Humankind and Environment*. 2d ed. Toronto: University of Toronto Press.

Goin, Peter. 1996. *Humanature*. Austin: University of Texas Press.

Groening, Gert, and Joachim Wolschke-Buhlman. 1992. "Some Notes on the Mania for Native Plants in Germany." *Landscape Journal* 11(2): 116–126.

—1994. "Response: If the Shoe Fits, Wear It!" *Landscape Journal* 13(1): 62–63.

Habermas, Jurgen. 1983. "Modernity: An Incomplete Project." Pp. 13–15 in *The Anti-Aesthetic*, ed. Hal Foster. Port Townsend, WA: Bay Press.

Haraway, Donna. 1991. *Simians, Cyborgs and Women: The Reinvention of Nature*. New York: Routledge.

Harrison, Robert Pogue. 1992. *Forests: The Shadow of Civilization*. Chicago: University of Chicago Press.

Harvey, David. 1989. *The Condition of Postmodernity*. Oxford: Blackwell.

Jung, C.G. 1973. *Synchronicity: An Acausal Connecting Principle*. Translated by R. Hull. Princeton, NJ: Princeton University Press.

Kohak, Erazim. 1984. *The Embers and the Stars*. Chicago: University of Chicago Press.

Koolhaas, Rem, and Bruce Mau. 1995. *S, M, L, XL*. New York: Monacelli Press.

Kovel, Joel. 1993. "The Marriage of Radical Ecologies." Pp. 406–417 in *Environmental Philosophy*, ed. Michael Zimmerman, et al. Englewood Cliffs, NJ: Prentice Hall.

Kwinter, Sanford. 1993. "Rem Koolhaas, OMA: The Reinvention of Geometry." *Assemblage* 18: 83–85.

Latour, Bruno. 1993. *We Have Never Been Modern*. Cambridge, MA: Harvard University Press.

Leopold, Aldo. 1949. *A Sand County Almanac*. New York: Oxford University Press.

Lucan, Jacques. 1991. *OMA—Rem Koolhaas*. Princeton, NJ: Princeton University Press.

MacKenzie, J. 1987. *The Empire of Nature*. Manchester: Manchester University Press.

McHarg, Ian. 1969. *Design With Nature*. Garden City, NY: Doubleday/Natural History Press. 1992. Reprint, New York: John Wiley and Sons.

Merchant, Carolyn. 1992. *Radical Ecology*. New York: Routledge, Chapman and Hall.

Merleau-Ponty, Maurice. 1962. *The Phenomenology of Perception*. Translated by Colin Smith. Suffolk, UK: Routledge and Kegan Paul.

Nietzsche, Friedrich. 1984. *Human, All Too Human*. Translated by Marion Faber. Lincoln: University of Nebraska Press.

Oelschlaeger, Max. 1991. *The Idea of Wilderness: From Prehistory to the Age of Ecology*. New Haven: Yale University Press.

Rorty, Richard. 1979. *Philosophy and the Mirror of Nature*. Princeton, NJ: Princeton University Press.

Rose, Dan. 1994. *Active Ingredients*. Unpublished manuscript, University of Pennsylvania.

Snyder, Gary. 1990. *The Practice of the Wild*. Berkeley, CA: North Point Press.

Sorvig, Kim. 1994. "Natives and Nazis: An Imaginary Conspiracy in Ecological Design." *Landscape Journal* 13(1): 58–61.

Spies, Werner. 1991. *Max Ernst: Collages*. Translated by John William Gabriel. New York: Harry N. Abrams.

Steiner, George. 1984. *George Steiner: A Reader*. Oxford: Oxford University Press.

Stevens, Wallace. 1981. *Collected Poems*. New York: Knopf.

Taylor, Mark. 1990. *Tears*. Albany: State University of New York Press.

Vanderbilt, Paul. 1993. *Between the Landscape and Its Other*. Baltimore: Johns Hopkins University Press.

Wilson, Alex. 1992. *The Culture of Nature*. Cambridge, MA: Blackwell.

Worster, Donald. 1979. *Nature's Economy: The Roots of Ecology*. New York: Anchor Press.

Zimmerman, Michael E., J. Baird Callicott, George Sessions, Karen J. Warren, and John Clark, eds. 1993. *Environmental Philosophy*. Englewood Cliffs, NJ: Prentice Hall.

Ecosystem dynamics are the normal pattern of observed changes to prevailing ecosystem conditions, functions, and their related ecological structures. As the consequence of complexity inherent in living systems, the dynamics are inevitable and to some extent, unpredictable as to the time and scale of occurrence.

Nina-Marie Lister

DYNAMICS

But operational dynamics and choreographies also extend to (designed) landscapes and entire cities, and they hint at the blurring, overlap, interdependence and/or full hybridization of environmental and urban systems. The scoring of pedestrian and human movements analytically or projectively; the productive alignments of bird and bee behaviors with building- and flood-scale infrastructures; the movements of wastes and resources and pollution and water across large metropolitan harbors; and inventive ways to record and project the movement of individual agents—digital particles or even pigeon-mounted cameras—across real and fictional topographies together form an expanded array of ways in which the world is constructed and depicted from a movement, performance, and operational standpoint.

Chris Reed

Lawrence Halprin & Associates. Motation Study. Nicolett Mall Between 6th and 7th Streets. Date of publication 1969. (SEE POSTER)

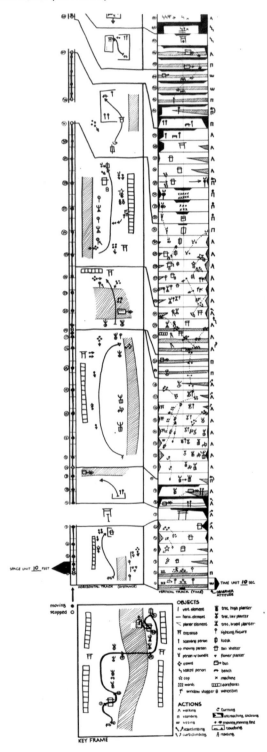

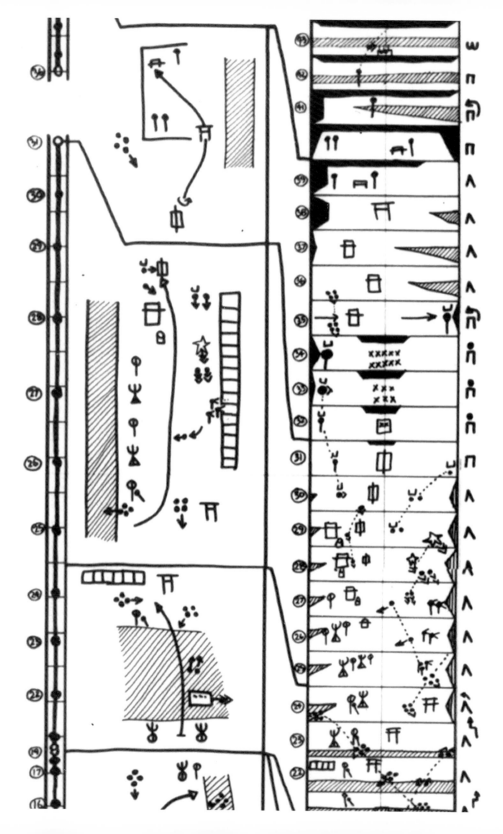

H.T. Odum. Energy and Matter Flow Through an Ecosystem, adapted from Silver. 1971.

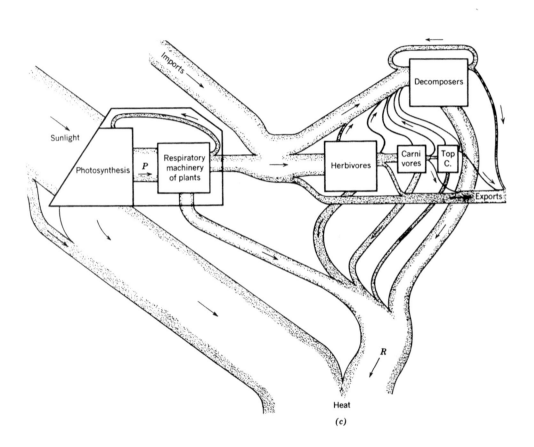

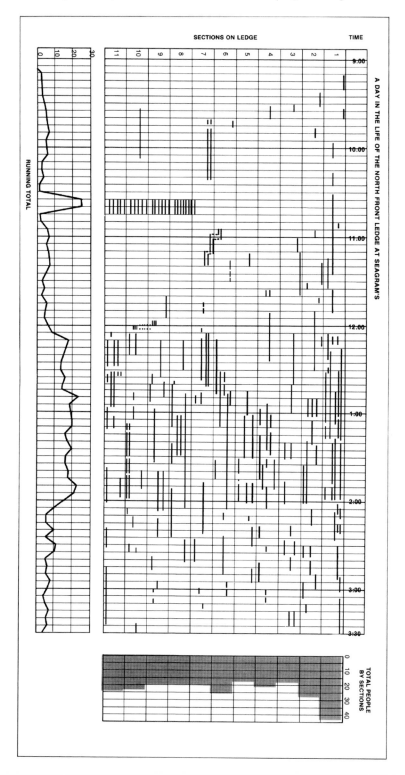

West 8. Mimicry, Coastal Birds and Shell Fields. Eastern Scheldt Storm Surge Barrier, Zeeland, the Netherlands. 1990.

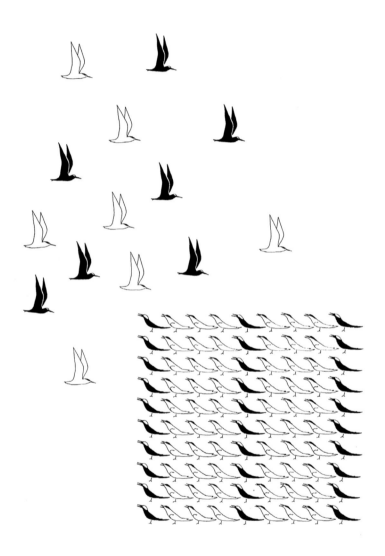

GROSS.MAX + Mark Dion. Delirious Piranesi in Bloom. Vertical Garden, London, United Kingdom. 2005.

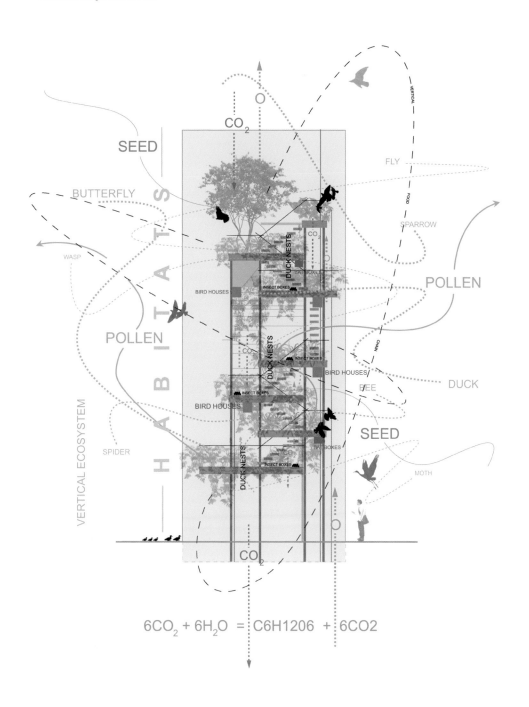

$$6CO_2 + 6H_2O = C6H1206 + 6CO2$$

Andrea Hansen. Tokyo Bay Marine Fields. 2009.

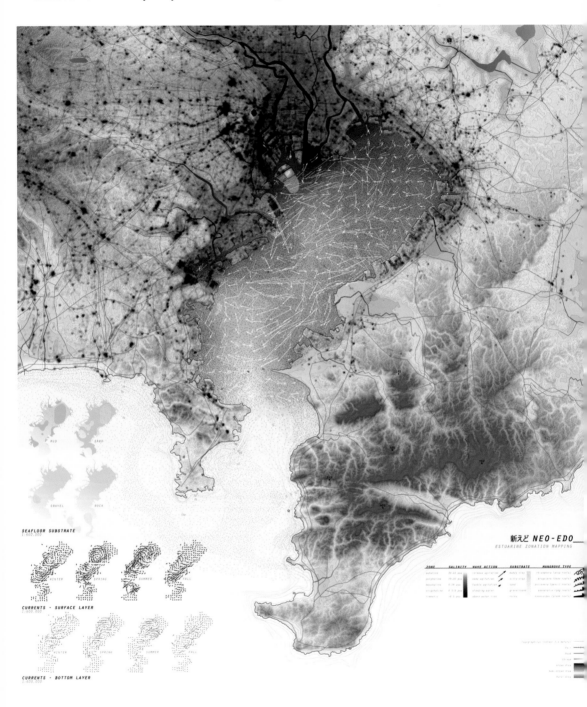

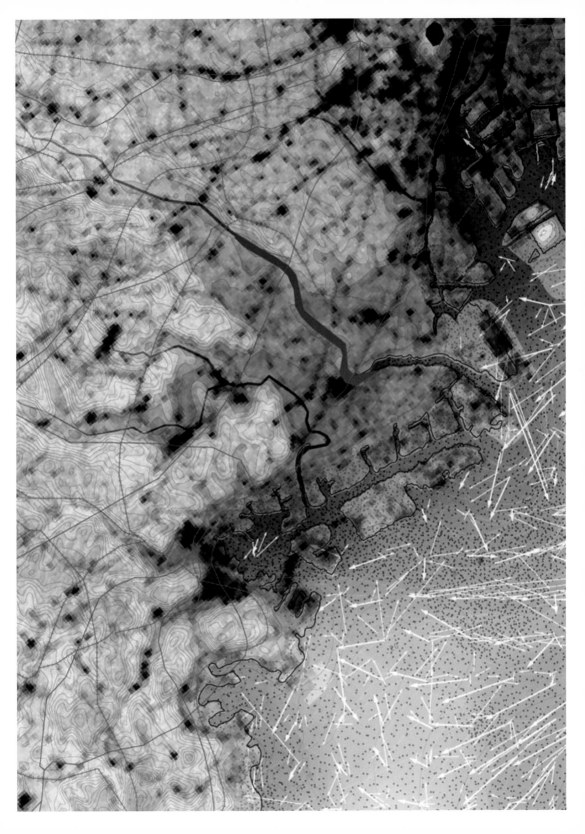

OPSYS/Pierre Bélanger. Waste Flows, Backflows, and Reflows. Maas-Rhine River Delta, Rotterdam, the Netherlands. 2009.

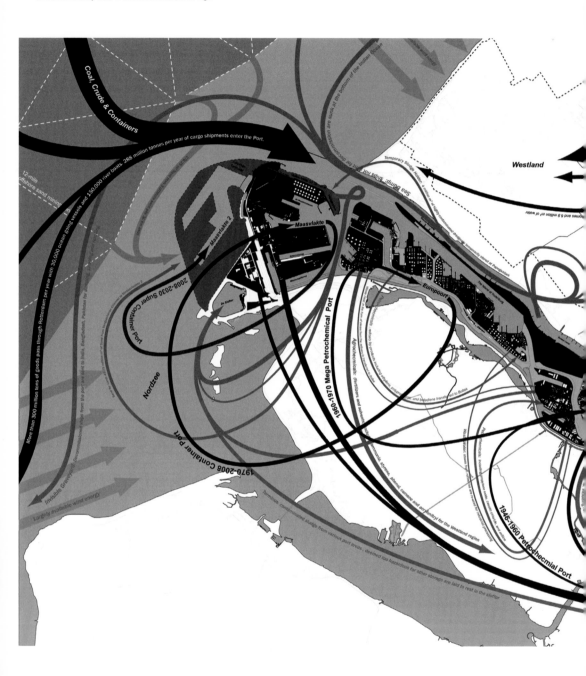

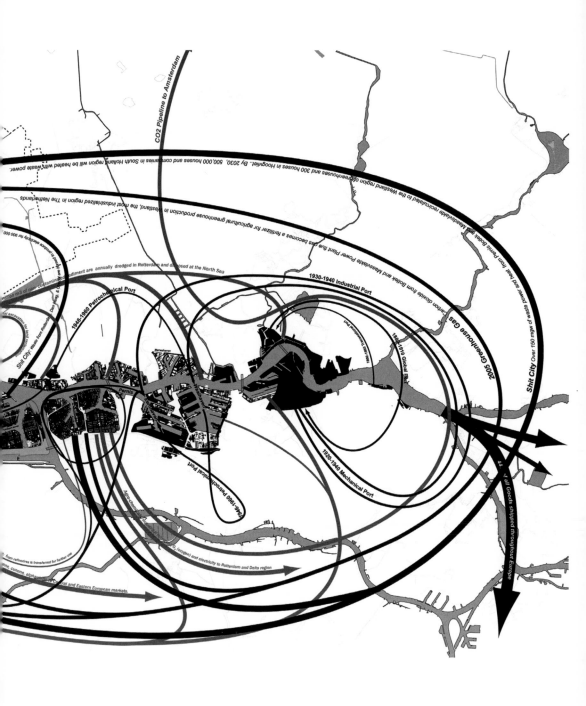

CO2 Pipeline to Amsterdam

By 2030, 500,000 houses and companies in Hoogvliet, 300 houses and companies in the Westland region will be heated with waste power.

Westland, the most industrialized greenhouse production in The Netherlands

Maasvlakte recirculated to the Westland region of greenhouses and 300 houses and companies in South Holland region will be heated with waste power.

Carbon dioxide from Botlek and Maasvlakte Power Plant flue gas becomes a fertilizer for agricultural greenhouse production in Westland, the most industrialized region in The Netherlands

million m3 of new containing sediment are annually dredged in Rotterdam and disposed at the North Sea

2005 Greenhouse Gas

1930-1940 Industrial Port

1946-1980 Petrochemical Port

Shit City: Waste from Rotterda

1870-1910 Global Pilot

Shit City: Over 150 mgw of waste and heat from Botlek

Pernis

Maasvlakte

1920-1940 Mechanical Port

1946-1980 Petrochemical Port

Afrohaven?

(toegave) and electricity to Rotterdam and Delta region

from refineries is transferred for further use

cumene, alphagene... Central and Eastern European markets.

44 of all Goods shipped throughout Europe

temporarily stored at Papegaaibek

Koelwaterkanaal

Europoort

The Island of Rozenburg

Scheur Car

...propylene, and butadiene transferred to Boltek

Waste Water: steam from refine...

Petrochemicals: including propyl...

Dredge City: 14 million m3 of non-contaminated sediment are annually dredge

Sand for Land: Dredgeate from channel excavation for land reclamation.

Shit City: Waste from Rotterdam, Den Haag, & Utrecht are burned t

1946-1960 Petrochemical Po

Steinweg

Pern

Botlek

3e Petroleum haven

1e Petroleum haven

Petro-chemica

A

Aranda Lasch. The Pigeon Project. 2004.

Designing Ecologies

Christopher Hight

What we need is an ecology without nature: the ultimate obstacle to protecting nature is the very notion of nature we rely on.
Slavoj Žižek, *In Defense of Lost Causes* (2008)

If environmental transformation is this century's greatest concern and central narrative, ecology is perhaps our most important epistemological and ontic framework for understanding and projecting possible futures.[1] The term "ecology" simultaneously refers to a general epistemological and ontological framework as well as scientific study of interaction between systems and their assemblages into (temporal) coherences. In recent design, ecology has served as a poetic metaphor, techno-scientific imperative, and aesthetic justification. It has been employed to argue for a return to traditional architecture and used for the most rococo parametricism; ecological awareness has become an accreditation requirement and a marketing tool. Thus, even as ecology increasingly serves as a general paradigm and central organizing narrative for our culture and the contemporary imagination, as the term proliferates, it is in danger of becoming a shibboleth applied to everything yet meaning almost nothing. Once transposed from science and nature, it can all too easily be reduced to quotidian truisms that everything is interlinked and interacting in complex ways. Greater specify is therefore required, along with a theoretical problematization of the transposition of ecological concepts into the design fields.

Modern narratives of rupture, progress, and utopia are being rewritten as eschatologies of environmental calamity—both ongoing disruptions (droughts, hurricanes, etc.) and novel threats (massive coastal flooding of newly constructed megacities due to sea-level rise, superbugs resistant to antibiotics and spread via global transport, and so on). Walter Benjamin famously presented Paul Klee's *Angelus Novus* as an iconic image of modern progress and its history, propelled incessantly into the future on the winds of change, its startled look taking in the debris field left its wake.[2] It was upon this tabula rasa that the Radiant City and other utopian urban visions were to be constructed. The modern angel of progress has been recast as a vengeful Gaia, or Mother Nature (this volume's excerpt of Daniel Botkin's *Discordant Harmonies* tracks such anthropomorphic personifications of Nature). The tabula rasa has become the thick infrastructural strata, and the future utopia has inverted as the "remediation" of toxic brownfield sites. The debris field of modernization and progress has been supplanted by what C.S. Holling terms "creative destruction" as systems lurch out of one steady-state and into a different pattern of organization.

Even as delineations of the constructed and "natural" environments have blurred, the capacity of design to articulate their relationships seems to have withered, with experimental architecture relegated to the role of compensatory icons and urbanism dominated by the palliative confections of New Urbanism. Paradoxically, certain designers and related scholars articulated the promise of renewed agency via the ecological. By the mid-1990s, the urban environment could no longer be usefully understood through the dualisms of Culture versus Nature.[3] Rem Koolhaas famously declared in *S,M,L,XL*'s paradigmatic text, "The Generic City," that what we used to call the "city" now worked and looked more like landscapes. His novel presentation of architecture and urbanism culminated with a series of images of a rainy Singapore taken through a car window. The images are more haptic than optic: one can smell the ozone produced as rain is vaporized by superheated pavement and feel the humidity more readily than delineate form or recognizable figures of architecture, landscape, or the city. In these photographs of a generic landscape-city, Koolhaas deployed the very technology of reproduction that Benjamin once said drained the original of its aura into a endless cycle of exchange, to produce a powerful environmental ambience and presence. Modernist space was here replaced by literal atmosphere. Buildings, trees, sky, smog, and pavement blurred in the mist through the rearview mirror as our Dutch angel of the new sped down the motorway.

Koolhaas's images of the environmental dissolution of architecture and urban form evoke the sorts of entangled blurring of an ecological worldview while also presenting it as an existential crisis for the design fields in an uncanny epistemological parallel of Holling's concept of creative destruction: the urban environment has suddenly transformed from one coherent state (that of the classical city) into another organization, necessitating radical adaptation of the discrete systems of knowledge that had evolved within the previous state lest they go extinct because they are no longer fit for the new environment. Charles Waldheim, for example, has argued that landscape design effectively "usurped" architecture's place at the top of the professional and professorial food chain.

Thus ecology operates for the design disciplines as both catalyst of innovation and eternal disruptive force in a similar way that industrialization did for Modernist architecture in the early twentieth century, or as technology served following World War II. For example, in his conclusion to *Theory and Design in the First Machine Age*, Reyner Banham mapped two ways out of the impasse that he had chronicled through his account of modern architectural history: choose either to conserve the discipline and risk becoming irrelevant to a technological age, or utterly retool architectural knowledge and practice, but in doing so "discard" the cultural identity of architecture as a field of knowledge.[4] A series of subsequent articles extended *Theory and Design's* conclusion.[5] There were, Banham argued, two Janus-faced identities of "Architecture." One was "tradition," the disciplinary and cultural identity given by accumulated knowledge upon which one would operate and innovate. The other was "technological," an attempt to determine design as a science. Both presented problems for Banham. He was concerned that the technological and science-driven architectures could all too easily lead to "unorganized hordes of uncoordinated specialists [who] could flood into the architects' preserves."[6] Rather than make architecture relevant, this inundation would simply dissipate its sophisticated design knowledge. Yet Banham also believed that formalism was profoundly retrograde and amounted to disciplinary navel-gazing.[7] To extend Banham's colorful metaphor of the architectural discipline as a fortress of knowledge, while retrenchment into cultural tradition may fortify its walls against the "hordes" of technological barbarians outside, it may also lose any strategic importance as the would-be invaders simply sweep around it. Those who guard the gates will soon discover that they have become docents in a museum of fossils.

Banham presented a route out of this impasse in his subsequent book, *Architecture of the Well-Tempered Environment*, via the modulation of the environment. Echoing his arguments about technology in general, environmental control systems are both disruptive to the tradition of architecture and the condition of possibility for a truly contemporary architecture by shifting from a focus on form, mass, and stability to program, atmosphere, and systems of exchange. Environmental control systems served as his literal example, and while far from "green," they were seen as a harbinger of the realignment of architectural knowledge and practice from walls and form to environment and interactive systems. In his narrative, the origin story of the primitive hut was to be replaced by the campfire.

Thus, in the nine years between *Theory and Design* and *Well-Tempered Environment,* a significant shift appears to have occurred in which a critical diagnosis of a crisis is converted into a projection of an alternative. Banham's work is of course just one coordinate within a broader transformation and reemergence of ecology and the environment in the 1960s. One might also point to Rachel Carson's 1962 *Silent Spring,* often understood as marking a new period of environmental awareness and political action, while Ian McHarg's 1969 *Design With Nature* delineated an environmental determinist paradigm of landscape design.

Banham's two "Architectures" of the science/technological and the cultural/social reflect what Bruno Latour has called the "modern constitution" of knowledge. In *We Have Never Been Modern,* Latour details this constitution as consisting of two domains that "must remain absolutely distinct."[8] These domains were Nature and Society, and as a corollary, Science and Culture. Drawing from his previous work in the history and theory of science, Latour maps this bicameral division in specific scientific experiments and abstract philosophical concepts. This separation began, he argues (unsurprisingly), by the so-called Kantian revolution in which *phenomena* and concepts on the one hand and *noumena* and things in themselves on the other were purified into two distinct areas in a way they were not previously, with the latter accessible only though their concepts within the subject. This division allowed Kant to construct what he believed to be a stable and systematic philosophical "architectonics."[9] Yet once this purification occurred, Latour argued, many schools of thought tried to "overcome" this divide. However, he also claims that most of these attempts simply managed to widen the gap by collapsing into one pole (phenomenology and logical positivism are two opposed examples). Such apparent "bridges" did not overcome Kant's epistemological structure so much as it reified a logical distinction into ontology and pathos. Things are thus continually "purified" into one pole or the other. At its postmodern terminus, everything becomes a construction of social, cultural, and linguistic conventions. There is no truth or reality, just ideological tropes and "reality-effect."[10] At its scientific extreme, everything cultural or social should be treated as if it were natural and studied as such. Nature or Society, Science or Culture, is alternatively transcendent or immanent. Yet, Latour argues, this creates a series of paradoxes, among them that Nature is understood as immanent (socially and culturally constructed) even though we simultaneously embrace the anti-anthropocentric notion that there is a vast realm that exceeds us; similarly Society-Culture is treated as transcendent even though of course it is constructed. One can see here how such paradoxes provide the armature for Banham's two Architectures of Science and Culture.

While one might think we have moved beyond Banham's obvious Nature/Culture binaries, the encounter between ecology and design has followed Latour's paradoxical modernity. Significant leaders in landscape architecture and architecture have positioned ecology (and the environment) as antagonistic or even fundamentally disruptive to the cultural tradition of their respective disciplines.

For example, Preston Scott Cohen and Erika Naginski's contribution to *Ecological Urbanism* approaches ecology has a harbinger of disciplinary doom. In their presentation, nature seems a vengeful and uninvited guest at a the salon of culture as ecology that threatens to "negate the project of architecture."[11] They argue that positioning ecology and biology as a model for digital design and an ethical imperative for sustainable architectures necessarily, "reject[s] the cultural, social and symbolic life of forms."[12] For them, architecture is a system of knowledge that requires autonomy from its "environment" in terms of the discipline and, to a large degree, the building's relationship to its surroundings. Moreover, it is this separation (purification) that allows for evolution of the environment (because it is constructed). Rather than embrace ecology, they seek to turn the tables and position the discipline as a means of critical thinking, "provoking" and "demystifying" the camouflaged ideologies that are smuggled in under the banner of the ecological and sustainable.

Likewise, Penelope Dean's "Never Mind All That Environmental Rubbish, Get On With Your Architecture" is a scathing indictment of scientifically determined applications of ecology and environment in architecture. For Dean, William McDonough and Ken Yeang exemplify an approach to the environment in architecture as "applied scientific solution over sociocultural projection or formal innovation."[13] If techno-scientific discourse is given the authority to determine design, then environmental "performance criteria no longer serve the discipline *per se*, but rather the über-category of 'environment'."[14] Here the terms environment, nature, and action are positioned as an isomorphic negation of the discipline, culture, and thought (respectively). Dean argues for "a reorientation of architectural ambitions back towards the ends of a larger disciplinary agenda where the production of ideas and concepts would be reasserted, once again, as one of the central tasks of architecture."[15] Environmental issues would not necessarily be excluded but they would be "subordinate" to architecture, "understood first and foremost as an intellectual discipline—a sociocultural practice—as opposed to an applied science."[16] Her principal example of this approach would be the inclusion of environmentally focused architects within historical and theoretical curricula. While this may contribute to "advancing the plurality of ideas" about the environment and its problems, it is also an argument for what Latour describes as "purification" of science and nature from society and culture (respectively).[17] Such arguments occupy Latour's paradoxical modernity. For Dean techno-scientific discourses dangerously assert a despotic authority through claims to natural "truth" even as culture is presented revealing the true constructed "nature" of these concepts. Dean concludes by proposing that history and theory courses should pay closer attention to the history of the environment in order to develop cultural resistance to the techno-scientific authority. In this way, historical and theoretical scholarship serves as a vaccine, inoculating the body of architectural (culture) knowledge with a bit of dead viral matter from Nature.

Other designers and theorists have taken the converse approach, in which ecology becomes a critical instrument for the questioning and expansion beyond historical cultural conventions of the design disciplines. For example, recent arguments for operational processes and organization have often explicitly attacked representational aspects that could be considered constitutive to landscape architecture since it emerged as a distinct field. In "Eidetic Operations and New Landscape," James Corner claimed that a renewed agency for landscape architecture required breaking with the disciplinary, semiotic, and cultural derivation of the term landscape itself, the Old English *landskip*. Because this genealogy had become exhausted, ideologically suspect, and even ecologically hazardous, Corner proposed pivoting to the Old German *landschaft* associated with the "working landscape," with the organization and interplay between things, processes, and material conditions.[18] Just as Banham identified a crisis between two "Architectures" (one descended from culture and one determined by science), Corner's juxtaposition of *landskip* and *landschaft* differentiates the field into two realms of cultural representation and natural processes. Rather than produce representations of nature as seen from a distance through the window of culture, such a practice would occupy the horizontal ground, the base material. Design qualities emerge from these operations, soft control of processes, and the interlinking of systems to produce autocatalytic complexity.[19]

Likewise, in his manifesto "Infrastructural Urbanism," Stan Allen argued that while the cultural turn of postmodernism provided critical distance from naïve functionalism and technological determinism, it had become a "semantic nightmare" (quoting Koolhaas),[20] collapsing into exactly the sort of solipsistic irrelevance where Banham feared postwar fascinations with Renaissance proportion would lead. To remediate this condition, Allen argued for shifting from understanding architecture as a discursive or linguistic practice, and reclaiming a lost identity of architecture as a "material practice" that can act in the world rather than comment on it from the balcony of high culture.[21]

Far from turning design into an applied science of problem solving, such arguments positioned the environment and ecology as a critical rubric for an expanded and reconfigured field of experimentation. Moreover, the industrial, economic, social, and other anthropogenic factors enfolded with natural processes are also key to these practices. Corner emphasized that *landshaft* incorporates industrial, economic, and social processes as well as natural processes. One of the most significant intellectual and political differences between the practices that coalesced around Landscape Urbanism and those aligned either with the environmental determinism of those like McHarg and McDonough or the project of disciplinary autonomy is its emphasis not on purification but on hybridity (one embedded in its name).[22] This hybridity is crucial for projective design ecologies, and I will return to in the second part of this chapter.

For now, we can also see that industrial, technological processes are positioned, like Nature, in contrast to cultural and representational "traditions." For example, Allen directly counterpoises architecture as a "discursive practice" that draws on other cultural fields (linguistics, deconstruction, and the "material practice" of Infrastructural Urbanism). Infrastructural systems are "artificial ecologies" that manage "the flows of energy and resources on a site, and they direct the density and distribution of a habitat. They create the conditions necessary to respond to incremental adjustments in resource availability, and modify the status of inhabitation in response to changing environmental conditions."[23] Infrastructure operates prior to cultural signification and meaning; design is not a language but the expression of these dynamic processes and organizations.

While not an exhaustive survey, these examples exhibit a specific pattern of disagreement and share a common ground on which the problem is posed.[24] Landscape Urbanism reconfigures the discipline by bracketing cultural and representational traits and develops an alternative approach mapping processes, whether natural, economic, or social. Its proponents do not want to dissolve the discipline into applied science but rather see an opportunity and need for expanding their field of operation and knowledge. Nevertheless, to survive in the future, the discipline must break with a significant part of its past, the part determined by cultural baggage. In contrast, proponents of autonomy argue that the cultural practices of architecture must resist those discourses that seek to determine design by Nature or Science. This does not mean that ecological and environmental issues are to be ignored, but that they are to be kept in their proper place along with things like fire code. The cultural determinations of design must be fortified lest the "uncultured scientists" and eco-barbarians flood the gates.[25]

Out of this pattern, a new set of paradoxes emerge. First, the cultural traditions of a discipline are to be bracketed because they produced an idealized image of Nature that is no longer relevant to contemporary society. A new lineage (or at least a Lucretian swerve) is to operate at the level of natural materials and forces to rejuvenate and empower its social and cultural relevance, that is, to develop representations with greater symbolic meaning. A material practice is still a "practice," or in other words, a cultural and social endeavor. The subsequent history and critiques of Landscape Urbanism, including Corner's work, have demonstrated that representations and disciplinary connections are not so easily bracketed, nor is it evident how much is gained in the process. Below I will argue for a projective ecological design that reinstates aesthetics, form, and representation as central topoi.

Second, if the value of a work is to be determined by its disciplinary autonomy, it is no less determined by its situation within its cultural environment (a system of ideas) than an ecological determinist would have it determined by its natural environment. Something called the "Discipline"—a conceptual, cultural, historical, and constructed system of knowledge—is consistently invoked as an authoritative discourse, but is too often treated as if it transcends these cultural contingencies. Within cultural studies jargon, it seems far too "naturalized." What is this Discipline? Who belongs to this Discipline, and more instructively, who and what are excluded from its sovereign domain? By definition, any disciplinary formation is a specific formation, operating at specific places, times, and milieus. The unity and continuity of what is called a discipline is to be demonstrated, not presumed and projected on other formations.[26] Perhaps counterintuitively, the more authoritative this abstracted identity of the Discipline becomes, the more it dilutes the specificity of disciplinary knowledge and practices while tending toward a purification (of what coheres to this identity of Architecture), as it will produce a plurality of dissent. Science may not be blindly accepted as the arbiter of truth, but an abstracted Discipline can also provide an uncritical authoritative discourse of power. If we should be concerned about techno-science barbarians of Nature beating at the gates of Culture, we should be equally circumspect of Disciples guarding the gates.

In that regard, Dean's proposal for rigorous historical and theoretical research and reexamination of environment and design is especially important because such work will also necessarily problematize now conventional histories and disciplinary identities from within more radically than could supposed forces outside. With that in mind, I propose that recent arguments are at least in part caught in a very modern opposition of Nature and Culture. Such a rubric underestimates the design fields (especially architecture) while it impedes the development of ecological design. In turn, a theory of "projective ecology" in design requires, perhaps before anything else, displacing the opposition of Nature vs. Society, or Science vs. Culture, determinism vs. autonomy.

Biopolitics of the *Unheimlich:*
From States of Exception to Projective Ecology_____

Having mapped the existing terrain (metaphor intended), I will try to locate a few coordinates within it, identifying a very preliminary and partial path for a projective ecological design project. In that regard, C.S. Holling's work on resilience and ecosystems theory, as well as the "ecosophical" frameworks of Gregory Bateson and Félix Guattari, can be useful in renovating epistemological models of disciplinarity and expertise in relationship to their broader social, political, and yes, natural contexts.

As we have seen, ecology and the environment are often associated with ontological crises and calamity even as they are presented and understood as external and existential threats to the design disciplines.[27] Such existential threats and "catastrophes" are common causes for establishing what Giorgio Agamben defines as a "state of exception," a spatial and temporal condition in which the social, cultural, and political facets—along with their legal protections–are set aside, and biological rather than cultural or social sense is controlled directly.

Such a "state of exception" is an extreme actualization of a biopower, a concept sketched in a very preliminary manner by Foucault and since extrapolated by many theorists including Agamben. Biopower operates at the "level of life" itself,[28] exercised via techniques and technologies through the body of the individual, integrating it into larger systems; it can also operate as a biopolitics, regulating populations through biological life processes.[29] It requires that knowledge of biological (vital) life is a central knowledge and can be employed in an authoritative manner upon social and political conditions, often in the name of sustaining or protecting them. In addition, biopower deploys a specific form of subjectification wherein biological life processes becomes means to alter the self.

Ecology is the central administrative knowledge for the ordering of things within an age of biopower. Ernst Haeckel first coined the word as *Ökologie,* roughly meaning the "science of the household of Nature." The metaphor of the house is not accidental or cozy. Agamben follows Hannah Arendt's work on the dynamic between the Athenian *oikos,* or household, and the *polis.* The former is the domain of biological life processes, both private and understood to be governed by natural laws and the site of the threshold conditions of life (birth, death), while the latter was the public realm of political representation. The head of the household, the male citizen, held absolute authority over the literal lives of those within the household, and it is this power that established his sovereignty. Agamben argues that distinctions between Culture and Nature, between Human and Animal, Public and Private have collapsed into *oikonomia* in which the "depoliticizations of biological life itself [is] the supreme political (or rather impolitical) task."[30] Given this, it is not unreasonable to propose that ecology is a central epistemological paradigm much in the way that history was in the nineteenth and early twentieth centuries.

As Agamben ruefully notes, "Living in the state of exception ... has now become the rule...our private biological body has become indistinguishable from our body politic, experiences that once used to be called political suddenly were confined to our biological body, and private experiences present themselves all of a sudden outside us as body politic."[31] Impending environmental calamity can easily be mobilized to produce an indefinite state of exception because its narratives of conservation, harmony, and wholeness are integral to eschatological narratives of crisis.

For example, William McDonough's "Cradle to Cradle" system operates according to this state of exception via a binary opposition of healthy equilibrium versus crisis. As the name suggests, it conceives a logistical accounting system for industrial and social processes in terms of metabolic health and "material" healthiness. Moreover, it is a conceptually closed system, a proprietary certification scheme to be applied infinitely "at every scale, from countries and economies down all the way to molecules,"[32] reflecting an ambition unmatched by any architect since Le Corbusier's attempt to patent the Modulor as a universal measure that would make the "good easy." While it seeks to certify the entire spectrum of cultural and social production, McDonough's system would operate as a sovereign entity. Forms of life cultural, industrial, or biological are to be converted into a form of intellectual property.[33] McDonough has presented all of this as an example of "design humility,"[34] in contrast to the presumably egomaniacal architects content with designing buildings rather than saving the world. Aesthetic experimentation and expression are implicitly degenerate aberrations unless regulated. The problem with such arguments is not that they determine design by scientific concepts but that they use "environmental crisis" to establish a state of exception in which to create an administrative and normative regime premised on the sustainability of a steady state. Design that does not obey this orthodoxy becomes a crime against the state of nature.

Ecosystems theories of resilience offer a powerful alternative in which transformation and fluctuation is not an exception to equilibrium. If a system is highly equilibrated, it actually has less of its ecological potential because is has less capacity for transformation. Moreover, an ecosystem may have multiple states of relative stability rather than a single ideal condition, and the patterns of transformation are at least as important as any pattern at a certain moment, or range of time. There are seeds that need the heat of fire to germinate, new growth that would otherwise be choked by dense brush and occluding canopies; storm surges destroy habitats but also redistribute substrates to produce even more robust matrices for life. Such changes do not usually occur gradually. Instead ecosystems tend to jump from one "state" to an entirely different condition.

This can be compared to theoretical ontologies of events, differentiation and multiplicity. As Alain Badiou writes, "Everything (which is natural) is (belongs) in everything, save that there is no everything." In other words, there is no organic state of oneness; each state in an ecosystem exists in "universal intrication" with its virtual states.[35] The moment of transition from one state to another is an event, a rupture in normative representations through which we can "discern the possibility of moving beyond its current state of impasse by application of new-found conceptual resources discovered or devised precisely in response to that same predicament."[36]

Such dynamics necessitate shifting from "the environment" as a singular world or nature to an immanent multiplicity of environments. To a large extent, modern concepts of the environment derive from the work of Jacob von Uexküll, which Sanford Kwinter's contribution to this volume addresses in detail. Through empirical research—often performed on bodies stimulated with electricity or other such forces—Uexküll argued that the organization of two anatomical networks, sensory and motor (*mertznetz* and *werknetz*, respectively) affected the way information was processed. The interaction and organization between these networks determined the organism's experience and understanding of its life-world (*umwelt*). This means that while there is an objective material reality, the environment of one organism would be rather different and perhaps incommensurable from an organism with differently organized bodies and sensoria. Uexküll tried to demonstrate the strangeness of other organisms' life-worlds though evocative prose that described the world of a tick, for example. Such accounts mediated between the human *umwelt* and provided a glimpse of the manifold of life. The other life-worlds he mentions are to some extent familiar because they are described according to familiar cultural tropes and literary forms, but that which is recounted is utterly strange. The effect is not unlike stories by Edgar Allen Poe or H.P. Lovecraft, and sometimes horrifyingly sublime. (Of course we can never really know the world of the tick or the frog, but what is most significant is the recognition and sensation of our contingency.)

The plurality of *umwelten* is central to Guattari's sketch of a projective and critical biopolitics. His "The Three Ecologies" diagrams a trifold plenum of *umwelten* as epistemological-ontological schema in which the categories of Nature and Culture are displaced by three interlinked social, subjective, and natural ecologies. He does not define these as domains in Kantian terms. Though the essay's tripartite organization echoes Kant's structure, the three ecologies do not constitute three legs in a stable tripod of reason but instead are more like three axes on a landscape or air plenum occupied by many material conditions and concepts. Rather than having either a transcendental or purely phenomenological schema of an environment, coherence is produced through the networking between these "ecologies." Guattari expands and transforms Gregory Bateson's mid-twentieth-century theories of ecology based on cybernetic and systems theory, which in turn was heavily influenced by Uexküll. For Bateson, ecology is not a discrete science so much as a general epistemological schema for the "study of the interaction and survival of ideas and programs (i.e., differences, complexes of differences, etc.) in circuits"[37] Bateson defined information not as the "difference that makes a difference"— that is, that shifts a system qualitatively in some way, whether toward a complete state change or legible alteration. The sensation and recognition of such differentials precipitates as figures of legibility through the organization of "minds." For Bateson there is never "a" mind. Instead, "multiple 'minds' or subsystems [are] organized in relationship to other such 'minds.'" Every mind is immanent to other minds and participates in their construction, not an object set apart from its context[38]—that is, there is not an organism and its environment. As another systems theory reiterated, "Everything that happens belongs to a system (or to many systems) and always at the same time to the environment of other systems."[39] Again, we see that this form of ecological thought is that of the many, of immanence and of difference. There is no singular unified *umwelt* but rather a plurality of *umwelten* and an immanent sense of alternatives.[40] Rather than a univocal totaling of Being against a ruptured crisis, there is an immanent multiplicity, or pluriverse.

A projective program of ecological design therefore does not need to oppose representational mimesis of the human *umwelt* (*landskip*) to performative orderings (*landshaft*). If all machines are social before they are technical,[41] urban landscapes such as Central Park have long been a technology of the self and social life, biopolitical instruments for improving the physical and moral health of the populace.[42] However much the traditional aesthetics of landscape referred to painterly tradition, its scenography was not simply a cultural idealization of Nature so much as a diagram of subjectification and power.[43] The question is how the biopolitics of ecology can not only be an instrument of control but also at once reveal the normative subjectifications and habitual organizations of life and construct alternatives.

A projective ecology is a biopolitical practice that tracks the "unreliability of our common sense itself which, habituated as it is to our ordinary life-world, finds it difficult to really accept that the flow of everyday reality can be perturbed."[44] Allen quoted Benjamin's adage that "construction fulfills the role of the unconscious" to indicate how infrastructure could also operate as a scaffold for the collective unconscious. Similarly, the biopolitical problem today is to operate at the level of life and the self in a way that opens onto plurality.[45] Anamorphosis, the uncanny, the glitch, the modulated, the hyperorganized—all are techniques of deterritorialization aimed at disrupting the quotidian life-worlds to manifest a common ground occupied by different systems. Its geometries intensify the entanglements of systems in strategic ways and turn mere overlaps of *umwelten* into intersections and encounters. The subjectification of a projective ecology foregrounds the environment as aesthetic encounter with radically other conditions of being. Its soundtrack has more to do with an engine run through autotune so that it sounds like cybernetic birdsong than harmonic music of the spheres.

A projective ecological program of design is thus a framework of mediation and assemblage. It takes as its baseline multiplicity and differentiation, intertwining social, subjective, and natural systems as "events" not simple in the objective but also in the subject or the many subjects. These events do not organize matter or even catalyze processes into a organic performance so much as research the critical junctions and "pressure points" of these systems—research in the sense of discovery and of remembering all that we have forgotten because they are the set of commonplaces, presumptions, and anthropocentric prejudices that reify our momentary environment as the environment. If ecology and performance often seems to return us to a metanarrative of Nature versus Culture, it can also provide for projections of alternative, inhuman dramas that our actions effect and which we are affected by but often either choose to ignore or cannot directly experience. Natural objects and processes are real and exceed us, but as such they do not articulate in themselves; the objects and transformations of Culture are just as real, but their articulations do not simply turn everything into the mere projection of humanity.[46]

Here it is useful to return to Latour's presentation of the modern constitution. He argued that even as modern thought categorically separated and purified Nature and Culture, the practices of modernity continually produce concepts, objects, and phenomena that exceed any such dualisms. An example Latour provides is "global warming"; the empirical reality and effect of global warming is not diminished by its equally real social and political reality and affect. Indeed, he argued in a rather resilient way, that what distinguishes modernity is not a rupture with a stable culture or natural order but its unprecedented proliferation of hybrid assemblages that traverse the categories of Nature and Culture.[47] These are not "intermediaries" between natural forces and cultural value, but "mediators" through which configurations are produced and then reconfigured, "actors endowed with the capacity to translate what they transport, to redefine it, redeploy it, and also to betray it."[48] Subsequently, Latour shifted from describing the "modern constitution" that separated Nature and Culture into two branches toward proposals for a "parliament of things" and "political ecology." In Latour's recent books and his exhibition "Making

Things Public," mediation is the primary mode for a political ecology, providing legibility for that which remains outside the realm of human representation. It is not that facts or truths are socially constructed but that they are so inhuman that they require some form of mediation in order to become a problem of thought or of action.[49] The implication here is that a projective "political ecology" has little to do with modern concepts of Nature as opposed to society. In this regard, perhaps the recent anxiety about ecology in design results exactly from the recognition that the way the disciplines have been constructed in modernity can no longer effectively deal with our world of hybridity.

In the Anthropocene age, where human actions have become the most influential factor in the environment, such an approach to hybridity offers the best chance to negotiate dramatic transformations in our environment. As Erle Ellis's maps in this book show, while humans have been reshaping their environment for millennia, they did so in a relatively steady state. The beginning of the Anthropocene epoch is marked by a quantitatively measurable increase in the speed and scale that creates a qualitative change that began in the Industrial Revolution but crosses a critical threshold in the late twentieth century, when human activity became the most significant single source of perturbation for geological, biological, and climatological conditions.[50] We have also crossed into a "critical stage" of urbanization.[51] For the first time, the majority of humans now live in urbanized zones.[52] By the middle of the twenty-first century, the total world urban population will probably equal the total number of people alive at the beginning of the century.[53] The size of urban conglomerations is also increasing. In the early 1970s there were two megacities (10 million people or more); now there are thirteen. By 2025 around fifty-nine cities are expected to have between 5 and 10 million inhabitants.[54] In other words, our environment—both constructed or affected—is irreducibly hybrid.

Architecture, landscape architecture, and urban design are not just autonomous disciplines. Even at their most conventional, the practice of architects and landscape architects depend on the elaboration of system of mediation, their expertise is that of mediation, translating, and transposition. This includes: the strategic use and innovations of drawings and other notational systems to coalesce heterogeneous and often contradictory social, cultural and natural factors into coherent expressions; the capacity of same (or similar) drawings to translate these notations into construction via the manifold expert knowledges this translation depends upon; and finally, the affect of the design in altering, constructing, or reconfiguring both the social subject and the environment around it. Moreover, a projective ecology in design concerns the development of new synthetic hybrids that entangle natural processes with social/cultural process, *through* the mediating domain of the subjective and affect. Here the aesthetic is interwoven into the history of discourses of the environment and the production of ecological concepts, such that an ecological design ethic is not detachable from its formal, graphic, and spatial concepts. This does not produce harmony between Nature and Culture, but brings the inhuman into the realm of our senses and sensation, and constructs alternative assemblages between processes and forms.

In an urbanized global environment, anxieties about conserving design from ecology only rehearse oppositions that neither describe our condition nor are useful for developing projective alternatives. Moreover, this view misses what is actually at stake for the design disciplines. Rather than understand ecology as a dominant and authoritative imposition that threatens the traditions of the design disciplines (for better or worse), with the advent of an ecological Anthropocene, design becomes the nexus of mediation between the social, the subjective, and the ontological. Ultimately then, ecology is not the new "technology." From authorizing design through scientistic metaphor or mandate, design becomes perhaps the central practice and way of thinking about our ecological condition and of intervening within it. Instead of adopting nature as a model, we need to urbanize ecology.

In conclusion, the films *Jaws* and *The Perfect Storm* provide parables of disciplinary resilience regarding the overwhelming prospect of climate change and ecological calamity.[55] In *Jaws*, Police Chief Martin Brody must find a way to eradicate the monster menacing his island town. When he finally is confronted with the enormous size of the creature, Brody famously declares, "You're gonna need a bigger boat." Brody does not have time to literally get a bigger boat as the shark chomps away even as traditional killing methods fail one after the other. However, he had already constructed an epistemologically expanded platform for action. Recognizing that he was well out of his usual "landlubber" context, he gathered a team of consultants not usually engaged in police work.

Brody combines his expert practices with the knowledge of his new colleagues to adapt. In contrast, when faced with *The Perfect Storm,* valiant Captain Billy Tyne turns inward to rely on singular expertise and sheer bravado and battens down the hatches. However, no degree of virtuosity would have saved Tyne from the massive convergence of weather systems that swallowed him, his crew, and his precious cargo without a trace. One film's lead character attempts to expand and transform disciplinary knowledge while the other doubles down on autonomous expertise. Captain Tyne is a macho disciple of romanticized autonomy. Chief Brody practices resilience, recognizing a suddenly altered context, enfolding what yesterday seemed alien, creating new collaborations, experimenting, and improvising.

Notes

1_ Of course, globalization, urbanization, and digitalization share the stage, but each of these is increasingly appearing as a supporting player in a larger mise-en-scène of its environmental effects. See Charles Waldheim, ed., *The Landscape Urbanism Reader* (New York: Princeton Architectural Press, 2006).

2_ Walter Benjamin, *Illuminations* (Houghton Mifflin Harcourt, 1968), 249.

3_ Charles Waldheim has remarked that Koolhaas and Frampton both claimed a new centrality of landscape that displaced the traditional dominance of architecture. That each made this claim from rather different intellectual positions and to different ends, Waldheim argues, indicates the breadth of this transformation. Waldheim, *The Landscape Urbanism Reader*, 42.

4_ Reyner Banham, *Theory and Design in the First Machine Age*, 2d edition (Cambridge, MA: MIT Press, 1980), 329.

5_ This formalism was catalyzed by Rudolf Wittkower and Colin Rowe's work on proportion. See Christopher Hight, *Architectural Principles in the Age of Cybernetics* (New York: Routledge, 2007), and Anthony Vidler, "Troubles in Theory Part III: The Great Divide: Technology vs. Tradition," *The Architectural Review* (July 24, 2012).

6_ Reyner Banham, "1960: Stocktaking," *AR*, February 1960, p. 100, as quoted in Vidler, "Troubles in Theory."

7_ Vidler, "Troubles in Theory."

8_ Ibid.

9_ Architecture serves as the privileged model and metaphor for systematic and rigorously ordered thought.

10_ Bruno Latour, *We Have Never Been Modern*, 32. Latour drew upon his previous—groundbreaking and controversial—sociological research on the practices of natural science to outline the rules of this constitution, which both challenged aspects of his previous work and set the stage for his subsequent work in political ecology.

11_ Preston Scott Cohen and Erika Naginski, "The Return of Nature," in Mohsen Mostafavi, ed., *Ecological Urbanism* (Cambridge, MA and Basel: Harvard Graduate School of Design and Lars Müller Publishers, 2010), 136.

12_ Ibid.

13_ Penelope Dean, "Never Mind All That Environmental Rubbish, Get On With Your Architecture," *Architectural Design* 79, no. 3 (2009), 27.

14_ Ibid., 26–27.

15_ Ibid., 28–29.

16_ Ibid., 29.

17_ Ibid., 28.

18_ James Corner, "Eidetic Operations and New Landscapes," in *Recovering Landscape: Essays in Contemporary Landscape Theory* (Princeton Architectural Press, 1999), 158.

19_ See Sanford Kwinter, "Politics and Pastoralism," *Assemblage* 27, Fall 1995.

20_ Stan Allen, *Points + Lines: Diagrams and Projects for the City* (Princeton Architectural Press, 1999), 54.

21_ Ibid., 53.

22_ Richard Weller, "An Art of Instrumentality," in Waldheim, ed., *The Landscape Urbanism Reader*, 76.

23_ Allen, *Points + Lines*, 57.

24_ What Foucault termed a "discursive formation," or a "dipositif" a concept that seems to have a great deal in common with Latour's concept of the "constitution" of modernity.

25_ There is an implied "architectural" metaphor at work that treats the discipline as if it were a fortress, with a continual locus across time (albeit with various additions).

26_ Michel Foucault, *The Archaeology of Knowledge* (New York: Routledge, 2002), 23–61.

27_ Moreover, because ecology is presented as a relatively recent problem that arose outside the design fields, it foregrounds the problematic relationship between science and nature and culturally based disciplines, such as urban planning, landscape design, and architectural design.

28_ Michel Foucault, *The History of Sexuality: An Introduction* (New York: Random House, 2012), 143.

29_ Michel Foucault and François Ewald, *"Society Must Be Defended": Lectures at the Collège de France, 1975–1976* (New York: Macmillan, 2003), 139.

30_ Giorgio Agamben, *The Open: Man and Animal* (Stanford: Stanford University Press, 2004), 72.

31_ Giorgio Agamben, *State of Exception* (Chicago: University of Chicago Press, 2008), 137.

32_ "Ask the Experts: Why Hasn't Cradle-to-Cradle Design Caught On Yet?," *TreeHugger*, accessed August 1, 2013, http://www.treehugger.com/sustainable-product-design/ask-experts-why-hasnt-cradle-to-cradle-design-caught-on-yet.html.

33_ It makes little difference if it is owned by McDonough or branded and managed as a nonprofit, Cradle to Cradle Products Innovation Institute.

34_ *William McDonough: Cradle to Cradle Design | Video on TED.com*, accessed August 2, 2013, http://www.ted.com/talks/william_mcdonough_on_cradle_to_cradle_design.html.

35_ Alain Badiou, *Being and Event* (London: Bloomsbury Academic, 2013), 140–141.

36_ Christopher Norris, *Badiou's "Being and Event": A Reader's Guide* (London: Continuum, 2009), 115.

37_ Gregory Bateson, *Steps to an Ecology of Mind: Collected Essays in Anthropology, Psychiatry, Evolution, and Epistemology* (Chicago: University of Chicago Press, 1972), 491.

38_ Ibid., 466.

39_ See for example, Niklas Luhmann, *Social Systems* (Stanford: Stanford University Press, 1995).

40_ Félix Guattari, Ian Pindar, and Paul Sutton, *The Three Ecologies* (London: Continuum, 2008).

41_Gilles Deleuze, *Foucault* (London: Continuum, 2006), 39–40.

42_Dorceta E. Taylor, "Central Park as a Model for Social Control: Urban Parks, Social Class, and Leisure Behavior in Nineteenth-Century America," *Journal of Leisure Research* 31, no. 4 (September 22, 1999), 420.

43_W. J. T. Mitchell, *Landscape and Power,* 2d edition (Chicago: University of Chicago Press, 2002).

44_Slavoj Žižek, *In Defense of Lost Causes* (London: Verso, 2009), 444–445.

45_Allen, *Points + Lines*, 54.

46_To draw from an analogy once made by Rem Koolhaas in a presentation of the Paranoid-Critical Method in design, facts are like the individual cards and their overlapping sets (suits, number, color, etc.) within a deck; however, their status is also governed by the game, the other cards in our hands, and moreover by their moment of appearance. Innumerable games can be invented from this finite set, and even within known rules, we can invent new strategies. Facts are, in this way, approached as events, ones to be composed.

47_See, Jonathan Crary, "J.G. Ballard and the Promiscuity of Forms," in Michel Feher, Sanford Kwinter, eds., *Zone 1/2 The [Contemporary] City* (New York: Zone Books, 1987), 162–163.

48_Latour, *We Have Never Been Modern*, 81.

49_Graham Harman, *Tool-Being: Heidegger and the Metaphysics of Objects* (Chicago: Open Court Publishing, 2002).

50_J. Zalasiwicz, M. Williams, et al., "Are We Now Living in the Anthropocene?," *GSA Today,* vol. 18, no. 2, February 2008, p. 5, figure 1.

51_Henri Lefebvre, *The Urban Revolution* (Minneapolis: University of Minnesota Press, 2003).

52_The World Bank estimates that the majority threshold was crossed in 2008 and that by 2012, 52.5 percent of the world's population lived in urban areas. World Bank, http://data.worldbank.org/indicator/SP.URB.TOTL.IN.ZS/countries/1W?display=graph.

53_United Nations Department of Economic and Social Affairs, Population Division, *World Urbanization Prospects, the 2011 Revision* (New York: United Nations, 2012), 3.

54_Ibid., 8.

55_Cinema has provided many previous anxieties of modernity, from Godzilla and post-Hiroshima Japan to Martians and the Red Menace.

Ecology and Planning

C.S. Holling and M.A. Goldberg

Published 1971

To offer an ecological view of urban systems to a planning audience is risky. But, the possibilities for collaboration appear to outweigh the risks. Ecologists and planners have much to learn from each other.

Since ecology emerged from its descriptive phase in the 1920s, its emphasis has been on understanding the operation of complex ecological processes and ecological systems. There has been little effort to develop effective *applications* of ecological principles. Within the last few years, however, there has been a major shift toward an interest in application; but ecologists' first efforts in this direction have been blundering and naïve. The central role of planners, on the other hand, has been application and policy formulation and implementation. Ecologists can benefit enormously from an infusion of the pragmatic realism that is, of necessity, forced upon the planning profession. Perhaps, at the same time, planners may gain some insights about urban systems from ecological theory.

As a basis for dialogue between planners and ecologists, we propose a conceptual framework based on ecological concepts of ecosystem structure and stability. This framework suggests an approach for planning based on a presumption of ignorance rather than on a presumption of knowledge. Since the area of our knowledge of man/environment interaction is minutely small in comparison with our ignorance, this conceptual framework may have some merit for the planning process.

The Nature and Behavior of Ecological Systems

Rather than presenting an exhaustive treatment of ecological concepts and terms, we hope to apply the philosophy of the ecological approach to solve problems of a kind that recur in all complex systems.[1] The key insight of this approach is that ecological systems are not in a state of delicate balance. Long before man appeared on the scene, natural systems were subjected to traumas and shocks imposed by climatic changes and other geophysical processes. The ecological systems that have survived have been those that are able to absorb and adapt to these traumas. As a result, these systems have considerable internal resilience, but we know that this resilience is not infinite. A forest can be turned into a desert, as in the Middle East, or a lake into the aquatic analog of a desert. The key feature of the resilience of ecological systems is that incremental changes are absorbed. It is only when a series of incremental changes accumulate or a massive shock is imposed that the resilience of the system is exceeded, generating dramatic and unexpected signals of change.

This has considerable consequence for planning, since, inherent in the philosophy of planning and intervention, is the presumption that an incremental change will quickly generate a signal of whether the intervention is correct or not.[2] If the signal indicates the intervention produces higher costs than benefits, then a new policy and a new incremental change can be developed. But because of the resilience of ecological systems, incremental changes do not generate immediate signals of their effect. As a result, planners can set in motion a sequence of incremental steps and face the reality of the inadequacy of the underlying policy only when the interventions accumulate to shatter the bounds of resilience within the system. By that time it can be too late. In order to demonstrate these features of ecosystems we will discuss two specific case histories, each based on man's intervention. The consequences of the interventions reveal some of the key properties of ecosystems.

Malarial Control in Borneo

Since the Second World War, the World Health Organization (WHO) has developed a remarkably successful malarial eradication program throughout the world. We wish to emphasize that, in this example of intervention, there is no question that there has been a dramatic improvement in the quality of life of people in affected regions. But, we wish to explore a specific case in which the World Health Organization sprayed village huts in Borneo with DDT in order to kill the mosquito that carries the plasmodium of malaria. This case has been documented by Harrison (1965).

The inland Dayak people of Borneo live in large single homes or long houses with up to 500 or more under one roof. This concentration of population allowed WHO to develop a thorough and orderly spraying of every long house, hut, and human habitation with DDT. The effect on health standards was dramatic, with a remarkable improvement in the energy and vitality of the people—particularly those remote tribes who had not previously had access to medical aid. Nevertheless, there were interesting consequences that illuminate some of the properties of ecological systems.

There is a small community of organisms that occupy the thatched huts of these villages—cats, cockroaches, and small lizards. The cockroaches picked up the DDT and were subsequently eaten by the lizards. In consuming the cockroaches, the lizards concentrated the DDT to a somewhat higher level than was present in the cockroaches. The cats ate the lizards and, by eating them, concentrated the level of DDT still further—to the point that it became lethal. The cats died. When the cats disappeared from the villages, woodland rats invaded, and it suddenly became apparent that the cats had been performing a hidden function—controlling rat populations. Now, with the rats came a new complex of organisms—fleas, lice, and parasites, and this community presented the new public health hazard of sylvatic plague. The problem became serious enough that finally the RAF was called to parachute living cats into these isolated villages in order to control the rats.

The story isn't finished at this point, however, since the DDT also killed the parasites and predators of a small caterpillar that normally causes minor damage to thatch roofs (Cheng 1963). The caterpillar populations, now uncontrolled, increased dramatically, causing the roofs of the huts to collapse.

We cite this example not because it has great substance, but simply because it shows the variety of interactive pathways that link parts of an ecological system, pathways that are sufficiently intricate and complicated so that manipulating one fragment causes a reverberation throughout the system. In addition, this case provides a simple example of a food chain in which energy and material moves from cockroaches to lizards to cats. Typically, in these food chains the number of organisms at a higher level in the chain are less abundant than those lower in the chain. This is the inevitable result of the loss of energy in moving from one trophic, or nutritional, level to another, and the consequence is a biological amplification that concentrates certain material at higher and higher levels as one moves up the chain. A contaminant like DDT, for example, can be present in the environment in very low, innocuous levels but can reach serious concentrations after two or three steps in the food chain. Actually, this example is highly simplified; usually in such situations there is a food *web* rather than a single linear food chain. Several species operate at more than one trophic level. Moreover, there are competitive interactions that further complicate and link species within an ecosystem. Even in this example, however, it is clear that the whole is not a simple sum of the parts and that there are a large number of components in a system acting and interacting in a variety of complex ways.

*A Cotton Ecosystem in Peru*_____

Unlike the preceding example, the case of cotton agriculture in many parts of the world has had a more serious outcome. Pest control practices in cotton have, until recently, been both ecological and economic disasters. A particularly well-documented case has been prepared by Smith and Van den Bosch (1967).

There are a series of valleys on the coast of Peru formed by streams running from the high Andes to the Pacific Ocean. Many of these valleys are under intensive agriculture and, because of the low rainfall, are irrigated. The result is that each valley is essentially a self-contained ecosystem isolated from others by barren ridges. In one of these valleys, the Canete, during the 1920s, the crop shifted from sugar cane to cotton. Over the years a group of seven native insects became significant cotton pests, including plant-sucking insects, the boll weevil, the tobacco-leaf worm, and some moths. The pest problem, however, was essentially modest, and the farmers of the region lived with the resulting economic damage. In 1949, chlorinated hydrocarbons like DDT, benzene hexachloride, and toxaphene became widely available, and the opportunity to dramatically decrease pest damage and increase crop yields arose. The characteristics of these insecticides seemed admirably suited to achieve the goal of pest reduction or elimination in this case:

1_ The insecticides are lethal to a large number of insects and are so mobile that they quickly and easily concentrate within insects.
2_ They are highly toxic to invertebrates and less so to mammalian forms.
3_ They have a long life in the environment so that, in theory, one application can have an effect over some time. It has been shown, for example, that DDT and its bio-logically active breakdown products have an environmental halflife of over a decade.
4_ They can be easily and inexpensively applied from aircraft.
5_ The contained nature of the valley ecosystem made it possible to spray the entire area with the insecticide.

We emphasize these details because the general features of this policy seem to be shared by many of man's actions. First, the objective is *narrowly defined*—in this case elimination of seven insect pests. Second, the plan developed is the simplest and least expensive means to achieve the narrow objective. But the consequences of this approach generated a series of unexpected and disastrous consequences explicitly because of the narrow definition of the objectives and the intervention.

The initial response to the insecticide treatment was a dramatic decline in pests and a one and one-half times increase in cotton production. This lasted, however, for only two or three years, when it was noticed that new pests were appearing that had never been a problem during the history of cotton production. Six new species of insects became as serious a problem as the original seven. The reason for the appearance of these new pests was the elimination of parasites and predators that were selectively killed because of the biological amplification of the insecticides through the food web. Within six years the original seven insect pests began to develop resistance to the insecticide, and crop damage increased. In order to control this new resurgence the concentration of the insecticide had to be increased, and the spraying interval reduced from two weeks to every three days. As these responses began to fail, the chlorinated hydrocarbons were replaced by organophosphate insecticides, which deteriorated more rapidly in the environment. But even with this change the cotton yield plummeted to well below yields experienced before the synthetic insecticide period.

The average yield in 1956 was the lowest in more than a decade, and the costs of control were the highest. The agricultural economy was close to bankruptcy, and this forced the development of a very sophisticated ecological control program that combined changed agricultural practices with the introduction and fostering of beneficial insects. Chemical control was minimized. These new practices allowed the reestablishment of the complexity of the food web with the result that the number of species of pests was again reduced to a manageable level. Cotton yields increased to the highest level experienced in the history of cotton production in the valley.

As in the Borneo example, this case demonstrates the complexity and the structure of one ecological system that gives the system the resilience to absorb unexpected changes. Application of the insecticide enormously reduced the complexity and diversity of the ecosystem with a dramatic loss in resilience. But there is a difference between the two examples. In the first example, the area of intervention was local, and although there was destabilization within the local region, the consequences never became serious enough to defeat the original purpose of the intervention. In the Peruvian example, on the other hand, the intervention was more global since the whole valley ecosystem was literally blanketed with insecticide. As a result, the short-term success of the narrow intervention led in the longer term to the complete opposite of the original goal.

*Nature of Ecological Systems*_____

These two examples illuminate four essential properties of ecological systems. By encompassing many components with complex feedback interactions between them, they exhibit a *systems* property. By responding not just to present events but to past ones as well, they show an *historical* quality. By responding to events at more than one point in space, they show a *spatial* interlocking property, and through the appearance of lags, thresholds, and limits they present distinctive *nonlinear* structural properties. First, ecosystems are characterized not only by their parts but also by the interaction among these parts. It is because of the complexity of the interactions that it is so dangerous to take a fragmented view, to look at an isolated piece of the system. By concentrating on one fragment and trying to optimize the performance of that fragment, we find that the rest of the system responds in unsuspected ways.

Second, ecological systems have not been assembled out of preexisting parts like a machine: they have evolved in time and are defined in part by their history. This point does not emerge clearly from the examples quoted; nevertheless, the resilience described in the examples is very much the consequence of past history.

When a large area is stripped of vegetation, a historical process begins that leads to the evolution of a stable ecosystem through a series of successional stages. Early in this succession, pioneer species occupy the space, and the diversity and complexity are low. The species that can operate under these circumstances are highly resistant to extreme conditions of drought and temperature and are highly productive. Competition is low, and a large proportion of the incident solar energy is converted to the production of bio-mass (the standing stock of organic material). As this accumulates, the conditions of the area begin to improve and to permit the appearance of groups of plants and animals that otherwise could not survive. The result is a gradual increase in the variety of species and the complexity of interaction and this increase in complexity is accompanied by an increase in the resilience of the system and a decrease in productivity. Under stable conditions this successional history can continue until a stable climax ecosystem evolves.

Man's objective in agricultural management is to halt this history at an early successional stage when the productivity is high. The price of doing this is a continual effort to prevent the system from moving to its more stable and less productive stage: hence herbicides and cultural practices eliminate or reduce those organisms that compete with man for food. But by emphasizing high productivity as a narrow objective, man develops the simplest and most direct policy, and the result leads to decreased complexity—large monocultures, heavy use of chemical herbicides, insecticides, and fertilizers. For the short term, the narrow objective of increased productivity is achieved, but the price paid is a dramatic decline in the resilience of the system. Third, complex ecosystems have very significant spatial interactions. Just as they have been formed by events over time so they are affected by events over space; ecosystems are not homogeneous structures but present a spatial mosaic of biological and physical characteristics. The differences noted above between the Borneo and Peruvian examples are explained, in part, by the difference in the spatial scale of the intervention. In the Borneo example, the intervention was local and, in fact, increased the spatial heterogeneity. In the Peruvian example, the intervention was global and dramatically decreased the spatial heterogeneity. The consequence was that the resilience in the cotton ecosystem vanished. Finally, there are a variety of structural properties of the processes that interrelate the components of an ecosystem. We do not wish to dwell on these details other than to say they present singular problems in mathematical analysis for they relate to the existence of thresholds, lags, limits, and discontinuities.

Behavior of Ecosystems

The distinctive behavior of systems flows from these four properties. Together they produce both resilience and stability. Even simple systems have properties of stability. Consider the example discussed by Hardin (1963). Every warm-blooded animal regulates its temperature. In man the temperature is close to 98.6°F. If through sickness or through dramatic change in external temperature, the body temperature begins to rise or fall, then negative feedback processes bring the temperature back to the equilibrium level. But we note this regulation occurs only within limits. If the body temperature is forced too high—above 106°F—the excessive heat input defeats the regulation. The higher temperature increases metabolism, which produces more heat, which produces higher temperature, and so on. The result is death. The same happens if temperature drops below a critical boundary. We see, therefore, even in this simple system, that stability relates not just to the equilibrium point but to the domain of temperatures over which true temperature regulation can occur. It is this domain of stability that is the measure of resilience.

In a more complex system, there are many quantities and qualities that change. Each species in an ecosystem and each qualitatively different individual within a species are distinct dimensions that can change over time. If we monitor the change in the quantity or quality of one of these dimensions, we can envisage results of the kind shown in Figure 1. Within the range of stable equilibrium, if we cause a change in the quantity being measured, it will return to equilibrium over time. But there is a limit to which we can perturb these quantities, and that limit is defined as a boundary of stability.

The domain of stability is contained within the upper and lower boundaries. In simple physiological and engineering control feedback systems, regulation is strong enough and conditions are stable enough that most of our attention can be fixed on or near the equilibrium. This is not true of ecological systems (Holling and Ewing

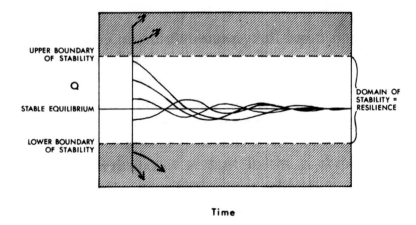

Figure 1. An example of a system with a stable equilibrium in which stability is possible within distinct boundaries.

1969). Ecological systems exist in a highly variable physical environment so that the equilibrium point itself is continually shifting and changing over time. At any one moment, each dimension of the system is attempting to track the equilibrium point but rarely, if ever, is it achieved. Therefore, each species is drifting and shifting in both its quantity and quality. Because of this variability imposed upon ecological systems, the ones that have survived, the ones that have not exceeded the boundaries of stability, are those that have evolved tactics to keep the domain of stability, or resilience, broad enough to absorb the consequences of change. The regulation forces within the domain of stability tend to be weak until the system approaches the boundary. They are not efficient systems in an optimizing sense because the price paid for efficiency is a decreased resilience and a high probability of extinction.

This view of stability is, of course, highly simplified. There may not be just one stable equilibrium at any instantaneous point in time; there may be several. Moreover, the stable condition might not be a single value but a sequence of values that return to a common starting value. This stable condition is termed a *stable limit cycle* (Figure 2). Finally, the sequence of stable values need never return to some common starting point. The earlier description of an ecological succession really represents such a condition—a *stable trajectory* as illustrated in Figure 3.

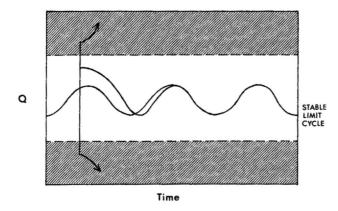

Figure 2. An example of a bounded limit cycle.

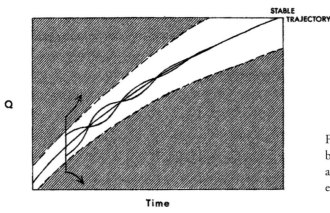

Figure 3. An example of a bounded stable trajectory analogous to that found in an ecological succession.

But, however the equilibrium conditions change, they are all bounded, and what we must ask in judging any policy is not only how effectively an equilibrium is achieved, but also how the resilience, or the domain of stability, is changed. The two insecticide examples illustrate the point. The policies used in these cases were characterized by three conditions:

1_ The problem is first isolated from the whole; that is, pests are damaging cotton.
2_ The objective is defined narrowly; that is, kill the insect pest.
3_ The simplest and most direct intervention is selected; that is, broad-scale application of a highly toxic long-lived insecticide.

Each of these conditions assumes unlimited resilience in the system. By adopting these policies, the problem and the solution are made simple enough to be highly successful in the short term. So long as there is sufficient resilience to absorb the consequences of our ignorance, then the success can persist for a long time. It is successful in the sense that an agriculturist can return his system almost instantly to an equilibrium point of one crop and no competing pests. The price paid, however, is the contraction of the boundaries of stability, and an equilibrium-centered point of view can be disastrous from a boundary-oriented view.

It is this boundary-oriented view of stability emerging from ecology that can serve as a conceptual framework for man's intervention into ecological systems. Such a framework changes the emphasis from maximizing the probability of success to minimizing the chance of disaster. It shifts the concentration from the forces that lead to convergence on equilibrium to the forces that lead to divergence from a boundary. It shifts our interest from increased efficiency to the need for resilience. Most important, it focuses attention on causes, not symptoms. There is now, for example, growing concern for pollution, but the causes are not just the explosion of population and consumption, but also the implosion of the boundaries of stability.

The Nature and Behavior of Urban Systems

Arguments related exclusively to the nature and behavior of ecological systems obviously cannot be uncritically transferred to urban systems. Analogies are dangerous instruments, and in this case the transfer should be made only when the structure and behavior of urban systems appear to be similar to the structure and behavior of ecological systems.

Ecology is the study of the interactions between organisms and the physical environment. Planning concerns itself with the interaction between man and the environment of which he is a part. But does this analogy go deeper than a simple verbal parallelism? There are specific examples that point to similarities between certain ecological and social processes.[3] But the real substance of an analogy between ecological and urban systems lies not in the similarities between parts and processes, but in fundamental similarities in the structure of entire systems. We earlier described four key properties of ecological systems, which concern system interaction and feedback, historical succession, spatial linkage, and nonlinear structure. The same properties seem to be important for urban systems.

In the first place, both urban and ecological systems are true systems functioning as a result of interaction between parts. Just as a narrow intervention in an ecological system causes unexpected reverberations, so will it in an urban system. A freeway is constructed as an efficient artery to move people, but the unanticipated social consequences stimulate urban sprawl and inner-city decay. A ghetto is demolished in order to revitalize the urban core, and disrupted social interactions trigger violence.

A tax subsidy is given to attract industry, leading to environmental pollution deteriorating the quality of life. Such narrow interventions demonstrate that the whole is not a simple sum of the parts.

Second, the city region, like an ecological system, has a history. The modern cities of North America are, to a major extent, the product of history since the industrial revolution. The technology of the industrial revolution removed the constraints imposed by limitations in the environment, permitting development to take place as if there were no environmental limitations. If, for transient moments of time, the signals of these limitations became apparent through the appearance of plague or famine, the problems were generally resolved by looking elsewhere for the solution. So long as there was an "elsewhere"—an undeveloped continent, an undeveloped West—then this approach provided the quickest solution. The only constraints were placed by economic needs, hence the great emphasis on economic growth. The result, therefore, is an urban system with many of the characteristics of an early stage in an ecological succession. The system is changing rapidly in time and is not closed. Without any apparent limitation, water and air are considered as free goods to receive, at no cost, the wastes of the system. Only now is it becoming generally recognized that there are environmental constraints, that water and air are not free goods, and that wastes cannot simply be transported "elsewhere." In a sense, the urban system, like an ecological one, has a memory that constrains it to respond to current events only as it has been conditioned by past events. In a rapidly changing present the responses can become dangerously inappropriate.

Third, the urban system has significant spatial characteristics and interactions. Just as the city has been formed by events over time, so it is affected by events over space. The city is not a homogeneous structure but a spatial mosaic of social, economic, and ecological variables that are connected by a variety of physical and social dispersal processes. Each individual human has a variety of needs—for shelter, recreation, and work. These activities are typically spatially separate, and any qualitative or quantitative change of a function at one point in space inevitably affects other functions at other points of space.

Finally, the same nonlinear, discontinuous structural properties noted in ecological systems apply to urban systems. Thresholds and limits exist with regard to city size. We know that a city of 500,000 residents has more than five times the variety of activities a city of 100,000 has. We also know that below certain threshold levels, certain activities do not occur. Thus, suburban areas and smaller cities just do not have great art museums, operas, symphonies, and restaurants. These activities appear to occur above certain population, or density, thresholds. Finally, such notions as agglomeration and per capita servicing costs are all nonlinear relationships with respect to city size.

Both the structure of the parts of an urban system and the whole system itself appear to have close similarities to ecological systems. Since we have argued that in ecological systems these distinctive structural features account for their behavior, it follows that urban systems must behave in similar ways. There must be a set of urban equilibrium conditions. But more important, these equilibrium states must exist within a domain of stability that defines the resilience of the urban system.[4] And, as in ecological systems, the consequences of intervention in a city can be viewed very differently depending on whether we take an equilibrium condition. If this is true, then we should be able to demonstrate, through samples of interventions, the same kinds of effects we showed with the insecticide examples.

Urban Programs with Unanticipated Consequences

For this purpose, we have selected examples of reasonably narrow interventions. A number of unexpected consequences emerge, and from them we can infer that the internal dynamics of urban systems are similar to ecological ones, and continued narrow interventions can lead to effects analogous to those that occur in natural systems. Our examples are chosen to demonstrate that simplification of urban systems, through such simple but large-scale interventions as urban freeway programs, urban renewal, and rent control, leads to large-scale unexpected consequences and a high likelihood of failure even with respect to the narrow objective of the intervention. This is the lesson from natural systems, and this, we think, is the experience to date in urban systems.

Three examples should suffice. The first two—rent control and residential urban renewal—represent simple and direct approaches to housing lower-income people. Our third example is freeway construction, which represents a similarly simple and direct approach to the "urban transportation problem." Each of these solutions has been carried out on a broad scale; each represents a considerable simplification of the real world; and each has had either little effect or negative effects vis-à-vis the original objective.

Rent control is a reasonable starting point. As in the insecticide examples, there are three explicit policy conditions. First the problem is isolated from the whole; in this case it is defined as inadequate low-cost housing. Second, the objective is narrowly defined: to limit the price increase in rental housing during periods of rapid economic growth. Third, the simplest and most direct policy is proposed: to apply government control of the prices. Finally, the implicit assumption is that there is sufficient resilience in the system to absorb unexpected consequences.

Strong economic arguments have been presented against this narrow approach to rent control by Turvey (1957), Needleman (1965), and Lindbeck (1967), and empirical evidence supports the thesis that rent control in the long run can diminish the supply of housing and therefore extend or guarantee a shortage (Fisher 1966, Gelting 1967, and Muth 1968).[5] Available evidence thus indicates a negative effect.

Residential urban renewal yields another instance where the desired result is reversed. Slum clearance programs have been aimed at revitalizing the hearts of urban regions. In their broadest context, they include a multiplicity of land uses. For present purposes we are interested only in slum clearance programs aimed at providing better housing for low-income families and individuals.

It is fairly clear at present that these programs have not had the intended effect of providing more low-income housing. Hartman (1964) presents strong evidence that the programs have failed. Gans (1968) and Anderson (1964) have documented the shortcomings and have demonstrated that the reverse effect has often been achieved. They claim that the program has resulted in a decline in housing for low-income people and that the price of the remaining housing has in fact increased in the face of dubious increases in quality. In light of this evidence, Fried's (1963) criticisms of the social impact of relocation appear especially damning. It appears, therefore, that slum clearance has failed to provide more housing to low-income people, has failed to significantly upgrade the quality of their housing, has imposed a high psychic cost on slum residents, and perhaps has even had the reverse effect of removing low-income housing stock from existence.

Our final example concerns *freeways* and is meant to illustrate a variety of unexpected consequences, not only those that have effects opposite to the desired ones, but also those that produce significant "side effects" outside the narrow bounds of the original intervention. Our scenario runs as follows. Current dependence on the automobile has led to urban sprawl and congestion. This, in turn, has induced us to treat these symptoms with large-scale urban freeway programs. These have induced further sprawl and changed land-use patterns that, in turn, have generated the need for more travel and therefore more traffic. The positive feedback of freeways to create traffic is illustrated in almost every major urban freeway system. Peak capacities are reached well ahead of design. The need for a more integrated and comprehensive transportation and land-use planning program has been called for every year during the 1960s. Levinson and Wynn (1962) and Wendt and Goldberg (1969) summarize the arguments for such an integrated approach. Without it, freeway programs are bound to have an effect opposite to that desired (that is, creation of traffic congestion rather than alleviation of congestion).

Freeways have also brought with them a wide variety of environmental side effects. Freeways have changed the morphology of cities, stimulating sprawl that typically utilizes agricultural land. Each city can argue, with reason, that increased efficiency of agriculture and the development of marginal agricultural lands can partially fill the gap. But the price paid for this increased efficiency is the consequence of yet another "quick technological fix"—the increased dependency on chemicals to control insect pests and weeds and on chemicals to fertilize the land. Initially, the natural environment can absorb and cleanse these additives, but this resilience is limited and, when exceeded, results in the signals of pollution that are now so evident.

Interestingly enough, freeway planners have claimed that freeways should reduce air pollution by increasing average vehicle speed and facilitating the more complete burning of gasoline. Bellomo and Edgerley (1971) provide interesting evidence that this is not necessarily the case. They note that there are three major automobile pollutants: carbon monoxide, hydrocarbons, and oxides of nitrogen. Both carbon monoxide and hydrocarbon emissions are reduced as a result of increased speed and more complete burning. Oxides of nitrogen, however, are produced in proportion to fuel consumption, which increases with vehicle speed. Thus, the Los Angeles freeway system, by increasing vehicle speeds, does reduce both carbon monoxide and hydrocarbon emissions. Unfortunately, it also increases the production of oxides of nitrogen, and it is these oxides that give Los Angeles its notorious photochemical smog. Here again we have the reverse of the desired state of affairs.

These examples illustrate the dangers inherent in focusing too narrowly on a component or symptom of a system problem. They have been chosen to relate the ideas developed for biological systems to urban systems to demonstrate that there are functional analogies that can be drawn from one to the other. Having illustrated these relationships, we can move on to some system-oriented solutions of the kind that are evolving in the biological sciences and that (again hopefully) can successfully be transplanted to urban systems.

*Ecological Principles and Urban Plans*_____

A variety of suggestions that have been made for urban systems are analogous to ecological control schemes in nature. They revolve around smaller-scale interventions and decentralized efforts rather than large-scale monolithic approaches.

There is a common theme running throughout the criticisms of the approaches to urban housing and transportation problems as well as through the suggestions for change. The criticisms concern the narrowness of the original approach and the failure to achieve stated goals while causing a variety of side effects. The suggestions for change are analogous to the ecological control schemes and basically state that the system can cure itself if given a chance. The chance is provided if our interventions give credence to the basic complexity and resilience of our urban systems. Such basic respect for the system eliminates a host of policies like those that have been previously sketched out. The idea is to let the system do it, while our interventions are aimed at juggling internal system parameters without simplifying the interactions of parameters and components.

In this vein, Gans (1969), Anderson (1964), Fried (1963), and Cogen and Feidelson (1967) argue for increased flexibility and more decentralized approaches to the urban housing problem. Instead of large-scale clearance and public housing programs or rent control, they advocate smaller-scale projects of rehabilitation, rent and income subsidies, tax credits and subsidies for property owners, and so on. These solutions allow individuals to make decisions as they see fit, while government decision-makers provide them with information in the form of subsidies and credit as to the kinds of decisions society is willing to pay for. This decentralized approach will likely be more efficient in the long run and certainly more humane and enduring, since individuals will be making decisions about their future and will necessarily feel more a part of the future.

Completely analogous suggestions have been made for transportation planning. Again the central concept is to let individuals choose for themselves their transportation, the locations of their housing relative to their jobs, and the convenience they desire for their travel. Transportation and urban planners again merely provided information that will guide people toward socially desirable ends.

Pricing is the most widely mentioned means of achieving this end. Meyer, Kain, and Wohl (1996) describe pricing schemes both for congestion and peak-hour use of roads and for parking. By changing the prices the individual traveler faces, he will more nearly bear the social costs that he creates in the form of congestion, pollution, and dispersed land patterns. It is then up to him whether or not he chooses to pay these new prices or switch his travel mode, house location, job location, or time of travel to a pattern that is more consistent with broader social goals of reasonable urban form, uncongested roads, and reasonably clean air. At the same time a variety of modes of travel and housing locations must be provided so that meaningful choices exist. Provision of such alternatives is entirely consistent with our thesis since it does not diminish the basic complexity of the urban system (it may well add to it) and does not diminish the system's resilience (again we may score gains where previously the system was stretched to capacity of the preexisting mode, be it freeway, subway, or ferry).

Conclusion

Given an intuitive understanding of our complex urban system, we would hope that practicing planners and other private and public decision-makers would draw several conclusions for themselves about the nature of their actions in the system. First, and most important, is that their actions be limited in scope and diverse in nature. Actions of this sort do preserve the complexity and resilience of the urban system and will limit the scale and potential harm of the inevitable unexpected consequences. Second, we feel that complexity is a worthwhile goal in its own right and should be preserved and encouraged. Finally, and really encompassing the above, we would hope decision-makers and their advisors will adopt a more boundary-oriented view of the world. We should be much more wary of success than failure. Again, rather than asking project directors to substantiate the ultimate success of their projects, they should be asked to ensure that unexpected and disastrous consequences be minimized. This is turning things around 180 degrees, but we feel this is the only way to proceed. Success has given us freeways, urban renewal, and public housing projects. We must reduce the size of our institutions to ensure their flexibility and respect for the system of which they are a small interacting part.

Notes

This text was originally published in the *Journal of the American Institute of Planners,* vol. 37, no. 2, March 1971.
Authors' note: This paper is very much a joint effort. Since both our names could not go first, the decision was relegated to a simple stochastic process—we tossed a coin.

1_ The reader specifically interested in an introduction to ecology can refer to Odum (1963) and Whittaker (1970).

2_ The notion of incremental (or "marginal" in the economist's jargon) changes is part and parcel of cost-benefit analysis. Non-marginal investments, which can change the structure of prices and the allocation of resources, are difficult to deal with under present cost-benefit approaches. Thus resilience is usually assumed by ignoring changes in prices induced by large-scale projects. See Prest and Turvey (1965) for a discussion of the assumptions concerning marginal and non-marginal projects.

3_ In one example (Holling 1969), a simulation model of recreational land use was developed. It was clear from this study that many of the qualities and processes in land acquisition were similar to those found in the ecological process of predation. Moreover, the similarity between land acquisition and predation extended to the structure of the interrelations among the components of each. They differed only in the specific form of the functions describing the action of each component. Therefore, even at the level of processes there is at least a structural identity that can be usefully explored so long as it is recognized that there are functional differences.

4_ See, Jacobs (1961, chapter 13), for some interesting descriptions of the destruction of formerly diverse and stable urban systems.

5_ The most complete study of the subject to date, by the RAND Corporation in New York, is not yet available, but preliminary evidence supports this statement.

References

Anderson, Martin. 1964. *The Federal Bulldozer* (Cambridge, MA: MIT Press).

Bellomo, S.J., and E. Edgerley. 1971. *Ways to Reduce Air Pollution through Planning Design and Operations*. Presented at the 50th Annual Meeting, Highway Research Board, Washington, D.C., January 1971.

Cheng, F.Y. 1963. "Deterioration of Thatch Roofs by Moth Larvae after House Spraying in the Course of a Malarial Eradication Programme in North Borneo," *Bulletin World Health Organization*, 28:136–137.

Cogen, J., and Kathryn Feidelson. 1967 "Rental Assistance for Large Families: An Interim Report," in J. Bellush and M. Hausknecht, eds., *Urban Renewal: People, Politics, and Planning* (New York: Doubleday Anchor), especially section VI, "New Directions," 508–542.

Fisher, E.M. 1966. "Twenty Years of Rent Control in New York City," in *Essays in Urban Land Economies* (Los Angeles: University of California Real Estate Research Program), 31–67.

Fried, Marc. 1963. "Grieving for a Lost Home," in L.J. Duhl, ed., *The Urban Condition* (New York: Basic Books), 151–171.

Gans, Herbert J. 1968. *People and Plans* (New York: Basic Books), especially chapter 18, "The Failure of Urban Renewal: A Critique and Some Proposals," 260–277.

Gelting, J.H. 1967. "On the Economic Effects of Rent Control in Denmark," in A.A. Nevitt, ed., *The Economic Problems of Housing* (London: Macmillan), 85–91.

Hardin, Garrett. 1963. "The Cybernetics of Competition: A Biologist's View of Society," *Perspectives in Biology and Medicine*, 7: 58–84.

Harman, Chester. 1964. "The Housing of Relocated Families," *Journal of the American Institute of Planners*, 30 (November): 266–286.

Harrison, Tom. 1965. "Operation Cat Drop," *Animals*, 5:512–513.

Holling, C. S. 1969. "Stability in Ecological and Social Systems," *Brookhaven Symposia in Biology*, 22:128–141.

Holling, C. S., and S. Ewing. 1969. "Blind Man's Bluff: Exploring the Response Space Generated by Realistic Ecological Simulation Models," in *Proceedings of the International Symposium of Statistical Ecology* (New Haven: Yale University Press, in press.)

Jacobs, Jane. 1961. *The Death and Life of Great American Cities* (New York: Random House).

Levinson, H. S., and F. H. Wynn. 1962. "Some Aspects of Future Transportation in Urban Areas," *Highway Research Board Bulletin*, 326: 1–31.

Lindbeck, Assar. 1967. "Rent Control as an Instrument of Housing Policy," in Nevitt, ed., *The Economic Problems of Housing*, 53–72.

Meyer, J., J. Kain, and M. Wohl. 1966. *The Urban Transportation Problem* (Cambridge, MA: Harvard University Press), especially chapter 13, 334–359.

Muth, R. F. 1968 "Urban Land and Residential Housing Markets," in H. S. Perloff and

L. Wingo, eds., *Issues in Urban Economics* (Baltimore: Johns Hopkins University Press), 285–333.

Needleman, Lionel. 1965. *The Economics of Housing* (London: Staples Press).

Odum, Eugene P. 1963. *Ecology* (New York: Holt, Rinehart and Winston).

Prest, A.R., and R. Turvey. 1965. "Cost-Benefit Analysis: A Survey," *Economic Journal*, 75.

Smith, Ray F., and Robert van den Bosch. 1967. "Integrated Control," in W. W. Kilgare and R.L. Doutt, eds., *Pest Control* (Academic Press).

Turrey, Ralph. 1957. *The Economics of Real Property* (London: George Allen & Unwin).

Wendt, P. F., and M. A. Goldberg. 1969. "The Use of Land Development Simulation Models on Transportation Planning," *Highway Research Record*, 285:82–91.

Whittaker, R. H. 1970. *Communities and Ecosystems* (New York: Macmillan Co.).

Selections from *Landscape Ecology Principles in Landscape Architecture and Land-Use Planning* >>>>>>>>>>>>>>>>>>>>>>>>>>

Wenche E. Dramstad, James D. Olson, and Richard T.T. Forman <<<<<<<<<<<<<<<<<<<<<<<<<<<<<<<<<<<<<<<<<<<<<<<<<

Published 1996

Development of Landscape Ecology

The key literature and concepts of landscape architecture and land-use planning are doubtless well known to the reader. However, a brief background in landscape ecology appears useful. The foundations may be traced back to scholars up to about 1950, who elucidated the natural history and physical environment patterns of large areas. Certain geographers, plant geographers, soil scientists, climatologists, and natural history writers were the "giants with shoulders" upon which later work stood.

From about 1950 to 1980 diverse important threads emerged, and their weaving together commenced. The term landscape ecology was used when aerial photography began to be widely available. The concept focused on specific spatial pattern in a section of a landscape, where biological communities interacted with the physical environment (Troll 1939, 1968). Diverse definitions of the term of course have appeared over the years, but today the primary, most widely held concept is as follows.

Ecology is generally defined as the study of the interactions among organisms and their environment, and a *landscape* is a kilometers-wide mosaic over which particular local ecosystems and land uses recur. These concepts have proven to be both simple and operationally useful. Thus *landscape ecology* is simply the ecology of landscapes, and *regional ecology* the ecology of regions.

Several other disciplines or important concepts were incorporated during this weaving phase of landscape ecology. The ecosystem concept, animal and plant geography, vegetation methodology, hedgerow studies, agronomic studies, and island biogeographic theory were important. Also quantitative geography, regional studies, human culture and aesthetics, and land evaluation were incorporated. Landscape architecture and land-use planning literature began to be included. This phase produced an abundance of intriguing, interdisciplinary individual designs, but no clear form of the overall tapestry was evident.

Since about 1980 the "land mosaic" phase has coalesced, where puzzle pieces increasingly fit together and an overall conceptual design of landscape and regional ecology emerges. Edited books tend to compile disparate, but sometimes key, pieces of landscape ecology. These include general concepts (Tjallingii and de Veer 1981, Ruzicka 1982, Brandt and Agger 1984, Zonneveld and Forman 1990), habitat fragmentation and conservation (Burgess and Sharpe 1981, Saunders et al. 1987, Hansson and Angelstam 1991), corridors and connectivity (Schreiber 1988, Brandle et al. 1988, Saunders and Hobbs 1991, Smith and Hellmund 1993), quantitative methodology (Berdoulay and Phipps 1985, Turner and Gardner 1991), and heterogeneity, boundaries, and restoration (Turner 1987, Hansen and di Castri 1992, Vos and Opdam 1992, Saunders et al. 1993).

The major authored volumes, in contrast, tend to integrate and synthesize theory and concepts. These books include land evaluation and planning (Zonneveld 1979, Takeuchi 1991), soil and agriculture (Vink 1980), logging and conservation (Harris 1984), total human ecosystem (Naveh and Lieberman 1993), hierarchy theory (O'Neill et al. 1986), statistical methodology (Jongman et al. 1987), river corridors (Malanson 1993), and land mosaics (Forman and Godron 1986, Forman 1995). Of course, to gain a solid and full understanding of the subject, articles in *Landscape Ecology* and many other journals are a must, and often a delight.

Landscape Ecology Today

The principles of landscape and regional ecology apply in any land mosaic, from suburban to agriculture and desert to forest. They work equally in pristine natural areas and areas of intense human activity. The object spread out beneath an airplane, or in an aerial photograph, contains living organisms in abundance, and therefore is a living system.

Like a plant cell or a human body, this living system exhibits three broad characteristics: structure, functioning, and change. *Landscape structure* is the spatial pattern or arrangement of landscape elements. *Functioning* is the movement and flows of animals, plants, water, wind, materials, and energy through the structure. And *change* is the dynamics or alteration in spatial pattern and functioning over time.

The structural pattern of a landscape or region is composed entirely of three types of elements. Indeed, these universal elements—patches, corridors, and matrix—are the handle for comparing highly dissimilar landscapes and for developing general principles. They also are the handle for land-use planning and landscape architecture, since spatial pattern strongly controls movements, flows, and changes.

The simple spatial language becomes evident when considering how patches, corridors, and the matrix combine to form the variety of land mosaics on earth. What are the key attributes of *patches?* They are large or small, round or elongated, smooth or convoluted, few or numerous, dispersed or clustered, and so forth. What about *corridors?* They appear narrow or wide, straight or curvy, continuous or disconnected, and so on. And the *matrix* is single or subdivided, variegated or nearly homogeneous, continuous or perforated, etc. These spatial attributes or descriptors are close to dictionary definitions, and all are familiar to decision-makers, professionals, and scholars of many disciplines.

The whole landscape or region is a mosaic, but the local neighborhood is likewise a configuration of patches, corridors, and matrix. Landscape ecologists are actively studying and developing principles for the biodiversity patterns and natural processes in these configurations or neighborhood mosaics.

For example, changing a mosaic by adding a hedgerow, pond, house, woods, road, or other element changes the functioning. Animals change their routes, water flows alter direction, erosion of soil particles changes, and humans move differently. Removing an element alters flows in a different manner. And rearranging the existing elements causes yet greater changes in how the neighborhood functions. These spatial elements and their arrangements are the ready handles for landscape architects and land-use planners.

Natural processes as well as human activities change landscapes. In a time series of aerial photographs, a sequence of mosaics typically appears. Habitat fragmentation is frequently noted and decried. But many other spatial processes are evident in land transformation, such as perforation, dissection, shrinkage, attrition, and coalescence, each with major ecological and human implications.

In short, the landscape ecology principles in this book are directly applicable and offer opportunities for wise planning, design, conservation, management, and land policy. The principles are significant from neighborhood to regional mosaics. They focus on spatial pattern, which strongly determines functioning and change. Their patch-corridor-matrix components have universality for any region. And their language enhances communication and collaboration. They will become central as society begins to seriously address the issue of creating sustainable environments.

Landscape ecology principles are listed below in four sections: Patches, Edges, Corridors, and Mosaics.

Patches

In a densely populated world, plant and animal habitat increasingly appears in scattered patches. Ecologists first considered habitat patches analogous with islands, but soon largely abandoned the analogy due to major differences between the sea and the matrix of countryside and suburban developments surrounding a "terrestrial" patch. Patches, however, do exhibit a degree of isolation, the effect and severity being dependent on the species present.

Four *origins* or causes of vegetation patches are usefully recognized: *remnants* (e.g., areas remaining from an earlier more extensive type, such as woodlots in agricultural areas); *introduced* (e.g., a new suburban development in an agricultural area, or a small pasture within a forest); *disturbance* (e.g., a burned area in a forest, or a spot devastated by a severe windstorm); and *environmental resources* (e.g., wetlands in a city, or oases in a desert).

Patches may be as *large* as a national forest, or as small as a single tree. Patches may be *numerous* in a landscape, such as avalanches or rock slides on a mountainside, or be scarce such as oases in a desert. The location of patches may be *beneficial* or *deleterious* to the optimal functioning of a landscape. For example, small, remnant forest patches between large reserves in an agricultural matrix can be beneficial. In contrast, a landfill located adjacent to a sensitive wetland may have a negative impact on the ecological health of the landscape.

Edges and Boundaries

An *edge* is described as the outer portion of a patch where the environment differs significantly from the interior of the patch. Often, edge and interior environments simply look and feel different. For example, vertical and horizontal structure, width, and species composition and abundance, in the edge of a patch, differ from interior conditions, and together comprise the *edge effect*. Whether a boundary is curvilinear or straight influences the flow of nutrients, water, energy, or species along or across it.

Boundaries may also be "political" or "administrative"—that is, represent artificial divisions between inside and out that may or may not correspond to natural "ecological" boundaries or edges. Relating these artificial edges with natural ones is important. As human development continues its expansion into natural environments, the edges created will increasingly form the critical point for interactions between human-made and natural habitats.

The shape of patches, as defined by their boundaries, can be manipulated by landscape architects and land-use planners to accomplish an ecological function or objective. Due to the diverse significance of edges, rich opportunities exist to use this key ecological transition zone between two types of habitat in designs and plans.

Corridors and Connectivity

The loss and isolation of habitat is a seemingly unstoppable process occurring throughout the modern world. Landscape planners and ecologists must contend with this continuing process if further reductions in biodiversity are to be slowed or halted.

Several dynamic processes cause this isolation and loss over time. The key spatial processes include: *fragmentation* (i.e., breaking up a larger/intact habitat into smaller dispersed patches); *dissection* (i.e., splitting an intact habitat into two patches separated by a corridor); *perforation* (i.e., creating "holes" within an essentially intact habitat);

Wenche E. Dramstad, James D. Olson, and Richard T.T. Forman

shrinkage (i.e., the decrease in size of one or more habitats); and *attrition* (i.e., the disappearance of one or more habitat patches).

In the face of continued habitat loss and isolation, many landscape ecologists stress the need for providing landscape connectivity, particularly in the forms of wildlife movement corridors and stepping stones. Despite residual discussion of the effectiveness of corridors in enhancing biodiversity, a growing empirical body of research underlines the net benefits accruing from incorporating higher-quality linkages between habitat patches.

Corridors in the landscape may also act as barriers or filters to species movement. Some may be population "sinks" (i.e., locations where individuals of a species tend to decrease in number). For example, roadways, railroads, power lines, canals, and trails may be thought of as "troughs" or barriers.

Finally, stream or river systems are corridors of exceptional significance in a landscape. Maintaining their ecological integrity in the face of intense human use is both a challenge and an opportunity to landscape designers and land-use planners.

Mosaics

The overall structural and functional integrity of a landscape can be understood and evaluated in terms of both *pattern* and *scale*. One assay of the ecological health of a landscape is the overall *connectivity* of the natural systems present. Corridors often interconnect with one another to form *networks*, enclosing other landscape elements. Networks in turn exhibit connectivity, *circuitry*, and *mesh size*. Networks emphasize the functioning of landscapes and may be used by planners and landscape architects to facilitate or inhibit flows and movements across a land mosaic.

A common landscape *pattern* is fragmentation, which is often associated with the loss and isolation of habitat. Alternatively, fragmentation is considered as one of several land transformation processes, which together may produce a diminution and isolation of habitat. Fragmentation also results from natural disturbances, such as fires and herbivore invasions, but has become an international land policy issue because of widespread alteration of land mosaics by human activities.

The spatial *scale* at which fragmentation occurs is important when identifying strategies to cope with continued habitat loss and isolation. For example, fragmented habitat at a fine scale may be perceived as intact habitat at a broad scale. Only by recognizing and addressing landscape changes across different scales (perhaps at least three) can planners and designers maximize protection of biodiversity and natural processes.

Note

This text is an edited selection from *Landscape Ecology Principles in Landscape Architecture and Land-Use Planning* (Cambridge, MA, and Washington, D.C.: Harvard University Graduate School of Design, Island Press, and the American Society of Landscape Architects, 1996).

References

Berdoulay, V., and M. Phipps, eds. 1985. *Paysage et Système*. Editions de l'Université d'Ottawa, Ottawa.

Brandle, J.R., D.L. Hintz, and J.W. Sturrock, eds. 1988. *Windbreak Technology*. Elsevier, Amsterdam. (Reprinted from *Agriculture, Ecosystems, and Environment* 22–23, 1988).

Brandt, J., and P. Agger, eds. 1984. *Proceedings of the First International Seminar on Methodology in Landscape Ecology Research and Planning*. 5 vols. Roskilde Universitetsforlag GeoRuc, Roskilde, Denmark.

Burgess, R.L., and D.M. Sharpe, eds. 1981. *Forest Island Dynamics in Man-Dominated Landscapes*. Springer-Verlag, New York.

Forman, R.T.T., ed. 1979. *Pine Barrens: Ecosystem and Landscape*. Academic Press, New York.

Forman, R.T.T. 1995. Land Mosaics: The Ecology of Landscapes and Regions. Cambridge University Press, Cambridge.

Forman, R.T.T. 1995. Some general principles of landscape and regional ecology. *Landscape Ecology* 10: 133–142.

Forman, R.T.T., and M. Godron. 1986. *Landscape Ecology*. John Wiley, New York.

Hansen, A.J., and F. di Castri, eds. 1992. *Landscape Boundaries: Consequences for Biotic Diversity and Ecological Flows*. Springer-Verlag, New York.

Hansson, L. and P. Angelstam. 1991. Landscape ecology as a theoretical basis for nature conservation. *Landscape Ecology* 5: 191–201.

Harris, L.D. 1984. *The Fragmented Forest: Island Biogeography Theory and the Preservation of Biotic Diversity*. University of Chicago Press, Chicago.

Hobbs, R.J. 1995. Landscape ecology. *Encyclopedia of Environmental Biology* 2, pp. 417–428.

Jongman, R.G.H., C.J.F. ter Braak, and O.F.R. van Tongeren. 1987. *Data Analysis in Community and Landscape Ecology*. PUDOC, Wageningen, Netherlands.

Malanson, G.P. 1993. *Riparian Landscapes*. Cambridge University Press, Cambridge.

Naveh, Z., and A.S. Lieberman. 1993. *Landscape Ecology: Theory and Application*. Springer-Verlag, New York.

O'Neill, R.V., D.L. DeAngelis, J.B. Waide, and T.F.H. Allen. 1986. *A Hierarchical Concept of Ecosystems.* Princeton University Press, Princeton.

Ruzicka, M., ed. 1982. *Proceedings of the Sixth International Symposium on Problems in Landscape Ecological Research.* Institute for Experimental Biology and Ecology, Bratislava, Czechoslovakia.

Saunders, D.A., G.W Arnold, A.A. Burbidge, and A.J.M. Hopkins, eds. 1987. *Nature Conservation: The Role of Remnants of Native Vegetation.* Surrey Beatty, Chipping Norton, Australia.

Saunders, D.A., and R.J. Hobbs, eds. 1991. *Nature Conservation 2: The Role of Corridors.*

Surrey Beatty, Chipping Norton, Australia.

Saunders, D.A., R.J. Hobbs, and P.R. Ehrlich, eds. 1993. *Nature Conservation 3: The Reconstruction of Fragmented Ecosystems: Global and Regional Perspectives.* Surrey Beatty, Chipping Norton, Australia.

Schreiber, K-F. 1988. *Connectivity in Landscape Ecology.* Münstersche Geographische

Arbeiten 29, Ferdinand Schoningh, Paderborn, Germany.

Smith, D.S., and P.C. Hellmund, eds. 1993. *Ecology of Greenways: Design and Function of Linear Conservation Areas.* University of Minnesota Press, Minneapolis, Minnesota.

Takeuchi, K. 1991. *Regional (Landscape) Ecology.* (In Japanese). Asakura Publishing, Tokyo. Tjallingii, S.P., and A.A. de Veer, eds. 1981. *Perspectives in Landscape Ecology.* PUDOC, Wageningen, Netherlands.

Troll, C. 1939. Luftbildplan und ökologische Bodenforschung. Zeitschrift der Gesellschaft für Erdkunde zu Berlin, pp. 241–298.

Troll, C. 1968. Landschaftsokologie. In Tuxen, R., ed. Pflanzensoziologie und Landschaftsokologie, pp. 1–21. Dr. W. Junk Publishers, The Hague, Netherlands.

Turner, M.G., ed. 1987. *Landscape Heterogeneity and Disturbance.* Springer-Verlag, New York.

Turner, M.G. 1989. Landscape ecology: the effect of pattern on process. *Annual Review of Ecology and Systematics* 20, pp. 171-197.

Turner, M.G., and R.H. Gardner, eds. 1991. *Quantitative Methods in Landscape Ecology: The Analysis and Interpretation of Landscape Heterogeneity.* Springer-Verlag, New York.

Vink, A.P.A. 1980. *Landschapsecologie en Landgebruik.* Bohn, Scheltema and Holkema, Utrecht, Netherlands. (1983 translation. Landscape Ecology and Land Use. Longman, London).

Vos, C.C., and P. Opdam, eds. 1992. *Landscape Ecology of a Stressed Environment.* Chapman and Hall, London.

Zonnevald, L.S. 1979. *Land Evaluation and Land(scape) Science.* 2nd edition. ITC Textbook VI1.4. Internalional Institute for Aerial Sunvey and Earth Sciences, Enschede, Netherlands.

Zonneveld, I. S., and R.T.T. Forman, eds. 1990. *Changing Landscapes: An Ecological Perspective.* Springer-Verlag, New York.

Succession is a process by which one ecosystem community is gradually replaced by another, which usually leads to communities more diverse in their structures and functions, and which imparts greater ecosystem stability for a limited period in time.[1] NML

1. After Clements (1916), Gleason (1926), and Cowles (1911).

SUCCESSION

Increasing complexity often brings along with it decreasing level of control, and varying degrees of possibility. Here, plant seeding, growth, and seasonal cycles can be activated in ways that create value for a project in its multiple formats over time; habitat cultivation and diversification become the engine of project evolution and phasing; linear trajectories of time and process and history expand the issues and inputs considered germane; and ecological-infrastructural-productive sequences are choreographed to suggest multiple possible futures. CR

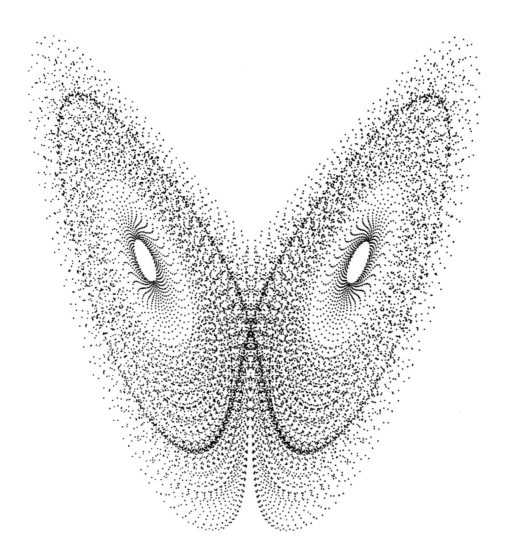

James Corner Field Operations with Nina-Marie Lister. Emergence through Adaptive Management. Downsview Park, Toronto, Canada. 1999. (SEE POSTER)

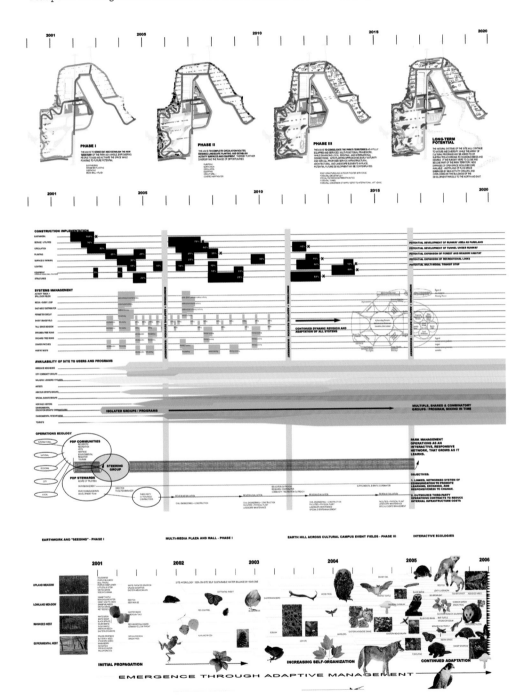

OMA. La Dynamique et L'Echelle du Temps, du Parterre a la Foret. Parc de la Villette, Paris, France. 1983/1985.

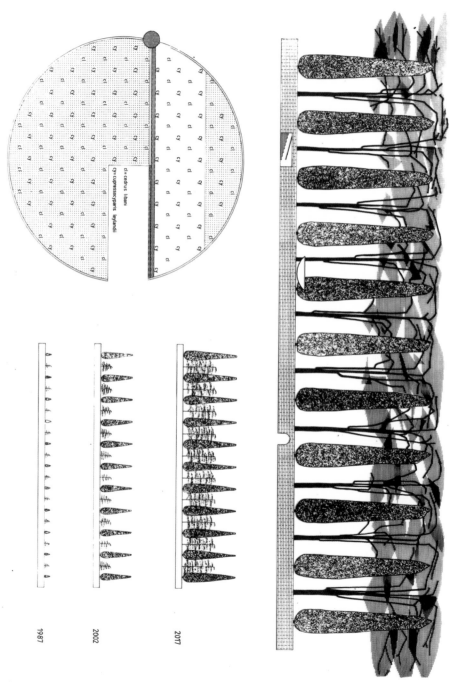

1987

2002

2017

Michel Desvigne Paysagistes. Thirty-Year Planting Development. Thomas Plant, Guyancourt, France. 1989.

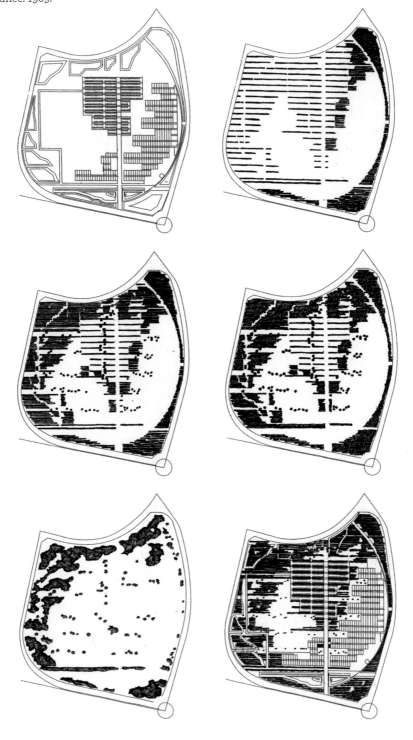

HABITAT PHASING

existing habitats

phase 1

phase 2

GRASSLAND
STRIP CROPPING

Strip cropping is an inexpensive, industrial scale technique for increasing the organic content of poor soils, chelating metals and toxins (inhibiting their uptake by plants), increasing soil depth, controlling weeds and increasing aeration.

A crop rotation system is proposed to improve the existing topsoil cover without importing large quantities of new soil.

The cultivated soils will support native prairie and meadow. In the wetter areas of the mounds, shallow-rooted successional woodland will ultimately diversify the grassland biotopes.

NORTH AND SOUTH MOUNDS west face 130 acres

CROP A ROWS	oats, mustard, sorhgum	ALLOW SUCCESSIONAL WOODLAND ON WET AREAS, MOW DRY AREAS EVERY 3 YEARS
ESTABLISH NATIVE PRAIRIE		ESTABLISH NATIVE PRAIRIE	ALLOW SUCCESSIONAL WOODLAND ON W
CROP B ROWS	sunflower, clover, barley	

NORTH AND SOUTH MOUNDS east face 95 acres

CROP A ROWS	oats, mustard, sorhgum	ESTABLISH NATIVE PRAIRIE
ESTABLISH NATIVE PRAIRIE		
CROP B ROWS	sunflower, clover, barley	

WOODLAND
ON THE MOUNDS

2 to 3 feet of new soil will be required for cultivation of denser, stratified woodland on the mounds in early stages of the park's development. The new soils would be stabilized and planted with native grassland intially to create a weed-resistant matrix for the gradual interplanting of young tree stock.

Proposed woodland on the mounds is located in areas adjacent to proposed lowland and swamp forests to widen the habitat corridor while conserving the amount of new soil to be imported.

A total of 220 acres of woodland on the mounds is proposed--with 65 acres on the north and south mounds, and 155 acres on the east and west mounds.

NORTH AND SOUTH MOUNDS 65 acres

20 A SOIL	ESTABLISH NATIVE PRAIRIE	PLANT	INTERPLANT
22 A SOIL	ESTABLISH NATIVE PRAIRIE	PLANT	INTERPLANT
22 A SOIL	ESTABLISH NATIVE PRAIRIE	PLANT	INTERPLANT

EAST AND WEST MOUNDS 155

22 A SOIL	ESTABLISH NATIVE PRAIRIE	PL
22 A SOIL	ESTABLISH NATIVE PRAIRIE	
22 A SOIL	ESTABLISH NATIVE P
22 A SOIL	ESTABLIS
22 A SOIL

LOWLAND FOREST

When a supply of native saplings and tree plugs are available (particularly in early years of park construction when other areas are being prepared for planting), lowland and swamp forests are planted in overlapping ecotonal bands on existing soil to build the woodland rim.

EXPRESSWAY CORRIDOR + NORTH AND SOUTH MOUNDS 160 acres

| PLANT | PLANT | PLANT | PLANT | PLANT | PLANT | PLANT |

EAST AND WEST MOUNDS

| PLANT | PLANT | | PLANT |

YEAR 1 2 3 4 5 6 7 8 | 9 10 11 12 13 14 15 16

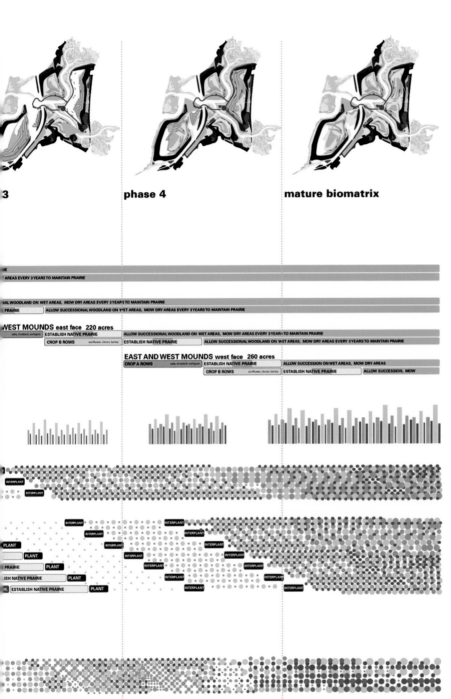

phase 4　　　mature biomatrix

19 20 21 22 23 24 25 26 27 28 29 30 31 32 33 34 35 36 37 38 39 40

OPSYS/Pierre Bélanger. The Agronomic Landscape, 6000 BC-2011 AD. 2011.

emerges the egyptian empire

Soil Erosion in Greece Causes Widespread Famine

the roman empir
from the nile's fe

Like the
Nile Delta

The slash and burn agricultural tactics that built
the Mayan empire were incapable of sustaining it.

"...rising demand for food and declining productivity
compelled cultivation of increasingly marginal land."

"By 400BC, Egypt and Sicily grew between one third
and three quarters of the food for Greek cities."

Greek soil's inability to support the empire's
expansion reduced its standing as a world power.

spice globalizes the world's
agricultural economy

famine and conges...
europe west for gr...

"Tobacco strips more than te...
more than thirty times the p...
than do traditional crops." 11...

"Real hunger, as much as the hunger
for empire or religious freedom, helped
launch europe toward the New World"

Wet weather for two straight years, combined with underperforming
land resulted in the great famine of 1315-1317, which toppled urban
settlements and lead to pervasive malnutrition, and the Black Plague,
ultimately killing one quarter of the European population.

Massive population growth around 1000AD resulted
in widespread urbanization of europe, the development
of a middle class, and global agricultural trade with Asia.

The Great Famine Kills 50 Million Europeans, Giving Rise to The Black Death

COMPLEAT BODY of HUSBANDRY

FOOD IS A WEAPON

SORRY NO GAS

15 McDONALDS 15
FAMOUS
HAMBURGERS
BUY 'EM BY THE BAG

TIME
FOOD PRICES:
The Big Beef

FLITE-FUEL

OR EUROPEAN RECOVERY
SUPPLIED BY THE
STATES OF AMERICA

BAYER
BASF
Chemical C

Tyson

Famine in Africa Kills 30 Million People in One Year

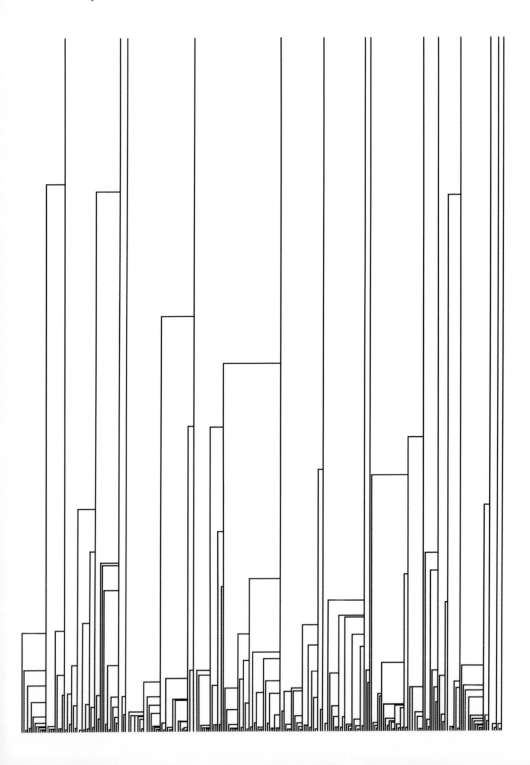

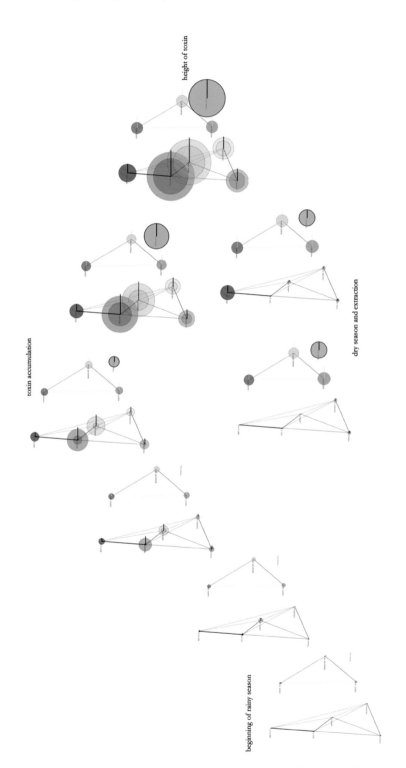

height of toxin

dry season and extraction

toxin accumulation

beginning of rainy season

Michael Ezban. Ichthyo Scenarios. 2012.

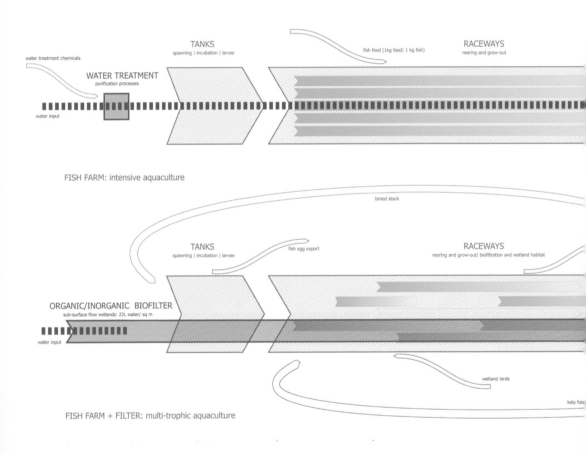

water treatment chemicals

TANKS
spawning | incubation | larvae

fish feed (1kg feed/ 1 kg fish)

RACEWAYS
rearing and grow-out

WATER TREATMENT
purification processes

water input

FISH FARM: intensive aquaculture

brood stock

TANKS
spawning | incubation | larvae

fish egg export

RACEWAYS
rearing and grow-out/ biofiltration and wetland habitat

ORGANIC/INORGANIC BIOFILTER
sub-surface flow wetlands: 22L water/ sq m

water input

wetland birds

kelp foo

FISH FARM + FILTER: multi-trophic aquaculture

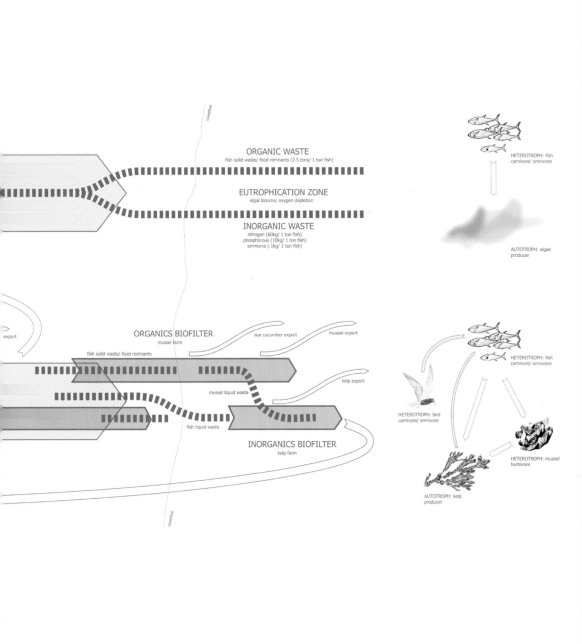

ORGANIC WASTE
fish solid waste/ food remnants (2.5 tons/ 1 ton fish)

EUTROPHICATION ZONE
algal blooms/ oxygen depletion

INORGANIC WASTE
nitrogen (60kg/ 1 ton fish)
phosphorous (10kg/ 1 ton fish)
ammonia (.1kg/ 1 ton fish)

HETEROTROPH: fish
carnivore/ omnivore

AUTOTROPH: algae
producer

ORGANICS BIOFILTER
mussel farm

sea cucumber export

mussel export

export

fish solid waste/ food remnants

mussel liquid waste

kelp export

fish liquid waste

INORGANICS BIOFILTER
kelp farm

coastline

HETEROTROPH: fish
carnivore/ omnivore

HETEROTROPH: bird
carnivore/ omnivore

HETEROTROPH: mussel
herbivore

AUTOTROPH: kelp
producer

Selections from
Discordant Harmonies >>>>>>>>>>>>>>>>>>>>>>>>>>

Daniel Botkin <<<<<<<<<<<<<<<<<<<<<<<<<<<<<<<<<<<<<<<<<<<<<<<<<
<<<<<<<<<<<<<<<<<<<<<<<<<<<<<<<<<<<<<<<<<<<<<<<<<<<<<<<<<<<<<<<<<<<
<<<<<<<<<<<<<<<<<<<<<<<<<<<<<<<<<<<<<<<<<<<<<<<<<<<<<<<<<<<<<<<<<<<
<<<<<<<<<<<<<<<<<<<<<<<<<<<<<<<<<<<<<<<<<<<<<<<<<<<<<<<<<<<<<<<<<<<
<<<<<<<<<<<<<<<<<<<<<<<<<<<<<<<<<<<<<<<<<<<<<<<<<<<<<<<<<<<<<<<<<<<
<<<<<<<<<<<<<<<<<<<<<<<<<<<<<<<<<<<<<<<<<<<<<<<<<<<<<<<<<<<<<<<<<<<
<<<<<<<<<<<<<<<<<<<<<<<<<<<<<<<<<<<<<<<<<<<<<<<<<<<<<<<<<<<<<<<<<<<
<<<<<<<<<<<<<<<<<<<<<<<<<<<<<<<<<<<<<<<<<<<<<<<<<<<<<<<<<<<<<<<<<<<
<<<<<<<<<<<<<<<<<<<<<<<<<<<<<<<<<<<<<<<<<<<<<<<<<<<<<<<<<<<<<<<<<<<
<<<<<<<<<<<<<<<<<<<<<<<<<<<<<<<<<<<<<<<<<<<<<<<<<<<<<<<<<<<<<<<<<<<
<<<<<<<<<<<<<<<<<<<<<<<<<<<<<<<<<<<<<<<<<<<<<<<<<<<<<<<<<<<<<<<<<<<
<<<<<<<<<<<<<<<<<<<<<<<<<<<<<<<<<<<<<<<<<<<<<<<<<<<<<<<<<<<<<<<<<<<
<<<<<<<<<<<<<<<<<<<<<<<<<<<<<<<<<<<<<<<<<<<<<<<<<<<<<<<<<<<<<<<<<<<
<<<<<<<<<<<<<<<<<<<<<<<<<<<<<<<<<<<<<<<<<<<<<<<<<<<<<<<<<<<<<<<<<<<
<<<<<<<<<<<<<<<<<<<<<<<<<<<<<<<<<<<<<<<<<<<<<<<<<<<<<<<<<<<<<<<<<<<
<<<<<<<<<<<<<<<<<<<<<<<<<<<<<<<<<<<<<<<<<<<<<<<<< Published 1990

Within the Moose's Stomach:
Nature as the Biosphere >>

An Afternoon on Isle Royale

One summer afternoon on Isle Royale, I came across a moose in a shallow pond that lay back from the shores, sheltered from Lake Superior's chilly winds. I stopped to rest my feet and view the scene, which appeared peaceful, calm, and pleasing. Feeding placidly, the moose seemed alone in the wilderness, breathing oxygen from an inert, lifeless but life-giving air and digging through dank, lifeless mud for a succulent morsel of green water plants. Yet looks are deceptive, and here, after our long journey through time and over the Earth's surface and among its many creatures, it is appropriate to take a lesson from Aristotle and view the "mean and despicable" creatures, for with this inquiry we can, at long last, begin to reinterpret nature for our time.

The moose—with its long spindly legs, which appear too thin for its stocky body, and its sagging belly—seemed an ungainly creature in the wilderness. Who would have designed such a creature? It has none of the attributes of classical beauty: a face without merit; a drooping hang-jaw and protruding lower lip; a hard gummy pallet instead of front upper teeth. The moose has inspired none of the rhapsodies to the grandeur or sublimity of nature, so important to Wordsworth's view of nature. Only a bull moose in the autumn, with its large antlers, presents any semblance of nature's magnificence— viewed, that is, from a distance; close up, the comical reappears.

If I had been hiking with another twentieth-century biologist versed in the Darwinian theory of evolution, he could have explained to me how well adapted a moose is to its environment, despite the superficial ugliness of the adaptations. Its lips, for example, are wonderfully adapted for pulling up underwater plants and tearing leaves from twigs: the lower front teeth push against the upper gums so that only the soft edible leaves are removed, leaving the twigs on the plants. I knew from past experience that the moose's long spindly legs can propel it at a surprising speed over the waters should I disturb it, enabling it to flee or chase me with great agility through the thickets and over dead logs, much faster than I could run. Watching the peaceful lakeside scene, under the bright blue sky against the tea-colored waters sheltered in the forest, I was reminded of those ancient questions that we have been considering.

All seemed constant beneath the sky, unchanging and permanent, without the slightest suggestion of the inevitable death of the moose or of the population explosions and crashes of its ancestors, without a sign of trampled vegetation or of water lilies and yew forced to the brink of extinction on the island by this ungainly herbivore. Although the moose seemed dependent on the wilderness—the air, the water, the soils, and the plants—it seemed to have little influence on its immediate environment or on the rest of nature beyond the island.

In this still-life, there seemed to be only one grazing moose, but in fact the moose was not alone. As an ungulate, a true ruminant with a four-chambered stomach, the moose carries within its intestines an intricate array of symbiotic microbes, just as do its many ruminant relatives, which include the rest of the cervids (the family of northern deer), domestic cattle, and many of the big-game animals of the African plains and savannas. Its stomach teems with microbes—1 billion per cubic centimeter—performing tasks that the moose cannot do for itself. Who would have designed a moose this way—of necessity harboring in its gut vast numbers of creatures on which its life depends, unable to make the enzymes to digest the vegetation that, in the northern wilderness, is its only food?

An ungulate's rumen is so complex that a textbook in animal physiology called it "an ecological system in dynamic equilibrium" with inputs (of food and saliva) and outputs (of those materials that the moose can digest).[1] There are many species of microbes in the rumen. The most important to the moose are bacteria, called anaerobes, that can live only in an oxygenless atmosphere. There are other species of bacteria and other unicellular organisms that feed on the bacteria—predators and prey, all growing, reproducing, feeding, and dying within the gut of this large mammal.

The anaerobic bacteria are truly symbiotic with the moose, making the moose's survival possible and depending on the moose to provide an environment without which they would die. A large fraction of the vegetation swallowed by the moose consists of cellulose and complex carbohydrates, which it cannot digest. The bacteria release enzymes that digest cellulose and other carbohydrates, breaking down these complex compounds into simple sugars that might make a good energy source for the moose, but it does not get a chance to use them. The bacteria take up the sugars and use them as their supply of energy before the lining of the moose's intestines can absorb these compounds. In the oxygenless atmosphere of the rumen, ordinary respiration, which requires oxygen, cannot take place. Instead, the bacteria ferment the sugars and give off fatty acids as the waste products of their metabolism. Of these, acetic acid, the acid in vinegar, is the most important. These acids become, in turn, the moose's food; they are absorbed by the walls of the rumen.

The moose, like all mammals, produces urea in the process of digesting its food. Urea is 47 percent nitrogen, an element essential for all living things and sometimes difficult for the moose to obtain in sufficient quantity, especially in the winter. The excretion of urea is a loss of this valuable resource. Instead of eliminating all the urea, as we do, the moose is able to transfer part of it through the blood to its saliva; when the saliva is swallowed, the urea is returned to the rumen. There, the bacteria are able to convert the nitrogen-rich urea, as well as ammonia, which is produced in other reactions, to proteins. The nitrogen in the urea is important to the bacteria, since it fertilizes their growth. The bacteria also synthesize vitamins that are necessary to the moose. Thus the moose can live on what would otherwise be a very poor diet—low in protein and vitamins, too low for its survival if it were not for the bacteria in its gut.

Of the plant material taken in by the moose, approximately 50 percent is digested by the bacteria; of the rest, about 10 percent is converted by the bacteria to methane, which is belched and released to the air unused by the moose. The remaining vegetation passes down the digestive system, along with a large mass of the bacteria (about 15 percent by weight of the original mass of vegetation taken in by the moose). These bacteria are digested by the moose, serving as high-quality food. The moose is also able to digest about half of the remaining vegetation by its own digestive process.

The moose contributes many things to this symbiosis. It provides the food for the bacteria and maintains an environment with a constant temperature of approximately 102°F. It swallows saliva along with vegetation. The saliva is slightly basic and neutralizes acids produced by the bacteria, helping to maintain an acidity in the rumen within a range that is acceptable, perhaps even optimal, for the bacteria. The bacteria live, grow, and multiply in a protected environment, with a special atmosphere and a steady input of food. The moose removes the fatty acids that are wastes of the bacteria that would otherwise poison the microbes and threaten their survival in the rumen. The rumen is an ecological system overwhelmingly biologically produced and controlled.

In some ways, the moose's rumen is a model in miniature of the biosphere—our planet's entire life-support system. Like the rumen, the biosphere is a system that includes and sustains life. But the rumen is also a system under biological control and is in steady-state within a certain range of conditions—as long as the moose is alive and healthy. In these qualities the stomach of a moose brings us back to the ancient questions about the characteristics of nature without human influence, and the question of whether nature is in a balance. The microbes in the moose's gut live in an environment that seems most bizarre to us and certainly unsuitable for human beings. There is little oxygen and in some parts of the intestine no oxygen at all. Noxious gases, such as methane and ammonia, abound, produced by the microbes and the moose's own digestive processes. The fluids are acidic, and the microbes withdraw nitrogen from the air—nitrogen is the most abundant molecule in air—and convert it to nitrate, nitric acid, ammonia, and other small and unpleasant chemicals.

The microbes that live in the rumen would die in the air outside, the air that was so clear and pleasant to me on that sunlit afternoon by the pond. Oxygen would kill the bacteria rapidly. But in the pond-bottom muds that the moose kicked at and waded through as it fed, there were similar bacteria that also can survive only where there is no oxygen; they live beneath the still waters of the pond where poisonous oxygen cannot penetrate. Nitrogen-fixing bacteria that live in the root nodules of leguminous plants, such as alders on the pond's edge, also cannot survive in an atmosphere rich in oxygen. For them, the nodules provide a home, an *ecos*, protecting them from the oxygen that is so deadly to them.

Global Nature

When some of the photosynthetic bacteria were buried but did not completely decompose, a slight imbalance resulted in the uptake and release of oxygen, which slowly built up in the atmosphere. Thus early life in the form of these lowly, seemingly insignificant mats began to change the entire planet. Free oxygen in the Earth's atmosphere is the result of 3 billion years of photosynthesis and is therefore a product of life. Like the atmosphere in the rumen in a modern moose's stomach, the Earth's atmosphere has been fundamentally altered by life.

Life appears to affect not only the air we breathe, but also the rocks on which we stand. Perhaps nothing seems less lifelike than a piece of steel or iron, a steel girder or a chunk of iron ore. But the origin of iron ores is intimately connected to life and its history on the Earth. The rocks that form the major economically important deposits of iron were laid down between 2.2 and 1.8 billion years ago, deposited because of the release of oxygen into the oceans by photosynthetic bacteria.[2] A vast amount of unoxidized iron was dissolved in those ancient oceans. Unoxidized iron is much more soluble in water than oxidized iron. Oxygen released into the ocean waters as a waste product by photosynthetic bacteria combined with the dissolved iron, changing it from a more soluble to a less soluble form. No longer dissolved in the water, the iron settled to the bottom of the oceans and became part of deposits that were slowly turned into rock. Over millions of years, these deposits formed thick bands of iron ore that are mined today from Minnesota to Australia. After most of the dissolved iron had been removed from the oceans, the oxygen produced by photosynthesis began to enter the atmosphere, leading to another major change in the biosphere, converting it from a reducing to an oxidizing environment.

From the chemistry of rocks such as stromatolites and iron-ore beds, geologists have been able to reconstruct the history of the Earth's atmosphere. The early atmosphere of the Earth, before the emergence of life, was composed primarily of hydrogen, methane, and ammonia. Approximately 3.5 billion years ago, about the age of the earliest fossils, there was a shift to an atmosphere with free nitrogen and carbon dioxide, which was followed by an increase in the concentration of oxygen and a decrease in that of carbon dioxide to approximately present levels. If the Earth had remained lifeless, the concentration of carbon dioxide and nitrogen in the atmosphere would have remained high, as would have the concentration of hydrogen, methane, and ammonia. Although oxygen would have increased as a result of the activity of sunlight, it would not have increased to the same concentration as found today. Carbon dioxide would have been ten times more abundant; free nitrogen, ten times less. [3]

Early life on the Earth altered not only the chemistry of the Earth's atmosphere, but also the heat budget of the Earth and the Earth's surface temperature. The temperature of the surface of the Earth is a result of energy exchange and of physical characteristics of the surface. Energy is received from the sun, and a very small amount is generated from the Earth's core (produced by radioactive processes that heat the center of the Earth). Energy is lost to space by radiation from the Earth's surface. The hotter an object, the more rapidly it radiates energy and the shorter the wavelength of the predominate radiation. A blue flame is hot; a red flame is cooler. The Earth's surface and the surfaces of animals and plants are so cool that energy is radiated predominately in the infrared, which is invisible to us. [4] If an object is cold and gives off less heat than it receives, it will warm up. But as it warms, it also radiates heat more rapidly. As a result, for any constant input of energy, a physical object will eventually reach a temperature that will allow it to radiate energy at the same rate that it receives energy.

The rate at which the Earth's surface radiates heat depends on its average "color" and temperature. A perfect emitter of heat is called an ideal black body, and black surfaces radiate heat much more readily than white surfaces. A white planet would radiate heat very differently from a black planet. Changes in the amount of ice and the distribution of vegetation over the Earth alter the reflecting and emitting characteristics of the planet's surface. Ice reflects 80 to 95 percent of light; a dry grassland, 30 to 40 percent; a coniferous forest 10 to 15 percent.[5] It has been estimated that under present atmospheric conditions, a 1 percent change in the amount of sunlight reflected by the Earth would cause approximately a 3°F change in the average temperature of the Earth's surface.

Changes in the absorption of energy can be due to changes in the cloud cover and in the amount of ice cover on the Earth's land surfaces. Organisms, particularly grasses and trees and algae, can also affect the absorption. Their absorption of light changes with the seasons. Marine algal mats can change from light and highly reflective in one season to almost black and highly emitting in another. Algae can also produce sediments such as calcium carbonate, which, when pure, is chalky white and has a different reflective characteristic than the sediments produced from a lifeless surface. Even a single-cell layer of algae spread over a large area of water could greatly alter the rate of energy exchange and therefore the temperature of the Earth's surface.

These examples suggest that life has greatly altered its environment at a global level over the history of the Earth; this explains in part the "fitness of the environment" that Lawrence Henderson observed in the early years of the twentieth century. The environment appears "fit" for life because life has evolved to take advantage of the environment and, conversely, has greatly changed the environment at a global level. This suggests that living things have a much more important effect on our planet than previously believed.

The Biosphere

Life and the environment affect each other at a global level. Together they form a planetary-scale system, the biosphere, that sustains life. The idea of the biosphere and the growth in understanding it can be traced back to several books published in the first few decades of the twentieth century, including Henderson's *Fitness of the Environment,* and to books published in the 1940s and 1950s by a very small number of scientists, including G.E. Hutchinson in the United States. However, it is only in the past two decades that this idea has gained momentum, helped by the popularization of the photographs of the Earth taken from space by the Apollo astronauts.[6] Just as the images of nearby planets, appearing as objects something like the Earth, with surface features and moons, affected ideas about the universe in the eighteenth and nineteenth centuries, so in the late 1960s photographs from space showing the Earth as a cloudy blue marble floating in inky blackness became profound images for our time. The pictures of our living planet floating alone, a unique cosmic island, evoked in the public consciousness strong feelings about the fragility of all life on our planet, in a way that could not have been possible in times past—not to Cicero, with his Earth-centered, divinely ordered cosmos; not to Galileo and Newton, with their exact calculations of the continual sweep of planets through the solar system; not to Wordsworth, with his challenges to a powerful nature. Perhaps more than any other single image or any single event these photographs of the Earth have done more to change our consciousness about the character of life, the factors that sustain it, and our role in the biosphere and our power over life. Those images from space have radically altered our myths about nature. The power of this image is demonstrated by its repeated use in recent years in many contexts, from advertisements to discussions of environmental problems. But behind this image, what are the characteristics of the biosphere? It is something like the stomach of a moose.

The Biosphere and the Balance of Nature

During the past decade, more and more scientists have acknowledged the significant impact of life on the Earth. This raises the possibility of another role of life—that life, in its entirety, might increase the stability of the biosphere, or, to put it in older terms, affect the balance of nature at the global level. The environment of the moose's stomach is maintained under very exacting conditions; the temperature, for example, remains within a very small range of variation. In the biosphere, conditions for the persistence of life are more flexible. There is a range of permissible conditions for life as we know it. For most life, temperatures must be approximately between 32°F and 122°F. The acidity of water must be close to neutral but can vary from slightly acidic to slightly basic. The elements essential to living organisms must be available, and in ratios that are acceptable to the needs of individuals. For life to continue, these factors must remain within certain ranges, but they need not be at single values continuously. Is the biosphere, then, at an exact steady-state? a precise balance of nature?

There are three schools of thought about a balance of nature at the global level. One assumes that the biosphere is in a steady-state, exactly as nature at a local level had been assumed to be in steady-state in nineteenth and twentieth-century management of biological resources. Speaking about the "biosphere" at "steady-state" is a twentieth-century way of saying that nature in the largest sense has a balance, a constancy of form and structure that, if undisturbed by human influence, will remain indefinitely. This idea is consistent with a machine metaphor and the idea of divine order. The second school of thought believes that life acts as the Earth's thermostat, requiring and creating constant conditions, like physiological feedback mechanisms in a moose that maintain its body temperature near 102°F. This is also consistent with a machine metaphor, but can be extended to have aspects that are organic. According to the third school, the biosphere is always changing and it is this very quality at the planetary level that has allowed life to persist.

Most current analyses of the biosphere are based on the first school of thought. Mathematical models and computer simulations of chemical cycles treat the biosphere as though it were a steady-state system operating at normal or optimum conditions except where disturbed by human influence.[7] James Lovelock and Lynn Margulis are proponents of the second school of thought. Lovelock has made an important and major contribution to the thinking of our time about the biosphere by proposing the "Gaia hypothesis." *Gaia* is the Greek Goddess Earth, and Lovelock uses the word as "a shorthand" for a hypothesis that "the biosphere is a self-regulating entity with the capacity to keep our planet healthy by controlling the chemical and physical environment." More specifically, he lists several of "Gaia's principal characteristics," which include "vital organs at the core" and a "tendency to keep constant conditions for all terrestrial life."[8] The first section of this book provided evidence that constancy and steady-state did not exist for nature at all levels smaller than the biosphere and that we had to abandon the machine metaphor for the entire range of ecological phenomena from individual populations to entire forests, to abandon the idea that they were like watches, car engines, or steam engines. With what can we replace that metaphor? Lewis Thomas asked the question "What is [the Earth] *most* like?" and answered, "It is *most* like a single cell."[9] How far can we push a new organic metaphor? How much is the biosphere like the internal organs of a large mammal? The metaphor holds for the influence of life on its environment and for the complex interplay between environment and life. But a fundamental difference between the environment within the moose's gut and the environment outside it is the matter of steady-state, of constancy, of a balance of nature.

Within the moose, all is in balance as long as the supply of food is constant and the moose is alive and healthy; that is, the moose is stable within certain limits.

In the nineteenth century, Charles Lyell considered the possibility of a global balance of nature in terms of uptake and loss in the cycling of the chemical elements through living things. Lyell thought that a balance was possible in theory and could in theory be affected by life, so that the supply of necessary "hydrogen, carbon, oxygen, azote [nitrogen] and other elements" might be obtained from the "putrescence of organic substances" and the release of the elements to the atmosphere. This would imply that "vegetable mould would, after a series of years, neither gain nor lose a single particle by the action of organic beings." Although Lyell concluded that this was "not far from the truth," he believed that most organic matter washed down from the land to the sea became "imbedded in subaqueous deposits" and would "remain throughout whole geological epochs before they again become subservient to the purpose of life."[10] The persistence of life seemed to Lyell to be made possible only by a continual release of the essential chemicals from the Earth's interior, which he assumed could not be affected by life, and not by the recycling of the elements by the biota. Lyell believed that life depends on the Earth, but life could not create a balance or constancy in the supply of the elements on which its survival depends.

Biological evolution has led to global changes in the environment, which, in turn, have led to new opportunities for biological evolution. In this way, a long-term process of change has occurred throughout the history of life on the Earth, which is an unfolding, one-way story. A machine is not a good metaphor for this system. You can stop a steam engine and start it again at a later time. You can move the wheels and levers and gears backward to some point and then restart the engine. But you cannot turn the biosphere backward from one of its major evolutionary steps to a previous one. Instead, the new emerging history of the biosphere is reminiscent, metaphorically, of the organic idea of the Earth. Like an idealized organism, the biosphere has had an origin and has passed through major stages. Like an idealized organism, the biosphere has had a history and what it will be tomorrow depends not only on what it is today, but also on what it was yesterday. Like an organism, the biosphere proceeds through its existence in a one-way direction, passing from stage to stage, each of which cannot be revisited.

The biosphere has been characterized by change at every time scale. The geologic processes of burial and return of chemical elements are among the slowest of these changes, on the order of hundreds of millions of years. At shorter time scales, climate has always been fluctuating. It is worth repeating that variations in climate are known for a large range of time scales, from 1 billion years to days. During ice ages, major changes occur in the patterns of the circulation of ocean currents and in the transfer of heat from the equator to the poles. As the climate has fluctuated, major changes have occurred in the distribution of life and the abundances of species. It would be highly unlikely if such fluctuations did not result in variations in the cycling of chemical elements necessary for life. Recent measurements of air trapped for thousands of years in pockets in glaciers indicate that the concentration of carbon dioxide in the atmosphere has varied considerably since the end of the most recent ice age, decreasing at the height of glaciation to about one-half of its value at the start of the industrial era. Thus in terms of climate, the cycling of chemical elements, the distribution of species and ecological communities, and the rate of extinction of species, we must reject the possibility of constancy in the biosphere. If the biosphere has not been in a precise steady-state, then life has not been a precise stabilizing device for the biosphere.

The remaining basic issue has to do with whether life has functioned to promote "the tendency to optimize conditions for all terrestrial life." The question itself can be best understood in terms of the relative roles of life and the nonliving aspects of the environment in determining the conditions on the Earth. If life functions to dampen changes that would have occurred had life not evolved and if such changes would have led to an environment outside the range that can support life, then it could be said that life has had a tendency to promote its own persistence. The geologic evidence as described by Peter Westbroek suggests that life has functioned in this fashion, against a background of large-scale changes in the environment. Whether the tendency is toward an optimum in any sense, however, cannot be answered at this time.

The image that emerges is of the biosphere made up of four dynamic parts—rocks, oceans, air, and life—each with its own characteristic ranges of movement and rates of change, rocks changing in composition most slowly, the oceans much more rapidly, and the atmosphere more rapidly still. Each part affects the others, and the inherent differences in their movement and rates of change can create complex patterns in time and space. Modulating all these changes is life. Life has greatly increased the rates of many chemical reactions and the transport of chemical elements from one part of the biosphere to another and has led to new patterns in the cycling of chemicals.

In spite of this new knowledge, the mechanistic ideas persist in attempts to explain and understand the biosphere. Such mechanistic explanations occur in the analyses of whether life tends to create negative-feedback mechanisms that maintain the environment in specific states that are in some way or other "optimal" for the continuation of life. The blending of new metaphors, the extent to which the biosphere is like a computer or like a rose, and the influx of some of the older machine-age ideas into these newer ones is a task for scientists to debate during the next decades, whether they recognize the underlying metaphors or not. The fact that the issues have come to this stage is in itself a fundamental change in the perception of nature. The biosphere is very different from a machine. The Earth is not alive, but the biosphere is a life-supporting and life-containing system with organic qualities, more like a moose than a water-powered mill. The biosphere is not a mystical organismic entity contraposed to rationality, but a system open to scientific analysis and to a new kind of understanding because of new knowledge and new metaphors. In its dynamic qualities, its one-way history, and its complexity, a new Earth is revealed. Like a pond on a quiet afternoon at Isle Royale, the reality of nature is revealed not by what is seen in the stillness, but by what is perceived within.

>>

Fire in the Forest: Managing Living Resources

Managing for Change

The management of the sequoia is reminiscent of the problem of the Rutland's warbler. The change in management policy to allow some fires to burn or to set controlled fires to protect the habitat of the warbler illustrated the beginning of a change in underlying assumptions about nature. The old ideas were no longer tenable, and controlled burning was one of the first examples of movement in a new direction. The attempt to move away from the "Bambi" and "Smokey the Bear" image of forest fires to a perspective that fires are a natural and desirable part of the patterns found in most forests, shrublands, and grasslands began, to the best of my knowledge, in earnest in the United States in the early 1940s. The change has come slowly, and episodes of large fires in famous parks repeatedly set the process back, as occurred in 1988 with the fires in Yellowstone National Park, but controlled burning is becoming widely accepted as part of the management of forests and shrublands.

The sequoia, the Kirtland's warbler, and similar cases posed a serious dilemma for the social and political movement known as environmentalism, a dilemma stated and explained in the first part of this book: much of the environmental ideology was based on the belief that nature undisturbed was constant and that this constant condition was most desirable, while in fact nature itself is highly variable, subject to change and requiring change in some cases. A question now arises: If we have a new perspective, has it helped us manage our environment better? If it has not helped, perhaps it is equally flawed. This brings us back to the second and third of the three ancient questions that people have discussed about nature throughout Western history: What is the influence of human beings on nature? What is humanity's role in nature?

We are living at a time of transition from the machine-age metaphor for nature to a new perspective that blends the older organic metaphor with a new technological metaphor. Our management of the environment has only begun to make the transition.[11] The difference between the old and the new approaches to management of biological resources can be put simply. In the old management, one managed for constancy and in terms of uncertainty (a lack of precise knowledge about the condition of the resource and its environment). In the new management, one accepts the need to manage in terms of uncertainty, as well as in terms of change, risk (the inherent unpredictability of events, such as the risk of death and extinction), and complexity. Complexity includes a number of qualities: the ecosystem context (a complex system of interrelationships, mutual causalities, and so forth), simultaneity of many events and conditions, and the possibility that there can be a variety of uses in different places at any one time so that there is complexity in the patterns of the landscapes and seascapes.

The underlying goal of both the old and the new approaches is the ideal of sustainability, but they differ in their interpretation of this ideal. Under the old management, a sustainable harvest could be obtained forever at the same rate in every time period. Under the new management, a sustainable harvest is one whose long-term time-averaged yield does not decline, but the rate of harvest may vary from time period to time period and may have to vary in the short run in order to lead to long-term sustainability. Under the new management, sustainability can be expressed in terms of a specific planning period, a planning time horizon, although in the ideal case this would be, from a human perspective, no different from a plan that would appear to last forever.

Under the old management, management for conservation and management for utilization (such as harvesting fish and cutting forests for timber) appeared to be different and, in general, incompatible goals. From an old preservationist perspective, nature undisturbed achieved a constancy that was desirable and was disrupted in an undesirable way only by human actions. From an old utilization perspective, the forest was there to cut, take apart, replace, and put back together as one chose. If nature was like a watch, then one had to choose between the stereotyped preservationist's approach—appreciate the beauty of the watch, and use it to tell time—and the stereotyped engineer's approach—attempt to take the watch apart and improve it, or use the parts for something else. Under the new management, our role in conservation is active; for example, harvesting may serve the interests of conservation as well as of utilization, and the goals of utilization and conservation can be part of one approach. This statement, however, must be considered with great care. It has become common to speak of "sustainable development," but as the British economist David Pearce has pointed out, this phrase is an oxymoron if strictly interpreted.[12] The rate of use of a resource cannot be increased forever, so in realistic terms a sustainable development must lead through a period of increasing rates of use of a resource to a range of levels that is not exceeded.

An important warning is necessary in regard to the new management. It is worth repeating that admitting that change is necessary seems to open a Pandora's box of problems for environmentalists. The fear is simple: Once we have admitted that some kinds of changes are good, how then can we argue against any changes—against any alteration of the environment? There are several answers to this question. First, as we have seen with the story of the elephants at Tsavo, the failure to accept change leads to destructive, undesirable results. It is only by understanding how nature works and accepting this understanding that our management of nature can really succeed.

Second, to accept certain kinds of change is not to accept all kinds of change. Moreover, we must focus our attention on the rates at which changes occur, understanding that certain rates of change are natural, desirable, and acceptable, while others are not. As long as we refuse to admit that any change is natural, we cannot make this distinction and deal with its implications. With the sequoia, for example, neither complete suppression of fire nor fires that burn every year are desirable; neither fires that are too intense nor those that are too weak are desirable. There is a rate and intensity of fires to which the sequoia have adapted over the millennia and which provides a basis for management. Somewhere in between is a rate of disturbance that would keep the forest in an actively growing state, and thus fires, when they did occur, would have a relatively small destructive impact and a relatively large beneficial effect, promoting recovery and regeneration. Dealing with natural resources is reminiscent of the passage in *Through the Looking-Glass* in which Alice discovers that she can reach a looking-glass house only by walking away from it; every time she tries to walk toward it, she winds up somewhere else. To maintain the forests in the dunes of Australia, the rain forests of the coast of New Zealand, or forests along the coast of Alaska, change is necessary; the soil must be disturbed and turned over to bring to the surface the chemicals required for life.

Third, there are novel aspects about some of the changes that we have brought about, some of which are desirable, but many of which are not. For example, plowing is a novel alteration of soils, as is the introduction of many new chemicals into the environment; since they are novel, they should be used extremely carefully. Another guideline for management is: minimize the use of new technologies when these lead to novel alterations of the environment.

Our approach to management of the environment has been dominated by the machine image of nature, which has been reinforced by the idea of divine origin. But we are now free to let go of that idea because we have new ideas and images that are equally powerful and equally well founded in science and mathematics. We must release ourselves from the grip of this image because it is contrary to the facts about nature and leads us down a path to misguided, destructive, and costly management policies.

Notes

This chapter presents selections from Daniel Botkin, *Discordant Harmonies: A New Ecology for the Twenty-first Century,* chapters 9 and 10 (New York: Oxford University Press, 1990).

1_ M.S. Gordon, G.A. Bartholomew, A.D. Ginnell, G.B. Jorgensen, and F.M. White, *Animal Physiology* (New York: Macmillan, 1997).

2_ L. Margulis and R. Guerrero, "From Planetary Atmospheres to Microbial Communities: A Stroll through Space and Time," in *Changing the Global Environment: Perspectives on Human Involvement,* eds. D.B. Botkin, M.F. Caswell, J.E. Estes, and A.A. Orio (Boston: Academic Press, 1989).

3_ For a history of the Earth's atmosphere, see J.C.G. Walker, *Evolution of the Atmosphere* (New York: Macmillan, 1977). The early concentration of oxygen and hydrogen is discussed by Walker in "Oxygen and Hydrogen in the Primitive Atmosphere," *Pure and Applied Geophysics,* 116 (1977): 222–231. The preceding two paragraphs are from D.B. Botkin and E.A. Keller, *Environmental Studies: The Earth as a Living Planet* (Columbus: Merrill, 1982), 57.

4_ D.M. Gates, *Biophysical Ecology* (New York: Springer-Verlag, 1980).

5_ Ibid.

6_ D.B. Botkin, ed., *Remote Sensing of the Biosphere* (Washington, D.C.: National Academy Press, 1986). The term *biosphere* is used here to mean the planetary system that includes and sustains life. The term has had other meanings; it was coined in the late nineteenth century by Edward Suess to refer to the total amount of organic matter on Earth—which we now refer to as "total biomass," and it has been used to mean simply the place where life is found on Earth, that is, the extent of the distribution of life. The term *ecosphere* is synonymous with biosphere.

7_ As an example, see C.A. Ekdahl and C.D. Keeling, "Atmospheric Carbon Dioxide and Radiocarbon in the Natural Carbon Cycle. I. Quantitative Deductions from Records at Mauna Loa Observatory and at the South Pole," in *Carbon and the Biosphere,* eds. G.M. Woodwell and E.V. Pecan, Brookhaven National Laboratory Symposium, no. 24 (Springfield, VA: U.S. Technical Information Service, 1973).

8_ J.E. Lovelock, *Gaia: A New Look at Life on Earth* (New York: Oxford University Press, 1979). The first quote is from p. xii; the second from p. 127.

9_ L. Thomas, *The Lives of a Cell: Notes of a Biology Watcher* (New York: Bantam Books, 1975), 4.

10_ C. Lyell, *Principles of Geology; Being an Attempt to Explain the Former Changes of the Earth's Surface, by Reference to Causes Now in Operation,* vol. II (London: John Murray, 1832), 189. Sir Charles Lyell lived from 1797 to 1875. His book is usually accepted as the first modern book on the science of geology.

11_ The modern discussions of the more specific aspects of these problems began at a symposium, the papers for which were published as W.L. Thomas, Jr., ed., *Man's Role in Changing the Face of the Earth* (Chicago: University of Chicago Press, 1956). They have continued with many reflective books and proceedings of conferences, including A.A. Orio and D.B. Botkin, eds., "Man's Role in Changing the Global Environment, Proceedings of an International Conference, Venice, Italy, 21–26 October, 1985," *The Science of the Total Environment,* 55 (1986): 1–399, and 56 (1986): 1–415.

12_ D. Pearce, "Sustainable Futures: Some Economic Issues," in *Changing the Global Environment: Perspectives on Human Involvement,* eds. Botkin, Caswell, Estes, and Orio.

(Anthropogenic Taxonomies) A Taxonomy of the Human Biosphere

Erle C. Ellis

Since prehistory, humans have altered ecosystems by hunting and foraging, using fire to clear vegetation, driving megafauna to extinction, and taking other actions that have produced long-term cascading effects across most continents [1]. However, the greatest transformation of the terrestrial biosphere ever wrought by humanity began more than 10,000 years ago, at the end of the last ice age, with the emergence of agricultural systems [2]. By domesticating species and transforming native ecosystems into agricultural fields, pastures, settlements, and other engineered environments in support of agricultural societies, our ancestors unleashed a process of unprecedented population growth, societal development, and planetary transformation that is now increasingly recognized as the dawning of a new geological epoch: the Anthropocene [1-5].

A Global Human Ecology

There is growing consensus that most of the terrestrial biosphere has now been transformed by human populations and their use of land [2, 6-9]. While climate and other geophysical and biotic factors continue to constrain the form and functioning of the terrestrial biosphere, human populations and their use of land increasingly determine the realized form and dynamics of terrestrial ecosystems, including the cycling of the elements, biodiversity, primary productivity, and the presence of trees and their successional state [9-11]. As a result, the classic approach to mapping, classifying, and understanding the global patterns of terrestrial ecology as a simple function of climatic and physiographic variables, the "classic" biomes, is no longer accurate (e.g., [12-16]).

Human interactions with ecosystems are diverse, dynamic, and complex, ranging from the relatively light impacts of mobile bands of hunter-gatherers to the wholesale replacement of native ecosystems by built structures [1, 4, 17, 18]. Population density is a useful indicator of the form and intensity of human/environment interactions, as larger populations are both a cause and a consequence of ecosystem modification to produce food and supply other needs [2, 18-20]. For this reason, most of the classic forms of human/ecosystem interaction are associated with orders of magnitude differences in population density, including foraging (< 1 person km^{-2}), shifting cultivation (> 10 persons km^{-2}), and continuous cultivation (> 100 persons km^{-2}). Populations denser than 2,500 persons km^{-2} are believed to be unsupportable by traditional subsistence agriculture [18-21].

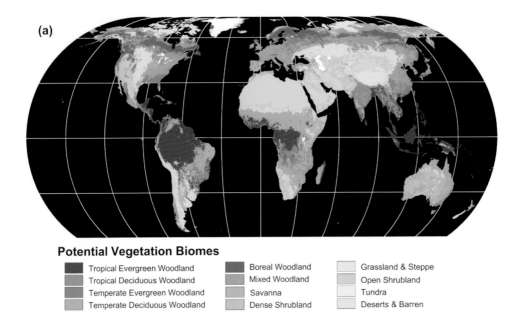

(a)

Potential Vegetation Biomes

Tropical Evergreen Woodland	Boreal Woodland	Grassland & Steppe
Tropical Deciduous Woodland	Mixed Woodland	Open Shrubland
Temperate Evergreen Woodland	Savanna	Tundra
Temperate Deciduous Woodland	Dense Shrubland	Deserts & Barren

A Taxonomy of the Human Biosphere

To characterize the global ecological patterns produced by sustained direct human interactions with terrestrial ecosystems, Ellis and Ramankutty [9] introduced the concept of anthropogenic biomes, or "anthromes," and developed a global classification and map of these as a new framework for global ecology and earth science. Anthromes were first classified and mapped empirically using statistical algorithms that identified globally significant patterns in global data on land use and human population density, an approach that was then modified using a rule-based classification system allowing long-term changes to be measured over time using historical data [22].

Figure 1. The classic "potential vegetation" biomes (a; [16]) compared with anthromes (b; for year 2000, from [22]; class descriptions in Table 1). Eckert IV projection.

(b)

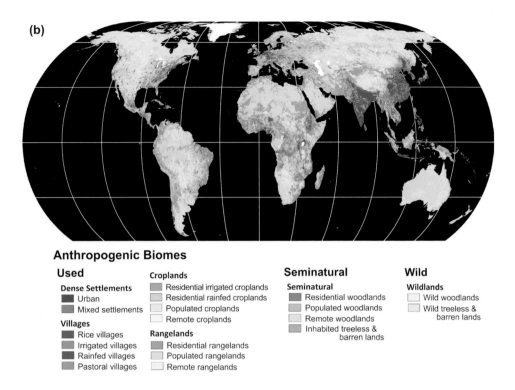

Anthropogenic Biomes

Used

Dense Settlements
- Urban
- Mixed settlements

Villages
- Rice villages
- Irrigated villages
- Rainfed villages
- Pastoral villages

Croplands
- Residential irrigated croplands
- Residential rainfed croplands
- Populated croplands
- Remote croplands

Rangelands
- Residential rangelands
- Populated rangelands
- Remote rangelands

Seminatural

Seminatural
- Residential woodlands
- Populated woodlands
- Remote woodlands
- Inhabited treeless & barren lands

Wild

Wildlands
- Wild woodlands
- Wild treeless & barren lands

The global extent of anthromes in year 2000 is mapped in Figure 1b, using the anthrome classes in Table 1 (maps viewable in Google Earth at http://ecotope.org/anthromes/v2). Based on this analysis, Wildlands covered just one quarter of Earth's ice-free land in year 2000, with the rest classified as anthromes. In 2000, more than half (> 55%) of global land area was under intensive use as Rangelands (32%), Croplands (16%), Villages (6.5%), and Densely Settled (1.2%) anthromes, leaving about 20% in Seminatural anthromes having low levels of land use for agriculture and settlements. These results also make clear that large extents of Wildlands remain only in the cold and dry biomes (Boreal, Shrublands, Deserts), and in the global regions with large extents of these (North America, Australia and New Zealand, Near East, and Eurasia).

Level	Class	Description
Dense settlements		Urban and other dense settlements.
	11 Urban	Dense built environments with very high populations.
	12 Mixed settlements	Suburbs, towns, and rural settlements with high but fragmented populations.
Villages		Densely populated agricultural settlements.
	21 Rice villages	Villages dominated by paddy rice.
	22 Irrigated villages	Villages dominated by irrigated crops.
	23 Rain-fed villages	Villages dominated by rain-fed agriculture.
	24 Pastoral villages	Villages dominated by rangeland.
Croplands		Lands used mainly for annual crops.
	31 Residential irrigated croplands	Irrigated cropland with substantial human populations.
	32 Residential rain-fed croplands	Rain-fed croplands with substantial human populations.
	33 Populated rain-fed cropland	Croplands with significant human populations, a mix of irrigated and rain-fed crops.
	35 Remote croplands	Croplands without significant populations.
Rangelands		Lands used mainly for livestock grazing and pasture.
	41 Residential rangelands	Rangelands with substantial human populations.
	42 Populated rangelands	Rangelands with significant human populations.
	43 Remote rangelands	Rangelands without significant human populations.
Seminatural lands		Inhabited lands with minor use for permanent agriculture and settlements (<20% of area used).
	51 Residential woodlands	Forest regions with minor land use and substantial populations.
	52 Populated woodlands	Forest regions with minor land use and significant populations.
	53 Remote woodlands	Forest regions with minor land use without significant populations.
	54 Inhabited treeless and barren lands	Regions without natural tree cover having only minor land use and a range of populations.
Wildlands		Lands without evidence of human populations or substantial land use.
	61 Wild woodlands	Forests and Savanna.
	62 Wild treeless and barren lands	(Grasslands, Shrublands, Tundra, Desert and Barren lands).

Table 1. Description of anthrome classes (from [22])

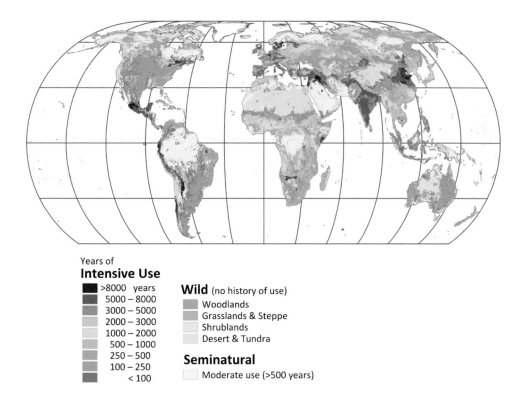

Years of
Intensive Use

- >8000 years
- 5000 – 8000
- 3000 – 5000
- 2000 – 3000
- 1000 – 2000
- 500 – 1000
- 250 – 500
- 100 – 250
- < 100

Wild (no history of use)
- Woodlands
- Grasslands & Steppe
- Shrublands
- Desert & Tundra

Seminatural
- Moderate use (>500 years)

Anthromes Are Ancient

Human effects on ecosystems have long been perceived by ecologists and conservationists as consisting primarily of recent disturbances to otherwise pristine ecosystems [23]. While the veracity of this conception has long been challenged by prominent ecologists [24], especially those of Europe and Asia [25], and by other disciplines [23], it remains a mainstream view. Recent evidence from spatially explicit global histories of land use across the terrestrial biosphere confirms that vast areas of the terrestrial biosphere were

Figure 2. Age of anthropogenic transformation of the terrestrial biosphere. Estimated based on years of intensive use determined from historical models of population density, land cover, and land use (based on [2]). Eckert IV projection.

first transformed for intensive agricultural use many thousands of years ago, especially in parts of the Middle East, India, China, Europe, and the Americas. In these regions of ancient use, the pre-human state of ecosystems can be assessed only through paleoecological reconstructions of the distant past— in some cases their state prior to the last ice age. The "native state" of these ecosystems is therefore best characterized as anthropogenic [2, 4, 26].

The precise historical timing of the terrestrial biosphere's transition from mostly wild to mostly used depends on how historical land use is assessed and reconstructed [2, 4]. If seminatural levels of use are considered sufficient to cause this transition, then some historical reconstructions date this at around 1000 B.C., while the most conservative reconstructions place the date just prior to the Industrial Revolution, around 1700 [4]. If intensive use is required to cause this transition, reconstructions tend to agree that the transition has occurred fairly recently, at the start or middle of the last century [2, 4]. Either way, about half of this transition resulted from anthropogenic transformation of lands still wild in 1700, and the other half by increasing the intensity of land use within the Seminatural anthromes that already covered at least half of the terrestrial biosphere by 1700 [22].

By as early as 3,000 years ago, nearly half of the terrestrial biosphere, including about 60% of all of Earth's Tropical and Temperate Woodlands, were most likely in use by shifting cultivators who may have cleared almost all of this area, one small patch at a time, at some point in history or prehistory [2, 27]. Even areas without measurable human populations or agriculture, considered "wild" in this analysis, may still have been significantly altered by anthropogenic fire regimes, exotic species introductions, and systematic foraging by sparse human populations [1, 23]. It is also important to note that Rangelands, which represent the lion's share of global land transformation since 1700, may have had relatively light impacts on ecosystem form and process compared with those of shifting cultivators in some regions. Nevertheless, by 1950 at the latest, most of the terrestrial biosphere had been transformed by direct human use of land and one of its most pervasive legacies; the remnant, recovering, and other less intensively managed ecosystems embedded within the otherwise used landscapes of anthromes [2, 26]

Even after thousands of years of human population growth and land use, more than 60% of Earth's ice-free land still remains without direct use for agriculture or urban settlements [22]. As of 2000, only about 40% of this area consists of Wildlands [22]. The other 60% represents lands without direct use that have become embedded within the working landscapes of Dense Settlements (1%), Villages (3%), Croplands (7%), Rangelands (19%), and Seminatural anthromes (29%) [22]. Taken together, these embedded unused lands now cover a greater global extent than all of Earth's remaining Wildlands combined, accounting for about 37% of all ice-free land, with 19% in Used and 18% in Seminatural anthromes [22]. More than half of these unused lands have been surrounded by agriculture and settlements for more than three centuries [22].

While the ecosystems of unused lands embedded within anthromes may often resemble the undisturbed ecosystems of a biome, they almost always exhibit novel ecological patterns and processes, even when never cleared or used directly, as a result of their fragmentation into smaller habitats within a matrix of used lands, the anthropogenic enhancement or suppression of fire regimes, species invasions, air pollution and acid rain, hydrological alteration, and low-intensity human use for wood gathering, hunting, foraging, or recreation [1, 4, 11, 28]. For this reason, anthromes are best characterized as heterogeneous, multifunctional landscape mosaics that combine used and novel ecosystems. This pervasive intermingling of used and novel ecosystems in anthrome mosaics is especially evident when landscapes are viewed from the air or when anthrome maps are compared with high-resolution satellite imagery in Google Earth (http://ecotope.org/anthromes/v2). Urban areas are embedded within agricultural areas, trees are interspersed with croplands and housing, and managed vegetation is mixed with seminatural vegetation (e.g., croplands are embedded within rangelands and forests). Though some of this landscape heterogeneity might be explained by the relatively coarse resolution of the global analyses used in anthrome mapping and classification, there is a more basic explanation: direct interactions between humans and ecosystems generally take place within heterogeneous landscape mosaics [9, 29, 30]. Regardless, direct human influence on ecosystem structure and function has spread far more widely than the 40% of Earth's ice-free land now in direct use for

agriculture and settlements because of the widespread intermingling of used and novel ecosystems in the anthrome mosaics that now cover more than three-quarters of the terrestrial biosphere [9, 22, 26].

The Ecology of Anthrome Mosaics

In undisturbed landscapes, ecosystem structure and function vary within and across landscapes in response to variations in terrain, hydrology, microclimate, dominant species, and stages of recovery from natural disturbances including fire [30-33]. Humans take advantage of this natural variation by using different parts of landscapes in different ways [4, 9, 28, 34]. The most productive, moist and fertile wooded plains are generally cleared and farmed first and most intensively, leaving steep hillsides for grazing, hunting, fuel gathering, or shifting cultivation [4, 9, 28, 34, 35]. Humans then build on the ecological legacies of this sustained use, expanding settlements into the oldest croplands, terracing denuded hillsides for agriculture once land is scarce and later abandoning agriculturally degraded lands to forestry or wildlife

Figure 3. Anthromes are mosaic landscapes composed of agriculture, settlements, and infrastructure in which remnant, recovering, and more lightly used novel ecosystems are embedded.

conservation [4, 17]. Humans also create entirely novel anthropogenic patterns by interconnecting and expanding settlements and other infrastructure [4, 36, 37]. These three sources of natural and anthropogenic spatial variation combine to form the complex, multifunctional, heterogeneous landscape mosaics of anthromes, which explains why they both conform to preexisting natural patterns and further stratify and enhance them [9, 29]. Further, all of these patterns are fractal in nature [38], producing similar patterns across spatial scales ranging from the land holdings of individual households to the global patterning of the anthromes and biomes [9].

As agriculture and settlements tend to concentrate where gentle terrain, fertile soils, available water, and other conditions are most suitable for these uses, "islands" of unused and less intensively managed ecosystems including planted forests, woodlots, parks, abandoned lands, and reserves tend to form on hills and in other less inviting environments embedded within the broader extents of working landscapes [4, 9, 34, 35, 39]. Yet it is never a simple matter to predict land-use patterns from the preexisting characteristics of landscapes, as these patterns emerge through the complex interplay of coupled human and natural systems over time and space, with a strong legacy effect of prior human activities. As a result, even where environmental and anthropogenic conditions are uniform, land-use patterns can still be heterogeneous and hard to predict [40]. For example, large-scale transportation networks or other infrastructure can restructure vast plains, and large cities can include major parks and even nature reserves [36].

A Global Ecology of Anthropogenic Landscapes

Despite the general complexity of anthrome mosaics, when they are studied empirically and theoretically, some general global patterns tend to emerge in response to variations in populations, land use, and land cover within and across anthrome levels, as illustrated in Figure 4. Natural variations within the biomes (Wildlands at left in Figure 4) combine with variations in population density and land-use systems (top), with lands most suitable for human use tending to be used and settled first, enabling populations to grow and develop, leading to increased land-use intensity over time [4]. Based on this basic model of anthrome pattern and process, global patterns in population density and land use are associated with variations in fundamental ecosystem processes including net primary production (photosynthesis—respiration of plants), carbon emissions (decomposition, combustion), the formation of reactive nitrogen (fertilizers, combustion) and the structure of biotic communities (native, exotic, domestic; see the lower part of Figure 4). While global models that can predict ecological pattern and process within anthromes remain at an early stage of development, empirical assessments have confirmed the utility of anthrome patterns as predictors of global patterns of biodiversity [41, 42], the biogeochemical cycles of soils [43], and their relation to market forces [44]. Given the long-term global trend toward ever-increasing anthropogenic transformation of the terrestrial biosphere, it seems likely that the degree to which anthromes can explain global patterns of ecosystem process and biodiversity will only increase over time.

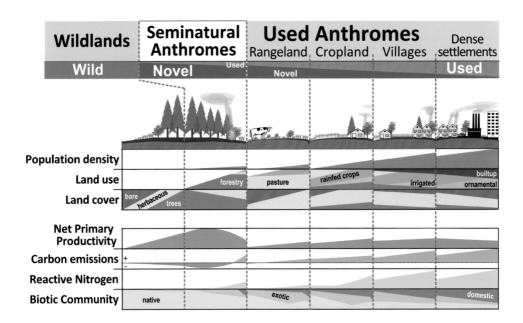

Figure 4. Conceptual diagram illustrating ecological variation across the terrestrial biosphere associated with variations in population density, land use, and land cover (based on [4]). Relative areas of used lands and novel ecosystems are illustrated at top. Response of selected ecosystem variables to variations is illustrated below.

Implications of an Anthropogenic Biosphere_____

Overwhelming evidence demonstrates that most of the terrestrial biosphere, including its biodiversity and ecosystem processes, has now been permanently reshaped by direct interactions between humans and ecosystems. At this point in history, nearly 40% of all ice-free land on Earth is in direct use for agriculture or urban settlements [7]. An additional 37% of ice-free land is not currently used for these purposes, but is embedded as novel ecosystems within anthromes having these uses [22, 26]. This leaves Wildlands in the minority, a mere 23% of global ice-free land area, with about 85% of these located only in the colder, drier, and less biodiverse biomes of the world [22].

Given that novel ecosystems embedded within anthromes now cover a greater global extent than Earth's remaining Wildlands, they offer an unparalleled opportunity for conserving the species and ecosystems we value [26, 45, 46]. The critical challenge therefore is in maintaining, enhancing, and restoring the ecological functions of the remnant, recovering and managed novel ecosystems formed by land use and its legacies within the complex multifunctional anthropogenic landscape mosaics that are the predominant form of terrestrial ecosystems today and into the future [11].

The mosaic structure of landscapes can be managed to enhance connectivity and habitat values, enabling high levels of native biodiversity to be sustained even in the urban and village anthromes where built-up lands and intensive cropping systems predominate, including the most ancient agricultural regions [2, 47-51]. Yet efforts to sustain and enhance biodiversity in anthromes are challenged by the trade-offs between conservation values and the benefits of using land for agricultural production and settlements [17, 51, 52]. Despite this apparent conflict, even under intensive use anthromes rarely consist entirely of farm fields and settlements; most anthrome landscapes take the form of multifunctional mosaics of used and novel ecosystems [9, 22]. For this reason, it is possible for global efforts to conserve, enhance, and restore biodiversity within anthromes, even without necessarily reducing land use overall [46, 53]. To make this possible, ecological research, monitoring, conservation, and restoration efforts must be expanded in novel anthropogenic ecosystems, as their optimal management, landscape and community structure, habitat connectivity, ecosystem processes, and dynamics remain poorly understood and cannot be reliably predicted from past trends or historical environmental constraints [11, 46]. Nevertheless, the evidence so far indicates that biodiversity and ecosystem services in novel ecosystems can match and even exceed those for the native ecosystems they have replaced [11, 54].

In the Anthropocene, there is no possibility of removing human influence from ecosystems: anthropogenic transformation of the terrestrial biosphere is essentially complete and permanent [4]. What has not already been altered directly, we are now altering indirectly through anthropogenic climate change and other effects mediated through the atmosphere. As a result, the future of all species, including our own, now depends on better understanding and managing the human ecology of our anthropogenic biosphere. To do so will require going beyond the mythology of humans as destroyers of a pristine and fragile nature. Anthromes tell a completely different story, of "human systems, with natural ecosystems embedded within them." This is not a minor change in the story of humans in the biosphere. Yet it is necessary for sustainable management of the biosphere in the Anthropocene. Nature is almost entirely in our hands now, for better or for worse, and there is no going back.

As we come to embrace our necessary role as stewards of Earth's ecological heritage, the challenges are many. Experience is very limited in managing the multifunctional landscapes needed to support the diverse needs of humanity while sustaining biodiverse ecosystems and resilient populations of native species over the long term at local and regional scales. Experience is even more limited at global scales.

Anthromes offer a rich global view of human interactions with ecosystems, helping move us toward a multidimensional perspective on humanity as permanent shapers and stewards of ecosystem structure and function, taking us beyond the conventional view that human interactions form only a single dimension of disturbance, impact, or domination (e.g., [6]). Advances in integrating agronomy, forestry, ecology, and the environmental sciences will help. Yet this is not enough. It will take bold action and experimentation at socially and ecologically relevant scales, great patience, careful observation, and perpetual adjustment to make substantial progress in learning how to design, create, and sustain the landscapes, anthromes, and biosphere that we want in the Anthropocene. We have never had more power to do great things, to design better landscape ecologies both for sustenance and for nature, to create beauty, and to manage a biosphere that will nurture, please, and honor our children, ourselves, and our ancestors. And with creation comes both opportunity and responsibility.

Notes

1_ Kirch, P.V., *Archaeology and Global Change: The Holocene Record*. Annual Review of Environment and Resources, 2005. 30(1): p. 409.

2_ Ellis, E.C., et al., *Used Planet: A Global History*. Proceedings of the National Academy of Sciences, 2013. 110(20): p. 7978–7985.

3_ Redman, C.L., *Human Impact on Ancient Environments*. 1999, Tucson: University of Arizona Press. 239.

4_ Ellis, E.C., *Anthropogenic Transformation of the Terrestrial Biosphere*. Proceedings of the Royal Society A: Mathematical, Physical and Engineering Science, 2011. 369(1938): p. 1010–1035.

5_ Steffen, W., et al., *The Anthropocene: Conceptual and Historical Perspectives*. Philosophical Transactions of the Royal Society A: Mathematical, Physical and Engineering Sciences, 2011. 369(1938): p. 842–867.

6_ Sanderson, E.W., et al., *The Human Footprint and the Last of the Wild*. BioScience, 2002. 52(10): p. 891–904.

7_ Foley, J.A., et al., *Global Consequences of Land Use*. Science, 2005. 309(5734): p. 570–574.

8_ Kareiva, P., et al., *Domesticated Nature: Shaping Landscapes and Ecosystems for Human Welfare*. Science, 2007. 316(5833): p. 1866–1869.

9_ Ellis, E.C. and N. Ramankutty, *Putting People in the Map: Anthropogenic Biomes of the World*. Frontiers in Ecology and the Environment, 2008. 6(8): p. 439–447.

10_ Vitousek, P.M., et al., *Human Domination of Earth's Ecosystems*. Science, 1997. 277(5325): p. 494–499.

11_ Hobbs, R.J., E.S. Higgs, and C.M. Hall, eds. *Novel Ecosystems: Intervening in the New Ecological World Order*. 2013, Wiley, Oxford: Oxford, UK. 384.

12_ Holdridge, L.R., *Determination of World Plant Formations from Simple Climatic Data*. Science, 1947. 105(2727): p. 367–368.

13_ Küchler, A.W., *A Physiognomic Classification of Vegetation*. Annals of the Association of American Geographers, 1949. 39(3): p. 201–210.

14_ Whittaker, R.H., *Communities and Ecosystems*. First ed. Current Concepts in Biology, ed. N.H. Giles, W. Kenworthy, and J.G. Torrey. 1970, New York: MacMillan. 185.

15_ Olson, D.M., et al., *Terrestrial Ecoregions of the World: A New Map of Life on Earth*. BioScience, 2001. 51(11): p. 933–938.

16_ Ramankutty, N. and J.A. Foley, *Estimating Historical Changes in Global Land Cover: Croplands from 1700 to 1992*. Global Biogeochemical Cycles, 1999. 13(4): p. 997–1027.

17_ DeFries, R.S., J.A. Foley, and G.P. Asner, *Land-Use Choices: Balancing Human Needs and Ecosystem Function.* Frontiers in Ecology and the Environment, 2004. 2(5): p. 249–257.

18_ Smil, V., *General Energetics: Energy in the Biosphere and Civilization.* First ed. 1991: John Wiley & Sons. 369.

19_ Boserup, E., *The Conditions of Agricultural Growth: The Economics of Agrarian Change under Population Pressure.* 1965, London: Allen & Unwin. 124.

20_ Boserup, E., *Population and Technological Change: A Study of Long-Term Trends.* 1981, Chicago: University of Chicago Press. 255.

21_ Netting, R.M., *Smallholders, Householders: Farm Families and the Ecology of Intensive Sustainable Agriculture.* 1993, Stanford, CA: Stanford University Press. 416.

22_ Ellis, E.C., et al., *Anthropogenic Transformation of the Biomes, 1700 to 2000.* Global Ecology and Biogeography, 2010. 19(5): p. 589–606.

23_ Cronon, W., *Changes in the Land: Indians, Colonists, and the Ecology of New England.* 1983, New York: Hill and Wang. 235

24_ Odum, E.P., *The Strategy of Ecosystem Development.* Science, 1969. 164(877): p. 262–270.

25_ Golley, F.B., *A History of the Ecosystem Concept in Ecology: More Than the Sum of the Parts.* 1993, New Haven: Yale University Press.

26_ Perring, M.P. and E.C. Ellis, *The Extent of Novel Ecosystems: Long in Time and Broad in Space,* in *Novel Ecosystems,* R.J. Hobbs, E.S. Higgs, and C.M. Hall, Editors. 2013, John Wiley & Sons, Ltd. p. 66–80.

27_ Ruddiman, W.F. and E.C. Ellis, *Effect of Per-Capita Land use Changes on Holocene Forest Clearance and CO_2 Emissions.* Quaternary Science Reviews, 2009. 28(27–28): p. 3011–3015.

28_ Butzer, K., *Archaeology as Human Ecology: Method and Theory for a Contextual Approach.* 1982: Cambridge University Press. 380.

29_ Forman, R.T.T., *Land Mosaics: The Ecology of Landscapes and Regions.* 1997, Cambridge; New York: Cambridge University Press. 632.

30_ Pickett, S.T.A. and M.L. Cadenasso, *Landscape Ecology: Spatial Heterogeneity in Ecological Systems.* Science, 1995. 269: p. 331–334.

31_ Jenny, H., *Role of the Plant Factor in the Pedogenic Functions.* Ecology, 1958. 39(1): p. 5–16.

32_ Whittaker, R.H., *Evolution and Measurement of Species Diversity.* Taxon, 1972. 21(2): p. 213–251.

33_ Sitch, S., et al., *Evaluation of Ecosystem Dynamics, Plant Geography and Terrestrial Carbon Cycling in the LPJ Dynamic Global Vegetation Model.* Global Change Biology, 2003. 9(2): p. 161–185.

34_ Huston, M.A., *The Three Phases of Land-Use Change: Implications for Biodiversity.* Ecological Applications, 2005. 15(6): p. 1864–1878.

35_ Wrbka, T., et al., *Linking Pattern and Process in Cultural Landscapes. An Empirical Study Based on Spatially Explicit Indicators.* Land Use Policy, 2004. 21(3): p. 289–306.

36_ Forman, R.T.T. and L.E. Alexander, *Roads and Their Major Ecological Effects.* Annual

Review of Ecology and Systematics, 2003. 29(1): p. 207–231.

37_Grimm, N.B., et al., *Global Change and the Ecology of Cities*. Science, 2008. 319(5864): p. 756–760.

38_Levin, S.A., *The Problem of Pattern and Scale in Ecology*. Ecology, 1992. 73(6): p. 1943–1967.

39_Daily, G.C., P.R. Ehrlich, and G.A. Sanchez-Azofeifa, *Countryside Biogeography: Use of Human-Dominated Habitats by the Avifauna of Southern Costa Rica*. Ecological Applications, 2001. 11(1): p. 1–13.

40_Verburg, P.H., et al., *From Land Cover Change to Land Function Dynamics: A Major Challenge to Improve Land Characterization*. Journal of Environmental Management, 2009. 90(3): p. 1327–1335.

41_Ellis, E.C., E.C. Antill, and H. Kreft, *All Is Not Loss: Plant Biodiversity in the Anthropocene*. PLoS ONE, 2012. 7(1): p. e30535.

42_Pekin, B.K. and B.C. Pijanowski, *Global Land Use Intensity and the Endangerment Status of Mammal Species*. Diversity and Distributions, 2012. 18(9): p. 909–918.

43_Richter, D.d. and D.H. Yaalon, *"The Changing Model of Soil" Revisited*. Soil Science Society of America Journal, 2012. 76(3): p. 766–778.

44_Verburg, P.H., E.C. Ellis, and A. Letourneau, *A Global Assessment of Market Accessibility and Market Influence for Global Environmental Change Studies*. Environmental Research Letters, 2011. 6(3): p. 034019.

45_DeFries, R., et al., *Planetary Opportunities: A Social Contract for Global Change Science to Contribute to a Sustainable Future*. BioScience, 2012. 62(6): p. 603–606.

46_Ellis, E.C., *Sustaining Biodiversity and People in the World's Anthropogenic Biomes*. Current Opinion in Environmental Sustainability, 2013. in press.

47_Ricketts, T.H., *The Matrix Matters: Effective Isolation in Fragmented Landscapes*. The American Naturalist, 2001. 158(1): p. 87–99.

48_Fahrig, L., *Effects of Habitat Fragmentation on Biodiversity*. Annual Review of Ecology Evolution and Systematics, 2003. 34: p. 487–515.

49_Lindenmayer, D., et al., *A Checklist for Ecological Management of Landscapes for Conservation*. Ecology Letters, 2008. 11(1): p. 78–91.

50_Ranganathan, J., et al., *Sustaining Biodiversity in Ancient Tropical Countryside*. Proceedings of the National Academy of Sciences, 2008. 105(46): p. 17852–17854.

51_Chazdon, R.L., et al., *Beyond Reserves: A Research Agenda for Conserving Biodiversity in Human-modified Tropical Landscapes*. Biotropica, 2009. 41(2): p. 142–153.

52_Phalan, B., et al., *Reconciling Food Production and Biodiversity Conservation: Land Sharing and Land Sparing Compared*. Science, 2011. 333(6047): p. 1289–1291.

53_Turner II, B.L., et al., *Land System Architecture: Using Land Systems to Adapt and Mitigate Global Environmental Change*. Global Environmental Change, 2013. 23(2): p. 395–397.

54_Lugo, A.E., *The Emerging Era of Novel Tropical Forests*. Biotropica, 2009. 9999(9999).

Cultural Landscapes and Dynamic Ecologies: Lessons from New Orleans

Jane Wolff

New Orleans is an object lesson in the ecological complexity of cultural landscapes. In the 300 years since its founding at the bottom of North America's largest drainage basin, the city—like the regional and continental landscapes to which it is intimately linked—has become an environmental hybrid, shaped in equal part by cultural intention and natural process. Like other manifestations of the Anthropocene,[1] this landscape evolved incrementally and ad hoc, transformed by a series of reciprocal interactions between the dynamic forces of the Mississippi River's delta and interventions by people to create stable conditions there. Constructed and administered by a wide range of actors and agencies, infrastructure has reshaped the delta at scales from the city to the drainage basin. However, engineering and policy have redirected environmental change rather than stopped it: again and again, the unintended consequences of each intervention have produced the demand for another. This process, played out over three centuries and accelerated by the large-scale urban drainage projects of the last 100 years, set the stage that made Hurricane Katrina an unprecedented disaster.

New Orleans and its dilemmas provide a valuable case study for the discussion of how the understanding of ecology is inflecting contemporary design practice at metropolitan scales—or not. The city's environmental history illustrates the central themes of contemporary ecological thinking: that ecosystems are open and networked; that they change progressively and in ways predictable as tendencies rather than in exact detail; that they respond in complex ways to disturbance; that they must be understood across scales; and that they can flip suddenly from one state to another.[2] Over the last dozen years, the complex ecological systems approach has engendered extensive discussion in the landscape architecture community about the design of dynamic sites. Though design professionals and scholars have made a wide range of interesting proposals that capitalize on landscapes' fluctuating tendencies,[3] there has been much less conversation about the challenge of implementing such ideas. The struggle to rehabilitate New Orleans since Hurricane Katrina has revealed the difficulty of untangling, managing, and administering hybrid ecological systems, particularly at metropolitan and regional scales. First, the fundamental principles and strategies of its twentieth-century infrastructure are at odds with the dynamics of the landscape. Second, predicting and

managing the city's hybrid ecological conditions are technically challenging tasks, exacerbated by the uncertainties of climate change. Third, the city and the landscapes it depends on suffer from institutional and governmental fragmentation: policies and administrative structures have not been organized for the synthetic consideration or adaptive management of metropolitan ecology and infrastructure. Finally, because hybrid landscapes like New Orleans do not fall into clear, familiar categories, the city's complexities are not well understood by most of its inhabitants, and their collective decisions about the future do not take into account the landscape's ecological reality. Like the physical conditions of the landscape, these cultural issues exist in overlapping contexts and scales, from the city to the drainage basin.

All of this makes New Orleans a useful place to examine the implications of current ecological thinking for landscape architecture and urbanism. In its intense struggle for resilience,[4] the city offers a parable about contemporary metropolitan landscapes with implications far beyond southern Louisiana.

Figure 1. Aerial photograph of New Orleans, 11 September 2005, by the U.S. National Oceanic and Atmospheric Administration. The disaster was the predictable outcome of the city's twentieth-century drainage policy and infrastructure.

Famously described by geographer Peirce Lewis as an inevitable city in an impossible location,[5] New Orleans was founded in 1718 to take advantage of a portage connection between Lake Pontchartrain and the Mississippi River. This site promised both rewards and risks. Its proximity to the river and lake offered direct access from the interior of the continent to the Gulf of Mexico. However, the circumstances that made New Orleans an ideal entrepôt meant that it was also subject to the variable conditions of the dynamic Mississippi Delta. In addition to flooding seasonally, the river periodically eroded and deposited land along its banks. Soils behind the relatively stable natural levee were waterlogged and unstable. The subtropical climate fostered mosquito-borne illnesses such as yellow fever and malaria, and the swampy landscape was believed to harbor a wide range of ills.[6] The only land suitable for urban development was the high ground along the Mississippi's natural levee. Except for the Gentilly and Metairie Ridges, which followed an old trace of the river, and the Esplanade Ridge, which connected Bayou Saint John and the Mississippi, the land between the natural levee and Lake Pontchartrain was a cypress swamp whose mucky soils lay just above sea level and were too wet to inhabit intensively. Until the late nineteenth century, when initial attempts to drain the back-of-town swamps began, the city's expansion followed the river's edge.[7]

Like other American cities, New Orleans was substantially transformed by public works projects during the Progressive era of the late nineteenth and early twentieth centuries. Its unique emphasis on drainage made the New Orleans we know now: infrastructure and institutions established a century ago set the stage for Hurricane Katrina's destructive power. Draining New Orleans was driven by urban expansion and public health concerns and enabled by technology that seemed capable of overcoming the swampy city's ecological processes. In the late 1890s, the Louisiana state legislature chartered two public agencies to manage water. The New Orleans Drainage Commission was established to execute a comprehensive drainage plan in 1896, and three years later, the state chartered the New Orleans Sewerage and Water Board to "furnish, construct, operate, and maintain a water treatment and distribution system and a sanitary sewerage system for New Orleans."[8]

The two organizations merged in 1903, but their institutional mandates only became feasible after the development of new technology ten years later, when A. Baldwin Wood designed a screw pump that significantly increased the ability to move water out of the city. Eleven Wood screw pumps had been installed by 1915.[9] Urban development followed quickly. By 1925, the drainage system network was 560 miles long and served 30,000 acres,[10] and in the early 1950s, the last large unreclaimed tract of land in central Orleans Parish was drained

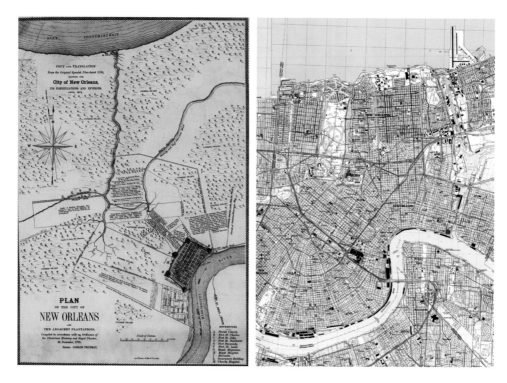

Figure 2 (left). "Plan of the City of New Orleans and adjacent plantations," by Charles Laveau Trudeau. This late eighteenth-century map of New Orleans shows the original fortified city at the river's natural levee; behind the levee lie cypress swamps.

Figure 3 (right). Map of New Orleans in the late 1990s, compiled from USGS quadrangles. The swampy ground depicted 200 years before has been replaced by uniform urbanization with almost no visible water.

and developed as the Pontchartrain Park and Gentilly Woods neighborhoods. In the space of less than fifty years, the back-of-town swamps were completely developed. Their subdivision and design left no room for water: parcellization patterns followed a standard grid interrupted only intermittently by canals that carried water from the city's pumping stations to Lake Pontchartrain.

The process and pattern of New Orleans's twentieth-century urbanization arose from the belief that engineering could overcome the hydrological and ecological processes of the Mississippi River and create a more controllable, more profitable, less hazardous landscape. However, the wholesale reclamation of land between the Mississippi's natural levee and Lake Pontchartrain has had an unexpected—and dynamic—consequence that requires ongoing intervention: it has caused the level of the drained areas to fall. This process, called subsidence, occurs through different mechanisms. Organic matter in the soil oxidizes, so soil volume is reduced. As pumping extracts water from the ground, soil particles collapse onto each other. In addition, the removal of the cypress swamps has brought an end to soil creation through organic decomposition, and the levees constructed along the length of the Mississippi to stop flooding have prevented the replenishment of soil by alluvial material. Without decomposition and alluvial replenishment, no new soil has been available to replace the ground lost to subsidence. Over the course of a century, the city's center, also known as Drainage Basin One, has become a giant sink. The elevations of reclaimed land have fallen to as low as 12 feet below sea level. The basin's north and south edges must be protected by levees along the Mississippi River and Lake Pontchartrain. Its upstream and downstream edges are formed by the levees of two constructed waterways, the Industrial Canal, which was excavated in the 1920s to create a shipping connection between the river and the lake, and the 17th Street Canal, which was dug in conjunction with railroad construction and became the largest outlet for the system that carries water out of Drainage Basin One.

Today, approximately half of Drainage Basin One lies below sea level. Groundwater, which comes to the surface as land sinks, must be constantly pumped out to avoid ponding in low areas. Because of the levees, all of the city's rainfall must be evacuated by mechanical pumping, even if it drains to the pumps by gravity. Rainwater enters the storm sewer system through drains

Historical Sections

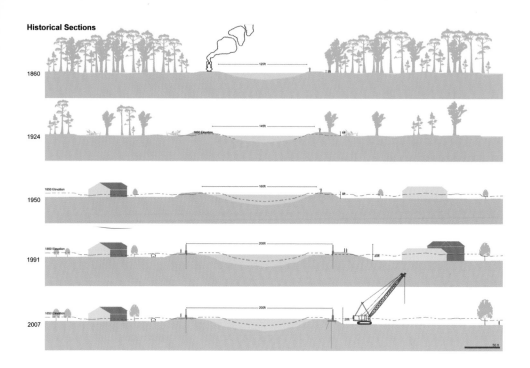

1860

1924

1950

1991

2007

Sections at Different Scales

Neighborhood Scale — The neighborhood scale shows the residential character of the 17th Street Canal.

9a

Canal Scale — The canal scale shows how the walls of the 17th Street Canal fully obscure the water from view.

9b

Canal Wall Scale — As shown at the canal wall scale, the soils underlying the 17th Street Canal reflect the history of the canal and played a key role in its breach during Katrina. The initial canal walls were built up using marsh soils and without modern compaction methods. Later improvemnts to the canal used stable clay soils and compaction, but were simply built upon the old soils. During Katrina, the pressure of the water undermined the canal wall in the interface between the marsh soils layer and the other layers, causing the canal to fail without being overtopped.

9c

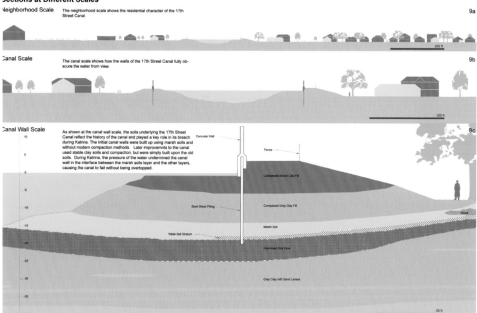

in the street and travels through pipes and canals to pumping stations, where it is mechanically lifted and sent through outfall canals to Lake Pontchartrain. The system can store half an inch of rainfall, and it can pump half an inch of rain in one hour. With storms of any higher intensity, which are not at all unusual in the city's subtropical climate, the city begins to flood. Hurricanes are not the only problem: New Orleans is subject to countless low-level inundations because its infrastructure cannot manage ordinary rainfall. This cycle of subsidence, pumping, and flooding demonstrates the city's hybrid ecology. A system built to dry the city out has merely redirected the water that is always present in a delta landscape.

Despite the clarity of this pattern (and its similarity to the historical evolution of other delta landscapes such as the western Netherlands or California's Sacramento-San Joaquin Delta[11]), public policy and popular understanding have not adapted in ways that have engendered management for greater resilience. Faith in technological solutions, coupled with the failure to acknowledge that the landscape would remain in flux no matter what engineering efforts were mounted, led to the disavowal of risk; eventually, awareness that New Orleans was and will always be shaped by the ecology of the delta and the river faded from the collective consciousness.

Figure 4a (top). The comparison of historical cross-sections of the 17th Street Canal shows the evolution of New Orleans's drainage dilemma. Originally dug through the cypress swamp during the construction of a rail line that connected the Mississippi River to Lake Pontchartrain, the canal now carries water away from approximately one-third of Drainage Basin One. Raised to the elevation of Lake Pontchartrain by Duty Pump Station 6, water travels through the canal at sea level, far above the level of the land beside it.
During Hurricane Katrina, when the storm surge from the lake forced water back into the canal and overwhelmed the pumps, the canal walls were breached, flooding huge areas of the city. In 2011, booster pumps were added where the canal meets Lake Pontchartrain to reduce the risk of failure.

Figure 4b (bottom). These detailed cross-sections of the 17th Street Canal as it exists today show how water is pumped through large areas of New Orleans at elevations much higher than ground level.

New Orleans's welfare is closely linked to the wetlands that lie between it and the Gulf of Mexico. The wetlands of Saint Bernard Parish, the city's downstream neighbor, have served historically to break the force of storms and surges before they reach New Orleans. Saint Bernard has also been used as protection for flooding from upstream. In 1927, during the Mississippi's record floods, New Orleanians argued for and effected the breach of levees downstream to alleviate pressure on their own boundaries, and the countryside was inundated to save the city.[12] Saint Bernard's hydrological boundaries[13] include essential service zones for New Orleans: oil and gas refineries and pipelines, substantial suburban development, water and sewer storage and treatment areas, and most recently, an extensive storm surge protection system.

Like New Orleans, Saint Bernard Parish has evolved over the past century into an ecological hybrid, transformed by the interaction between the delta's dynamic processes and infrastructure created for navigation, drainage, industry, and urbanization. The city's first line of storm and surge defense, Saint Bernard

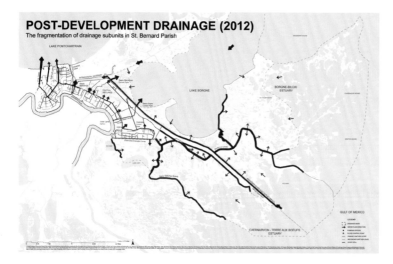

Figure 5. Saint Bernard Parish extends from metropolitan New Orleans to the Gulf of Mexico. It includes both reclaimed land, Saint Bernard Polder, and unreclaimed marsh. Saint Bernard Polder includes the Lower 9th Ward of the city of New Orleans, in Orleans Parish.

is itself threatened by subsidence, degraded wetlands, saltwater intrusion, and inadequate infrastructure. Until the 1920s, Saint Bernard Parish was part of the same hydrological system as New Orleans. Like its denser neighbor, it included human settlements along the Mississippi River's natural levee and bayous and swamps extending to Lake Borgne. Since 1923, when the construction of the Industrial Canal divided the landscape's continuous bayous, Saint Bernard's drainage patterns have been separated from central New Orleans (Drainage Basin One).[14] Today, the populated part of the parish comprises a self-contained drainage unit called Saint Bernard Polder.[15] This area, like New Orleans, has suffered significant subsidence in conjunction with urban and industrial development. Protected by levees and drained by pumps, it includes urban and suburban areas and an extensive complex of oil and gas refineries.

Its water is evacuated to the Saint Bernard Central Wetlands, whose storage capacity is limited by two factors. Along the wetland's Lake Borgne levee, floodgates must be closed to protect against surges of 1 foot or more above sea level, which threaten low-lying commercial and industrial development at the area's upstream boundary. However, along the wetland's landward levee, pump outlets will be swamped if water rises to 2.5 feet above sea level. The region's rainy climate means a constant balancing act for the Lake Borgne Levee District, which manages the polder's drainage regime: in 2011, the outlet to Lake Borgne had to be closed fifty-three times.[16]

Beyond the polder's boundary, the parish's wetlands have suffered terrible degradation from several causes. First, countless canals and pipelines excavated to bring oil and gas to Saint Bernard's refineries have created long edges subject to erosion. Second, the Mississippi River-Gulf Outlet (MR-GO), constructed in the 1950s to provide a direct route from the Gulf of Mexico to the Port of New Orleans, has produced not only catastrophic erosion along its length[17] but also saltwater intrusion. Allowing saltwater to migrate inland has led to the death of more than 15,000 acres of brackish and saltwater marsh and cypress swamp that served to dampen wave action during storms, to retain soil and sediment that supported the wetlands, and to replenish soils through decomposition.[18] The MR-GO was closed in 2011 to prevent further saltwater migration, but enormous damage had already been done. Finally, the wetlands have been starved of new sediment and freshwater by the closing of the Mississippi River's distributary channels, or bayous, over the last century.

New Orleans may not look like a national problem, but it is. Like a set of Russian dolls, the overlapping issues at play in the city and its region are nested in a hybrid ecosystem at continental scale: the Mississippi River and its drainage basin, which stretches from the Appalachian Mountains to the Rockies and includes thirty-one American states and two Canadian provinces. The Mississippi and its watershed have been radically transformed since the Louisiana Purchase extended American territory beyond the Continental Divide, and changes made to the drainage basin for local, regional, and national benefit have cast long shadows in the Mississippi Delta.

Since the early nineteenth century, the Mississippi and its tributaries have been dammed for navigation and power generation; levees have been built along their lengths to prevent flooding; and floodplains have been intensely developed. Beyond that, the watershed has been mined, forested, farmed, and urbanized. As Pare Lorentz showed in his 1937 film *The River*, the exploitation of the drainage basin's natural resources had catastrophic ecological results.[19] Even well-intentioned attempts to manage the river have had unexpected and problematic effects. The Corps of Engineers' attempts to improve navigation and control flooding have speeded the river's eventual migration to a new channel.[20] Building levees, limiting floodplains, and paving the drainage basin have meant more and more water in the river. Constructing dams on the river's tributary branches and closing its distributary channels have deprived coastal wetlands of sediment. The consequences for New Orleans and southern Louisiana are enormous. The subsidence and wetlands loss created by metropolitan and regional forces are made even more dangerous by increased water volumes and decreased sediment loads in the Mississippi and its main tributary, the Missouri. Ironically, decisions made to control flooding have exacerbated the problems they were meant to address. An increase in the threshold for catastrophe[21] means that many small floods have been replaced by a smaller number of large ones. The system may seem to fail less often, but the consequences are worse when it does.

Progressive-era infrastructure worked well enough during the twentieth century that levees and pumps came to seem normal to New Orleanians. Flood culture disappeared, and even after the catastrophic failures that attended Hurricanes Katrina and Rita, most citizens, even those involved in landscape and urban design and policy work, did not have a clear picture of the city's drainage regimen. The planning process for rehabilitation did not tackle the city as a landscape problem, and for the most part public conversation about the future took other directions. Attention focused on the rebuilding of the city and on the construction of additional engineering infrastructure, like booster pumps at the drainage canals' outlets. Proposals to remove low-lying land from redevelopment exposed the intersection between issues of racial inequity and problems of ecology and infrastructure. For example, late in 2005 the Urban Land Institute's Green Dot map identified zones that the Institute considered unsuitable for rebuilding by large, abstract green circles rather than carefully delineated areas.[22] The neighborhoods to be removed from redevelopment were disproportionately African-American and economically mixed or marginal. When the map was published in the *Times-Picayune*, New Orleans's daily newspaper, controversy erupted, and Mayor Ray Nagin asserted the right of all citizens to return to their homes, whatever the risk.

Today, nearly eight years after the storm, the city's policy divisions—planning districts, wards, neighborhoods—do not correlate with its physical subdivision into drainage pump service areas. Jurisdictions are fragmented and overlapping: for instance, the Department of Public Works controls and maintains drainage pipes under 36 inches in diameter, while the Sewerage and Water Board controls and maintains drainage pipes over 36 inches in diameter. The lack of clear information about the city's ecological circumstances is an enormous problem. Accurate base data about the city's terrain and soils were not available for several years after the storm. The only widely accessible representation of the drainage system was created by an independent academic research project, *Gutter to Gulf*.[23] Lack of funding for landscape projects has meant that efforts have been undertaken at smaller scales than necessary or that projects simply couldn't be carried out.

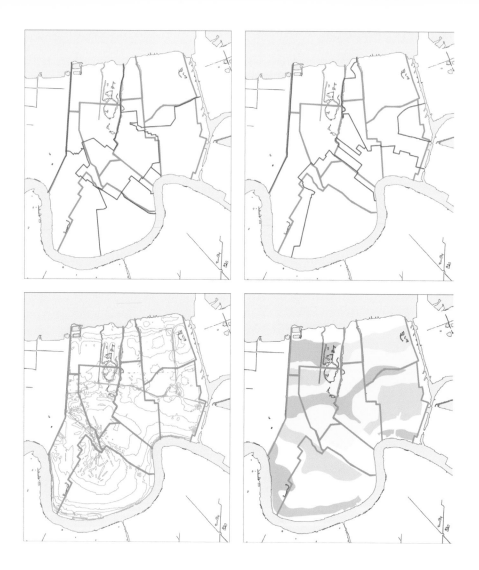

Figure 6. These drawings juxtapose the pumping service areas—or watersheds—within New Orleans's Drainage Basin One with other policy and physical structures, including planning districts (top left), council districts (top right), topography (bottom left), and groundwater elevations (bottom right). There is no spatial correlation between the hydraulic drainage units and any other city system.

Saint Bernard Parish, New Orleans's historic protector against storms, now contains a new, federally funded coastal defense system described by the *New York Times* as a "133-mile chain of levees, flood walls, gates and pumps too vast to take in at once, except perhaps from space."[24] The entire project, built by the Army Corps of Engineers to protect the city from a 100-year storm, cost $14.5 billion. A significant portion of the system, including a 27-mile-long levee known locally as the Great Wall of Louisiana and the Lake Borgne Surge Barrier, comprises the lake edge of Saint Bernard Polder. These structures, built by the Corps at a cost of $2 billion, will be maintained and administered by the Lake Borgne Basin Levee District, an organization comprising fewer than ten people and operating on an annual budget of between $3 million and $4 million.[25] The federal government's enormous investment in fixed infrastructure has not been matched by funding for local maintenance and upkeep. The new infrastructure presents other problems as well. In the *Times* coverage, Tim Doody, "president of the levee board that oversees Orleans and St. Bernard Parishes," says, " 'we all need to be behind protection that's greater than'...100-year protection, which means it was built to prevent the kind of flooding that has a 1 percent chance of occurring in any given year...Katrina is generally considered to have been a 400-year storm, and rising seas and more numerous hurricanes predicted in many climate-change models suggest harsher conditions to come."[26] In addition to the concerns raised by the *Times* article, the current system relies on the same model of fixed infrastructure that set southern Louisiana's dilemmas into motion 100 years ago. Calls for adaptive management, such as the Louisiana Coastal Protection and Recovery Act's (LACPRA) plans for wetland restoration, have begun to address the need to develop management strategies that can evolve to meet changing environmental conditions that can't be exactly predicted. Unfortunately, these proposals are also subject to the difficulties of administrative fragmentation. LACPRA calls for increasing freshwater diversions through Saint Bernard Polder by factors of seven to eight, but the Lake Borgne Basin Levee District will be called upon to maintain and dredge the new channels and to deal with the increased complexities of water storage in its Central Wetlands Unit.

New Orleans and the National Attention Span

Nearly eight years after Hurricane Katrina, most Americans have lost track of New Orleans's dilemmas. Superstorm Sandy's demonstration that much of the eastern seaboard of the United States is vulnerable to the consequences of sea-level rise has attracted attention to New York, but has not rekindled public discussion about post-Katrina Louisiana. To the extent that national attention is directed toward New Orleans, it focuses on expenditure for fixed infrastructure such as the Corps of Engineers flood barrier. More complicated topics—the mismatch between the Corps' approach and the dynamic character of the delta landscape, the relationship among national, regional, and local management strategies, New Orleans's role as the canary in a coal mine for other cities vulnerable to flooding—seem to have been left behind.

Complex Systems and New Tools for Metropolitan Design

Viewed through the lens of the complex systems approach, New Orleans poses an urgent question: what can be done to address the tension between what we know (or should know) and what we do? Given the regularity of systemic failure, sometimes with catastrophic consequences, that gap is a paradox. With enough public investment, the technical dilemmas posed by New Orleans and southern Louisiana could be addressed successfully.[27]

Figure 7. The Great Wall of Louisiana, Saint Bernard Parish, February 2012.

The most significant obstacles to progress are cultural. Until more people understand the need for a new management paradigm, policies and politics will not shift away from the support of big, monolithic infrastructure projects. The city's circumstances urgently need interpretation for a range of audiences, including policy makers and politicians; technicians, designers, and engineers; and the citizens whose aggregated choices shape the landscape at large scales. Its complex systems and invisible infrastructure need to be made legible.

The need for public literacy about New Orleans's hybrid ecology—its history, current state, and latent possibilities—suggests a new role for landscape and urban designers, who have the skills to mobilize, represent, and synthesize information about current conditions and more resilient alternatives. *Gutter to Gulf*, a research, teaching, and public information initiative that arose from the observation of crippling information gaps in post-Katrina New Orleans, offers a model for this type of work. The initiative was conceived to develop a place-based vocabulary for citizens, designers, and policy makers.[28] Its premise is that design advocacy and agency depend on a clear understanding of what exists: ideas for change make sense only in the context of the landscape's evolution. *Gutter to Gulf* makes sophisticated information about water infrastructure in New Orleans available to the varied audiences with a stake in the city's future. Its website synthesizes primary- and secondary-source research, original graphic documentation and analysis, and speculative design proposals to tell a comprehensive story about how water has shaped—and continues to shape—the metropolitan landscape. This means laying out the hydrological history of the city and the region; explaining the infrastructure systems that regulate water today; revealing the gaps among the city's physical, administrative, and policy structures for managing water; and proposing a series of flexible, incremental, and complementary tactics that can shift New Orleans's landscape toward adaptive management with ecological, infrastructural, and civic benefits.

New Orleans, the New Ecology, and Beyond

New Orleans demonstrates the urgency—and the difficulty—of putting the principles of complex systems ecology into practice at metropolitan scales. The circumstances that made Hurricane Katrina so devastating and that continue to make the city's rehabilitation so difficult constitute a Gordian knot

of dilemmas about ecology, infrastructure, and cultural ambitions. The city's history and current condition demonstrate the importance of management strategies that can adapt to unexpected consequences. They reveal the need for integrated regional structures of administration and governance. Most of all, they speak to the need for public education about the complex ecological realities of urban settlements in dynamic landscapes. These dilemmas face every metropolitan landscape in North America, and the intensity of their expression at the bottom of the continent's largest drainage basin makes New Orleans a compelling and vivid site to work toward a more resilient paradigm.

Figure 8. Gutter to Gulf home page, www.guttertogulf.com. This website, produced by Jane Wolff, Elise Shelley, and Derek Hoeferlin, presents research and design work on New Orleans's urban hydrology and hydraulics by students from the University of Toronto and Washington University. The site's design was realized with assistance from Karen May and Denise Pinto.

Notes

I would like to thank my *Gutter to Gulf* partners Elise Shelley and Derek Hoeferlin and our students at the University of Toronto and Washington University, without whose efforts I would never have known so much about New Orleans; my New Orleans friends and colleagues Richard Campanella, Louis Jackson, Ray Manning, Elizabeth Mossop, Carol Reese, Hilairie Schackai, and David Waggonner for generously sharing their insights and experiences; and my invaluable research assistants, Michael Cook and Elise Hunchuck of the University of Toronto.

1_ To make the point that human activities have profoundly transformed all of Earth's ecological systems, atmospheric chemist Paul J. Crutzen defined the Anthropocene as a new geological epoch "supplementing the Holocene—the warm period of the past 10-12 millenia. The Anthropocene could be said to have started in the latter part of the eighteenth century when analyses of air trapped in polar ice showed the beginning of growing global concentrations of carbon dioxide and methane. This date also happens to coincide with James Watt's design of the steam engine in 1784." He introduced the term in his paper "Geology of Mankind," in *Nature* 415 (2002): 23.

2_ These principles, which emerged twenty-five years ago as the New Ecology and more recently as the Ecosystem Approach or Complex Systems Approach, emphasize the need to understand flux and process in landscapes. My summary refers both to work inside the field of ecology, including work by C.S. Holling, Sven Erik Jørgensen, and James Kay, and work designed to translate ecological ideas for designers, particularly the writing of Nina-Marie Lister. See C.S. Holling, "Resilience of Ecosystems; Local Surprise and Global Change," in *Sustainable Development of the Biosphere*, eds. W. C. Clark and R. E. Munn (Cambridge: Cambridge University Press, 1986), 292–320; Sven Erik Jørgensen, *A New Ecology: Systems Perspective* (Amsterdam, Boston: Elsevier, 2007), 3-4; David Waltner-Toews, James J. Kay, and Nina-Marie E. Lister, *The Ecosystem Approach: Complexity, Uncertainty, and Managing for Sustainability* (New York: Columbia University Press, 2008); Nina-Marie E. Lister, "Sustainable Large Parks: Ecological Design or Designer Ecology," in *Large Parks*, eds. Julia Czerniak and George Hargreaves (New York: Princeton Architectural Press, 2007), 35–58.

3_ Prominent examples include the competition entries for Parc Downsview Park and Fresh Kills Park. Please see Julia Czerniak, *Downsview Park Toronto* (Cambridge, MA, and New York: Harvard Design School and Prestel Publishing, 2002); "Fresh Kills Park Project: Project History," New York City Department of City Planning, accessed February 1, 2013, http://www.nyc.gov/html/dcp/html/fkl/fkl2.shtml.

4_ Resilience is defined as the "rate at which a system returns to a reference state or dynamic after a perturbation." Stuart L. Pimm, quoted by the Stanford Encyclopedia of Philosophy in "Ecology," accessed May 17, 2013, http://plato.stanford.edu/entries/ecology/.

5_ Peirce F. Lewis, *New Orleans: The Making of an Urban Landscape* (Santa Fe and Harrisonburg: Center for American Places, 2003), 19.

6_ Richard Campanella, *Time and Place in New Orleans: Past Geographies in the Present Day* (Gretna: Pelican Publishing Company, 2002), 50, 59–62. Campanella's work, which also includes *Bienville's Dilemma: A Historical Geography of New Orleans, Geographies of New Orleans: Urban Fabrics Before the Storm* and *New Orleans Then and Now* (with Marina Campanella), provides an encyclopedic account of New Orleans's evolution. For an account of the landscape's role in shaping cultural practices and institutions, see Ari Kelman's *A River and Its City: The Nature of Landscape in New Orleans* (Berkeley: University of California Press, 2006).

7_ Craig E. Colton's *An Unnatural Metropolis: Wresting New Orleans from Nature* (Baton Rouge: Louisiana State University Press, 2005) and Richard Campanella's *Time and Place in New Orleans: Past Geographies in the Present Day* provide detailed accounts of the development of the city's drainage infrastructure.

8_ See "A Historical Look at the Sewerage and Water Board," Sewerage and Water Board of New Orleans, accessed July 7, 2012, http://www.swbno.org/history_history.asp.

9_ Campanella, *Time and Place in New Orleans*, 60.

10_ Ibid.

11_ My scholarship on the history of land reclamation in the Netherlands is summarized in my unpublished paper, "Nature Process and Cultural Form: Water in the Dutch Landscape" (paper presented to document my work as a Charles Eliot Traveling Fellow at the Harvard Graduate School of Design, Cambridge, Massachusetts, April 1996). For a discussion of how ecological complexity has been exacerbated by competing cultural and programmatic demands on the landscape, see my book, *Delta Primer: A Field Guide to the California Delta* (San Francisco: William Stout Publishers, 2003).

12_ Kelman, *A River and Its City*, 161.

13_ In Louisiana, counties are called parishes.

14_ Saint Bernard Polder, the self-contained drainage unit that contains the parish's populated areas, also includes New Orleans's Lower Ninth Ward and Bayou Bienvenue. New Orleans East comprises its own drainage unit.

15_ Polder is a Dutch word, now used in English, meaning self-contained drainage unit. New Orleans's Drainage Basin One is also a polder.

16_ From a conversation with Stuart Williamson, former executive director of the Lake Borgne Levee District (February 6, 2012).

17_ Originally dug at 650 feet wide, the canal's sides have slumped to expand its average width to 1,970 feet in 2005.

18_ The MR-GO also played a catastrophic role during Hurricane Katrina, when its direct connection to the gulf allowed the attendant storm surge a direct route inland. This trajectory brought high water into the Industrial Canal, whose levee failures flooded the Lower Ninth Ward.

19_ Pare Lorentz's 1937 film *The River*, one of the Works Progress Administration's Films of Merit, can be watched online at http://archive.org/details/TheRiverByPareLorentz

20_ John McPhee, "Atchafalaya," in *The Control of Nature* (New York: Farrar, Straus and Giroux, 1989), 3–94.

21_ See Holling, "Resilience of Ecosystems," 292–320.

22_ This map, published by the *New Orleans Times-Picayune*, has been removed from the paper's web archive. See "Katrina: One Year Later," *New Orleans Times-Picayune*, November 29, 2005.

23_ I am one of the authors of this project, a collaborative research and teaching initiative of the University of Toronto and Washington University in Saint Louis described in greater detail at the end of this chapter. My co-authors are Elise Shelley and Derek Hoeferlin.

24_ John Schwartz, "Vast Defenses Now Shielding New Orleans Against Big Storms," *New York Times*, June 15, 2012, A1, A28.

25_ From a conversation with Stuart Williamson.

26_ Schwartz, "Vast Defenses Now Shielding New Orleans Against Big Storms."

27_ For instance, the Dutch initiative "Room for the River" provides an administrative, technical, and economic model for adaptive management that permits controlled flooding in the eastern and central Netherlands to protect urban areas. The initiative's aims, methods, and projects are detailed in its comprehensive website, "Ruimte voor de rivier," http://www.ruimtevoorderivier.nl/ and translated into English at "Room for the river programme," http://www.ruimtevoorderivier.nl/meta-navigatie/english/ (both accessed July 10, 2012).

28_ The initiative's website is at http://www.guttertogulf.com.

Emergence is a phenomenon characteristic of complex systems and, in particular, of patterns observed in nature through the study of biology and ecology—patterns that arise through the collective actions of many individual entities and a multiplicity of their interactions.[1] NML

1. After Peter Corning (2002).

EMERGENCE

Collectivity and multiplicity predominate, whereby multiple internal protocols and external inputs interact and inform the (re-) conceptualization of landscapes and infrastructures, at a range of scales. Individual agents play ongoing roles in existing and proposed landscapes and cities; hydrologic, ecological, and jurisdictional mechanisms intersect and play off one another, often muddying the waters; the life and seasonality of protective metropolitan infrastructure and the crafting of humid and thermal atmospheres are all part of an understanding of the world in an eternal state of becoming. CR

Wenche E. Dramstad, James D. Olson, and Richard T.T. Forman. Movement Diagrams: Patches, Edges, Corridors, Mosaics. 1966.

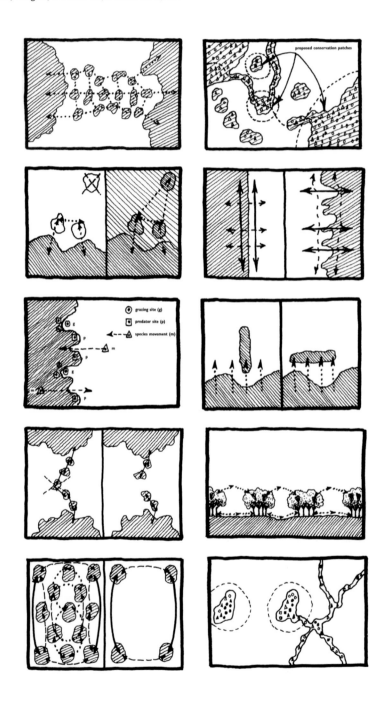

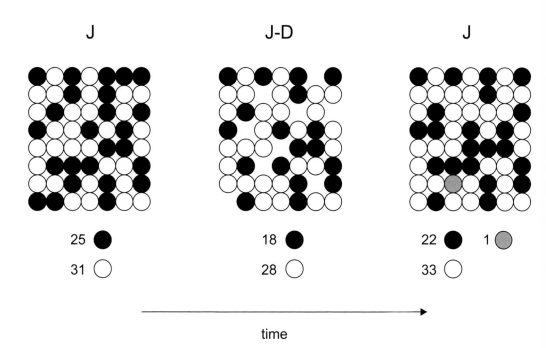

Bernard Tschumi Architects, Dereck Revington Studio, and Sterling Finlayson Architects.
Spatial Temporal Dynamics of Ecosystem. 1999.

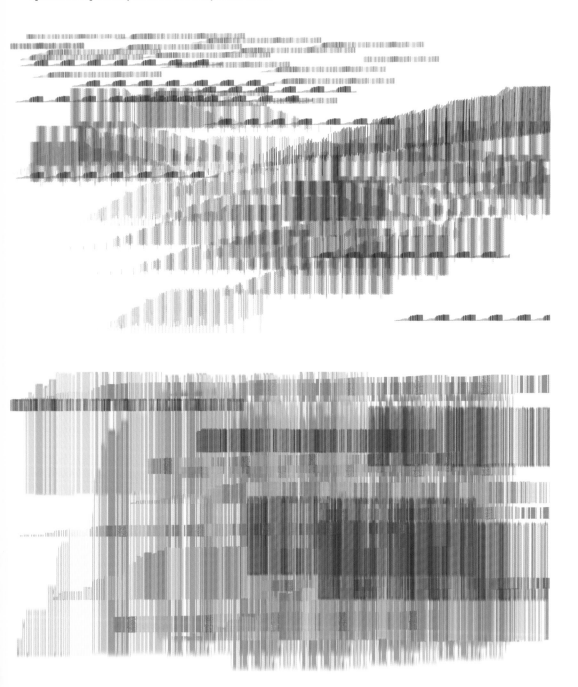

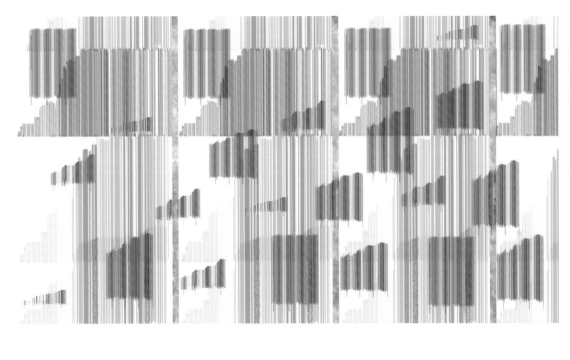
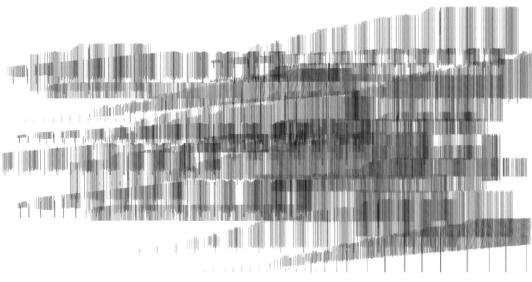

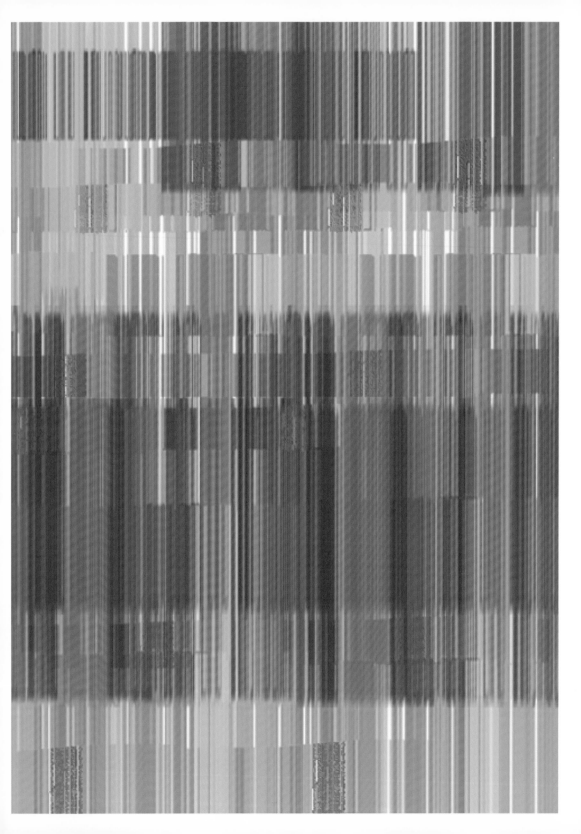

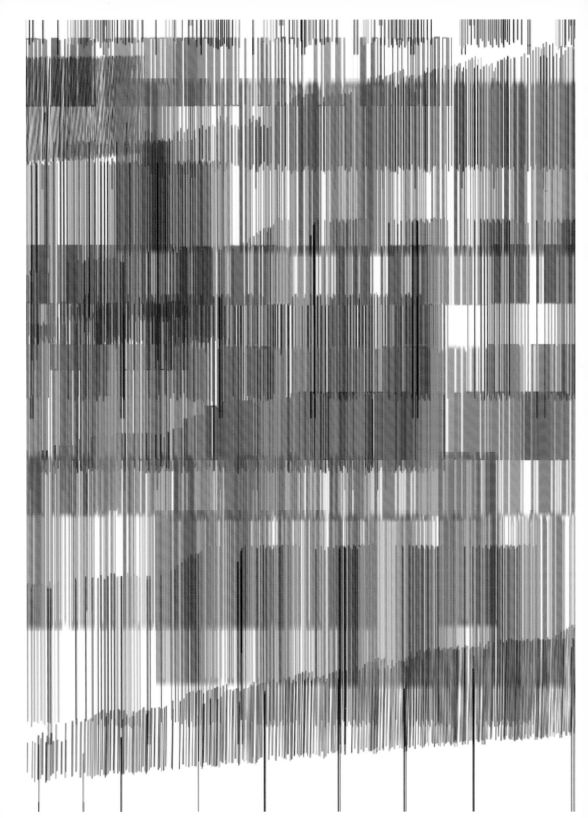

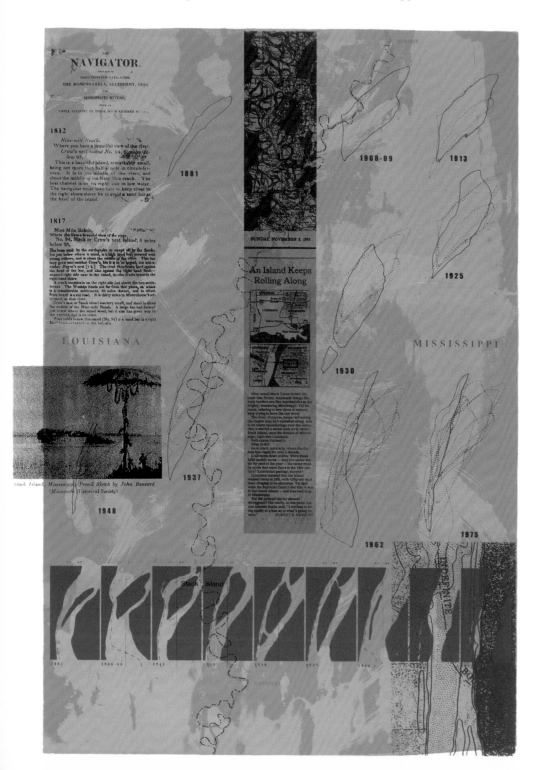

Stoss/Chris Reed, Aki Omi. Seed choreographies. 2004.

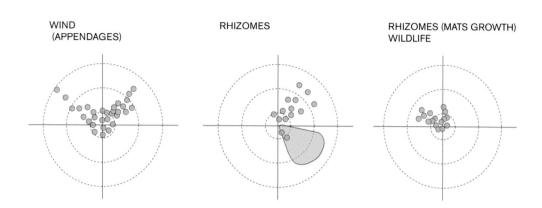

WIND
(APPENDAGES)

RHIZOMES

RHIZOMES (MATS GROWTH)
WILDLIFE

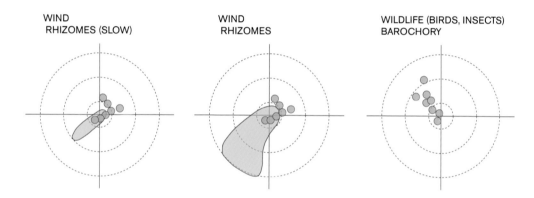

WIND
RHIZOMES (SLOW)

WIND
RHIZOMES

WILDLIFE (BIRDS, INSECTS)
BAROCHORY

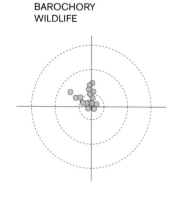

BAROCHORY
WILDLIFE

James Corner Field Operations. Diversification in Time. The High Line, New York, USA. 2004.

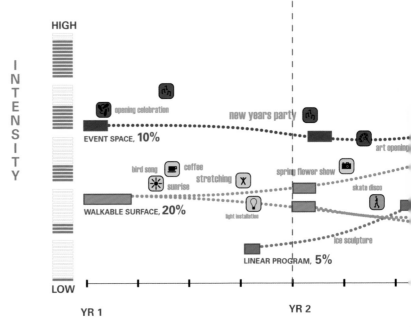

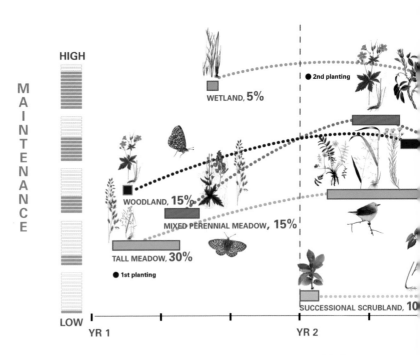

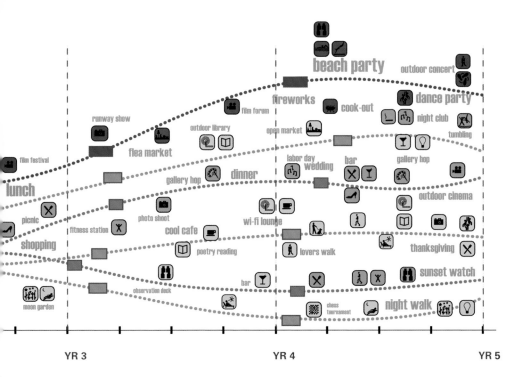

beach party

outdoor concert

fireworks
cook-out
dance party

runway show
film forum
night club

outdoor library
open market
tumbling

flea market

film festival
labor day
wedding
bar
gallery hop

lunch
gallery hop
dinner
outdoor cinema

picnic
photo shoot
wi-fi lounge

fitness station
cool cafe

shopping
thanksgiving

poetry reading
lovers walk

bar
sunset watch

moon garden
observation deck
chess
tournament
night walk

YR 3   YR 4   YR 5

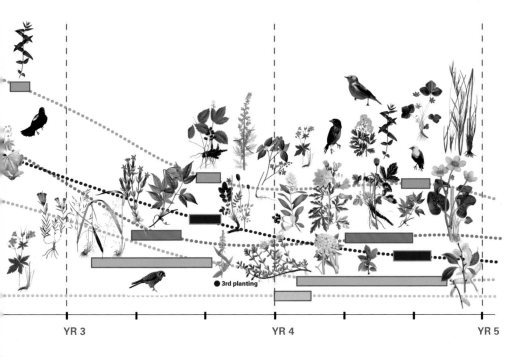

● 3rd planting

YR 3   YR 4   YR 5

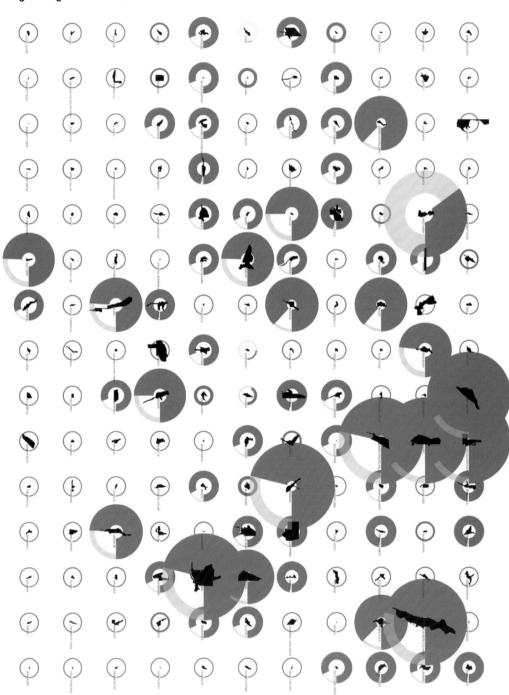

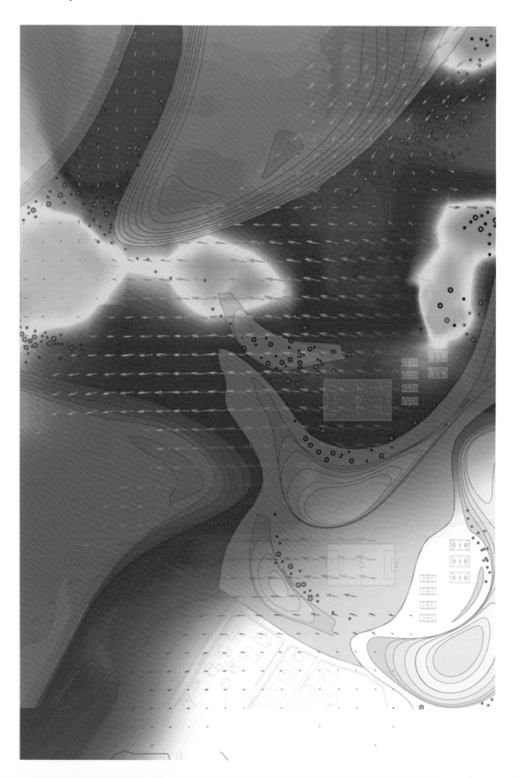

Do Landscapes Learn? Ecology's "New Paradigm" and Design in Landscape Architecture

Robert E. Cook

Published 1999

For the past two decades, the field of ecology has been undergoing a quiet shift in the concepts and philosophy that shape ordinary theoretical and field investigations. The "new paradigm" that has emerged in this shift centers on an understanding of the natural world as a setting of dynamic change and uncertainty, placing the underlying assumptions that now support ecological research in marked contrast to the perspective that has influenced our understanding of the natural world over the last century.[1]

One may ask, what implications does this "new paradigm" have for disciplines with ecological applications, such as conservation, ecological restoration, and landscape architecture?[2] The value of this new perspective depends upon how ecological knowledge is used in practice. On the face of it, an understanding of ecology can assist landscape architects in their work in two obvious ways. A design project usually involves a serious intervention and rearrangement of the land, and a biological understanding of the consequences may help the architect predict and control the outcome of the intervention. Second, the narrative of ecology and the feelings an ecological perspective may provoke can serve as inspiration for the aesthetic challenge facing the designer.

There may also be a third value in understanding the work of ecologists and the implications of a shift in perspective: the designer may begin to see the conduct of ecological studies as an engagement with the land and its inhabitants, analogous to but philosophically distinct from landscape architecture. This third value may then serve to initiate a deeper dialogue between the ecologist and the designer.

What led to my own such engagement with the land as a practicing ecologist was a seemingly unremarkable population of wild violets growing in the woodlands of New England. The question behind my research was simple: Why would female plants bother with sex when asexual reproduction is perfectly adequate? Female plants frequently reproduce without sex, leading to the cloning of identical individuals. I wanted to understand why, in an evolutionary sense, sex ever evolved.[3]

The chosen species of particular interest to me was a white-flowering, short-stemmed violet called *Viola blanda*, familiar to anyone who frequents the wetter parts of our New England woodlands. Every year in early May, it forms a rosette of leaves in the leaf litter of the forest floor. Out of the axil of its leaves, where the leaf stem, or petiole, meets the main stem, emerges a new shoot. It grows somewhat like a branch except that it remains just below the surface of the soil. This runner, or stolon, is leafless and grows through the summer to distances of twenty or more inches from the mother plant.

As the days of autumn grow shorter, extension growth ceases, and the tip of the stolon shoot turns up to barely emerge from the soil. It overwinters in this form, and the warming of the soil in April stimulates the emergence of leaves and the initiation of roots that will give this daughter plant independence from its mother. Throughout the following season, the daughter now repeats the cycle, forming one or more stolons that in turn create granddaughters and great-granddaughters, all at different locations across the forest floor.

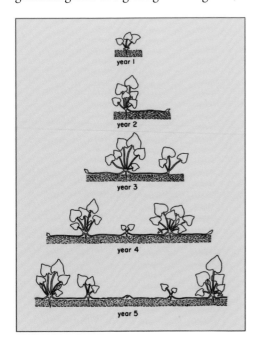

I studied the formation of these clones by marking seedlings and censusing each one repeatedly through the season and over a number of years. When the growth of any new stolons stopped each fall, I would mark the new locations of the potential daughter plants. If they survived winter and emerged the following spring, I would add them to my census population. In this way I could track the formation of clones and know the underground connections among the plants in my population. Obviously, such a demographic approach to watching violets grow involved many, many hours spent on my knees tracking individual plants. Over the eight years of my research I encountered about 8,000 violets and discovered that any one individual lives a relatively short life, perhaps four or five years. Yet this plant is replaced by her genetically identical daughters and granddaughters, although in different locations. In this sense, the plant is capable of surviving indefinitely through the asexual production of new generations.

There was, however, an entirely different interpretation one can place on this pattern of life and death. Because daughters and granddaughters are genetically identical to the mother plant, they are the same individual from an evolutionary point of view. The 'adaptation' of the clone in the forest understory is its "movement" across the forest floor.

Schematic sketch of the life cycle of a *Viola blanda* plant showing the way in which the distribution of growth shifts to younger generations as the clone moves slowly across the forest floor, continually acquiring new locations.

Understanding this spatial pattern required tracking the clone's temporal pattern of new questions about clonal behavior: was this movement random, or could it be directed, perhaps to locations of higher resources such as sunlight or mineral nutrients? Were the clones foraging for "food" over the forest floor?

After 1983, my career turned away from the investigations that could answer such questions, but the perspective toward the natural world that they embraced—a dynamic, constantly changing nature—reflected the influence of the new paradigm that was then overtaking academic ecology. The significance of this influence is best conveyed through an understanding of the old paradigm and how it became established.

Ecological Theory_____

Ecology as a science really began as plant ecology before the turn of the century. Botanists were developing taxonomic schemes to describe and classify diverse plant communities. This included both different-looking communities with different plant species growing in different regions of the world and different-looking communities growing at different times in the same location. By the end of the nineteenth century, botanists understood that, for any one location, there was a recognizable sequence of plants that invaded a site following a severe disturbance, such as fire or land clearing for agriculture. The sequence of species that appeared in stages usually ended with a community composition similar to that found before the disturbance, a process called succession.

The intellectual father of ecology was Frederick E. Clements, a botanist who grew up in the grasslands and prairie regions of this country. His prolific writings over fifty years left an enduring imprint on the science of ecology, particularly the establishment of the old paradigm. Trained in floristic taxonomy characteristic of nineteenth-century botany, Clements believed that one could understand the proper classification of plant communities if one could understand how those communities came to occupy land rendered bare by disturbance. Clements brought a holistic perspective to his beliefs about vegetation that was consistent with much of the intellectual thought at the time. He argued that the plant community, the whole assemblage of species found growing together on a site, was actually a single living organism. As such, it displayed characteristics of development, integration, and homeostasis similar to an individual plant or animal. In 1905 he published his first ecological book called *Research Methods in Ecology*, which describes the plant community, then called a formation: "Vegetation an Organism" [sic]—The plant formation is "an organic unit." This unit, he writes, "exhibits activities or changes which result in development, structure, and reproduction.... According to this point of view, the formation is a complex organism, which possesses functions and structure, and passes through a cycle of development similar to that of the plant....As an organism, the formation is undergoing constant change."[4]

Clements's concept of vegetation as a kind of "superorganism," propounded in numerous books and papers in the first half of this century, had an enormous appeal for many individuals entering the discipline of ecology as a subfield of botanical study. His theory became an alternative to the strongly reductionist tendencies seen in physiology and genetics, and its spiritual qualities reinforced the emotional feelings experienced by scientists who spent thousands of hours in the field investigating the natural world. Also at this time, the organism as a metaphor was influencing the intellectual development of disciplines well outside ecology.[5]

During the old paradigm's long hold over the field of ecology in this country, one important transformation developed in the decade before World War II. The concept of the plant community was not only expanded to include all of its animal inhabitants, but also redescribed in terms of two fundamental processes that give life to the "superorganism"—the flow of energy through the community and the cycling of nonorganic elements such as hydrogen, oxygen, nitrogen, and carbon. The "superorganism" was transformed into the "system," now called an "ecosystem." Following the war, the science of ecosystem studies began to grow rapidly, and a new language describing the dynamics of energy and nutrients came to dominate the discipline of ecology.

Although describing a natural system in energetic terms might seem reductionist in nature, ecosystem ecology retained a strongly holistic interpretation: the healthy ecosystem as an integrated, efficiently functioning entity that can be defined, described, and measured quantitatively. Reference to the superorganism disappeared from the narratives of ecologists, but descriptions of functional properties drew on a language heavily characterized by organismic attributes. Ecosystems, ecologists now recognized, displayed homeostasis and self-regulation. When disturbed by outside forces, they exhibited a process of regeneration described as a predictable series of developmental stages that continued until a mature and healthy equilibrium was reached. The leading textbook of the time, *Fundamentals of Ecology* (1954) by Eugene Odum, contains a summary chapter, "The Strategy of Ecosystem Development," that states, "Ecosystem development, or what is more often known as ecological succession...is an orderly process of community development [that] is reasonably directional, and, therefore, predictable....Succession is community-controlled....It culminates in a stabilized ecosystem in which maximum biomass and symbiotic function between organisms are maintained per unit of available energy flow....The development of ecosystems has many parallels in the developmental biology of organisms, and also in the development of human society."[6]

The influence of this holistic paradigm, also called the "equilibrium paradigm," went well beyond academic ecology, especially with the rise of environmentalism in the 1960s. Ian McHarg's *Design with Nature* (1969), the classic study that merged ecology and landscape planning, is suffused with a spiritual and holistic interpretation of the natural world. McHarg writes, "Ecologists describe the thin film of life covering the earth as the biosphere, the sum of all organisms and communities, acting as a single superorganism."[7]

Four major elements characterize this equilibrium paradigm. First, ecological systems in their natural state are closed, self-regulating systems. Energy efficiently sustains the maximum state of biomass, and nutrients cycle within the system without significant loss. Second, the system in its most mature state is in a condition of balance or equilibrium. The forces of nature causing change (i.e., disturbance) are external to the system. Third, when the system is disturbed by outside forces and degraded to an earlier developmental, less efficient state, an ecological process known as succession changes the system through a sequence of predictable stages to restore the original conditions and return the system to an equilibrium condition. Finally, the activities of humans are not part of the natural world and are often in conflict with its operation. The influence of human culture is largely negative, acting as an agent of disturbance that undermines the balanced, stable equilibrium of the mature and healthy system.

The transition from one paradigm to another was brought about in the 1980s by several factors.[8] The first was the influence of evolutionary theory on ecology through its causal explanations, especially the mechanism of natural selection. New ecology textbooks began to appear in the 1970s that fully incorporated population genetics and population biology into ecological theory and practice. From this perspective, a community, or ecosystem, is a collection of populations, and the whole is not greater than the sum of the parts.

Along with a population approach to ecology came a statistical and probabilistic perspective for understanding complex natural phenomena. Ecologists increasingly recognized the large role that chance played in the way the natural world works. Finally, the accumulation of evidence from long-term, historically oriented studies of natural systems overwhelmingly indicated that nature was very unruly and seldom behaved in a way that was consistent with the ideal models and predictions of the old paradigm. Despite the tenacious, century-old hold of a holistic ecology over the minds of ecologists and its popularization for political and religious ends, the metaphor of the organism has been gradually replaced by the new paradigm.

If the older paradigm can be characterized by its equilibrium, the new paradigm emphasizes the dynamic and changing nature of communities and ecosystems.[9] These systems are no longer seen as closed, self-regulating entities, since their boundaries are much more complex and difficult to define than this would imply. Changes in the composition of a community can be greatly influenced by factors outside the system, further expanding the scope and complexity of the ecological knowledge required to understand its local dynamics.

Disturbance is a frequent, intrinsic characteristic of ecosystems. They are constantly subject to varying degrees of physical disruption from natural forces, and species exhibit a wide range of adaptations to disturbance. Fire, windstorm, landslide, flooding, and the mortality of plants and animals that result are all intrinsic elements of every natural setting, leaving most communities resembling a patchwork mosaic of species usually representing very different stages of succession.

Succession itself is now viewed as a highly probabilistic process that can be greatly influenced by local conditions and the particular order of events that occurs. In other words, what was formerly considered a highly predictable, universal process is actually highly contingent on history and content. Successions may display multiple pathways and multiple end states, if an end state is ever reached.

Finally, in the new paradigm humans can be and usually must be considered part of the system. This is a recognition of the overwhelming influence of human culture on all natural systems and the worldwide impact of certain cultural practices such as the burning of fossil fuel, the release of ozone-destroying chlorofluorocarbons, and the introduction of alien species. The new paradigm challenges any clean distinction between culture and nature.

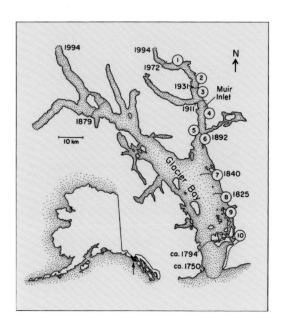

Case Studies

The use of the word *paradigm*, whether old or new, implies a certain language used within a discipline, almost independent of the underlying concepts and assumptions. A detailed review of two case studies from the practice of ecology demonstrates this play between evidence, concepts, and language.

The first case is the classic example of succession that has been cited in many leading textbooks since it was first described in 1923.[10] At Glacier Bay, Alaska, the resident glacier has been melting and retreating north at a rate of about half a kilometer a year since 1750. The valley left in its wake filled with seawater to form Glacier Bay, and all along the shore the glacier has deposited till consisting of a variety of silty and sandy sediments containing pebbles, stones, and large rocks in a homogeneous outwash with no nutrient content.

Location of ten study sites at Glacier Bay, including positions of glacier termini established from historical maps and photographs (1794 and 1879–1994) or from the measurement of tree cores (1750, 1825, 1840). Arrow indicates location of Glacier Bay National Park and Preserve in southeastern Alaska (redrawn after Christopher L. Fastie, "Causes and Ecosystem Consequences of Multiple Pathways of Primary Succession at Glacier Bay, Alaska," *Ecology* 76 [1995], 1900.

Succession began when plants invaded the shoreline. An initial community of mosses and herbaceous species was followed by low-growing willows, cottonwoods, and alders. The alders soon spread into thickets, which were in turn invaded by Sitka spruce. After a century, the spruce forest completely shaded out the lower-growing alders and was itself infiltrated by mountain and western hemlock. This mixed spruce-hemlock forest is considered to be the final, or climax, stage of succession, reached after a period of 200 years.

Studies conducted after World War II revealed a parallel pattern of soil development.[11] Nitrogen-fixing herbaceous species and alders increased the nitrogen content of the soil, and the decomposition of acidic alder leaves lowered the initially high, alkaline condition of the glacial till. These changing conditions permitted the seedlings of spruce and hemlock to successfully colonize, and the increasing level of nitrogen accelerated tree growth and the accumulation of organic carbon in the soil. This tidy narrative—a predictable sequence of plant species parallel with, and presumably caused by, a predictable sequence of soil development—exemplified primary succession until the present decade. Yet this process is not based on observations of a single site over a 200-year period; obviously, no ecologist is that dedicated or long-lived. Instead, study plots were established at different distances south along the shoreline of Glacier Bay. Sites nearest the edge of the glacier were the youngest, and sites 100 kilometers away at the mouth of the Bay were the oldest. This methodology assumes that the sequence of plant communities seen in space accurately describes the sequence of plant communities that will occur at one site over a 200-year period; that is, spatial variation is presumed to mirror temporal variation.

Beginning in 1987, Christopher Fastie, a graduate student at the University of Alaska, decided to see if a historical reconstruction of single sites over time actually matched the description of the successional sequence of Glacier Bay as seen in the spatial comparison of multiple sites. To do this he took core samples out of all tree trunks growing at each of ten study areas in a sequence from north to south (see Figure 2) and reconstructed the history of each tree's growth by measuring every annual growth ring under a microscope. The history of the site could then be reconstructed from a knowledge of the growth of its individual trees. In addition, he did a soil analysis at all ten study areas. Using meticulous statistical methods, he recreated the forest history at each site based on the direct evidence displayed by the wood of each tree.[12]

Fastie found that the actual history sometimes differed considerably from the classic successional narrative. The three oldest sites closest to the open sea displayed an invasion of spruce and hemlock much earlier than expected, and there was little evidence that alder thickets were ever a dominant part of the early forest history of these sites. The middle-aged sites were covered with alder thickets, which seemed to have greatly delayed the invasion of spruce and hemlock. At the very youngest sites, over 60 kilometers from the sea and closest to the glacier, cottonwood rather than alder was coming to dominate the earlier phases of vegetational change.

Thus Fastie identified three distinct patterns of succession at Glacier Bay, all within a comparatively short distance of each other. In addition, he noted that the oldest sites were under attack from the spruce bark beetle, which was killing all canopy spruce in some stands. This new disturbance may have been facilitated by declining tree vigor due to low nitrogen availability in the soil. Fastie speculates that spruce trees colonizing younger sites, where nitrogen-fixing alder thickets have previously been dominant, may have greater resistance to such insect outbreaks and may therefore experience a very different history as much as a century later. He concludes:

> The existence of qualitatively distinct pathways at similar sites at Glacier Bay demonstrates that no single sequence of species replacements and no single mechanistic model of plant community change is mandatory....Multiple pathways of compositional change at Glacier Bay appear to be a function of landscape context, which, in conjunction with...dispersal capabilities and generation time, affects seed rain to newly deglaciated surfaces and thereby alters the arrival sequence of species.... The single species differences early in succession at otherwise similar sites at Glacier Bay therefore could have substantial consequences for successional pathway and ecosystem function for many centuries.[13]

The second case is drawn from much closer to home. For more than eighty years, the Harvard Forest in Petersham, Massachusetts, has been a study site for the effects of catastrophic natural disturbance on forested landscapes. Established as part of a traditional forestry school after the turn of the century, large tracts of white pine and hemlock growing on its lands were severely damaged by the 1938 hurricane that destroyed forests throughout central New England. After World War II, the direction of research at Harvard shifted from questions of applied biology such as forest production to more basic issues involving the structure and functioning of natural ecosystems.

David Foster, director of the Harvard Forest, and his colleagues have conducted a series of studies that have revealed the role of natural disturbance in the temperate forests of the northeastern United States.[14] One small forest of particular interest in southwestern New Hampshire is the Pisgah Tract, which has never been cut for timber. This primeval forest today looks like many of the second-growth woodlands found throughout New England growing on abandoned farmland, except that on the forest floor, surrounded by sixty-year-old birch, maple, and oak trees, lie the fallen, decaying trunks of huge, 100-foot white pine and hemlock trees that were once part of the old-growth forest. The trees were all blown down in four hours on 21 September 1938, and a new forest has grown up around them.

Through methods of historical reconstruction similar to those used by Fastie in Glacier Bay, Foster meticulously traced the history of this site back to 1635 when a powerful hurricane destroyed the forest and was followed, thirty years later, by widespread fire. Over the subsequent 300 years, the site was subjected to seven damaging windstorms or hurricanes, six widespread fires, and three broad-scale attacks by pathogens. This pattern of regular disturbance shaped the composition of the forest through the death of large trees and the recruitment of new seedlings. It was this patchwork plant community, dominated by large hemlocks and white pines, that was destroyed in 1938 and followed by a forest of a very different composition.

Foster's interest in the functioning of the temperate forest ecosystem was not limited to an understanding of its past, however.[15] He wanted to discover how human cultural activities were affecting the forests. Over the past century, we have been increasing the concentration of carbon dioxide in the atmosphere by 30 percent, with every indication that this and future increases will lead to a worldwide rise in the average temperature of the Earth's surface. In addition, the amount of nitrogen being introduced into natural systems worldwide has more than doubled and promises to continue increasing, creating a very large fertilization experiment with unknown consequences. While we ordinarily think of human disturbance to nature in terms of forest clearing and agricultural production, a much more global and chronic source of disturbance involves fundamental changes to biogeochemical cycles. How, Foster asked, do the responses of forests to these chronic disturbances compare to similar responses to catastrophic disturbance?

To find out, Foster set up a series of experimental plots in 1990. In one, he used a power-driven winch to pull over all the trees in one direction, thereby simulating the effects of a hurricane. In a second, he placed heating coils below the soil surface and raised the average temperature by 5 degrees centigrade. Finally, he fertilized a third plot with nitrogen monthly between May and October. He subsequently measured the plants' responses to these three experimental manipulations. Following each treatment, he also tracked changes in key nutrient processes in the water and soil of the forest.

While the experiment has only been running for six years, some preliminary conclusions are quite interesting. As one might expect, pulling over more than 250 mature trees in the middle of a forest caused immense structural damage, with an additional 400 trees more or less affected. In addition, the uplifted root systems created a series of huge holes in the forest floor, and the erosion of the soil clinging to roots formed mounds of soil beside these pits. The forest floor was covered with broken debris and litter.

Despite this bleak picture, regeneration of the forest began immediately. Snapped and fallen trees sprouted new shoots from branches and roots. Forty percent of the trees pulled over managed to survive and recover. New seedlings and saplings soon appeared and quickly grew in the open sunlight. Within four years a new canopy of young trees and survivors had formed.

Foster had anticipated that such chaotic disruption of the forest and soil structure would have a great impact on the water and nutrient processes that are critical to ecosystem functioning. But he found no evidence of any change. The movement of carbon and nitrogen was very similar in the hurricane simulation plots and the controls that experienced no disturbance.

Such was not the case in the fertilizer and soil-warming experiments, however. These plots showed no changes in the structure and composition of the forest, at least not yet. While there was some increase in leaf litter production in the fertilizer experiment, the forests looked very similar in appearance to their controls. Despite this, measures of carbon and nitrogen cycling indicated major changes. Heating the soil greatly increased the release of carbon dioxide from the soil into the atmosphere and more than doubled the rate of nitrogen mineralization, a measure of nitrogen release in the soil. This implied a profoundly altered soil environment. Similarly, in the fertilizer experiment, the rate of nitrogen immobilization in the soil increased nearly 100 percent during the six years of the experiment without any effect on the rate of carbon dioxide release. Where this nitrogen is being stored remains a mystery.

Although he intends to continue monitoring these experiments for many years to come, Foster has made some initial conclusions:

Whereas the blowdown site appears severely disturbed, internal processes have not been altered significantly, and the stand is on a path to recovery of structure and function in keeping with the cyclic pattern of disturbance and development of this forest type. By contrast, the chronic nitrogen and soil warming plots are visually intact and apparently healthy, yet the subtler measures of ecosystem function suggest serious imbalances, with possible future implications for community structure, internal ecosystem processes, and exchanges with the global environment.[16]

From these two ecological examples, the picture of the natural world that emerges is one of continual change—the flux of nature rather than the balance of nature. The pattern of this change is highly local and contingent on a particular sequence of historical events, and the effect can create a very heterogeneous spatial pattern on the land. The causes of the visible changes may be quite invisible, and the outcome of particular causes may be highly probabilistic; that is, chance can have a strong influence on change. Moreover, the pattern of change at one site may be complexly related to causes a great distance away or to large-scale processes with small, cumulative effects. Many of these causes are related to humans, who have come to dominate the natural world in the past century.

Ecology and Landscape Architecture

How can this picture of a contingent, fluctuating, and dynamic nature be of any use to the practice of landscape architecture? Some answers begin to surface if we return to the framework of possibilities noted earlier—ecology as knowledge, ecology as inspiration, and ecology as a basis for a conceptual dialogue.

Most landscape architects, if given the choice, would prefer to design landscape interventions that maintain or improve the ecological health of the land—thus the term *sustainable design*. To this end, a deeper understanding of the workings of the natural world is helpful. The problem, of course, is knowing how any particular intervention affects the health of the land.

Landscape architects seem to be at great odds over the role of ecology versus aesthetics in their work.[17] And the concern seems to be, almost to the point of dogma, that anything really creative or fun must be "unhealthy" and bad. But do we know this to be true, at least true the way scientists understand truth? Is there a literature of statistical studies that measure and document the impact of ordinary landscape interventions on the degree of health exhibited by the land in a way analogous to clinical trials that measure pharmaceutical effectiveness and side effects? I suspect there is not, leaving the matter prey to ideology and politics. We ecologists are at least partly to blame. Who wants to spend several years monitoring the biomass production, nitrogen dynamics, and water budget of the Dumbarton Oaks garden when you could be freezing your toes taking tree cores at Glacier Bay?

When it comes to measuring ecosystem health, the problem becomes even more complex. Ecologists are rather good at declaring the patient near death or dead, and the measurements to back up this judgment are rather easy to acquire and understand. But detecting a slight temperature rise or an arthritic limp is not nearly as simple. Natural systems are naturally resilient, and hide their illnesses until they are really ill. And ecologists have not developed methodologies to measure the more subtle effects of cultural manipulations of the land.

With the ascendancy of the new paradigm, this may change. Humans are now recognized as being a part of the natural world, and the ecological study of human interventions, even on the scale of landscape architecture, has become acceptable for sympathetic ecologists. Within the past year, the National Science Foundation awarded a multimillion-dollar grant to a study entitled "Human Settlements as Ecosystems: Metropolitan Baltimore, Maryland, from 1797 to 2100." [18] Can clinical trials on the ecological impact of the perennial border or the linden allée be far behind?

Given the difficulties in defining health and the lack of empirical evidence to prove that ordinary landscape design interventions are unhealthy or ecologically irresponsible, perhaps a neutral stance in the war between aesthetics and ecology is needed. My own bias inclines toward the position recently articulated by Louise Mozingo, who sees no necessary zero-sum game between ecologically sensitive design and the aesthetic expression of the designer.[19] She calls for the infusion of a new aesthetic into traditional ecological design. The latter, she argues, often leads to boring, unexciting landscapes invisible to ordinary people: "The lack of aesthetic value of most ecological design lends it a ploddingness that is neither appealing to us as designers, nor as humans. It creates a kind of landscape hairshirt that may make some feel holy but sends too many of us running to the nearest Italian garden."[20]

Mozingo's new ecological aesthetic would be built on five qualities that traditionally contribute to the creation of iconic designs of notable aesthetic value—visibility, temporality, reiterated forms, humanistic expression, and metaphor. In each of these domains, Mozingo finds the rhetoric of ecological design in conflict with any aesthetic language. But it is not at all clear that in the preservation of critical ecological processes negates the actual use of such a language in constructed landscape projects. She challenges ecological designers to reassess their morally superior, functionalist perspective: "While ecological design is clearly an ethic, it is not, at present, fully conceived as an aesthetic…Successfully promulgating ecological design requires the recognition and application of culturally based aesthetics."[21]

The value of such a new ecological aesthetic, successfully integrated into the practice of landscape design, would seem to rest on a deep and subtle understanding of the natural world by the designer. This calls for a rigorous scientific understanding that distinguishes fundamental ecological processes from the visual and superficial ecology of natural history. Armed with such an understanding when approaching a particular site, the designer is much freer to identify a set of aesthetic possibilities that will preserve or have minimal impact upon the critical ecological functions of the land. Landscape architects must be prepared to acquire, either as practitioners or students, the necessary level of scientific literacy that this implies.

There may be growing opportunities for defining a scientifically grounded aesthetic in the expanding field of ecological restoration.[22] Highly disturbed sites are readily accessible to this science, and the recovery of process is often more forgiving of experimentation. The aesthetic challenges are usually obvious, yet landscape architects have not, as yet, taken any leading role in the intellectual development of this field. The theory of ecological restoration seems to have been largely the province of engineers, ecologists, and the New Age philosophers.[23]

A deeper scientific understanding of the natural world can also be a source of inspiration to landscape architects, both as motivation and as artistic idea. The results of such inspiration can be delightfully evocative, but care should be taken to understand where science ends and aesthetics begins. A scientist sees a clear distinction between a decision based on a disciplined and critical understanding of a phenomenon, grounded in community consensus, and a decision based on a more personal, hypothetical perception of that phenomenon. Both are equally valid, but they are different. Too often in writings about design in landscape architecture, science is evoked to lend authority to designs that are not based on a true scientific understanding, and the hybrid becomes more of a politically correct imperative than a personal expression of feelings. Several years ago Anne Whiston Spirn captured this point perfectly: "Ecology as a science (a way of describing the world), ecology as a cause (a mandate for moral action), and ecology as an aesthetic (a norm for beauty) are often confused and conflated.... It is important to distinguish the insights ecology yields as a description of the world, on the one hand, from how these insights have served as a source of prescriptive principles or aesthetic values, on the other."[24]

The new paradigm, by its contrast with the old, is key to a third way that the scientific nature of ecology can inform landscape architecture. Ecologists and designers think about their work in entirely different ways, which are revealed most conspicuously in the language landscape architects and ecologists use. Look, for example, at the conceptual language Elizabeth Meyer chooses to serve as the theoretical frame of her essay "The Expanded Field of Landscape Architecture":

> The *figured ground* is that undulating body between the figural object and neutral field, between mass and void. It finds structure in the ground, its topographic and geological structure. The *articulated space* is the space between figural space framed by buildings and open space, homogeneous and undefined. This is the realm of the spatiality of plants, hedges, hedgerows, allées, bosques, orchards, and forests; it is a space of layering, ambiguity and change. The *minimal garden*, also called the garden without walls, relies on patterning the ground plane to create a visible landscape. The surface—what is usually undefined—is transformed into a horizontal object that defines an implied space above it—like a Persian rug on the floor.[25]

What is so striking about Meyer's language is how spatial it is. Landscape architects think spatially and practice their discipline spatially. The very roots of the compound word that defines their work, *land* and *scape*, derive from spatial references, as noted by J. B. Jackson: "As far back as we can trace the word, land meant a defined space, one with boundaries....Scape...once meant a composition of similar objects...Landscape is... synthetic space, a man-made system of spaces superimposed on the face of the land."[26]

A design is a spatial object, usually represented in the two-dimensional plan and the three-dimensional model. Designers give form to their inspirations through the manipulation of objects on the surface of the land and the creation of unique spaces. How different this way of thinking is from that of the ecologist.

Take the new paradigm compared with the old. The superorganism as a metaphor for the climax, steady-state plant community or ecosystem is an idealized concept of a relatively static, unchanging natural world. The new paradigm replaces this fixed, nature-inbalance model with one that is dynamic, contingent, and full of change and uncertainty. For an ecologist, what is interesting about nature is what happened yesterday and how it informs us about what might happen tomorrow. The temporality of nature *is* nature, and insights based on spatial perceptions alone are highly suspect without an understanding of the underlying dynamic processes that created the spatial configuration. This is why an ecologist will carefully measure the annual growth rings of 10,000 tree cores or spend six years on his knees watching violets grow.

If the language of landscape architecture is essentially a spatial language, what is the analogous language for ecologists? I think it is mathematics. Scientists use mathematics to describe the dynamic flux of nature, whether it is the probability of events (statistics) or the description of rates of change (calculus). For the designer, spatial language seems closely linked with the eye and the translation of its perceptions into new spatial configurations. The ecologist distrusts the eye and brings great effort and discipline to the process of acquiring data that unmask the guises of the eye. No wonder "ecological design" is sometimes treated as an oxymoron. Laurie Olin, discussing his own collaborative work with ecologists practicing wetland restoration, makes this difference clear:

> Of great interest to me was their disinterest in what their work looked like....
> In their early work, they tried to make their new and restored habitats look like those they had studied....They had discovered, however, that many things died, some grew by leaps and bounds...and other things just turned up. They found themselves engaged in a sort of wilderness gardening for a few years until the systems and various populations took hold....As a result, they said now they do not bother trying to make a site look "pretty."...What nature looks like, or is supposed to look like, appears to be our problem, a cultural matter; it has little to do with ecology.[27]

Landscape architects may not need to worry about the march of time: clients care a lot about how things look, especially while they are paying the fee; they deal with the effects of time later—long after the designer has cashed the check. But this view may be too cynical. A positive alternative sees ecology's new paradigm suggesting a renewed acknowledgment of temporality in landscape design. Such a temporality is one critical element of Mozingo's call for a new aesthetic: "Landscape aesthetics prizes a static vision imposed upon the land... Conventional design sees landscape change not as a vital, imaginative force but as a frightening or disappointing one....The acceptance of change, of moving beyond the fixed vision of the landscape, is ecologically necessary."[28]

An analogy with architecture can be equally persuasive in acknowledging change. Throughout my reading of Stuart Brand's *How Buildings Learn: What Happens After*

They're Built, I found myself creating a parallel volume by substituting the words *landscape architect* for *architect* and *landscape* for *building*. What might this second book look like?

Brand argues that architects do not care about buildings once they are built: "I recall asking one architect what he learned from his earlier buildings. 'Oh, you never go back!' he exclaimed. 'It's too discouraging'...Facilities managers have universally acid views about architects. One said, 'They design it and move on to the next one. They're paid their fee and don't want to know.'"[29] Brand encourages architects to "examine buildings as a whole—not just whole in space but whole in time....In the absence of theory or standard practice in the matter, we can begin by investigating: what happens anyway in buildings over time?...Time is the essence of the real design problem."[30] "If you think about what a building actually does as it is used through time—how it matures, how it takes the knocks, how it develops, and you realize that beauty resides in that process—then you have a different kind of architecture. What would an aesthetic based on the inevitability of transience actually look like?"[31] The real life of buildings, Brand argues, begins with occupancy: "A building 'learns' only through people learning....Loved buildings are the ones that work well, that suit the people in them, and that show their age and history... What makes a building learn is its physical connection to the people within."[32]

Brand sees the need for a new body of research on the study of buildings in time: "There is a shocking lack of data about how buildings actually behave. We simply don't have the numbers. To get beyond the anecdotal level...will take serious statistical analysis over a significant depth of time and an adventurous range of building types.... What might be learned from highly detailed longitudinal studies of buildings in use? What changes from hour to hour, day to day, week to week, month to month, year to year, and over decades? This kind of study is the norm in ecology and some of the social sciences; there's no lack of lore about how to do it."[33]

Applying Brand's reasoning to the landscape, the new-paradigm ecologist might rightly ask: How do designed landscapes behave after they are built? Do we have any longitudinal studies that document their interactions with their inhabitants, how they "learn" and adapt, are adapted to, and come to be loved? Do landscape architects want to go back and find out what happened? How would one study the evolution of some famous landscapes after they were built? Would such a temporal aesthetic, informed by the real life of landscapes, give new meaning to "ecological design?"

Perhaps the new paradigm in ecology, then, may stimulate a different dialogue between ecologists and designers around a renewed acknowledgment of temporality in landscape architecture. In one sense, all landscapes are vernacular landscapes, in that they are designed to work and to be worked by people. A working landscape (a landscape that works) is dynamic in ways that ideally express the designer's intent to create not just a spatial object but a successfully designed system of processes. Perhaps the language and literature of landscape architecture could begin to acknowledge that the learning of landscapes is as important as their creation. "A building is not something you finish, notes Brand. "A building is something you start."[34]

Notes

This chapter originally appeared in Michel Conan, ed., *Environmentalism in Landscape Architecture,* Dumbarton Oaks Colloquium Series in the History of Landscape Architecture 22 (Washington, D.C.: Dumbarton Oaks, 2000).

1_ Daniel Simberloff, "A Succession of Paradigms in Ecology: Essentialism to Materialism to Probabilism," in *Conceptual Issues in Ecology,* ed. Esa Saarinen (Boston: D. Reidel, 1982), 63–99.

2_ Robert E. Cook, "Is Landscape Preservation an Oxymoron?" *George Wright Forum* 13, no. 1 (1996): 42–53; Stuart T. A. Pickett, Victor T. Parker, and Peggy L. Fiedler, "The New Paradigm in Ecology: Implications for Conservation Biology above the Species Level," in *Conservation Biology,* ed. Peggy L. Fiedler and Subohd K. Jain (New York: Chapman Hall, 1992), 66–88.

3_ Robert E. Cook, "Clonal Growth and Reproduction in Plants," *American Scientist* 71 (1983): 244-53.

4_ Frederick E. Clements, *Research Methods in Ecology* (Lincoln, NE: University Publishing Company, 1905), 199.

5_ Robert P. McIntosh, *The Background of Ecology: Concepts and Theory* (New York: Cambridge University Press, 1988), 383 ff.

6_ Eugene P. Odum, *Fundamentals of Ecology* (Philadelphia: Saunders, 1954), 251.

7_ Ian L. McHarg, *Design with Nature* (Garden City, N.Y.: Natural History Press, 1969), 47.

8_ Simberloff, "A Succession of Paradigms," 63–99.

9_ Pickett, Parker, and Fiedler, "The New Paradigm," 66–88.

10_William S. Cooper, "The Recent Ecological History of Glacier Bay, Alaska: The Interglacial Forests of Glacier Bay," *Ecology* 4 (1923): 93–128.

11_Richard L. Crocker and John Major, "Soil Development in Relation to Vegetation and Surface Age at Glacier Bay, Alaska," *Journal of Ecology* 43 (1955): 427–448.

12_Christopher L. Fastie, "Causes and Ecosystem Consequences of Multiple Pathways of Primary Succession at Glacier Bay, Alaska," *Ecology* 76 (1995): 1899–1916. To give you a feel for the scale of Fastie's sampling plan, he set up ten 10-by-15-meter study plots at each of the ten study areas. He supplemented this with thirty-five additional plots as needed. Within each of these plots, he counted and measured all seedlings and saplings by species, and he cored every tree. He even cored any dead trees in the plots to determine the time of germination and the time of death. Each tree was cored six times, and each core was sanded smooth and its growth rings measured to within 0.02 millimeter accuracy. I estimate that Fastie carefully looked at and measured 10,000 to 12,000 tree cores.

13_Fastie, "Causes and Ecosystem Consequences," 1913.

14_David R. Foster, "Disturbance History, Community Organization, and Vegetation Dynamics of the Old-Growth Pisgah Forest, Southwestern New Hampshire, U.S.A.," *Journal of Ecology* 76 (1988): 105–134.

15_David R. Foster, et al., "Forest Response to Disturbance and Anthropogenic Stress," *BioScience* 47 (1997): 437–445.

16_Ibid., 444.

17_Anne Whiston Spirn, "The Authority of Nature: Conflict and Confusion in Landscape Architecture," in *Nature and Ideology: Natural Garden Design in the Twentieth Century*, ed. Joachim Wolschke-Bulmahn (Washington, D.C.: Dumbarton Oaks, 1997), 249–261.

18_Stuart T.A. Pickett, "Human Settlements as Ecosystems: Metropolitan Baltimore, Maryland, from 1797 to 2100," available at http://baltimore.umbc.ecu/lter/proposal.htm.

19_Louise A. Mozingo, "The Aesthetic of Ecological Design: Seeing Science as Culture," *Landscape Journal* 16 (1997): 46–59.

20_Ibid., 58.

21_Ibid., 57.

22_Andrew P. Dobson, Anthony D. Bradshaw, and Arnold J. M. Baker, "Hopes for the Future: Restoration Ecology and Conservation Biology," *Science* 277 (1997): 515–522.

23_The intellectual development of this field has been chronicled in the pages of *Restoration and Management Notes*, published at the University of Washington; see also A. Dwight Baldwin, Judith DeLuce, and Carl Pletsch, *Beyond Preservation: Restoring and Inventing Landscapes* (Minneapolis, MN: University of Minnesota Press, 1994).

24_Spirn, "The Authority of Nature," 256.

25_Elizabeth K. Meyer, "The Expanded Field of Landscape Architecture," in *Ecological Design and Planning*, ed. George F. Thompson and Frederick R. Steiner (New York: John Wiley, 1997), 52.

26_John B. Jackson, *Discovering the Vernacular Landscape* (New Haven, CN: Yale University Press, 1984), ii.

27_Laurie Olin, "Landscape Design and Nature," in *Ecological Design and Planning*, ed. George F. Thompson and Frederick R. Steiner (New York: John Wiley, 1997), 109–139.

28_Mozingo, "The Aesthetics of Ecological Design," 52.

29_Stuart Brand, *How Buildings Learn: What Happens After They're Built* (New York: Viking Penguin, 1994), 66.

30_Ibid., 2.

31_Ibid., 71.

32_Ibid., 189, 209.

33_Ibid., 213, 215.

34_Ibid., 189.

The Flora of the Future

Peter Del Tredici

The concept of ecological restoration, as developed over the past twenty years, rests on the mistaken assumption that we can somehow bring back past ecosystems by removing invasive species and replanting native species. This overly simplistic view of the world ignores two basic tenets of modern ecology—that environmental stability is an illusion, and that an unpredictable future belongs to the best adapted.[1]

Many landscape architects feel conflicted by the restoration debate, trapped between the profession's idealistic rhetoric about the innate superiority of native ecosystems and the constraints imposed by the financial and ecological realities of a particular site. Over the past 250 years, people have altered the basic trajectory of modern ecology to such an extent that going back to some earlier native condition is no longer possible and is certainly not a realistic solution to the increasingly complex environmental problems that we face.

Landscape architects—and anyone else who works directly with vegetation—need to acknowledge that a wide variety of so-called novel or emergent ecosystems are developing before our eyes. They are the product of the interacting forces of urbanization, globalization, and climate change, and are made up of organisms that have been brought together by the elimination or neutralization of barriers that had kept them separated for millions of years.[2] The concept of a novel ecosystem applies not only our cities and suburbs but also to many landscapes that have been subjected to the disturbance-intensive practices of agriculture, industry, and mining. It is unrealistic to assume that turning back the ecological clock will be any easier than turning back the economic clock that created these landscapes.[3]

Landscape architecture can be a charged discipline, especially when it has to resolve the competing interests of its human clients with those of the other organisms that seek to inhabit the same space. The dichotomies that separate people from nature, and native from non-native species, present problematic contradictions that landscape architects must resolve if they hope to have a lasting impact on the environments they design. All of which brings me to the main purpose of this essay: to articulate an ecologically oriented vision for human-dominated landscapes that does not define them as intrinsically negative, valueless, or alien.

The range map from my book *Wild Urban Plants* covers much of the northeast United States and eastern Canada, from Detroit in the west to Montreal in the north, Boston in the east and Washington, D.C., in the south.[4] This is an intensively urbanized area, whether defined by the density of human population (500 to 1,000 people per square mile) or by the percentage of impervious surface. From a plant's perspective, the latter matters more than the former. Recent research by geographers at Boston University has shown that in the greater Boston area, most of the land inside the Interstate 95 beltway (along a westward transect) has an impervious surface coverage greater than 30 percent.[5] This figure is significant because it provides a convenient and easily measurable definition of urbanization from the biological perspective.

The preponderance of buildings and pavement in cities not only reduces the amount of land available for plants and animals but also has a profound effect on hydrology by decreasing water infiltration, increasing runoff, and compacting adjacent soil.[6] More than one study has shown that for urbanized riparian habitats, the number of native species relative to non-natives declines in direct proportion to the amount and proximity of impervious surfaces.[7]

From the ecological perspective, cities display a suite of distinctive environmental characteristics, the most significant of which is the ongoing physical disturbance and fragmentation associated with the construction and maintenance of infrastructure. Such disturbances can drastically alter soil and drainage conditions, which in turn destabilize existing plant communities. In economically vibrant cities, a significant portion of the urban infrastructure fabric is always in the process of being torn up and rebuilt, which tends to create a shifting mosaic of opportunistic plant associations dominated by disturbance-adapted, early-successional species. In economically depressed cities, where portions of the urban core have been abandoned for relatively long periods of time, plant succession has been allowed to proceed without interference (i.e., maintenance), and stable plant associations of woody plants (forests) have developed. Casual observations in a number of cities suggest that the amount and maturity of spontaneous vegetation that they contain is inversely proportional to their economic prosperity.[8]

A functional wetland dominated by common reed (*Phragmites australis*) has developed in this abandoned factory loading dock in Detroit.

In many ways, urbanization is analogous to the geological process of glaciation—a force that levels everything in its wake and then retreats, leaving behind a substrate of compacted glacial till. From the ecological perspective, a freshly bulldozed urban site exists in a state of primary succession where the biota has to develop from scratch. In contrast, sites undergoing secondary succession contain plants or seeds that sprout back following disturbance.

The urban glacier leaves compacted glacial till in its wake.

Another characteristic of urban environments is their high temperatures relative to the surrounding non-urbanized land. This phenomenon is referred to as the "urban heat island" effect and is a function of the abundance of concrete buildings and asphalt paving. Because such structures absorb and retain heat—to say nothing of the cars, air conditioners, heating units, and electrical equipment that generate heat—the annual mean temperatures of large urban areas can be up to 5° F (3° C) higher than the surrounding non-urban areas, and in extreme cases the temperature difference between the city and the countryside can be as much as 21° F (12° C).[9] One particularly interesting implication of the urban heat island effect is that cities offer us a preview of coming attractions when it comes to climate change. Essentially cities have already warmed up to the extent that the rest of the countryside is predicted to reach over the next twenty to thirty years, and thus they present valuable opportunities to study how climate change will play out in the future.

Soil quality is another important issue facing plants that grow in the urban environment. In some cases, pockets of native soil will support a remnant native ecosystem, but large areas of non-native soil have often been brought in as fill from outside the area. In some cases it is construction rubble, and in others reasonably good soil that has been brought in from adjacent agricultural land. Urban soil quality is thus highly variable and dependent on the history of the site. One of the more serious problems associated with urban soils is the high level of compaction produced by heavy foot or vehicular traffic, or use of heavy equipment. On most construction sites where topsoil has been removed and stockpiled, the underlying subsoil is compacted to a density approaching that of concrete, precluding the growth of all but the toughest plants. Another common problem is the presence of toxic chemicals such as heavy metals, petroleum by-products, and industrial solvents—the legacy of past land uses. When severe, such contamination has the capacity to inhibit plant growth, limit vegetation succession, and damage human health.

Perhaps the most ubiquitous form of urban soil pollution is the widespread use of road salt in areas with cold winters. Sodium chloride (and to a lesser extent calcium chloride) can have a number of negative impacts on both soil and vegetation, including the degradation of soil aggregates, the increase in the osmotic potential of soil (making it harder for plants to get water), and the alteration of basic soil chemistry by elevating its pH.[10] The abundant use of

road salt along our highways selectively favors the growth of plants adapted to alkaline soil conditions—such as mugwort (*Artemesia vulgaris*) and tree-of-heaven (*Ailanthus altissima*). Mugwort is a common inhabitant of vacant lots throughout the northeast United States, especially those that have been mulched with limestone-rich construction rubble.

Taxonomy of Urban Landscapes

Urban landscapes can be divided into three broad categories based on their soils, their land-use history, the vegetation they support and, by extension, their maintenance requirements.[11] The first type is the remnant native landscape that consists primarily of native plants growing in relatively undisturbed native soils. Given a consistent level of maintenance, they can be preserved as features within the urban context; without maintenance, they are often overwhelmed by non-native species. Second are the managed, functional landscapes, including gardens, parks, ball fields, cemeteries, etc. These are dominated by cultivated plants, with rich manufactured soils, and they have medium-to-high maintenance requirements. And finally there are the ruderal or abandoned landscapes—the least studied of the three types and the focus of the remainder of this essay. These consist of post-industrial or post-residential vacant land, and infrastructure edges dominated by spontaneous vegetation, either native or introduced, on

Mugwort (*Artemesia vulgaris*) growing along a salted street in Watertown, Massachusetts.

relatively poor and often compacted soils. They have extremely low maintenance requirements—so low in fact that they can be considered self-sustaining.

One important research question concerning ruderal landscapes is how much land in any given city does spontaneous vegetation occupy? With the help of my Harvard Graduate School of Design students using GIS technology, we calculated that roughly 9.5 percent of the surface area of Somerville, Massachusetts (one of the most densely populated cities in the state) is dominated by spontaneous vegetation. This is land that no one maintains, and it exceeds the land area occupied by maintained parks.

In Detroit, roughly 40 percent of the total land area has been abandoned —a remarkable figure, equivalent to the total area of the city of Boston. Some of this land consists of abandoned buildings, but about half can be classified as open space. While Detroit is clearly a tragic story from the socioeconomic perspective, it is a paradise for spontaneous vegetation. In a typical residential Detroit neighborhood, not more than a mile from downtown, perhaps only one in five or ten houses are left standing, while the others have been torn down and hauled away. The remaining compacted subsoil may or may not have fresh topsoil and grass seed spread on top of it. Orchard grass (*Dactylis glomerata*) and a variety of other European grasses quickly get established and create a remarkably pastoral-feeling landscape. In areas where this grass is not mowed, trees, shrubs, and vines move in and, given enough time, develop into forests.

An orchard grass (*Dactylis glomerata*) meadow in Detroit.

The plants that grow spontaneously in urban areas—whether native or non-native—are performing important ecological functions. Ecologists refer to these functions as environmental services and they include: excess nutrient absorption in wetlands, heat reduction in paved areas, erosion control, soil and air pollution tolerance and remediation, food and habitat for wildlife, and food and medicine for people (even if we don't use it).[12]

Near the Vince Lombardi exit on the New Jersey Turnpike, for example, one can't miss noticing the extensive stands of common reed (*Phragmites australis*). The plant is a European ecotype of the species, and conservationists tend to consider it highly invasive. But the New Jersey Meadowlands is a landscape of landfills—more than 500 of them occupy the area. From a functional perspective, *Phragmites* is helping to clean up the Meadowlands by absorbing abundant excess nitrogen and phosphorous throughout this highly contaminated site. Nevertheless, some people talk about restoring the native vegetation of the New Jersey Meadowlands, and to them I say: It's really not that hard—just remove the New Jersey Turnpike and reestablish the tidal flow of water, and the *Phragmites* will disappear. The plant is an indicator of impeded drainage and as such, is a symptom of environmental degradation, not its cause.

All plants, regardless of where they originate, can play an important role in stabilizing streams and riverbanks. Along many urban rivers in the northeast, leadwort (*Amorpha fruticosa*) was widely planted at the turn of the last century to control erosion. Land managers appreciate this midwestern native because it can be cut down to the ground in fall and will sprout back up in spring, never getting tall enough to obstruct views of the river. It's a socially and ecologically functional plant throughout New England despite the fact that it's not native to the region.

Common reed (*Phragmites australis*) dominates the Meadowlands along the New Jersey Turnpike.

Leadwort (*Amorpha fruticosa*) along the Hudson River north of New York City.

The seaside rose (*Rosa rugosa*) is another plant that people often assume is a native species. It was introduced from northeast Asia and now grows spontaneously just above the high-tide line all along the New England coast. It's easy to recognize because of its beautiful pink flowers and large, edible rose hips, and it plays an important role in stabilizing coastal sand dunes. When I served on the Massachusetts Invasive Species Council, we decided not to list this species as invasive because it wasn't displacing any native woody species in the specialized niche where it typically grows.

A counterexample is the autumn olive (*Elaeagnus umbellata*), which was planted extensively along interstate highway banks in the 1970s and 1980s. It fixes atmospheric nitrogen with the help of symbiotic bacteria that live in its roots, and it produces large quantities of bright red, edible fruit. Twenty years later, the plant has been reclassified as an invasive species—a perfect example of a plant that did its job too well and has spread beyond its planting sites with the help of migratory birds (both native and non-native). It's easy to forget that many of the woody plants now listed as invasive were once considered valued ornamentals and planted by the millions with the encouragement of various state and federal agencies. The spread of these species across the landscape is as much a sociological as a biological problem, and we ignore this fact at our peril.[13]

New Infrastructural Taxonomies

The plants that appear spontaneously in urban ecosystems are remarkable for their ability to grow under extremely harsh conditions—most notably in soils that are relatively infertile, dry, unshaded, and alkaline.[14] Through a quirk of evolutionary fate, many of these plants have evolved life-history traits in their native habitats that have "preadapted" them to flourish in cities. Stone or brick buildings, for example, are analogous to naturally occurring limestone cliffs.[15] Similarly, the increased use of de-icing salts along walkways and highways has resulted in the development of high pH

Princess tree (*Paulownia tomentosa*) colonizing an abandoned building in New London, Connecticut.

microhabitats that are often colonized by either grassland species adapted to limestone soils or salt-loving plants from coastal habitats. Preadaptation is a useful idea for understanding the emergent ecology of cities because it helps explain the patterns of distribution of plants growing in a variety of distinctive urban habitats, including the following:

_____The **chain-link fence** is one of the more specialized habitats of the urban environment. They provide plants—especially vines—with a convenient trellis to spread out on and a measure of protection from the predation of maintenance crews. Chain-link fences also provide "safe sites" for the germination of seeds, a manifestation of which are the straight lines of spontaneous urban trees that one commonly finds in cities, long after the fence that protected the trees is gone. Root suckering species such as *Ailanthus* grow particularly well along chain-link fence lines.

Two "bonsaied" American elms (*Ulmus americana*) are well adjusted to their chain-link fence habitat in Hartford, Connecticut.

Tree-of-heaven (*Ailanthus altissima*) root sprouts growing along a fence line in Boston.

_____**Vacant lots** that have been cleared of buildings are often mulched with masonry and construction rubble. Their soils typically have high pH levels, and they are usually colonized by a suite of plants that I like to refer to as a "cosmopolitan urban meadow." Many of these plants, including mugwort (*Artemesia vulgaris*) and curly dock (*Rumex crispus*), are common in the dry, alkaline grasslands of Europe.

A typical urban meadow dominated by mugwort (*Artemesia vulgaris*) and curly dock (*Rumex crispus*).

_____The highway **median strip** is typically only a few feet wide, with minimal topsoil above a compacted subsoil layer. Initially these areas may have been planted with lawn grasses, but they usually end up dominated by crabgrass (*Digitaria* spp.). As most homeowners know, crabgrass comes up in lawns in late spring, when temperatures consistently get above 70 or 80 degrees. It's a warm-season grass that thrives when it's hot and dry, and because it is an annual species, the road salt used in winter has no effect on its development. In short, the median strip is perfect for crabgrass.

Crabgrass (*Digitaria* spp.) in the median strip.

_____**Stone walls** and masonry building façades provide great habitats for plants—especially when their maintenance has been neglected. From the plant's perspective, these structures are good stand-ins for a limestone cliff, and many cliff species are well adapted to growing on city walls.[16]

_____**Pavement cracks** are among the most distinctive niches in the urban environment. Wherever you have two types of paving material coming together, you have a seam, and the different materials expand differentially in response to summer and winter temperature to create a crack. We tend to think of pavement cracks as stressful habitats, but in fact, as the water sheets off the pavement, it flows right into the crack, making it a rich site in terms of its ability to accumulate moisture and nutrients. With oil from cars as a carbohydrate source available for decomposition by fungi and bacteria, cracks can develop significant microbial diversity.

Ailanthus altissima on the Great Wall in China (left) and on a lesser wall in Boston (right).

Grasses growing in pavement cracks in Boston.

_____**Specialized microclimates** are as important in cities as they are in natural environments. As an example, carpetweed (*Mollugo verticillata*), a summer annual from Central America, subsists only on air-conditioner drip. Its seeds germinate under a window air-conditioning unit when it is turned on in early summer, and it dries up and sets seed when the unit is turned off in September. Many annuals common in cities display similar capacities to exploit ephemeral urban niches.

_____**River corridors**, annually disturbed by fluctuating levels of water during the course of the year, are typically dominated by spontaneous vegetation with broad environmental adaptability. They serve as important pathways for the migration of both plants and animals into and out of the city. The same is true for **railway corridors**. At the Arnold Arboretum in Boston, where I have worked since 1979, coyote, deer, fox, and pheasant are commonly sighted, often coming up from the suburban south following the railroad line that borders the eastern edge of the property.

Cultural Significance_____

Any discussion of urban ecology would be incomplete without a consideration of the cultural significance of the plants that grow in cities. This is an important topic because it explains not only why certain plants were brought here but why so many have spread so rapidly. Most people treat the invasive plant issue as a biological problem, but the introduction and distribution of most of these plants was the result of deliberate decisions by people that reflected specific goals relating to economic, ornamental, or conservation values of the day.[17]
If we fail to take into account their historical associations with people, we can't fully understand their present ecological spread. To put it another way, the invasive species issue is as much a cultural as an ecological problem. Stories to illustrate this point are legion, but I have selected a few examples:

Carpetweed (*Mollugo verticillata*) subsisting on air-conditioner drip in Boston.

_____Purslane (*Portulaca oleracea*) is an annual plant of uncertain origin that grows everywhere—in the tropics as well as the temperate zone—and everywhere it grows, people eat it. Specifically, people use the foliage, which is a little mucilaginous, for thickening soups; and because of its high omega-3 oil content, it's very nutritious. Obviously this is a plant that was originally brought here for culinary purposes and has managed to escape and spread on its own.

_____Japanese knotweed (*Polygonum cuspidatum*) was introduced into Europe from Asia in the 1860s as an ornamental plant. It spread across the Atlantic to the United States around 1880 and was widely planted for its dramatic presence in the landscape and because it grew well in poor soil. But by the 1920s it was widely considered a weed, and in the 1990s it was reclassified as an invasive species. Despite its checkered history, the plant is cultivated in Asia as the commercial source of resveratrol, the compound in red wine that is thought to promote longevity in humans.

Purslane (*Portulaca oleracea*) with its strong taproot and prostrate growth habit is preadapted to growing in sidewalk cracks and being stepped on.

Japanese knotweed (*Polygonum cuspidatum*) in flower amid a sea of pavement in Boston.

_____And finally, there's Queen Anne's lace (*Daucus carota*), which was featured in the Herbal written by Dioscorides some 2,000 years ago. He noted that when ingested, a decoction of the seeds can have birth-control effects—an organic morning-after pill, if you will. Indeed, modern research has shown that Queen Anne's lace is biologically active and can affect a woman's menstrual cycle. With the invention of the printing press, knowledge of this particular use of the plant was deleted from Dioscorides' Herbal as well as from our culture. Recent research by John Riddle of the University of North Carolina, however, has shown that the information was not lost but merely hiding underground.[18] He discovered that in the 1970s, women in Appalachia learned of this traditional European use of Queen Anne's lace from their mothers, who had learned about it from their mothers, going back to their immigration from Europe.

Changes in urban vegetation over time clearly reflect constantly shifting human value judgments, socioeconomic cycles, and evolving technological advances in transportation, communication, and construction.[19]

Ecology of Aesthetics

Aesthetic issues associated with spontaneous urban vegetation are particularly problematic because such standards are subjective and culturally determined. What looks unkempt to one person can look natural and robust to another. Aesthetics are also context dependent: a plant growing in a vacant lot in Boston is considered a weed, while the same plant growing in a meadow in the countryside is deemed a wildflower. This relativity becomes most apparent when discussing the merits of native versus non-native species. Many of the plants we vilify as unsightly weeds in urban areas of North America are considered dry-meadow natives in their European homelands.

Queen Anne's Lace (*Daucus carota*) and chicory (*Cichorium intybus*) make a stunning combination along roadsides in July and August.

Many spontaneous urban plants (e.g., mugwort) can grow quite tall and become unsightly as they mature. Such plants are typically interpreted by inner-city residents as indicators of dereliction and neglect as well as havens for vermin. This image problem is exemplified by the fact that most people refer to spontaneous vegetation as "weeds"—a term with no biological meaning. "Weed" is simply a word used to describe a plant that a person does not like or does not want in the yard. It is a value judgment that reflects personal preferences. Remarkably, there seems to be no Latin word for an unwanted plant, and in many languages "bad plant" (e.g., *mala hierba* in Spanish) is the only available term.

To counteract this stereotype, I suggest the term "cosmopolitan urban vegetation" as a way of celebrating urban botanical diversity, in much the same way that we celebrate the diversity of the human population. I like to promote the concept of the cosmopolitan urban meadow, which consists of a selection of herbaceous species—both native and non-native—that will flourish in compacted urban soils with minimal maintenance and look good for most of the growing season. By selecting plants that are long lived, that don't get to be too tall, and produce showy flowers, one has a potential strategy for dealing with vacant urban land.[20] It doesn't take a lot of resources to establish such a meadow from seed (the soil should be on the lean side) or to maintain it with one or two mowings per year. Once established, the meadow will hold the ground until another use for the land is implemented.

The beach on Fisher's Island off the coast of Connecticut—not a native plant anywhere.

Working with spontaneous vegetation does not have to be an "all or nothing" proposition. There are some plants that should, if possible, be deleted from the landscape, including toxic native species such as poison ivy (*Toxicodendron radicans*) and ragweed (*Ambrosia artemesifolia*). Vines, in general, are problematic because they aggressively climb up trees, overwhelm them with foliage, and pull them down. In extreme cases, high-climbing vines can flatten whole forests, creating what is politely referred to as a vinescape. The exotic Asian bittersweet (*Celastrus orbiculatus*), porcelain berry (*Ampelopsis brevidunculata*), and the Asian wisterias (*Wistaria* spp.) are especially problematic, as are our native grapevines (*Vitis* spp.).

With spontaneous woody vegetation, the *modus operandi* should be one of management—design by removal of the unwanted rather than insertion of the wanted. The name for this process is "intaglio," from the engraving process, where one creates an image by removing unwanted material.[21] The black locust trees (*Robinia pseudoacacia*) shown here are a beautiful feature because somebody had the sense to leave them alone except to remove the vines that would otherwise have strangled and knocked them down. Learning how to manage vegetation with sensitivity requires a fair amount of experience and skill; it is a promising niche for young, enterprising horticulturists.

Monet with weeds in Detroit: chicory (*Cichorium intybus*), yellow sweet clover (*Melilotus officinalis*), and spotted knapweed (*Centauria biebersteinii*).

Porcelain berry (*Ampelopsis brevipedunculata*) vinescape along the Saw Mill River Parkway north of New York City.

The current leaders in this field are the Germans, and the famous Landschaftspark in Duisburg-Nord is perhaps the best example. In this park designed by Peter Latz, an abandoned steel mill is embedded in a landscape that combines spontaneous vegetation with designed gardens. In Berlin, the Natur-Park Südegelände was established on the site of an abandoned rail yard that had been colonized by spontaneous vegetation following the construction of the Berlin Wall.[22] It's a remarkable landscape with an eclectic mix of native and non-native plants that support a remarkable array of invertebrates.

The Germans have a lot to teach us about the appreciation and uses of spontaneous vegetation in the urban landscape, but their approach needs to be modified to fit the conditions—both economic and sociological—of American cities.

The task facing tomorrow's landscape architects is not so much how to eliminate these novel ecosystems but rather how to manage them to increase their ecological, social, and aesthetic values.[23]

This mature stand of black locust (*Robinia pseudoacacia*) has been enhanced through the process of intaglio, or the creation of a landscape by the judicious removal of unwanted plants.

European birch (*Betula pendula*) growing amid abandoned railroad tracks in Berlin's Natur-Park Südegelände.

Notes

1_ Daniel Botkin, *Discordant Harmonies: A New Ecology for the Twenty-first Century* (New York: Oxford University Press, 1990).

2_ Richard J. Hobbs, Eric Higgs, and James A. Harris, "Novel Ecosystems: Implications for Conservation and Restoration," *Trends in Ecology and Evolution* 24 (11, 2009): 599–605; Ingo Kowarik, "Novel Ecosystems, Biodiversity, and Conservation," *Environmental Pollution* 159 (2011): 1974–1983.

3_ Mark Davis et al., "Don't Judge Species by Their Origins," *Nature* 474 (2011): 153–214; John G. Kelcey and Norbert Muller, eds., *Plants and Habitats of European Cities* (New York: Springer, 2011).

4_ Peter Del Tredici, *Wild Urban Plants of the Northeast: A Field Guide* (Ithaca, NY: Cornell University Press, 2010).

5_ Max Brondfield et al., "Modeling and Validation of On-Road CO_2 Emissions Inventories at the Urban Regional Scale," *Environmental Pollution* 170 (2012): 113–123.

6_ Chester L. Arnold and C. James Gibbons, "Impervious Surface Coverage: The Emergence of a Key Environmental Indicator," *Journal of the American Planning Association* 62 (2, 1996): 201–217.

7_ Derric N. Pennington et al., "Urbanization and Riparian Forest Woody Communities: Diversity, Composition, and Structure within a Metropolitan Landscape," *Biological Conservation* 143 (1, 2010): 182–194; Sandrine Godefroid and Nico Koedam, "Urban Plant Species Patterns Are Highly Driven by Density and Function of Built-Up Areas," *Landscape Ecology* 22 (2007): 1227–1239.

8_ Deiter Rink, "Wilderness: The Nature of Urban Shrinkage? The Debate on Urban Restructuring and Restoration in Eastern Germany," *Nature and Culture* 4 (3, 2009): 275–292.

9_ Monika Sieghardt et al., "The Abiotic Environment: Impact of Urban Growing Conditions on Urban Vegetation," in *Urban Forests and Trees*, eds. Cecil C. Konijnendijk, Kjell Nilsson, Thomas B. Randrup, and Jasper Schipperijn (Berlin: Springer, 2005), 281–323.

10_ Ibid.

11_ Peter Del Tredici, "Spontaneous Urban Vegetation: Reflections of Change in a Globalized World," *Nature and Culture* 5 (3, 2010): 299–315; Norbert Kühn, "Intentions for the Unintentional Spontaneous Vegetation as the Basis for Innovative Planting Design in Urban Areas," *Journal of Landscape Architecture*, Autumn 2006: 46–53.

12_ Steward T.A. Pickett, et al. "Beyond Urban Legends: An Emerging Framework of Urban Ecology, as Illustrated by the Baltimore Ecosystem Study," *BioScience* 59 (2, 2008): 139 150; Per Bolund and Swen Hunhammar, "Ecosystem Services in Urban Areas," *Ecological Economics* 29 (2, 1999): 293–301.

13_ Ingo Kowarik, "Human Agency in Biological Invasions: Secondary Releases Foster Naturalization and Population Expansion of Alien Plant Species," *Biological Invasions 5* (2003): 293–312; Richard N. Mack, "Cultivation Fosters Plant Naturalization by Reducing Environmental Stochasticity, "*Biological Invasions 2* (2000): 111–122.

14_ Sonja Knapp et al., "Changes in the Functional Composition of a Central European Flora over Three Centuries," *Perspectives in Plant Ecology, Evolution, and Systematics* 12 (2010): 235–244.

15_ Peter Del Tredici, "Green Blacktop," *New Geographies* 3 (2011): 86–89.

16_ Douglas Larson, Uta Matthes, Peter E. Kelly, Jeremy Lundholm, and John Garrath, *The Urban Cliff Revolution* (Markham, Ontario: Fitzhenry and Whiteside, 2004).

17_ Philip J. Pauly, *Fruits and Plains: The Horticultural Transformation of America* (Cambridge, MA: Harvard University Press, 2008).

18_ John N. Riddle, *Contraception and Abortion from the Ancient World to the Renaissance* (Cambridge, MA: Harvard University Press, 1992).

19_ Nancy B. Grimm et al., "Global Change and the Ecology of Cities," *Science* 319 (5864, 2008): 756–760; Knapp et al., "Changes in the Functional Composition of a Central European Urban Flora over Three Centuries," 235–244.

20_ Del Tredici, *Wild Urban Plants;* Nigel Dunnett and James Hitchmough, eds., *The Dynamic Landscape: Design, Ecology and Management of Naturalistic Urban Planting* (London: Spon Press, 2004).

21_ Warren G. Kenfield, *The Wild Gardener in the Wild Landscape: The Art of Naturalistic Landscaping* (New York: Hafner, 1966).

22_ Ingo Kowarik and Andreas Langer, "Natur-Park Südgelände: Linking Conservation and Recreation in an Abandoned Railyard in Berlin," in *Wild Urban Woodlands*, eds. Ingo Kowarik and Stefan Körner (Berlin: Springer, 2005), 287–299.

23_ Peter Del Tredici, "The Role of Horticulture in a Changing World," in M. Conan and W. J. Kress, eds., *Botanical Progress, Horticultural Innovation, and Cultural Changes* (Washington, D.C.: Dumbarton Oaks, 2007), 259–264.

Flood Control Freakology:
Los Angeles River Watershed

David Fletcher

Published 2008

The Los Angeles River runs through one of the most complex urban watersheds in the world. From its headwaters in the Santa Monica and San Gabriel Mountains, it flows 51 miles through the San Fernando Valley, past downtown Los Angeles to the Pacific Ocean just east of the nation's busiest seaport. As it does so, the river channel weaves its way through thirteen municipalities and crosses over forty-seven political boundaries. Once a meshwork of meandering rivers, streams, arroyos, and washes, the river is a fully engineered flood-control system. No longer a natural aqueous phenomenon, it is now a man-made web of vascular networks, many of which channel other flows besides water: freeways, streets, bridges, railways, power lines, cell towers, as well as sewage infrastructures. Embedded within the fabric of the watershed are political structures and bureaucracies, environmental conditions, economic organizations, and cultural relations. These fluid systems are more evident in their political and social operations than physical form: rivers of energy, streams of revenue and resources, movement of goods and services.

In the 1954 film *THEM!* the city's massive storm-drain networks hosted a colony of radioactive ants. Long Hollywood's favorite local symbol of dystopia, the Los Angeles River is perceived by many residents as unnatural or nonexistent. This "narrative of loss" has dominated river discourse for the last quarter-century and is used by many to promote visions of bucolic transformations, irrespective of existing land uses and the need for flood control.

If freakish, the river is a living ecology. In spite of many voices that suggest it is an ecological disaster, it contains a vibrant mix of varied ecologies—vegetable, animal, and human. To be sure, these are not the Arcadian ideals of bucolic and pure nature. Instead, this is an infrastructural ecology, opportunistic and emergent, that lives off human excess, with many of its values and functions unknown or misunderstood. We need to develop new narratives to understand and appreciate urban watersheds and how they function: where the water flows, what flows in them, who uses, owns, and manages them, how they function, what they are connected to, and what ecologies exist within them.

Technocratic Flow

Embracing freakology rather than bucology is the key to understanding the contemporary river, its watershed, and our place within it. The Los Angeles River offers an extreme example of how an urban river becomes enmeshed in infrastructure and urbanism and generates new life. Combining nature and infrastructure while tying together—even defining—the basin, the Los Angeles River is the single most powerful space in Southern California: our Golden Gate Bridge, our Yosemite.

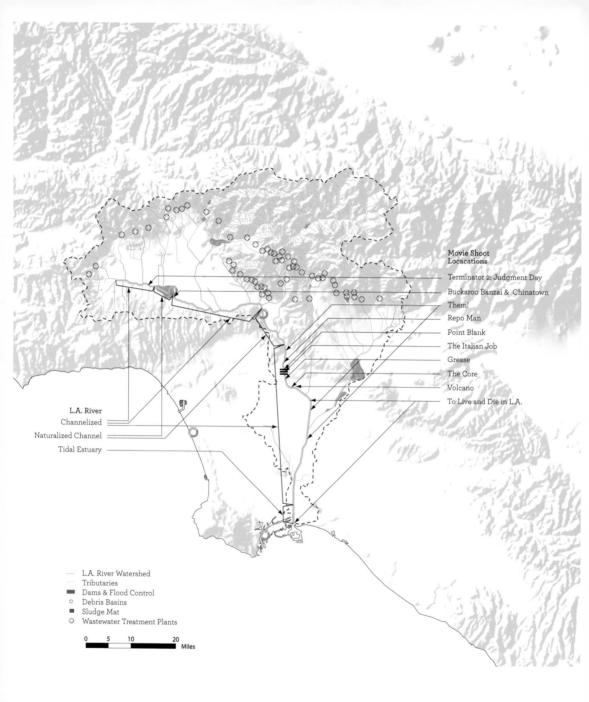

Movie Shoot
Locacations

Terminator 2: Judgment Day
Buckaroo Banzai & Chinatown
Them!
Repo Man
Point Blank
The Italian Job
Grease
The Core
Volcano
To Live and Die in L.A.

L.A. River
Channelized
Naturalized Channel
Tidal Estuary

···· L.A. River Watershed
— Tributaries
▬ Dams & Flood Control
○ Debris Basins
▤ Sludge Mat
◎ Wastewater Treatment Plants

0   5   10   20
                 Miles

Points of Interest in the Los Angeles River Watershed.

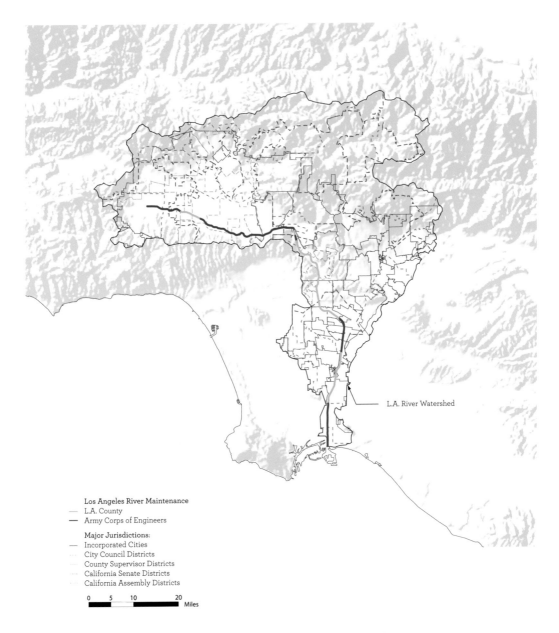

L.A. River Watershed

Los Angeles River Maintenance
— L.A. County
— Army Corps of Engineers

Major Jurisdictions:
— Incorporated Cities
— City Council Districts
— County Supervisor Districts
— California Senate Districts
— California Assembly Districts

0   5   10   20
                          Miles

Political Jurisdictions in the Los Angeles River Watershed.

Historically, as the river flooded and meandered across the floodplain, the watershed boundary constantly redefined itself. Originally, the river ran through a broad alluvial floodplain, the result of meandering dendritic flows that constantly redefined and disturbed the landscape and its ecologies. These natural disturbances produced a great diversity of habitats including riparian woodlands, coastal dunes, and freshwater and brackish wetlands. Vast forests of oak and walnut, along with dense willow thickets, dominated the riparian environment. The river would join with springs from surrounding hills to form shallow lakes, ponds, and vast marshes. Sedges, cattails, and bulrush thrived in open wetlands and sloughs. As late as 1872, a Coast Guard survey shows a continuous series of tidal estuaries, lagoons, mudflats, and salt marshes from the mouth of the Los Angeles River east to the San Gabriel River.

Today, that boundary encompasses an 834-square-mile drainage area defined not only by topography but also by wastewater and stormwater infrastructure. The river begins at the confluence of two tributaries, the Arroyo Calabasas and Bell Creek, and absorbs eleven other tributaries as it flows to the Pacific Ocean at Queensway Bay in Long Beach. As reconstructed by the United States Army Corps of Engineers, the County Flood Control District, and the Works Progress Administration, the river and its tributaries are largely channelized and lined with concrete. The resulting landscape is an exercise in the oblique, composed of graceful patterns of flumes—vertical, trapezoidal, and transitional structures—that craze throughout the basin. This technocratic flood-control system was designed to serve a projected population of 3 million; today, Los Angeles's population is 10.4 million and expected to increase 15 percent by 2020.

The present-day river functions mainly as a flood-control system consisting of tributary debris basins that capture sediment from the mountains, dams and reservoirs that regulate and detain water, and a concrete riverbed engineered to conduct water to the ocean as quickly as possible. Urbanization, oil extraction, port activities, agriculture, coastal development and channelization have virtually eliminated the historic ecologies. Overall, this has resulted in the loss of all of the original riparian habitats, the dry arroyos, and 98 percent of the lakes and ponds.[1]

The river itself has ceased to exist as a single entity. Rather it is a jurisdictional matrix of boundaries, rights-of-way, easements, and liabilities. More even than a physical thing, it is a zone comprised of an invisible pattern of ownership and maintenance jurisdictions, railroad lands, and utility easements. Through its many reaches, the river channel is a shattered mosaic of public and private ownerships, with parcels going into and through the channel. Often these federal, state, county, city, and private territories overlap, as air rights, water rights, and mineral rights are superimposed on rights to movement, maintenance, and law enforcement. No single agency controls the river: the City of Los Angeles owns the water that flows within the city boundary, the Water Master manages groundwater, the County of Los Angeles Department of Public Works maintains the channel for flood safety, and the Army Corps of Engineers ensures the structural integrity and capacity of the channel to "effectively convey flows." Together, the Corps and the County are responsible for maintenance and operations in the channel right-of-way. Finally, the State of California certifies that the water meets the requirements of the Clean Water Act. Standing under a bridge, in the river, you might be on private property, in city-owned water, in a channel built and maintained by the federal government within a county easement, and in the air rights of the California Department of Transportation. Railways and utility easements will flow on either side of you, conducting goods from the port and power to adjacent municipalities.

The river is also a place of illicit boundaries, with gang territories crisscrossing its pathways and spaces, and human encampments within storm drains and under bridges. Bisecting the Los Angeles basin, it serves to define the "other side of the tracks."

In the unurbanized past, the river did not exist in the summers. Its flow was seasonal, dry in the summer and flooded during winter storms, but now effluent and urban runoff allow it to flow more consistently, year round. Such extremes inspired settlers to view the river as a violent flood machine, something to be restrained.[2] Today, there is no distinct seasonal change in flows. With increased irrigation, the summer flows increase while winter rains still occasionally result in flash floods. Throughout any given year, Los Angeles averages 15.4 inches of rainfall, but more than 85 percent of the total precipitation occurs through high-intensity storms between January and March.[3] River flows can rise and fall rapidly during storms, reaching flow levels of 36 billion gallons per day. Within a five-hour period, the water level in the channel can rise from 3 inches to 25 feet. Because of the great volume of water entering the system, adjacent urban areas would flood every time it rained, if not for the coordinated choreography of stormwater control. During storm events, Corps and County dam commanders are in constant communication to coordinate their responses to specific storm event and downstream conditions, releasing water before their individual flood basins overflow. Storm events result in a massive flow of not only water but also debris in the riverbed. While the County is mobilized to remove debris from the channel, the Los Angeles City Fire Department's Swift Water Rescue Teams remove people.

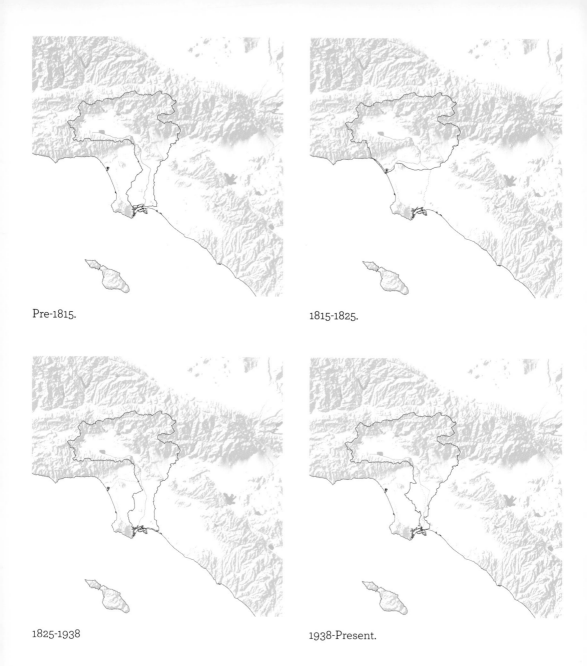

Pre-1815.

1815-1825.

1825-1938

1938-Present.

Historical Extent of the Los Angeles River Watershed.

Between rain events, flows are considerably lower, between 64 and 99 million gallons per day (mgd). Over the past seventy years, urbanization, channelization, and discharge within the watershed dramatically altered flow conditions. The river's present baseline water flow of 88 mgd, equating to a depth of 4 inches, is a relatively new phenomenon, the product of increased urbanization, water use, and water waste. From the 1930s to the late 1970s, when municipal sewage treatment plants began discharging into the river, the average flow was 10 mgd. Today, flow in the river is dictated by the amount of wastewater discharged from the Tillman, Burbank, and Los Angeles/Glendale sewage treatment plants, which contribute 55 mgd collectively. The next greatest quantity is the 30 mgd of dry-weather urban runoff introduced through over 2,200 storm-drain outlets collecting water from excess irrigation, car washing, as well as sidewalk and street cleaning. The remaining flow is 3 mgd of upwelling groundwater, which is contaminated in many areas. With new sewage discharges, the average daily flow increased 25 mgd during the early 1980s. In the sense that the river has more continually running water than it has had in its post-colonial history, it is by many definitions more a "river" today than it ever was.[4]

Freakology

The government considers the river and most of its tributaries to be "impaired water bodies." Development, over the past century, along with the use of fertilizers, pesticides, and household chemicals, has resulted in the degradation of surface and ground water within the region. The most recent report lists trash, fecal coliform bacteria, lead, ammonia, scum, pesticides, fertilizer, and last but not least, odors as key factors impacting the river.[5]

The most significant visual blight on the river is the omnipresent urban trash from illegal dumping, wind deposition, and malicious action. Stolen or junk cars are driven into the riverbed, shopping carts are rolled off bridges, and pit bulls that have lost fights are dumped into the channels. Many recent investigators are astounded by the amount of trash in the river, but also mention its unlikely role in creating riparian structure.[6] After winter storms, thousands of multicolored bags—known as "Los Angeles moss"—hang from trees, often as high as 30 feet in the air. Bedframes and automobile fenders can be seen stacked and wedged in trees and wrapped around bridge supports. Shopping carts are remarkably common; one study counted twenty-five within a 60-foot-diameter circle.[7] The remaining trash is a mix of clothing, paper, and spray cans from the multitude of "graffiti universities" that exist under bridges.

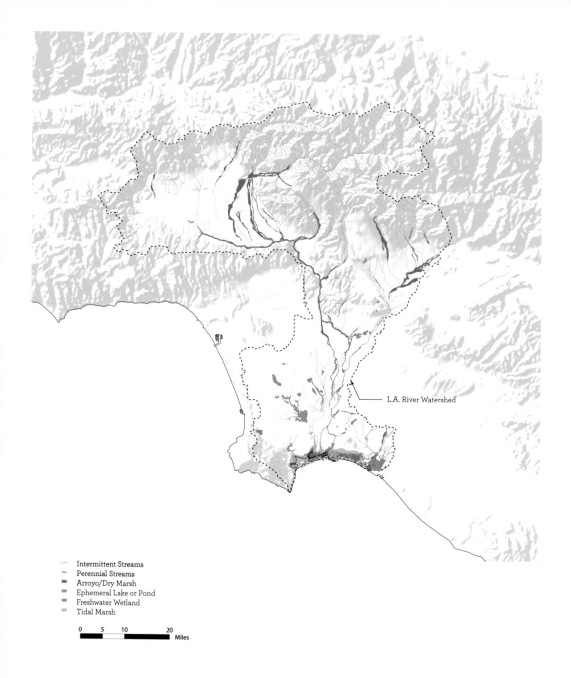

L.A. River Watershed

··· Intermittent Streams
—   Perennial Streams
▬   Arroyo/Dry Marsh
▬   Ephemeral Lake or Pond
▬   Freshwater Wetland
▬   Tidal Marsh

0   5   10   20
                          Miles

Historic Features of the Los Angeles River Watershed, 1994.

Every year, the river is purged at the ocean's expense, as winter storms wash out the manmade debris and all but the largest stones in the riverbed, eliminating most of the fine sediments vital to life such as silts and organic materials. Recent studies suggest that, although trash obviously has its own set of hazards for ecology, it has become a vital component to the riparian ecosystems; loose debris gets incorporated into the vegetative community, binding and forming a structural substrate that holds organic nutrients and silts.[8]

Some of the most vigorous stands of new vegetation have been observed growing through and around dense stands of inorganic trash and debris.

The river has many elaborate and well-furnished human encampments, which have become established in the channel storm drains, riverbeds, and under bridges and freeways. The inhabitants harvest aluminum and plastics daily from its flows and redeem them for cash at local recycling centers. On any given day, individuals and groups, some of whom have made the river a home, may be seen washing and socializing in the low-flow channel. Fires can be seen in the channel at night, with smoke emanating from well-furnished storm-drain apartments.

The present river ecology is a churning soup of exotic and native vegetative communities that have been introduced since the nineteenth century, some by design, others by accident. Tourism, shipping, rail, industry, agriculture, and ornamental vegetation have brought humans, animals, insects, and seeds from around the globe to colonize the river's naturalized reaches. These reaches have established a curious equilibrium with their ecologies, depending on nutrient-rich flows from sewage treatment and urban runoff.[9] Most (82 percent) of the river is lined with concrete channels, with the remainder divided among five "naturalized" reaches. Three of the naturalized reaches are termed "soft-bottom," because strong groundwater pressure and tidal activity made them impossible to line with concrete. The Sepulveda Basin, the Glendale Narrows, and the Willow Street tidal estuary are all ecologies rooted in soft sediment, cobbles, and boulders. With their riparian willow woodlands and wetland habitats of bulrush and cattails, these reaches appear to be the healthiest of the river's habitats. Such ecologies provide for a variety of native and endangered species, including Swainson's thrushes, night herons, ospreys, wood ducks, and many reptile and amphibian species, otherwise rare or nonexistent in the lower reaches.[10] They also serve as conduits for many mammals, including deer and coyotes that use the channels to connect to ecological patches and habitats across the basin. Many of the river's bridges house bat colonies and swallow nests. These species are critical to urban disease vector control, feeding on the mosquito populations that emerge from pools and standing water.

These reaches have also become habitat for thriving parrot colonies, ragtag teams of birds that escaped private homes as well as from the old Busch Gardens amusement park, closed in the early 1980s. Vegetated islands emerge throughout these channel segments, composed of a ruderal mixture of agricultural and ornamental landscape plants with origins in all of the world's continents, except Antarctica. These islands are populated with tree-of-heaven from China, eucalyptus from Australia, the castor bean plant from Ethiopia, the ubiquitous Mexican fan palm, passion flower vine from Brazil, and the extremely aggressive giant reed from Nepal, the latter growing to 30 feet at a rate of 3 feet per week.[11] New invasive species and biomass are constantly introduced to the river through wind and through storm drains. The County regularly clears vegetation from the channel to maintain flood capacity, which is considered to be at 50 percent in most of the naturalized reaches, due to the maturity of existing stands.

The Willow Street tidal estuary runs 2 miles from Willow Street to the river mouth, at Long Beach. Here, the banks are covered with rock riprap, and the area absorbs significant sediment deposit from upstream zones.[12] Most of the sediment load is dropped at the river mouth or beyond, at Queensway Bay. As a result, the port must be dredged annually to maintain navigability. Tidally influenced, this zone supports a great diversity of estuarine invertebrates such as barnacles, mussels, annelid worms, and small crustaceans. These ecologies are not federally protected, yet have a powerful and vocal constituency among the many naturalists and birders, who visit and study them regularly.

The Lower Los Angeles River, which runs 6 miles to the tidal estuary zone, is perhaps one of the most interesting ecologies. In this reach, the increased nutrient-rich waters spill out of the low-flow channel, a 1-foot-deep by 20-feet-wide channel running through most of the river. This channel was originally designed to concentrate and conduct silt-laden water out to sea and to allow steelhead trout up the river to spawn. But the original design did not anticipate the increased flows from the sewage treatment plants. This effluent-enriched water spreads out across the concrete sills, forming a thriving and vast algal zone, the "Sludge Mat." Invertebrates have extensively colonized this zone, creating the most biologically productive stopover for migrating shorebirds in Southern California. It has the largest concentration of black-necked stilts in the United States.[13]

As an artificial ecology, the Los Angeles River is by no means unique in the Golden State. Large-scale artificial ecologies have replaced many of the historic ecologies in Southern California. One example is the Salton Sea, an enormous brackish lake in the Imperial Valley resulting from the failure of a water canal. Serving as a waste sump for adjacent agriculture and unprotected by environmental regulations, the Salton

Sea is nevertheless the second most biologically productive body of water in the state. These infrastructural ecologies are systems in uneasy equilibrium, and their uncertain futures depend on water supply, policy, and demand. Called the "Salton Stink" by local residents, this water body has become undesirable for recreation and development. It is this relative isolation, born of "undesirability," that strengthens its ecological viability. It should be noted that all of the water on which these riparian freakologies depend is imported at great expense to the environmental health of watersheds across the West. The diversion of water to the Salton Sea has resulted in ecological devastation at the former outlet in Baja California. Despite the very real regional consequences of such accidental ecologies, and their negative perceptions, we need to come to terms with their benefits, so that they may be better understood, protected, and enhanced.

The widespread perception that native is good and exotic is bad has a corollary in the river itself, whereby the engineered solution is perceived as an eyesore and a travesty. The waterway has many names, each revealing an ideological stance: to engineers it is "the invert," to managers a "storm channel," to politicians and activists it is simply "the river."

Succession

The naive desire to return the river to a "natural" state amid an asphalt metropolis is, in fact, a threat to the urban ecologies that have emerged in response to the river's modifications. Recent guidelines call for the total removal of exotic species and the planting of vegetation that was historically native to the watershed. But this narrow agenda does not take into account the many thriving species, native or otherwise, that are now dependent on the existing condition and the exotic species that occupy it. Many of these infrastructural freakologies serve as green infrastructures, cleansing and processing excess nutrients, controlling erosion, and providing habitat that survives independent of human agency. Certainly many invasive species are damaging and should be removed, but a blanket eugenic response fails to respect how non-native landscapes perform significant ecological functions. Nor is eradication safe: exotic plant eradication is presently performed by volunteer groups using herbicides of various types or by government agencies with bulldozers. The proposals that call for eradication assume that native vegetation will return to dominance, restoring the balance of nature.[14] Yet often, new invaders replace the old ones, or the offending plants simply return. Moreover, because soil and hydrologic conditions have so radically changed, native vegetation would require careful maintenance to survive.

Central to understanding the river's ecology is the concept of ecological succession, the changes due to the disturbance of animal and plant communities over time. Recent approaches to ecology put forth the theory that "natural" disturbances—fire, flood, tornado, earthquake—are integral to ecological processes. Stability in nature is an illusion; moreover, non-natural factors such as urbanization, global warming, and the heat-island effect all have to be included in the ecological equation.[15] Thus the native-versus-exotic debate is oversimplified: the landscape assemblages should not be mistaken as the cause of environmental degradation, when they are actually an ecologically appropriate result.

Nor can we imagine that the river will stay in its current form. The future of the river and its infrastructural ecologies depends on water availability and flood-control policy.

With prolonged drought conditions and growing pressure on water supplies in the American West, Los Angeles will have to become more self-reliant, turning to conservation and grey water reuse as major sources of water savings. Los Angeles uses more fresh water than any other American city. But the way that water is used is unusual: 22 percent is for non-agricultural irrigation and only 2 percent is for human consumption.[16]

Both the city and county have plans for greater wastewater reuse, water recycling, and groundwater infiltration on an urban scale.[17] As water becomes more expensive, wastewater storage and reuse will also be a lucrative source of income for the city's Department of Water and Power (LADWP). As the city grows rapidly over the next decades—primarily through sprawl and infill densification—and as wastewater is reappropriated for that growth, the city forecasts that the amount of water reaching the river will drastically decrease. Decreased water supplies due to climate change and increasing water demand for recycled water means that soon there will not be enough water to sustain the river's ecologies and landscapes.

To put the problem in perspective, a LADWP study recently determined that merely topping off its two river-adjacent artificial lakes—Balboa and Wildlife Lakes—and irrigating its Japanese gardens alone requires 27 mgd, while the amount of water needed to maintain all of the currently existing effluent-dependent ecologies along the river is approximately 35 mgd.[18] Studies suggest that the reduction in water supply will concentrate pollutants and salts in the river, resulting in the degradation of freshwater habitats, while marine species downstream will thrive, thereby extending their habitats up the river.[19]

The LADWP recently funded a team of engineers and landscape architects to produce the Los Angeles River Revitalization Master Plan.[20] This study proposes to extensively retrofit the existing channel with new multi-objective parks, open-space networks, habitat enhancements, channel modifications, as well as constructed scenarios for urban and economic responses. The plan promotes a vision of the river as a ligamentous void, a 221-mile connective system of channels, offering an unparalleled alternative transportation and wildlife corridor network, linking commuters and connecting ecological patches throughout the basin. Yet many of the channel modification scenarios and major transformations are predicated on wholesale changes in the way the city deals with water. Realization of much of the plan depends on watershed management, property acquisition, transformation of existing detention basins, and the establishment of new water detention infrastructures on a gigantic scale. The study also recommends an integrative governance structure, combining the forces of the Corps, the county, and the city into an entity that can implement projects and guide new development. Unprecedented in its scope, this plan will result in many benefits for Los Angeles and its watershed. But if the plan is broad in its ambition, ultimately it is doubtful that there will be enough water to support these new landscapes and ecologies, let alone those that already exist. Public expectation, rooted in an unsustainable, Arcadian image of "the river," has shaped public desires and influenced revitalization efforts.

The term "revitalization" implies regrowth as a recuperative agent for societal wrongdoings and suggests that it is desirable to correct the freakological conditions in which virtually any invader can thrive. During the past twenty years, there has been an explosion of interest and of new constituents for the river, with causes ranging from complete floodplain restoration to the creation of waterfront development, parks, and habitats. Though there is strong advocacy for the river's renewal and restoration, there is as yet little constituency for understanding the river as it is and as it will be in the future, for the infrastructural sublime, for the freakological, for the river as artifact.[21] Certainly, it is unfair to compare our river to the popular Edenic conception of "river," with all of its associated expectations and tidy bourgeois sentimentalities. Rather, we must reassess the very definition of "river," expanding our idea of "nature" to include the parrot, the shopping cart, the weed, the sludge mat, and the storm-drain apartment. We must develop new narratives and vocabularies for our vital urban freakologies, for these are the ecologies of the future. If not, the river will never be truly understood or integrated into the ongoing urban project. Only by integrating the river's complexities into planning efforts can we move forward realistically.

Notes

This chapter appeared originally in *The Infrastructural City: Networked Ecologies in Los Angeles,* Kazys Varnelis, ed. (Barcelona: Actar, 2008).

1_ Sean Woods, *Wetlands of the Los Angeles River Watershed* (Oakland: California Coastal Conservancy, 2000), 78.

2_ Jared Orsi, *Hazardous Metropolis: Flooding and Urban Ecology in Los Angeles* (Berkeley and Los Angeles, University of California Press, 2004), 11.

3_ City of Los Angeles Department of Public Works, "Rainfall Indices: For the Period October 1, 2002–September 30, 2003," http://dpw.lacounty.gov/wrd/report/0203/precip/indices.cfm.

4_ *A Joint Venture. Phase II City of Los Angeles Integrated Wastewater Resources Plan for the Wastewater Program* (Los Angeles: Department of Water and Power, 2005), ES-1.

5_ California Regional Water Quality Control Board, *Water Quality Control Plan for the Los Angeles Region* (Sacramento: EPA and California Regional Water Quality Control Board, 1998).

6_ Bureau of Reclamation, Natural Resources Group, *Los Angeles River Physical and Biological Habitat Assessment* (Los Angeles: Bureau of Reclamation, 2004).

7_ Ibid., 18.

8_ Ibid.

9_ Brown and Caldwell, *Greater Los Angeles County Integrated Regional Water Management Plan* (Los Angeles: Leadership Committee of Greater Los Angeles County IRWMP, 2006).

10_Peter Bloom, *Avifauna Along Portions of the Los Angeles River* (Los Angeles: FoLAR Riverwatch Biological Monitoring Program, 2002), 7–9.

11_Bill Neill, *Survey of Invasive Non-Native Plants, Primarily Arundo Donax, Along the Los Angeles River and Tributaries* (Los Angeles: California Coastal Conservancy, 2002), 8–11.

12_Hampik Dekermenjian, *Technical Memorandum 2, Los Angeles River Flow Evaluation Phase 2: Estuary Reach Literature Review* (Los Angeles: Department of Water and Power, 2004), 2–5.

13_Bureau of Reclamation, *Los Angeles River*, 16.

14_Los Angeles and San Gabriel Rivers Watershed Council, *Los Angeles River Master Plan: Landscaping Guidelines and Plant Palettes* (Los Angeles: County of Los Angeles Department of Public Works, 2004), 24.

15_Peter Del Tredici, "Neocreationism and the Illusion of Ecological Restoration" *Harvard Design Magazine* 20 (Spring/Summer 2004), 87–89.

16_United States Census Bureau, *Statistical Abstract of the United States 2004–2005* (Washington, D.C.: United States Census Bureau, 2005), http://www.census.gov/prod /2004pu bs/o4statab/ geo.pdf.

17_City of Los Angeles Department of Public Works, Bureau of Sanitation, *Department of Water and Power. Recycled Water Evaluation Study Phase I Baseline Study* (Los Angeles: City of Los Angeles Department of Public Works, 1995), np.

18_Hampik Dekermenjian, *Technical Memorandum 1, Los Angeles River Flow Evaluation Phase 2: Projected Dry Season Flow in the Los Angeles River Based on IRP Alternatives* (Los Angeles: Department of Water and Power, 2005), and Jeff Friesen, *Technical Memorandum 8, Los Angeles River Flow Evaluation Phase 2: Low-Flow Channel Effects for a Range of Flow Alternatives* (Los Angeles: Department of Water and Power, 2005).

19_Hampik Dekermenjian, *Technical Memorandum 7, Los Angeles River Flow Evaluation Phase 2: Projected Dry Season Flow in the Los Angeles River Based on IRP Alternatives* (Los Angeles: Department of Water and Power, 2005), 5–7.

20_The author was a project manager and designer on the Master Plan team. The full Master Plan may be found at http://www.lariverrmp.orgf.

21_FOVICKS—Friends of Vast Industrial Concrete Kafkaesque Structures, http:ffseriss.com/people/erco/fovicks/. See the FOVICKS website for a comprehensive photo essay of the river from the headwaters to the Rio Hondo confluence.

Resilience refers to the ability of an ecosystem to withstand and, to some degree, absorb the effects of sometimes unpredictable and sudden changes to prevailing environmental conditions while still maintaining the majority of its structures and functions. Occasionally, such changes may result in a reorganization of the system's structures and functions into a new, or alternate steady state. As such, resilience implies transformative capacity, and straddles the tensions between stability and perturbation, constancy and change.[1] NML

1. *After Folke et al (2010), Gunderson & Holling (2002), Holling (1973, 1978, 1996), Lister (1998, 2008).*

RESILIENCE

Here, creative instabilities are invoked, and multiple states (of being) are possible, even within the same space or territory. Piscine occupation of dissimilar ecological space or horticultural occupations of varying geologic and hydrologic territories; the mapping and projection of fluctuating urban and hydrologic choreographies; appropriation of four-dimensional modeling techniques that simulate and project reciprocal growth and flow strategies; and the design of places and cities that can have very distinct and very different futures—yet still demonstrate their formational principles—are all brought into play. CR

C.S. Holling. Four Ecosystem Functions, redrawn and reinterpreted by Tomás Folch, Nina-Marie Lister, and Chris Reed. 2002/2012. (SEE POSTER)

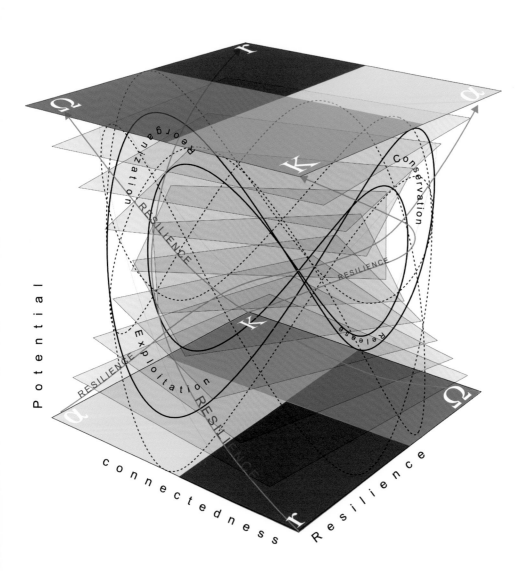

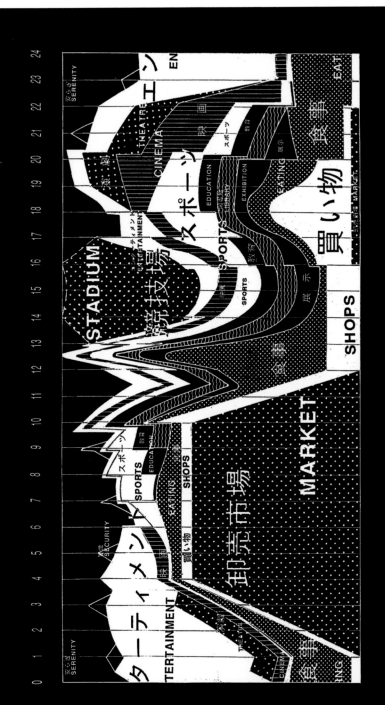

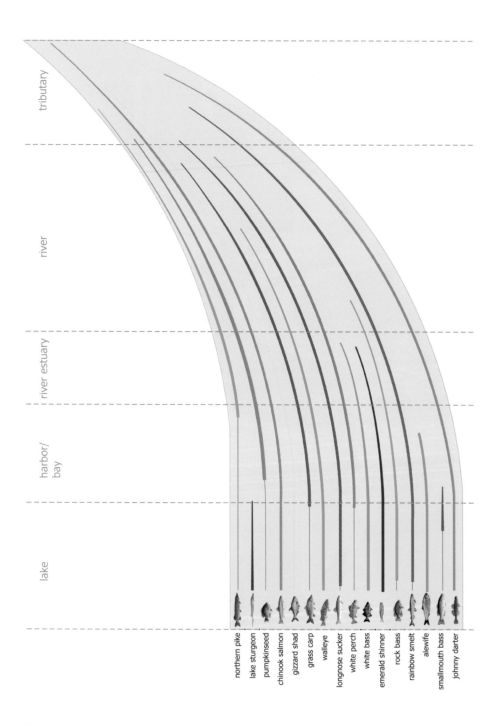

tributary

river

river estuary

harbor/
bay

lake

northern pike
lake sturgeon
pumpkinseed
chinook salmon
gizzard shad
grass carp
walleye
longnose sucker
white perch
white bass
emerald shinner
rock bass
rainbow smelt
alewife
smallmouth bass
johnny darter

Christopher Tuccio. Milkweed Habitats. 2008. (SEE POSTER)

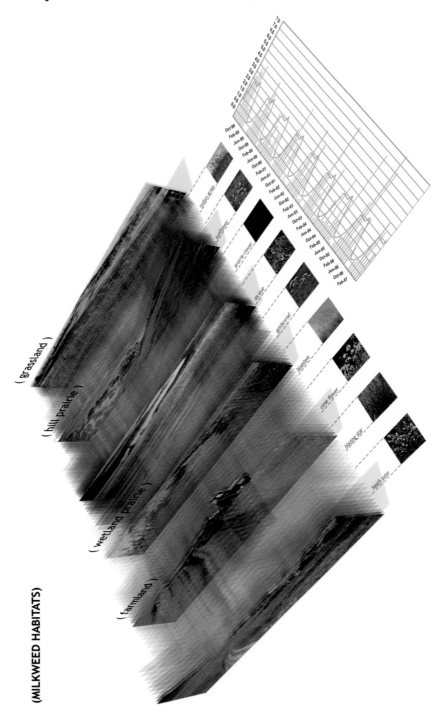

James Corner Field Operations. Habitat Nests. Downsview Park, Toronto, Canada. 1999. (SEE POSTER)

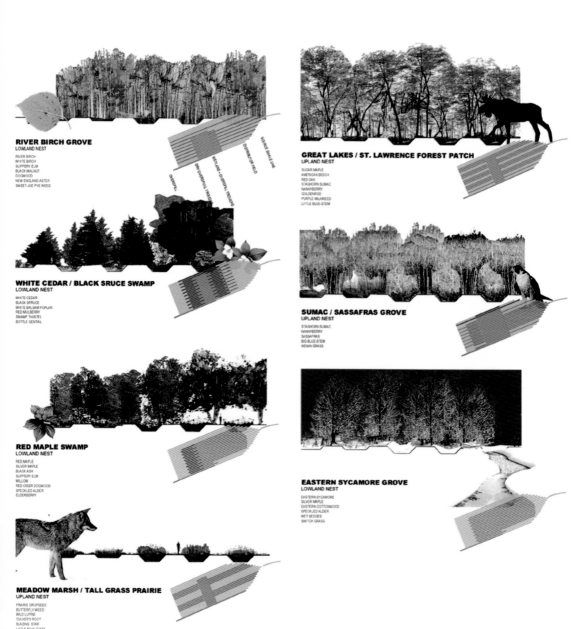

RIVER BIRCH GROVE
LOWLAND NEST

RIVER BIRCH
WHITE BIRCH
SLIPPERY ELM
BLACK WALNUT
DOGWOOD
NEW ENGLAND ASTER
SWEET JOE PYE WEED

WHITE CEDAR / BLACK SRUCE SWAMP
LOWLAND NEST

WHITE CEDAR
BLACK SPRUCE
WHITE BALSAM POPLAR
RED MULBERRY
SWAMP THISTEL
BOTTLE GENTIAL

RED MAPLE SWAMP
LOWLAND NEST

RED MAPLE
SILVER MAPLE
BLACK ASH
SLIPPERY ELM
WILLOW
RED OSIER DOGWOOD
SPECKLED ALDER
ELDERBERRY

MEADOW MARSH / TALL GRASS PRAIRIE
UPLAND NEST

PRAIRIE DROPSEED
BUTTERFLYWEED
WILD LUPINE
CULVER'S ROOT
BLAZING STAR
LITTLE BLUE-STEM
SWITCH GRASS

GREAT LAKES / ST. LAWRENCE FOREST PATCH
UPLAND NEST

SUGAR MAPLE
AMERICAN BEECH
RED OAK
STAGHORN SUMAC
NANNYBERRY
GOLDENROD
PURPLE MILKWEED
LITTLE BLUE-STEM

SUMAC / SASSAFRAS GROVE
UPLAND NEST

STAGHORN SUMAC
NANNYBERRY
SASSAFRAS
BIG BLUE-STEM
INDIAN GRASS

EASTERN SYCAMORE GROVE
LOWLAND NEST

EASTERN SYCAMORE
SILVER MAPLE
EASTERN COTTONWOOD
SPECKLED ALDER
WET SEDGES
SWITCH GRASS

Christopher Hall, for Bradley Cantrell's Illustrating Ecologies Class at Louisiana State University. River Bank Depositional Patterns. 2010. (SEE POSTER)

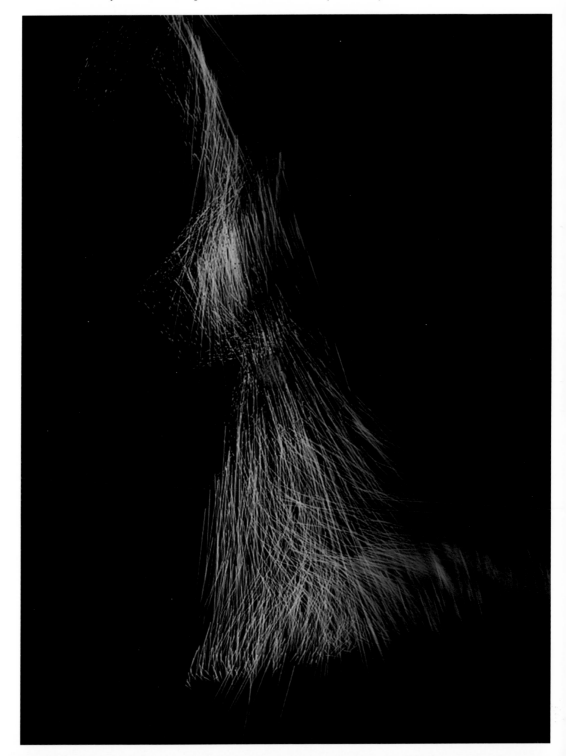

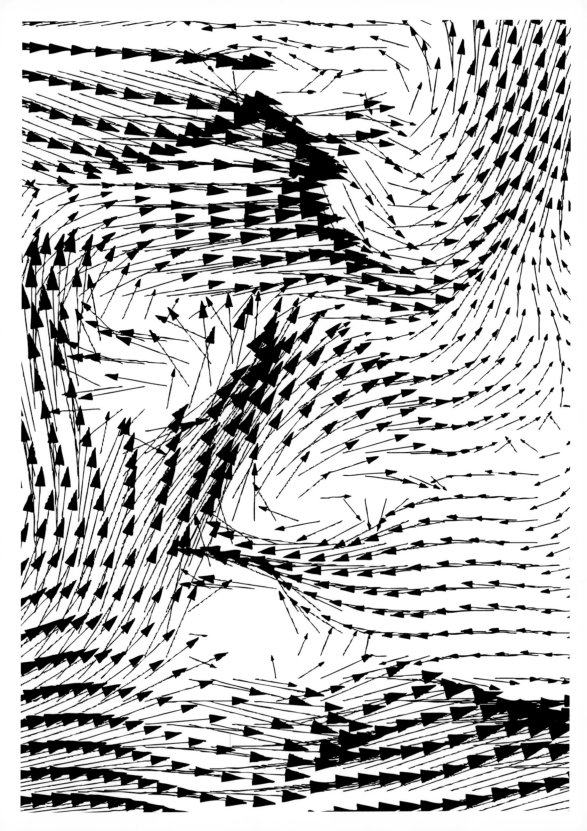

Tomás Folch and Chris Reed, after Tomás Folch, Amna Chaudry, Lauren McClure, and Sara Newey. Oyster Reef Flows. 2011.

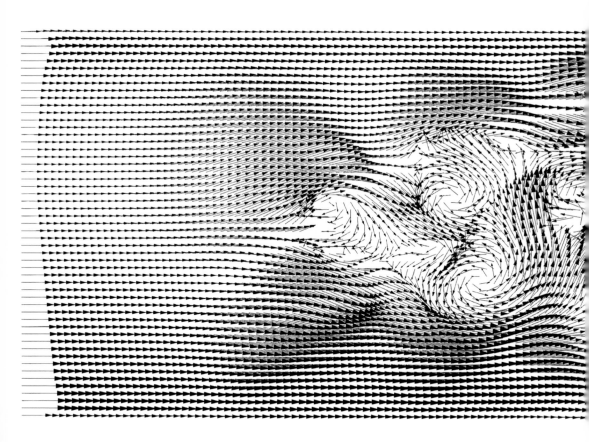

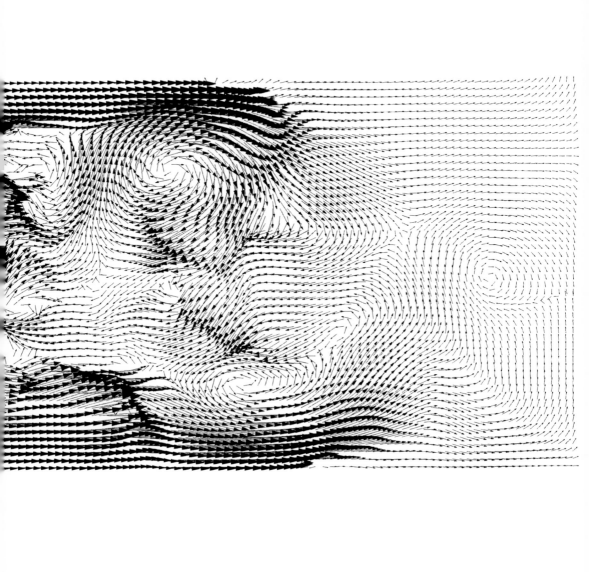

Stoss/Chris Reed, Tomás Folch, Megan Studer. States of Flux. Bass River Park, Massachusetts. 2011.

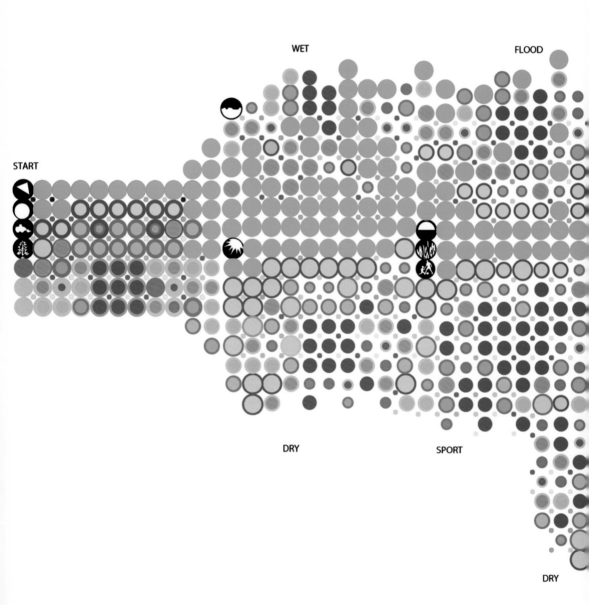

WET

FLOOD

START

DRY

SPORT

DRY

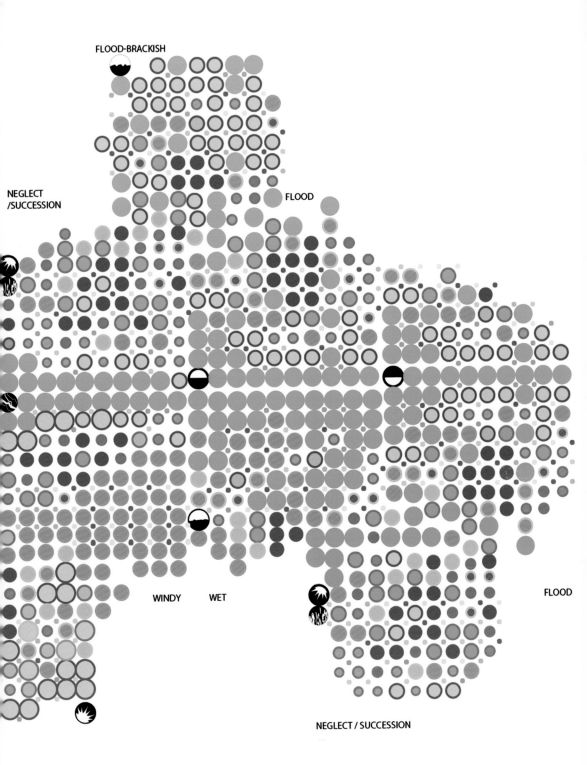

FLOOD-BRACKISH

NEGLECT
/SUCCESSION

FLOOD

WINDY   WET

FLOOD

NEGLECT / SUCCESSION

Design Thinking, Wicked Problems, Messy Plans

Frances Westley and Katharine McGowan

Scientists and activists concerned about the future of society and the planet have pointed to the urgent need for sustainability transitions.[1] Given the complex, systemic, and interrelated nature of the serious ecological, social, and economic problems confronting us, we need new forms of problem solving. These problems (and their resolutions) require decision makers to work across the system to engage in radical reorientations and demand shifts in deeply held values, beliefs, and patterns of social behavior, resulting in new multilevel governance regimes. To accomplish such radical shifts, we need to harness human creativity and innovation potential to tip interlinked social and ecological systems toward greater resilience and sustainability. While the imperative for such disruption is increasing, the challenge remains: how do we intervene in complex adaptive systems to catalyze such a shift?

What Is Design Thinking?

Design is ubiquitous; it is the creation of meaning, either in physical/material form or in less tangible outcomes like policies, plans, and programs. Design is "iterative, exploratory, and sometimes a chaotic process," that encapsulates both how the designer sees and therefore how he or she thinks.[2] The design process covers the "cognitive operations" of problem solving that includes "generation, exploration, comparison and selection" of potential solutions, designs, etc.[3]

This definition of the design process is the result of decades of intellectual and practical interest in improving human capacity. Richard Buchanan points to John Dewey's 1929 *The Quest for Certainty* as an important moment where technology was defined as "experimental thinking," where a physical product may or may not be the discrete outcome.[4] These designed technologies do not necessarily include all avenues of thinking, however; as Herbert Simon argued, design was specific to the creation of the artificial, as opposed to humans' interaction with the natural world: "Everyone designs who devises courses of action aimed at changing existing situations into preferred ones."[5] From a practical perspective, William Rouse argues that there existed a deficit of innovation in engineering in the second half of the twentieth century. Instead of adding new technologies to existing products, human-centered design offered a new perspective to potential designers that emphasized the importance of design to "enhance human abilities...[and] help overcome human limitations."[6]

An important aspect of understanding design is to distinguish between the thing itself, which can be defined as a specification of an object, manifested by an agent, intended to accomplish goals in a particular environment, using a set of primitive components, satisfying a set of requirements, subject to constraints and the design process.[7] A good analogy for the design process may be that of the square-dancing choreographer. In square dancing, ninety-odd different elements can be combined into 1,500 standard square dances. A skilled choreographer, however, can create chains of elements to match the music, the nature of the event, and the dancers' skill. Creativity is embedded in the relation between elements. Similarly, but in an even more complex way, the modern dance choreographer uses many elements to produce sequences of great originality and creativity, requiring highly skilled performers.

There is considerable divergence in the design world as to how such combinations are accomplished, some arguing for a linear, rational, and deliberate set of steps and others for something more emergent and improvisational.[8] In either case, the designer is someone who employs the design process to specify the object, arrange the components, and satisfy requirements, using a set of steps that together are the design process.

Until recently, design remained largely the purview of architects, landscape architects, engineers, and industrial and other designers, who used the skills and the steps in the design process to produce things—from products to technologies to infrastructures. This includes the development of human-centered design practice, which emphasizes how designed products should serve a social purpose (not always what can be done, but also what *should* be done), and to work effectively as teams (design for better design).[9] However, designers are now enlarging the claims for their approaches: perhaps design skills and approaches can be usefully employed to find innovative solutions to nontechnical issues. These claims have largely been packaged under the rubric of design thinking.

Tim Brown of IDEO has popularized human-centered ideas of design thinking and brought them into the mainstream. Design thinking differs from design as a professional activity because the former "puts the tools (of design) into the hands of people who may never have thought of themselves as designers and applies them to a vastly greater range of problems."[10] In this way, design thinking expands the concept of design beyond the "technocentric" interventions associated with traditional design to a broader range of complex problems, including social and potentially environmental problems.

Broadly construed, the discussion of design thinking can cover innumerable human activities, but if the goal is integrated knowledge with a useful purpose, it becomes important to distinguish among the types of problems that designers consider. In 1972, Horst Rittel and Melvin Webber categorized the problems that planners and designers address within two broad groups: determinate problems that could be resolved through the then-dominant linear design model (problem definition to problem solution), and indeterminate or so-called "wicked" problems that defied this orthodox method and appeared to resist resolution.[11]

In the business community, determinate problems continue to predominate. The design of both products and services is linked with competitiveness, as illustrated in a UK Design Council study, which found that over a ten-year period, design-aware companies outperform the market by 200 percent.[12] Similarly, government-sponsored "design" processes have proliferated, including the London (UK) Design Council, the Netherlands Department of Public Works and Water Management's use of design techniques such as scenario planning and visualization, and Brazil's CGEE, a government-run unit that uses similar techniques for forecasting and planning.[13] Part of the impetus for this search and experimentation is motivated by the current state of government and the welfare state internationally; under threat from austerity budgets, and facing increased citizen demand, government must try to do more with less.

For the second kind of problem—the wicked problem, which originated in the context of social planning—Rittel and Webber created a list of qualifications, including: these problems have no definite answer; there is no one "right" solution but only better and worse ones, evaluated largely through trial and error; and they are symptomatic of other "higher-level" problems.[14] Wicked problems are the main interest for those advocating for a design thinking approach. The design process is at once iterative, chaotic, and nonlinear, governed by constraints of desirability, viability, and feasibility.[15] Design thinking advocates suggest that its apparently chaotic and nonlinear aspects mean that design thinking has an elective affinity with complex problems, which are similarly characterized by emergence, nonlinearities, and thresholds. The discipline of constraints, on the other hand, means that design thinking solutions need to be grounded in such a way that they have the potential for broader system impact.

Wicked problems may serve as the basis for discussions between designers and scientists seeking collaborative solutions to complex environmental challenges. Here we see most clearly the emergence of an intellectual marriage of complexity, systems thinking, and design, and the possibilities for such an approach offering a useful interdisciplinary process for scientists, designers, planners, managers, and others concerned with environmental problems to engage diverse thinking in crafting solutions.

Nonetheless, the difference between science and design thinking should not be underestimated or obscured. Science emphasizes the study of the natural world, design the manipulation of the artificial world. The scientific method relies on controlled experiment and classification; design methods favor modeling, prototyping, pattern forming, and synthesis. Above all, science privileges objectivity, rationality, and neutrality, whereas design favors practicality, ingenuity, and appropriateness or fit.[16] Bringing scientists and designers together in an exercise of design thinking requires a capacity for "mode 2" knowledge generation,[17] transdisciplinary methods, and synthesis that is significantly helped by a careful design of the process of interaction itself. The concept of design labs offers a variety of multi-stakeholder creative problem-solving approaches specifically informed by design thinking.

What Are Design Labs?

At their core, design lab processes bring together various stakeholders to design a potentially innovative solution to a complex societal problem. Unsurprisingly, this is not a brief, one-off process but rather can extend over several months, and each design lab process is marked by stages of data collection, analysis, creative engagement, prototype development, and rollout. Unlike a workshop or studio, both of which also emphasize various perspectives' interaction and collaboration, laboratory processes are meant to create novel approaches that have transferability and scalability. This shares a charrette process's interest in stakeholder engagement (the inquiry-by-design method of charrette), but is less a method of consultation than of co-creation.

A multiplicity of design labs have sprung up around the world, many focused on government policy, some specifically on the environment. For example, Denmark's MindLab is a vehicle for the Danish government to take on such intractable problems as developing a Danish climate change agenda. A customized physical space was created within government buildings, with ambient lighting and whiteboard walls, in deliberate contrast to the surrounding office space. Through considerable trial and error, MindLab has worked out a process design that involves a long preliminary research phase to develop a clearer and more accurate design brief and, through qualitative methods, rich input to the lab itself. This process determines who should participate. Participants are then led through seven steps of framing, knowing, analyzing, synthesizing, creating, scaling, and learning.[18]

Other initiatives such as the Stanford D-Lab,[19] Toronto's Institute Without Borders, and Helsinki Design Lab have experimented with other formats,[20] but all retain a variation of research, exploration, prototyping, and experimentation. The Malmö Design:Lab creators have given considerable thought to the character and implications of a laboratory process, building on the collaborative practice of partner-engaged design; the designers organized sessions of twenty to thirty participants, with goals from "consensus around particular design artifacts" to visualization, theatrical enactment, and games.[21] They found the laboratory process was as much a beginning as an end in itself: "what seems the most important outcome was the opportunity for the partners involved to try out new approaches that can be accomplished in a collaboration spanning organizational and community boundaries."[22]

Based on this experience, the Malmö designers assert that a laboratory is more structured in content and outcome than a workshop—labs are experiments with scalability and portability, meaning that they are transparent in their process (not replicable in their results), so that the lab is a "sustainable practice that can continue to make sense of what is collaboratively envisioned."[23] In both design schools and client-oriented action research, the design laboratory is user-focused prototyping and scenario planning as a dominant form of design thinking.[24] Design thinking's roots in such fields as engineering show through clearly in these forms of research, however, as the process often begins with "abstract specifications" or a brief and ends with "the description of a product."[25]

Likely because of the association with trade and production rather than theory, the academic study of design (and particularly of design labs in their many forms) lags significantly behind its practice.[26] However, design thinking and design labs stand on the shoulders of rich if relatively recent intellectual developments that seek to understand and embrace "messy" complex problems.[27] These earlier approaches, sometimes termed "whole system processes" or more recently "change labs," were themselves based on breakthroughs in understanding of group psychology and complexity theory earlier in the twentieth century. Specifically, design labs rely to a varied extent on group dynamics, people's ability to share and collaborate effectively, and the tools necessary to express those interactions and specifically, their resultant designs.

As design labs seek to address messy, wicked, or complex social and ecological problems, there is considerable variation in their engagement in what might be called process design. For environmental scientists and activists seeking to engage stakeholders in an innovation process or action agenda, the importance of doing so with the full knowledge of group process and group dynamics means that a review of these earlier processes is important.

The Antecedents of Design Labs

In the late 1940s and early 1950s, members of disparate academic disciplines gathered periodically at the Beekman Hotel in New York City to discuss new paths for scientists. Members of the American Josiah Macy Jr. Foundation's Conference Program rejected traditional conference structure, eschewing long scholarly papers in favor of short presentations and long group discussions where no participant could simply appeal to his expertise to sway colleagues on any point.[28] In this collaborative environment, experts in fields as varied as anthropology, psychiatry, social relations, and zoology advanced thinking on two subjects: complex system thinking, and group processes and dynamics. The latter drew on the work of social psychologists such as Wilfred Bion, and, extending Freudian theory, put forward an early idea about how groups might structure activities to give rise to a particular set of experiences.[29] The workshops were explicitly interdisciplinary, based on the belief that scientific insights relied on the ability to overcome technical and philosophical barriers between disciplines.[30] Conference organizers warned against "unrecognized blind spots, prejudices, and over-attachment to or dependence upon an 'authority' or upon too narrowly conceived criteria of credibility" as impediments to scientific breakthroughs and meaningful intellectual cooperation.[31]

The Macy meetings were among the factors that contributed to the development of "a new set of ideas [that] impinged on the human sciences and began to transform some traditional fields of inquiry."[32] Although applied physics and mathematics had a more immediate effect on North American life, the shifts in inquiry thanks to the introduction of action research, complexity, and computing affected multiple disciplines and formed the basis for the transformative processes that predated design labs.

Group Dynamics and Group Psychology

Many social scientists who worked in the war effort developed an interest in "human sciences" and meaningful problem solving—a shift from changing individual behavior to improving social structures.[33]

Of particular interest to the organizers of the Macy conferences was the work emerging from the Tavistock Institute of Human Relations in the United Kingdom (created after World War I as part of the older Tavistock Clinic), many of whose eventual members were involved with action research that brought wartime insights to industry to achieve organizational change and development.[34] The Tavistock Clinic was created to treat the psychological problems of veterans, and when Britain entered World War II, the staff sought to ensure that their insights into psychiatry and the human being could benefit the war effort. In 1941, Tavistock psychiatrists influenced Parliament to create the Directorate of Army Psychiatry and used insights from their prewar research and wartime observations to inform officer selection, morale, etc.[35] Polish psychologist Kurt Lewin met Eric Trist of Tavistock in the interwar years, and Trist employed some of Lewin's thinking on Gestalt psychology in his work with the British Land Army.[36]

Another Tavistock clinician, Wilfred Bion, began at the same time to develop ideas about the dynamics of groups, which had an important shaping impact on the new field of group psychology. Bion argued that task accomplishment in groups is often derailed by psychological dynamics (which he labeled basic assumptions) not related to task. These include patterns of dependency, fight-flight behavior, and emotional pairing. Group therapists, by learning to recognize these psychological dynamics as they emerged, could help structure interactions to make them a learning experience and facilitate more creative task accomplishment.[37]

Meanwhile, across the Atlantic, the Connecticut State Inter-racial Commission approached Lewin, now at MIT's Center for Group Dynamics, to suggest solutions to religious and racial prejudice; the result was a "change" experiment, wherein workshop participants were trained in anti-prejudice community action and encouraged to reflect on their own experience and behavior, which informed research into what changed their attitudes.[38] These early collaborative workshops led to the creation of the National Training Laboratories in Bethel, Maine, in 1947, focused on interpersonal relations (specifically sensitivity training) that built on Bion's work as well as Lewin's.[39] Important to the eventual lab process, Lewin emphasized "creating 'here and now' data, analyzing it, and using feedback," in working with groups.[40] Lewin's action research in understanding and influencing group dynamics contributed to the rise of the academic fields of organizational behavior, organizational design, and organizational development (and much contemporary consulting practice): it enshrined process design and expert facilitation as key skills necessary for unstructured problem solving and creativity in groups and organizations.

After the war, Tavistock researchers sought to continue applying their "multi-disciplinary and integrative approach to behavioral science" such as social psychiatry, social psychology, and group dynamics to a civilian context.[41] And as they extended from groups to organizations to the broader society, they began to engage another group of scholars that the Macy workshops brought together: those interested in complex systems, cybernetics, and system design.

*Systems and Complexity Theory*_____

The Macy cross-disciplinary discussions not only stimulated a new way of understanding organizations as a dynamic process; they also contributed to the development of many elements of systems theory, such as cybernetics.[42] In the 1930s, Karl Ludwig von Bertalanffy's idea of systems—a set, open or otherwise, of interrelated components, marked by self-learning through feedback[43]—promoted systems thinking, an approach that seeks to unify different approaches (biology, anthropology, psychology, etc.) that considers circular causality, self-organization, and the "unpredictable emergence of order from disorder."[44] How do systems and the examination of complexity affect how we ask questions and seek solutions?

Cybernetics focused on a specific element of systems, as the "scientific study and mathematical modeling for an understanding of regulation and control in any system," although often in closed or human-machine systems.[45] Systems engineers employed cybernetics and computer simulations to create ever-more deadly weapons of war and declare American supremacy on the battlefield and in space.[46] Norbert Wiener's *The Human Use of Human Beings* (1950) set out the importance of cybernetics (the content and means of communication) to basic social understanding and foreshadowed the increasing importance of human-machine interaction.[47]

The Macy workshops brought together two groups of thinkers, one focused on group processes and dynamics and the design of human experience, and the other concerned with understanding system dynamics and their design. These intellectual collaborations and exchanges lay the groundwork for the fields of organization and system design, process design, and some of the fundamental properties of cybernetics and artificial intelligence. It also gave rise to new forms of intervention in social systems.

Although some observers expressed grave concerns about cybernetics-related systems as overly functionalist and rooted in control and predictability, thinking about systems through a complexity lens offered new avenues of inquiry and insight. Eric Trist, who had worked with Bion, applied this new thinking in an organizational restructuring process he called sociotechnical redesign. Trist's sociotechnical systems approach offered the potential of improving industry and opened up a new field of inquiry in organizational studies. Trist began work on the sociotechnical systems in 1954, and by 1957 Tavistock ran its first "laboratory" process with the University of Leicester, with influence from Lewin's National Training Laboratory.[48] In these laboratories, research, consultancy, and training were interwoven activities, as experts learned from participatory processes in the field. Organizations—the social systems under examination in these laboratories— were increasingly seen as a product of human design, and when their design was informed by group psychology and dynamics, they could become powerful vehicles for the realization of both social and technical goals.

By 1960, Trist had begun to recognize the limits of the organizational system focus. Organizations alone could only do so much. A complex adaptive systems lens helped identify the challenge of intervening in "megamesses," the label Trist and his colleague Fred Emery used to identify broad intractable problem domains such as the "environment," "poverty," or "health," which plagued society and burdened its organizations.[49] Building on his earlier insight that a fundamental change in communication was required if actors in complex systems were to change the system's direction, Trist and Emery developed a second lab-like process specifically geared to addressing complexity, Future Search.[50] Future Search was the first of the "whole system processes," designed to bring concerned stakeholders into the discussion to chart a common future. Trist likened it to a set of sailboats, tossed about in a storm. In this scenario, all the sailboats are unknowingly connected to each other by underwater flexible cables, so whenever one sailboat corrects for the wind and attempts to set a course to its safe harbor, it is pulled off that course by the unseen other boats, going in different directions to different ports. In Trist's view, the only way to reach safe harbor is to bring the "whole system," or representatives of it, together to set a common course.

Future Search was a robust design, which embedded an understanding of both group dynamics and complexity theory in a process that proved successful across contexts and cultures. It also catalyzed a variety of other whole system processes, now commonly known as change labs, including Appreciative Inquiry,[51] Deliberative Dialogue,[52] Reos Change Labs,[53] Theory U,[54] and to some extent, Scenario Planning.[55]

However, at this point the elements of these processes remain loosely coupled. It is interesting that in his seminal *Change by Design,* Tim Brown makes no mention of any of the whole system processes, save for the related Scenario Planning. This is characteristic of a field reaching out from its roots (design) and trying to address a new field (social change and complex systems). From the point of view of scientists and environmental activists, however, as well as those interested in social innovation, it is important to recognize that while there is an elective affinity or apparent fit between whole system processes and design lab approaches, their integration has not been fully realized, and each has strengths and weaknesses.

Design labs clearly share goals with whole system approaches, particularly those approaches that we have outlined above, which look to address wicked or difficult questions. However, despite some pronounced strengths over whole system approaches, the design approach seems less sensitive to the rich history of social psychological and complexity theory that undergirds the whole system approach. In this sense, despite their desire to apply a design approach to complex or wicked social as well as technical problems, many of the design lab approaches seem less able to manage for emergence (something to which process design and expert facilitation are geared). Second, despite the emphasis on prototyping, the problem of designing and testing social as opposed to technical interventions has not been fully conceptualized. Both of these drawbacks are important when it comes to making an argument that design lab approaches can be a useful support to scientific understanding and action in linked social-ecological perspectives.

Whole System ("Change Labs")	Design Labs
Strengths	*Strengths*
> Excellent understanding of group dynamics > Focus on shared vision > Focus on building collaboration	> Strong on up-front research > Focus on prototyping > Understanding innovation (maybe) > Good integration of expertise with lay knowledge
Weaknesses	*Weaknesses*
> Poor use of expertise/research > Weak on implementation/prototyping > No particular emphasis on innovation > Poor or no integration of cross-scale dynamics	> Tendency to default to technical innovation > Not clear on how to prototype complex systems change > Less strong on understanding social or political dynamics > Poor or no integration of cross-scale dynamics

Table 1 Comparative Strengths and Weaknesses of Whole System Processes and Design Labs

Tailoring Design Labs to Ecology? Dialing Up the Power of Design Labs for Transforming Complex Social-Ecological Problem Domains_____

Ecologists, particularly system ecologists, have long recognized the complexity of the problems that they are facing. Some of the most sophisticated models of system interactions in any field come from ecology. Work in nonlinear transitions, thresholds, bifurcations, and attractors have shaped such approaches as resilience theory and the work of a number of leading thinkers in the field.[56] In the 1970s, some ecologists became increasingly involved in action research as the reality of human impact on the environment became clear.[57] Scientific inquiry offered some useful answers to problems of climate change, but left unanswered or ignored important issues such as science's role in socioeconomic or political power dynamics, and the engagement of stakeholders became crucial to advancing "ecology-as-social-action."[58] The role of human activity, including resource management, economic exploitation, and earlier conservation efforts underlined the importance of approaching ecosystem resilience and sustainability as a linked human and environmental issue.[59]

Peter Taylor (2002) argues that the rise of ecology-as-social-action was linked with the ability of ecologists to inform public policy around environmental use, management, and conservation. However, as this work emerges from the recognition of connected social-ecological systems, Taylor underlines the importance of ecologists being aware of how those social systems they seek to influence work, and how their scientific conclusions will be seen, internalized, and used.[60] An argument could be made that with its combination of research, processes based on knowledge of social psychology and group dynamics, emergence and creativity, and prototyping to test solutions, design thinking and design labs may offer just such processes for engaging nonscientists more deeply in finding creative solutions to intractable problems. The current poorly integrated relationship between these two compatible processes is an opportunity for bringing the best elements to bear on the transformation of linked social and ecological systems.

Such approaches are not alien to science. In the seminal work on adaptive management, Holling postulated that to manage complex ecological systems, a "learning" approach was required, where managers treat interventions (including policy interventions) as experiments. Adaptive management also involved convening stakeholders on the assumption that effective collaboration between scientists, policy makers, managers, and the public are increasingly necessary for optimal results.[61] The University of Waterloo's James J. Kay's lab pioneered this work in what became the Ecosystem Approach (with many of Holling's students), which applied a social-ecological approach to planning and design.[62] This approach largely lacked a detailed process for engaging social actors or an awareness of process design that characterizes whole system processes, but it nevertheless has had a profound impact on attempts to manage social-ecological systems. The European NeWater project, for example, seeks to engage stakeholders in the development and implementation of adaptive water management.[63] According to Claudia Pahl-Wostl et al., an adaptive management regime involves information collection and the actors engaging with both that information (being able to "draw meaningful conclusions from it") and each other; the iterative process of problem definition, hypothesis development, testing, policy formation, and evaluation runs closely parallel to current thinking about design lab processes.

Throughout the 1990s, groups such as the IUCN Conservation Breeding Specialist group began to experiment with lab-like workshops, including some of the whole system design processes, such as collaborations with management and social scientists.[64] These workshops were designed to assess the status of endangered species and create strategies for conservation; additionally, they integrated complex system models into the decision-making process to test the sensitivity of policy and management options. As mentioned above, in the context of a multi-stakeholder workshop on complex problems, these models may be a proxy for prototyping, and this element should be built into design labs seeking to innovate in complex social or ecological problem domains.

However, these experiments have remained isolated, and many environmental scientists still have a weak understanding of the potential power of lab-like processes. Design labs, particularly when coupled with whole system approaches and computer simulations, represent the embodiment of a rich history of theory and practice in social psychology, process design, complexity thinking, design, and experimental prototyping.

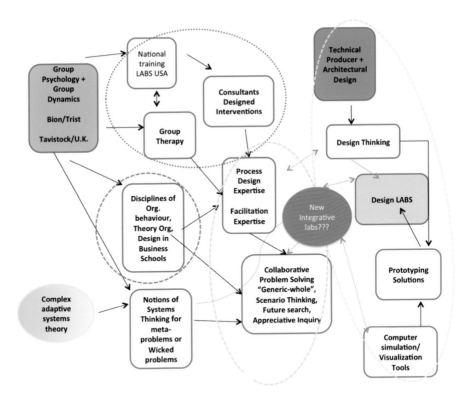

Figure 1. Affinities and Interactions in Design Lab Space.

One fruitful avenue for increasing the power of design labs with regard to innovation in social-ecological systems is to build in computer simulations. Increased computing power over the last sixty years has significantly improved our ability to make sense of systems and has allowed us to create simulations and rapid prototyping necessary for an effective design lab process. World War II, a strong undercurrent in much of the intellectual discussions of design and systems, had drastically advanced the capabilities—and therefore possibilities—of computation for managing data, representing ideas, and imagining solutions, and the Cold War kept up demand for new military innovation.[65]

Although the potential for computer systems may be clear from this example, the focus on control in midcentury cybernetics impeded many potential intellectual and practical applications of systems thinking in the 1960s.[66] However, the applications of computing reached beyond the management of information and into its expression. In the 1960s, architects started to explore new computer-based tools "to examine architecture and design as an emergent social, material and spatial system."[67] The ability of computing to express information, rather than simply manage it, came from the mixture of computing and art. This was not one movement but many simultaneous explorations in a relatively new and constantly evolving medium of computer-aided design and 3D modeling, as evidenced in such examples as Grasshopper (using Rhinoceros 3d) and FormZ.

In the late 1960s, MIT's Architecture Machine Group began work to develop computation tools for architects, and MIT's Center for Advanced Visual Studies sought to create a (computer-based) platform for art and technology to intersect and develop. The Institute of Contemporary Arts in London hosted an exhibit entitled "Cybernetic Serendipity" that coordinated the work of artists and scientists of various stripes.[68] The ability to model aspects of complex adaptive systems with these new computer-based tools (including genetic algorithms, cellular automata, neural networks, multi-agent systems, and even artificial life forms) has significantly advanced our understanding of these emergent, reactive learning entities.[69]

John Frazer's *An Evolutionary Architecture* emphasized the benefit of computer models to help architects "rethink explicitly and clearly the way in which we habitually do things."[70] Modeling behavior can be a useful heuristic to understand not just what we do now but also the range of options of what we could do. The ability to create virtual environments, which has grown exponentially since the 1980s, has allowed users to simulate behavior in multi-agent systems ranging from stock markets to land-use plans.[71] Importantly, these experiments allow for testing future possibilities, such as scenarios created in a design lab. Computer-based tools have expanded the capacity of design processes to trace and test transformation pathways. They are an ideal bridge between design thinking and ecological approaches and represent a strengthening of both.

The second promising avenue is to marry more explicitly the ideas of emergence, discontinuities, cross-scale dynamics, and resilience with the whole system approaches to process design, to strengthen the early stages of generation, exploration, comparison, and selection that in some design labs can become too linear to capture the full complexity of the problem domain under consideration. Even in situ simulations can be useful; the design charrette as a practice is being adopted by planning schools for social planning problems.

Many items that fit under the wide design umbrella are creations or communications of meaning—things, processes, and policies meant to disseminate and exchange information and ultimately solve human problems.[72] The problems facing ecosystems today, including pollution, loss of resilience and biodiversity, and the many emergent elements of climate change, are not uniquely environmental problems but are also social, technical, political, and economic problems. Their resolutions require a mechanism that can bring together stakeholders in these different domains and build these perspectives into an integrative whole. As Richard Buchanan explains, design thinking is not strictly an integrative approach to academic inquiry, but a bridging of knowledge from even widely disparate disciplines, to "serve the purpose of enriching human life."[73] Fortunately, in design thinking and the potential to combine it with whole system thinking and visual language, new processes are possible that take integrative ways of knowing and seek to create integrative ways of doing.

Notes

1_ Paul Gallopin and Paul Raskin, *Global Sustainability: Bending the Curve* (Florence, KY: Routledge, 2002).

2_ Rim Razzouk and Valerie Shute, "What Is Design Thinking and Why Is It Important?" *Review of Educational Research* 82.3 (September 2012): 330–348, 331, 334.

3_ Ibid., 337.

4_ Richard Buchanan, "Wicked Problems in Design Thinking," *Design Issues* 8.2 (Spring 1992): 5–21, 6, 8.

5_ Herbert Simon, *The Science of the Artificial*, 2d ed. (Cambridge, MA: MIT Press, 1981).

6_ William Rouse, *Design for Success: A Human-Centered Approach to Designing Successful Products and Systems* (New York: Wiley-Interscience Publication, 1991), 3–5.

7_ P. Ralph and Y. Wand, "A Proposal for a Formal Definition of the Design Concept," in K. Lyytinen, P. Loucopoulos, J. Mylopoulos, and W. Robinson, eds., *Design Requirements Workshop* (LNBIP 14, 2009), 103–136. doi:10.1007/978-3-540-92966-6_6

8_ Ibid.

9_ Clive Dym et al., "Engineering Design Thinking, Teaching, and Learning," *Journal of Engineering Education* (January 2005): 103–120, 103–104; Rouse, *Design for Success*, xiii.

10_ T. Brown, *Change by Design* (New York: Harper Collins, 2009), 2.

11_ Horst W. J. Rittel and Melvin M. Webber, "Dilemmas in a General Theory of Planning," working paper presented at the Institute of Urban and Regional Development, University of California, Berkeley, November 1972; published as "Dilemmas in a General Theory of Planning," *Policy Sciences* 4.2 (1973): 155–169.

12_ Christian Bason, *Leading Public Sector Innovation: Co-creating for a Better Society* (Bristol, UK: Policy Press, 2010), 136; Razzouk and Shute, "What Is Design Thinking and Why Is It Important?" 331.

13_ Bason, *Leading Public Sector Innovation,* 4.

14_ Ibid.

15_ Brown, *Change by Design*, 17–19.

16_ Nigel Cross, "Designerly Ways of Knowing," *Design Studies* 3.4 (1982): 221–227.

17_ M. Gibbons, Camille Limoges, Helga Nowotny, Simon Schwartzman, Peter Scott, and Martin Trow, *The New Production of Knowledge: The Dynamics of Science and Research in Contemporary Societies* (New York: Sage, 1994).

18_ Bason, *Leading Public Sector Innovation*.

19_ F. Westley et al., "Tipping Toward Sustainability," *Ambio* 40 (2011): 719–738.

20_ D-School Stanford: *http://dschool stanford.edu;* Helsinki Design Lab: *http://www.hel-sinkidesignlab.org*; Institute Without Boundaries: www.institutewithoutboundaries.com.

21_ Thomas Binder and Eva Brandt, "The Design:Lab as Platform in Participatory Design Research," *CoDesign* 4.2 (June 2008): 115–129, 116–117.

22_Ibid., 118.

23_Ibid., 119–121.

24_Ibid., 115–116.

25_Razzouk and Shute, "What Is Design Thinking and Why Is It Important?" 336.

26_Buchanan, "Wicked Problems in Design Thinking," 5–21, 5.

27_Russell Ackoff, "Systems, Messes, and Interactive Planning," in *Redesigning the Future* (New York: Wiley, 1974), chapters 1 and 2.

28_Bertram Schallner, ed., *Group Processes: Transactions of the First Conference, September 26, 27, 28, 29, and 30, 1954*, vol. 4 (Ithaca, NY: Josiah Macy Jr. Foundation, 1955), 7.

29_Ibid., 1, 7.

30_Ibid., 7.

31_Ibid.

32_Steve Joshua Heims, *The Cybernetics Group* (Cambridge, MA: MIT Press, 1991), 1.

33_Ibid., 3–4.

34_Eric Trist, "The Evolution of Socio-Technical Systems: A Conceptual Framework and an Action Research Program," *Occasional Paper No. 2*, Conference on Organizational Design and Performance, June 1981;tavinstitute.org/about/our_history.php.

35_Eric Trist and Hugh Murray, eds. *The Social Engagement of Social Science: A Tavistock Anthology, Vol. I: The Socio-Psychological Perspective* (Philadelphia: University of Pennsylvania Press, 1990), 1.

36_Alfred J. Marrow, *The Practical Theorist: The Life and Work of Kurt Lewin* (New York: Basic Books, Inc., 1969), 69.

37_W.R. Bion, *Experiences in Groups* (London: Tavistock, 1961).

38_Elizabeth Lasch-Quinn, *Race Experts: How Racial Etiquette, Sensitivity Training, and New Age Therapy Hijacked the Civil Rights Revolution* (New York: W. W. Norton, 2001), 65; Marrow, *The Practical Theorist*, 213.

39_Lasch-Quinn, *Race Experts*, 69.

40_Marrow, *The Practical Theorist*, 214.

41_Trist and Murray, eds. *The Social Engagement of Social Science*, 2; H.V. Dicks, *Fifty Years of the Tavistock Clinic* (London: Routledge and Kegan Paul, 1970), 7.

42_William Rasch and Cary Wolfe, eds., *Observing Complexity: Systems Theory and Postmodernity* (Minneapolis: University of Minnesota Press, 2000), 9; John Mingers and Leroy White, "A Review of the Recent Contribution of System Thinking to Operational Research and Management Science," *European Journal of Operational Research* 207 (2010): 1147–1161, 1147–1148.

43_Kenneth D. Bailey, *Sociology and the New Systems Theory: Towards a Theoretical Synthesis* (New York: State University of New York Press, 1994), 41, 44, 47.

44_Rasch and Wolfe, eds., *Observing Complexity*.

45_Mingers and White, "A Review of the Recent Contribution of System Thinking to Operational Research and Management Science," 1148; J.R. Beniger, *The Control Revolution: Technological and Economic Origins of the Information Society* (Cambridge, MA: MIT Press, 1986).

46_Jennifer S. Light, *From Warfare to Welfare: Defense Intellectuals and Urban Problems in Cold War America* (Baltimore: Johns Hopkins University Press, 2003); Mingers and White, "A Review of the Recent Contribution of System Thinking to Operational Research and Management Science," 1148, 1150; Rachel Plotnick, "Computers, Systems Theory, and the Making of a Wired Hospital: A History of Technicon Medical Information System, 1964–1987," *Journal of the American Society for Information Science and Technology* 61.6 (2010): 1281–1294.

47_Norbert Wiener, *The Human Use of Human Beings: Cybernetics and Society* (Boston: Houghton Mifflin, 1950), 16.

48_Dicks, *Fifty Years of the Tavistock Clinic*, 212.

49_F. E. Emery and E. L. Trist, "The Causal Texture of Organizational Environments," *Human Relations* (1965) 18: 21–32.

50_M. Weisbord, *Discovering Common Ground* (San Francisco: Berrett-Koehler, 1992).

51_D. L. Cooperrider, D. Whitney, and J.M. Stavros, *Appreciative Inquiry Handbook* (Bedford Heights, OH: Lakeshore Publishers, 2003).

52_W. Isaacs, *Dialogue: The Art of Thinking Together* (New York: Doubleday, 1999).

53_Adam Kahane, *Solving Tough Problems* (San Francisco: Berrett-Koehler, 2004).

54_Otto Scharmer, *Theory U* (San Francisco: Berrett-Koehler, 2009).

55_Peter Schwartz, *The Art of the Long View: Planning for the Future in an Uncertain World* (New York: Currency Doubleday, 1991).

56_Bailey, *Sociology and the New Systems Theory*, xiii, 1; Rasch and Wolfe, eds., *Observing Complexity*, 9; Marco Janssen, ed., *Complexity and Ecosystem Management: The Theory and Practice of Multi-Agent Systems* (Cheltenham, UK: Edward Elgar, 2002).

57_Peter Taylor, *Unruly Complexity: Ecology, Interpretation, Engagement* (Chicago: University of Chicago Press, 2005), xv.

58_Ibid.

59_Lance H Gunderson, C.S. Holling, and Stephen S. Light, eds. *Barriers and Bridges to the Renewal of Ecosystems and Institutions* (New York: Columbia University Press, 1995); David Waltner-Toews, James J. Kay, and Nina-Marie Lister, *The Ecosystem Approach: Complexity, Uncertainty, and Managing for Sustainability* (New York: Columbia University Press, 2008).

60_Taylor, *Unruly Complexity*, xvi.

61_C.S. Holling, ed. *Adaptive Environmental Assessment and Management* (Chichester, UK: Wiley, 1978).

62_Toews et al., *The Ecosystem Approach.*

63_Claudia Pahl-Wostl et al., "Managing Change toward Adaptive Water Management through Social Learning," *Ecology and Society* 12.2 (2007): 30.

64_F. Westley and P. Miller, *Experiments in Consilience* (San Francisco: Island Press, 2002).

65_Light, *From Warfare to Welfare*; Mingers and White, "A Review of the Recent Contribution of System Thinking to Operational Research and Management Science," 1148, 1150; Plotnick, "Computers, Systems Theory and the Making of a Wired Hospital," 1281–1294.

66_Bailey, *Sociology and the New Systems Theory*, xiii, 41; Rasch and Wolfe, eds., *Observing Complexity*, 10.

67_Theodore Spyropoulos, "Evolving Patterns: Correlated Systems of Interaction," *Architectural Design*, 2009.

68_Spyropoulos, "Evolving Patterns"; "History," *Computer Arts Society* www.computer-arts-society.com/history (accessed 15 November 2012).

69_Janssen, *Complexity and Ecosystem Management*, 1.

70_Spyropoulus, "Evolving Patterns," 84; John Frazer, *An Evolutionary Architecture* (London: Architectural Association, 1995).

71_Ibid., 3.

72_Bason, *Leading Public Sector Innovation*, 137.

73_Buchanan, "Wicked Problems in Design Thinking," 6.

The Shape of Energy

Sean Lally

Creating the boundaries that define and separate activities is an essential act in architectural design. A boundary distinguishes a change that allows two separate activities to exist adjacent to each other. The material characteristics that create these boundaries inform the shapes that architecture can take, influencing spatial organizations, conglomerations and subdivisions, and typologies, while simultaneously providing a measure of value, whether aesthetic or monetary.

The characteristics and behaviors of the boundaries on which architects have relied for so long (stone, steel, or glass) could be best described as solid-state materials; the boundaries that these materials create are static. But architects have worked with another range of materials with boundary edges that are anything but static— instead continently in flux and in a feedback relationship with their climatic context, requiring different standards for the value placed on the shapes they produce. These materials are the electromagnetics, thermodynamics, acoustic waves, and chemical interactions that surround us constantly, yet have largely resisted becoming architectural material to build with. Generally grouped together as energy associated with fuel or dismissed as simply air that fills architecture's volumes, these materials can be controlled and deployed to meet the spatial and organizational requirements needed to become their own architecture. In doing so, they become a set of building materials known as *material energies* that give the architect access to new types of boundary edges that move from points, lines, and surfaces to gradients of intensities and fallouts. The physical properties of material energies will influence the core understanding of how a geographic edge condition is defined. Therefore this discussion of shape as it pertains to energy has much more at stake than simply replacing one material system (solid state) with another (material energies). Before these proclivities can be witnessed or embraced by architecture, they must first be given shape.

Understanding the importance of giving shape to architecture through building materials might appear so fundamental as to not require clarification. Yet this is precisely what has been evading the architect as it pertains to working with energy. If asked to identify the shapes of energy in architecture today, an individual would point to the technologies that harness it (photovoltaic cells, wind turbines, generators) or the devices that release it (heating, ventilation, and air conditioning [HVAC] systems and light fixtures). This is because energy innovation is recognized today only in the technologies and devices associated with its collection and release, not in what architects do with the energy *after* it is released. Working in collusion with the technologies and devices that harness and release energy are the surface geometries that bind it; energy fills the interior cavity of an existing architectural form like air in a car tire. The devices of energy collection and release coupled with the armatures of mediation act as the sole means for defining the shapes given to architecture. All imaginable attention, aesthetics, and value have been placed on the mechanisms that control these energies; attention has been turned away from the energies themselves because it has been assumed that shape and value cannot be absorbed or achieved apart from solid-state materials. The ability to give architectural shape to energy is of primary importance in advancing future energy research within architecture and beyond, yet it appears to be one of the most elusive aspects of this current conversation.

To glimpse architecture's fundamental shapes, it is necessary to strip away the layers of surfaces and devices that have been built on top of the energy systems that support nearly any given activity in the first place. Other than the ergonomics associated with furniture and the body, it is the control of these energy systems that architects seek to facilitate a particular activity. Without giving shape to the energy systems that are at the core of our social experiences, architecture's most intrinsic characteristics are not being seen but are only being perceived through the restrained filters and signifiers believed to be the sole way to instill such value in architecture. Looking to energy as a material provides another medium for absorbing aesthetics and monetary value and also gives opportunities to contemplate and observe as-yet-unknown spatial and organizational ramifications that are shaped by the proclivities of the material systems used. It is through these material energies that the shape of architecture can be found, buried beneath and obfuscated by surfaces and shells, mechanisms that have long been assumed to be the architect's only option for designing the parameters necessary for these activities.

What begins as a conversation about the properties of material energies and the shapes that they are capable of producing eventually opens up to include these larger typologies, as more diverse organizational systems

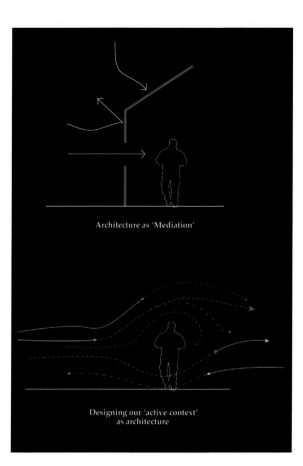

Architecture as 'Mediation'

Designing our 'active context'
as architecture

Beyond mediation

The use of a surface to mediate the existing energies and climates of a site to provide spaces for activities, people, and objects is without question architecture's defining characteristic. Surfaces of mediation currently hold all of the aesthetic values, technological advancements, and organizational controls associated with architecture. If architects stop seeing architecture as the result of mediation—a process of blocking, absorbing, or allowing various forms of energy inside, mainly without altering them—those same energy variables can become the subject of design. Architecture then becomes an act of amplification—strengthening and augmenting the characteristics and properties of the particles and waves that both the surrounding environment and architecture share. Amplification means designing the material composition of the local environment that the body moves through to meet the spatial and organizational needs associated with architecture. The action is similar to introducing currents into a body of water or using its thermoclines, those demarcations that are often sudden and striking in their contrasts in temperature from one region of water to another. The responsibility we currently place on surfaces and geometries to provide architectural systems would be taken up by the amplified energy that currently courses through the environment, making these various forms of energy the building blocks of architecture.

of circulation and density are required to accommodate more complex activities and programs. The intention here is first to better understand the characteristics and proclivities of the architectural shape of energy before seeking to draw out the spatial and organizational implications on activities and social experiences that emerge from developing new typologies. Architectural shape is more than the proclivities of the materials used to define a geographic space; it is the combined result of those material biases intertwined with the social pressures and forces placed on the activities they seek to facilitate.

Characteristics of Energy's Shape
*Feedbacks*_____

When energy is released, whether heat and light from a burning piece of wood, sound waves from a speaker, light from a flashlight, or steam from a hot cup of coffee, that energy seeks to dissipate into its surroundings. "Energy spontaneously disperses from being localized to becoming spread out if it is not hindered from doing so," states the second law of thermodynamics. The rate at which that energy spreads is based on the parameters of its surroundings, including existing temperature, light levels, humidity, and air velocity. For this reason, the shape of an architecture made of energy cannot have an unwavering and consistent form due to one primary feature; instead, it manifests the feedback between the energy exerted to create a physical space and the context of atmospheric conditions that interact with that energy. Such architectural shape is a boundary that represents the relationship between material energies and existing climate conditions. These two factors interact and exchange forms of energy that influence not only the architecture's initial shape but also the degree to which it can fluctuate over time, as external atmospheric conditions change. Architectural shape will therefore always be in a feedback loop between the existing environment and the system an architect produces. This feedback goes beyond the external forces acting on its shape to include those that enter the architecture. There is an "energy balance equation" in which anything that crosses that boundary (additional people—their body temperature, physical mass, or supporting objects) affects the energy system, that is, the architecture.

     Energy's shape has the potential to shift in size or resolution, among an array of other physical attributes, from one moment to another, because its climatic context is variable and interacts with the energies that make up the intended shape. A particular streetlight produces what the eye perceives to be a different boundary edge under a full moon than under a new moon, when less light is reflected back to Earth. The distance between the light source and the ground might not change; therefore the size of the circle of light on the ground remains the same. However, the edge between the area of light on the ground and the darkness beyond will appear less defined when more light is reaching Earth's surface and is being reflected from surrounding surfaces than on a darker night. The same effect can be observed using a flashlight outside during the transition from dusk to sunset. The definition of the boundaries that a particular light is able to produce as it pans out from your hand will increase as the sun sets. The darker the surroundings, the more defined the edge will become. The boundaries, and therefore an architecture defined by such properties, are not isolated closed systems standing in opposition to their contexts (solid-state construction and mediation), but are instead open systems, arrangements informed by the relationship between an architectural system and its environment.

This does not mean that the control that architects have in securing activities will necessarily waver as surrounding atmospheric variables or the "energy balance equation" changes, but it does mean that additional energy might need to be exerted or released to maintain such a configuration. This might very well affect other aesthetic characteristics of the architectural shape.

*Actual Color May Vary*_____

Neither a campfire nor street lighting needs to operate under the assumption that the inputs and output of heat and light to and from each of these sources are constant (for example, the same amount of wood or output of lumen from the lightbulb). In a campfire, more wood can be added as fuel that will increase the size of the flame to offset additional cold, wind, or darkness at the site and therefore maintain the geographical desired edge. When the external variables of ambient light, humidity, air particles, wind, and thermal conditions change, a specified boundary will either grow or shrink, because those external variables exert influence on the energy source creating the boundary. Additional energy can be exerted to offset external forces and maintain a desired geographic control, or it can be allowed to withdraw and go dormant, like a streetlight turned off until needed again. But as you place more wood on a fire to overcome the cold, the flame burns hotter and brighter and the color of that flame itself might change slightly (irrespective of fuel source and chemistry). The decision to maintain the thermal boundary around the fire as the surrounding climate pushes against it requires an increase in fuel, and that increase has an influence on the aesthetic qualities of the fire.

As external physical properties of the surroundings fluctuate, architecture produced through amplification must intensify or abate to maintain a specified series of boundaries needed for organizing spaces. This increase or decrease of intensity will manifest itself through other characteristics of the architecture, particularly the aesthetics of architecture's shape. A campfire is a simplistic example, but it serves to illustrate the basic principle clearly for all forms of architectural boundaries created from energy. These boundaries will always have a dialogue with their context, because they consist of the same material properties.

But this increase in energy intensity is not a proportional progression, just as increasing the length of a cantilever by 20 percent does not necessarily mean that the new overhang will require the same percentage increase in materials and structural depth. In that example, the energy in the increased cantilever will be stored in the solid masses used in the structure. However, in the case of material energies, the additional deployment of energy to offset external forces from the surrounding environment will have to be seen or felt within the physical characteristics of the boundary edges.

This fluctuation might occur to some degree from one minute to another, seasonally, or over decades, as climatic variables change and nearby design projects or construction influences the particular system. What this produces is a unique relationship between sustaining a particular set of physical boundaries needed to define the parameters of an activity and maintaining particular aesthetic characteristics, which could certainly change if the physical boundaries are upheld. A fluctuating relationship in an architectural shape between aesthetics and spatial boundaries differs rather substantially from what is now associated with architectural form, thought to be static and unwavering, with aesthetic qualities generally assumed to be inscribed into the solid-state boundaries produced.

Shape is not predetermined for recognition solely by the eye. The spectrum of energy's material properties sometimes extends well beyond the realm of what is visible to the human eye. Therefore the shape of energy in architecture might take on other characteristics, detectable beyond the visible spectrum through other sensory perceptions or because they influence secondary or tertiary systems that the eyes might be able to perceive.

Where does a campfire start and end? More specifically, can you define the edge that separates the resources of heat and light that the campfire delivers from the surrounding environmental context of ambient air temperature and light that already exists? Is that edge where you can see the light dissipating into the darker surroundings, or is it the thermal boundary your body can feel as you determine a location most accommodating for your chosen activity? What about the edges of a magnetic field or a frequency of sound, or even a thermal condition again, but this time without a visible indicator—the fire, for example—to give it a visual shape? The human eye can't perceive heat, but an exhaust grate on a swatch of land during the winter will produce a patch of growing green grass surrounded by snow. This shows that the temperature is unique to a given location. You can't see humidity levels either, but you can see condensation when air on one side of a window is colder than on the other side, as the air on the warmer side will hold more water and condense on the cold glass. Such invisible energy sources—important system signatures that are invisible but for their footprints or traces—might require a tracer to run in parallel to give us the indicators that fit with our predominant senses, like the scent tracers the gas industry places inside natural gas to alert people to its existence should there be a leak. The tracers used to track velocities of river currents' flow patterns below surface water currents are another example.

Being able to identify the boundary of these energy systems at any particular moment is important because those edges (after being more tightly controlled as an architectural material) will come to define architectural space, and will therefore require a shape that designers can articulate abstractly, through various representation techniques, and that inhabitants can identify in their occupation and use of the architecture. It also raises the question of how architects communicate such an architectural shape to an audience prior to delivery. The relationship of a representation used to convey design intentions and what is expected in a final deliverable when working with materials that are not always visible to the human eye and are inherently fluctuating is difficult to manage yet of critical importance. What is required is an ability to design and convey a specified bandwidth of change that is expected in this architecture's shape. Tracers coupled with the new activities that are made possible on a given site may help alleviate these issues. However, the tolerances associated with final dimensions, assembly of materials, and finishes used to judge the success of a project, from design on paper into construction, will certainly take on a slightly different meaning.

*Tolerances*_____

Our control over material energies is not definitive like our control over geometry. Tolerances in geometries as they relate to solid-state construction are expressed in fractions of an inch or millimeters, both in the required specifications for constructing a product and in conveying design intentions to a future audience. Conveying an image of architecture's shape so that it can be recognized and commodified is no small task with regard to energy systems, yet it is of considerable importance; not only does shape communicate intentions to a wider audience but it also acts as a means of refining architectural intentions during the design phase.

Being able to plan for these tolerances requires knowledge of the material energies deployed and of the activities a project requires and the atmospheric variables associated with the specific geographic locale in which the project will be situated. In some regards, this geographic locale produces a type of vernacular role in the production of this architecture, as the architecture's performative abilities, shapes, and organizational systems will most certainly be related to its climatic context. This is not because such an approach is seen as more appropriate or reasonable, but because the existing climatic or environmental variables of a given region or site may be more difficult to overcome or influence. The existing variables of a site will play a role in giving shape to architecture, whether that site is at a particular latitude or in a particular microclimate within a city. As a simple example: if you pick a house

from a catalog that is made of wood framing, steel, glass, or any number of other construction systems, its shape will be the same in Guadalajara, Mexico, as in Boston or Seattle (assuming the same precision of construction). Your energy bills may vary, but its shape in terms of spatial control—size of rooms, circulation, and even color—will not.

By contrast, the shape of a given project produced with material energies will most certainly be informed by the feedback from the existing atmospheric variables unique to each region and site (Guadalajara, Boston, or Seattle). This does not mean that a similar design intention and strategy cannot be deployed across these three climates when designing a house, but it does mean that unique qualities, as well as potential organizational implications, will vary from one site to another, making a singular, sellable image of the house difficult to devise. Unlike the catalog house with a reproducible image

Sean Lally/WEATHERS
Proof 001, Installation Proposal. Chicago, Illinois, USA, 2013.
The energy mass within the plaza creates a physical shape and space usable during Chicago's winter months. The shape of the space can be tuned in intensity to accommodate changing recreational and public programming needs and can even go dormant when not needed. Embedded into the existing stone paving of the plaza, the project sits flush on grade. Two openings are covered with a porous, walkable surface. The larger opening pushes air out and launches it on a circular course before it is pulled back down and recycled by the smaller opening to the rear.

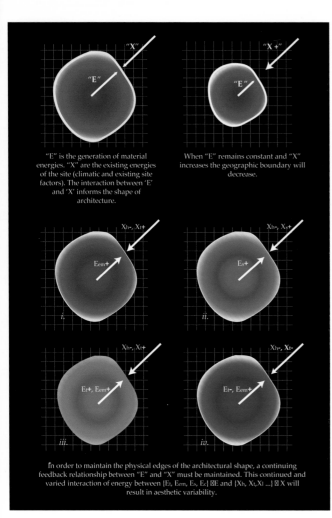

"X"

"E"

"E" is the generation of material energies. "X" are the existing energies of the site (climatic and existing site factors). The interaction between 'E' and 'X' informs the shape of architecture.

"X+"

"E"

When "E" remains constant and "X" increases the geographic boundary will decrease.

Xh-, Xt+

Eem+

i.

Xh-, Xs+

Es+

ii.

Xh-, Xt+

Et+, Eem+

iii.

Xh-, Xt-

Et-, Eem+

iv.

In order to maintain the physical edges of the architectural shape, a continuing feedback relationship between "E" and "X" must be maintained. This continued and varied interaction of energy between {Et, Eem, Es, Ec} ⊠E and {Xh, Xt,Xt ...} ⊠ X will result in aesthetic variability.

Shape succession

The physical properties of the boundaries that define this architecture are tied to the relationship between the intensity of the *material energies* used and the climatic variables of the surrounding context exerting pressure on those qualities. As the properties of the climatic surroundings fluctuate (i.e., increasing in humidity or wind speed, or dropping in temperature), the architectural shape must respond by either intensifying or decreasing the energy output needed to maintain the specified series of boundaries for refining and organizing a given space. Additional energy can be exerted to offset external forces and maintain a desired geographic control, or the boundary can be allowed to withdraw from the area or even go dormant. This feedback relationship between the material energies and the existing climatic variables influences aesthetic as well as physical boundaries and the spatial control of the architectural shape. Like a campfire, the flames can increase in size to offset the increasing cold, wind, or darkness of the site and therefore maintain the geographical desired edge, but this means the intensified flames are burning hotter and brighter in the center, changing the architecture's physical and aesthetic properties in the process.

that can be built nearly anywhere due to standardized assembly and building materials, architecture built of material energies produces a type of shape that is micro-vernacular, as each site creates a unique feedback relationship to the energy systems deployed. Seasonal variability in humidity levels, temperature, and winds might be a regional characteristic of a city that architects are aware of, but even the microclimates that make one site unique from another three blocks away will play a role in the project's shape. These differences yield a shape vernacular that transcends its predecessors, which are tied directly to surfaces and walls that mediate their surroundings, such as the porches and overhangs of homes of the southern United States before air conditioning, which select or reject breezes, or the massive walls of adobe structures in the Southwest, to name just a few. The vernaculars generated by material energies have their own characteristics.

Shape Succession

With a better understanding of the proclivities associated with the material energies that inform this architectural shape, attention can be turned to the social and organizational implications that are sure to emerge as notions of stasis and architectural boundaries are reframed. This feedback relationship between the energies that form architectural space and the climatic variables of its context produces a shape that differs greatly from what is traditionally associated with architecture as a static, unwavering condition. In actuality, though, this approach to shape coincides with currently changing characterizations of how environmental systems and ecosystems demarcate and define geographic locales. Perceptions of ecological systems have evolved substantially over the last century. Ecosystems were once thought of as closed systems seeking a state of equilibrium with predictable end states, but they are now thought of as dynamic and nonlinear, where "disturbance is a frequent and intrinsic characteristic."[1] Within this growing understanding of ecosystems and the boundaries utilized to define them, these diverse pockets are now recognized to have the possibility of multiple outcomes and no determined condition. An architecture in which shape is constructed by amplifying and harnessing shared contextual materialities can learn something from this change in thought.

Fire columns
Yves Klein's fire column represents material energies, which sit within a new lineage of symbolic column orders for the architectural profession.

Robert E. Cook, in his essay "Do Landscapes Learn?" (reprinted in its entirety in this volume), describes what he believes is a paradigm shift in how we think about ecologies and their changing characteristics over time, referred to as ecological succession. Succession is a term roughly a century old that explains the process through which an ecological community develops change in its configuration. This is the combined relationship of variables within a system of vegetation, fauna, and microclimates, including chemical compositions of air and soil that change from one geographic locale to another, separating one ecosystem from another. Ecosystems are discernible from one another by such variations, which can be demarcated along geographic boundaries.

This concept of "climax succession" undoubtedly resonates with traditional notions of architectural form made of geometries and solid-state construction, as both are predicated on the assumption of a closed system. We strive to protect a building (from earthquakes, hurricanes, fires, and decay, for example), but we understand its form (from representations to construction and occupation) as a singular, pinnacle condition. When that form eventually fails and succumbs to one of these forces, it will leave behind artifacts that others can attempt to piece together to identify the lost climax replaced in what we all consciously know to be a process of continuing succession (i.e., history). It almost goes without saying that the building material that defined that climax was never in a closed system. Everyone has a mental image of a building succumbing to the elements around it over time, eventually being absorbed into the changing environments around it, whether due to environmental conditions (decay) or political ones (demolition). But as a working state of architecture, its existence is contingent on perpetuating this climax state for as long as possible. When that climax state can no longer be held, it quickly falls into what is characterized as decline until it can be repaired back to its climax state. Very little variation is acceptable.

To fortify this notion, building materials for architecture have advanced in the pursuit of strength and durability against the variables around them that might degrade the "climax form" that the architect envisions. To maintain such an aesthetic or formal configuration, construction has sought out technologies and materials that produce these forms through trapped and ossified energy, marching forward from bundled grasses to wood, stone, iron, steel, glass, and plastics, all in an attempt to enforce a designed and unwavering climax form set within the environment. These solid-state material advancements create greater territorial control in construction precision, increasing a design's longevity by allowing it to outlast a growing list of external forces while also inscribing our exact aesthetic desires. When projects like the Guggenheim in New York, the Louvre in Paris, or the landscape gardens of Thomas Church or Garrett Eckbo are completed, they each exist with no visions other than their continued existence both in terms of territorial control and aesthetic value. The value of the project's form in these cases is judged on its ability to maintain the singular configuration envisioned and recognized by all those who have witnessed it in image or in person. They are considered "preserved" as long as they maintain these same characteristics through time.

The idea that architecture exists as a closed system comes from a clear and logical place, because architecture has a responsibility to secure and facilitate a wide range of activities, many of which cannot (as we prescribe them) vary in their organizational configurations or exist without some steady level of protection from outside forces. This, of course, is what makes architecture distinct from how we understand surrounding environmental ecologies. It is this need to meet the requirements of activities and social experiences beyond what an existing site might be able to offer prior to intervention that makes it architecture. Architecture demands a tighter specificity of control

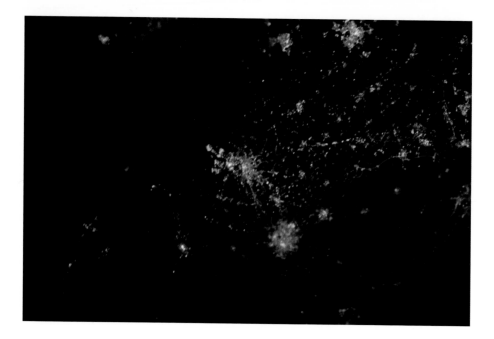

for social activities not generally associated with what existing environmental surroundings supply. A theatrical performance, gallery opening, or your ability to entertain in your own living room is not thought to be subject to the weather. Your guests' ability to arrive at the event may be impeded by those variables, but the staging of the event itself is not. Those programmatic activities are not thought of as being in repose or on hold.

The shape of architecture is determined by the extent to which the physical boundaries of a defined territory are held at any particular moment. As external climatic pressure increases, a choice is made either to increase the

Urban wash
The wash of artificial light, seen from this vantage point, not only highlights existing infrastructures of connectivity and overarching shapes of cities but produces new ones not seen during the day. If this wash were imbued with a broader spectrum of material energies beyond the visible spectrum of light, it might become an even stronger architectural typology to engage for design at the local as well as urban scale. Photograph of Antwerp, Belgium, at night shot from the NASA International Space Station, Mission-ISS026, Role-E, Frame-13692.

use of material energies to offset this pressure and maintain those boundaries or not to do so, which results in a diminished ability to control space. This architectural shape is created from gradient intensities that do not produce the same dichotomy we recognize with surfaces and walls, where the body exists on one side of a boundary or the other. An architectural shape consisting of material energies is made of the same materiality as the surrounding context, which makes the production of a historical artifact more difficult but also makes that shape more flexible, able to accommodate the shifting demands of changing activities, expansion, and recession. This is an embedded characteristic that can be held as tightly or nimbly as one chooses. Decisions can be made to reinforce an organizational system against one of these external forces on an hourly, seasonally, or yearly basis, but as was discussed earlier, aesthetic and sensory implications will be perceived elsewhere.

So how do we reconcile this ingrained association of stasis in architecture (climax form), or the demand to maintain a building's image and its defined spatial control, with what is ultimately a fluid and variable feedback relationship between material energies and an existing climatic context? It is important to recognize that the shape's resultant aesthetic value will become variable along a determined bandwidth as long as the shape maintains spatial and organizational specificity—or potentially, vice versa: a shape could maintain aesthetic criteria while letting spatial configurations ebb. Architects can manage this ever-changing balance through the approach of "shape succession."

Shape succession provides a window into being able to embrace intrinsic characteristics of the material energies that construct an architectural shape while simultaneously addressing the need to secure the parameters of social activities. What is necessary is a shape that is capable of holding those boundaries when needed, but is potentially able to release that grip if other opportunities to organize space are pursued. The question of whether material energies can facilitate the needs of architecture is less in doubt if architects and the individuals using a space are willing to recognize and accept a shifting notion of stasis, if not in terms of the geographic boundaries of that space at a given moment, then certainly in terms of their aesthetic qualities. This produces an architectural aesthetic that varies in some regard, as the material energies attempt to maintain properties of a defined and desired spatial boundary by overcoming the influence of external variables acting upon them.

Shaping Social Experiences

The boundaries constructed within the environment influence behavior both directly, by physically interacting with the body, as well as culturally, through constructed social norms. Architectural boundaries present difficulties should one try to question them, including the social responses of those who witness such behavior. Try to walk through the drywall partition in front of you or test the glass wall of the office building you're in and see what the response is, both from your own body and from the people around you. The physical properties of the boundary, as well as the actions available to the body in responding to it, create an understood datum related to both the property of the material—how our bodies sense it—and what happens if the body were to come in contact with it.

A concrete wall will provide greater security and privacy than a glass wall, but it won't allow the same engagement between two people on either side. A short picket fence will demarcate the edge of a house's property and prevent (most) family dogs from escaping while simultaneously making it clear to passers-by where trespassing begins, all while never obscuring views into or out of the property. The articulation of boundary edges as they are defined and interpreted for construction in architecture forms an objective reality, producing a datum of control. These datums of control may be overruled by a particular individual's mischievousness or confusion of cultural norms: a room with a door, two windows, seating, and a great video projector and sound system may be prescribed as a lecture room, for example, but this doesn't prevent someone from running through the door and out one of the windows at any given point. But two rooms connected by a single corridor certainly prescribe the path for that individual prior to coming through that door and exiting out the window. To put it another way, the physical boundaries created, predicated on our body's ability to perceive and interact with the properties of those boundaries, dictate our interactions with each other and space. Its not always possible to know how a space will be used, but by working with the physical properties of the boundaries that structure and organize architecture, a dialogue is created between the possible actions of people and the characteristics of the spaces defined.

Architectural shape is more than the manipulation of materials alone. It comes from a dialogue between the physical boundaries architects create to organize people and goods and larger social trends tied to economy,

politics, philosophy, and communication that originate outside the purview of architecture. Each applies pressure upon the other in ways ultimately unknown until they come into direct contact, only to then influence and reinform one another. The physical boundaries we define and then subdivide, conglomerate, and connect to manage complex social interactions (schools, public libraries) or highly specified activities (theaters, hospitals) influence the nature of those activities initially specified. Pairing the characteristics and opportunities of shape with social demands outside of architecture is how spatial typologies come about.

Discussions of shape may begin with the properties of the materials that construct it or the ways that it can foster a single chosen activity, but it is through these social pressures and the need for larger and more complex organizational strategies that architectural shape really emerges. Understanding the proclivities of a material system beyond the construction of

Sean Lally/WEATHERS
Proof 001, Installation Proposal. Chicago, Illinois, USA, 2013.
The boundary edge of the space can be held tightly as the air moves out from the source below and into the environment above. Air temperature, velocity, and the release of particulates into the air join together to inform the spatial boundary edge. Spatial boundaries can be both visually detected from a distance as well as sensed through tactile means, triggered by the thermal and electrical charges and resistance of air particulates that the human body comes in contact with as it approaches and enters the spaces.

a singular space and how it might inform larger typologies and organizations is what is most intriguing, and yet most difficult to predict. These results may be intentional at times, while in other cases the implications may trickle down and play out over longer stretches of time in unexpected ways, impossible to have planned for yet apparent in hindsight and consequently available for deployment once again through revisions and refinements in future design. As Louis Pasteur said, "In the fields of observation chance favors only the prepared mind." It is therefore only through identifying two variables simultaneously—the proclivities of materials and the larger social trends that inform architectural shape—that we can be prepared to recognize the opportunities stemming from this dialogue, which the architect can then exploit or suppress in creating architecture's shape.

Robin Evans reminds us that architecture is more than a practicality and that the shape and configurations it takes are never "neutral translations of such prerequisites." The configuration of rooms, systems of circulation, and visual connectivity that surround us appear so common that we forget the significance these configurations have had on defining our social dynamics and lifestyles, and that these configurations and typologies have an "origin."[2] The assumption that certain configurations of spaces and typologies within our daily lives are so simple and "ordinary" is a "delusion" because they in fact come from dozens if not hundreds of iterations of this dialogue, and in turn go on to influence our social lives.[3]

The example that Evans points to that most clearly illustrates this dialogue is what he refers to as the yet-unwritten history of the corridor. This typology of organizing a building's activity layout appears to be so ordinary and obvious to architect and inhabitant alike that it is assumed to lack a history, yet it is known to have given shape to countless architectures. In truth, the corridor is thought to originate in the last few years of the sixteenth century in John Thorpe's Beaufort House, in Chelsea, England, where it is notated on the plan as "a longe Entry through all."[4] Prior to the use of the corridor, rooms would exist in a matrix; each room contained multiple doors, making it necessary to pass through one room to reach another. This movement would obviously disturb the activities of those rooms as individuals passed through. The corridor provides the opportunity to move along a shared pathway connected to each of the rooms while simultaneously separating the activities within from the circulation of individuals looking to access a separate space.

SHAGG—San Fernando Corridor Temporary Artwork. WEATHERS/Sean Lally.
Installation proposal, 2009–10.
SHAGG picks up where Astroturf left off, creating an artificial carpet for the human body
to engage in the exterior environment. No longer accepting that the various energies
within our environment are beyond our control, SHAGG attempts to design these energy
systems and make them the new building blocks of architecture. The project SHAGG
creates an outdoor, carpet-sized garden that does not rely on the sun's light for warmth and
photosynthesis, so its color and bloom are no longer tied to the seasons, and the distracting
sounds of traffic and neighbors are overcome by white-noise emitters embedded under
the 30,000-square-meter surface area. Composed of a series of strategically placed carpets
that emit light, heat, and sound, SHAGG produces a level of artificial coziness, creating an
environment that enables social gathering. Rather than try to recreate the recognizable,
SHAGG is used to design its own microworlds.

The matrix of room configurations that existed prior to the seventeenth century treated the human body in domestic spaces much differently than the corridor would in the nineteenth century. If the matrix of rooms reinforced the overlap and intersection of bodies passing each other in space, the corridor would reinforce their separation. Much of this shift can be attributed to the changing notion of what the *interior* was.[5] Specifically in England, the notion of the interior underwent significant changes between the late fifteenth century (just prior the emergence of Robin Evans's example of the corridor) and the mid-nineteenth century. The late fifteenth century defined the interior as one's inner spirituality, separated from the outside world. The eighteenth century would see "interiority" as "inner character and a sense of individual subjectivity."[6] In the nineteenth century, it would come to mean the inside of a building or room and emerge with the significance of a physical three-dimensional space.[7] The hermetic effect produced in isolating rooms from one another reinforced the privacy and separation of physical bodies that was rooted in this changing psychological notion of the interior. As the notion of the interior grew beyond the individual body, the need to separate that body from other bodies also grew more acute. Material manifestations of the interior, including room and corridor planning in the mid-nineteenth century, did more than just articulate this change. Over the course of those 100-plus years, the articulation of space and movement was in dialogue with an ongoing change in individual subjectivity, and these two factors would influence social engagements, interactions, circulation, and aesthetics in those interior architectural spaces.

The example above is but one of many that illustrate that material change and fabrication alone are not responsible for the spatial typologies and shapes of architecture that emerge over time. It also serves to highlight that it takes a combination of tuning the proclivities of materialities afforded us at any particular moment with the social pressures of economics, communication, politics, and the like to bring us novel organizational systems and architectural shapes. But if architects fail to observe these two variables simultaneously in dialogue, questioning them so as to speculate on the potential spatial and organizational implications at play, they will fail to do anything more than attempt to mimic and reproduce known organizational systems. Regardless of the novelty of any forms, they will be only imitating existing typologies. Giving shape to this architecture is a means to avoid the passive aspects of designing that begin by defining activities and then constructing boundaries to facilitate them.[8]

The underlying interest within this discussion is to direct a conversation toward new spatial typologies that could develop from these material energies and suggest possibilities for how they might influence new social experiences. But in truth, the best we can do at the moment is to bookend the discussion by identifying characteristics of material systems on one end and current social trends on the other. In between will be iteration upon iteration by multiple voices seeking opportunities to strengthen and reinform both poles. The development of this architecture's shape requires simultaneous attention to selected social trends and a willingness to embellish the dialogue between those trends and the proclivities of the material energies that facilitate them. Over time, architects will recognize these organizational techniques as facilitating social standards and producing architectural types like those that have developed in the past (courtyard, tower, free plan, double-loaded corridor). The shapes and norms of architecture that we might instinctively dismiss as neutral and ordinary were not likely produced by singular decrees and immediate manifestations, but instead were developed by amplifying existing currents that course below the surface of architecture, requiring multiple iterations to rise to the top. A dialogue between multiple architects produces these typologies gradually, until they are exemplified by several individuals or traced back to a few earlier projects through recognizable elements of those now-ubiquitous shapes. An architecture of mediation has witnessed many voices and taken on many titles over the course of movements during or after their time (classical, Gothic, Renaissance, baroque, modern, postmodern). An architecture designed by amplifying environmental energy systems will hopefully encourage as many voices to take part in its manifestation, through not a singular directive but a multiplicity of efforts.

One implication is certain: continuous advancement of material energies will produce a material system (energy) that leaves less of a trace of our activities than the materiality that came prior to it. Petrified energy in the form of blocks of stone and beams of steel may leave evidence behind for centuries as artifacts of fallen "climaxes," but material energies will dissipate almost immediately, leaving little behind. Like turning a light switch off, material energies are quickly gone but easily brought back. The resultant architecture might appear almost to dissipate on command, when that localized energy is permitted to spread out. The building blocks of material energies attain entropy more quickly than those of solid-state construction, dissolving and dissipating their shapes when no longer attended to.

Such an image may portray them as more frail, but material energies might also be seen as more nimble. Unlike a climax form, which projects past accomplishments long into future decades, this architectural system might be more fleeting and therefore adaptable to change (climatic, economic, social, and aesthetic), offering a shape that could prove far more valuable. Shape succession looks to what some might point to be an architecture constructed of energy systems' greatest weakness and suggests it as its greatest attribute. This condition might one day cause people to recall those artifacts of monumental and ossified energy blocks as cold-blooded dinosaurs that existed prior to the warm-blooded architectures that by that point will move under their feet. Shape succession creates an architecture that is more agile and has an innate ability to be upgraded. The properties of material energies that require them to be continually active and reproduced to define edges and boundaries work to meet an ever-growing demand for updates, changes in spatial needs, and continued advancements in performance simulations, producing an architecture that is continually being regenerated and therefore easily enhanced and fine-tuned. Imagine an architectural shape (including its aesthetics and the intensity of its boundary control) that is continuously replenishable. The ability to renew more quickly and continuously throughout a project's lifespan seems pertinent today. The shapes might be entropic, but the social implications of these organizational opportunities and social experiences might be longer lived. This is a very different type of artifact for architecture to leave behind.

Notes
The following essay is a revised version of a chapter of the same name from my book *The Air from Other Planets: A Brief History of Architecture to Come* (Zurich: Lars Müller Publishers, 2013).

1_ Robert E. Cook, "Do Landscapes Learn? Ecology's 'New Paradigm' and Design in Landscape Architecture," in *Environmentalism and Landscape Architecture*, ed. Michel Conan (Washington, D.C.: Dumbarton Oaks, 2000).

2_ Robin Evans, "Figures, Doors, and Passages," in *Translations from Drawing to Building and Other Essays* (Cambridge, MA: MIT Press, 1997), 56.

3_ Ibid., 89.

4_ Ibid., 70.

5_ Ibid., 88.

6_ Charles Rice, *The Emergence of the Interior, Architecture, Modernity, Domesticity* (London and New York: Routledge, 2007), 2.

7_ Ibid.

8_ Rem Koolhaas and Bernard Tschumi, "Two Architects, Ten Questions on Program," *Praxis: Journal of Writing and Building* 8, ed. Amanda Reeser Lawrence and Ashley Schafer (2006): 6–15.

Combustible Landscape

Sanford Kwinter

Most textbooks and surveys fix the origins of the science of ecology in the work of Alexander von Humboldt, particularly his 1807 "Essay on the Geography of Plants."[1] There is little need to contest this genealogy, mainly because we do not know what it means in the first place to speak of the origin of a term that has never been concretely defined. What I would like to present here consists of a proposal not to radicalize ecology—since I am not an ecologist, that job would not be mine—but to ask in what ways "ecology" may uniquely be able to continue to radicalize *us*. The approach to this task will also be an approach toward a needed definition.

As a theorist, my interest is in what might be called "ecological thinking." The unity and power of ecology as a discipline, I would argue, is not to be reduced to its role at the foundations of biological thought (although it is also this), but for the habits of mind—the philosophical postures—that it has brought into play not only in the life sciences but in all aspects of both our knowledge systems and our experiential world. I will suggest that our contemporary world may be characterized by a recent passage in which space, architecture, and social life can no longer be understood in the conventional yet modern terms of relations of machines but that we are converging strongly toward a theory, and system of explanation, in which the animal and its flexible and especially creative relations play the central, paradigmatic role.

Von Humboldt showed how plant shapes, sizes, and behaviors depended on variables in the immediate environment such as altitude, climate, soil, latitude, etc. The same genotype was seen to express itself along a wide spectrum of variations according to which conditions it encounters in its temporal and spatial location. Von Humboldt was among the first to embed the study of forms within a field of influences and hence began a great series of fundamental changes in how we understand the concept of "environment." His phrase "Alles ist Wechselwirkung," typically translated as "Everything is connected," is more critically and accurately translated as "All is interaction." To von Humboldt we owe the habits of thinking about form and nature as an expression of interactions that more or less incorporate, or synthesize, the environment itself. In von Humboldt I would situate the notion, later dear to Romantic theorists and artists alike, that form is an expression of forces. Hence the beginning of ecological thinking.[2]

But von Humboldt's friend and elder Johann Goethe had completed a work on botany himself barely ten years earlier that many today view as the origin of dynamical systems thinking. In this work, *The Metamorphosis of Plants* (1790), Goethe supplies a single model of algorithmic explanation for the diversity of vegetal forms in the world as well as for the diversity of organ forms within a single plant and family.[3] Stem, leaves, calyx, and petal (and all forms in between) are related as organizational points in a space made up of three interacting fields of influence: a flexible "type," a continuous "gradient," and a closed but repeating "cycle." As Ernst Cassirer brilliantly summarized it: Goethe effectuated the transition from "generic" thinking—from the habits of thinking about form within the fixed and decidedly typological Linnaean tables of genera and species—to the "genetic" habit of mind that sees form as an active process of generation, improvisation, and expression.[4] Here is a second critical component of what will come to be known as "ecological thinking": the open communicative interplay—and integration—of continuums that possess very different temporalities or rates of unfolding. Every plant and plant part is an expression of one point and moment in this matrix of interactions.

Fifty years later, Charles Darwin, in his famous garden at Down House, notices the powerful tendency of a plot of ground—even "a [single] square yard of turf" as he describes it—to alter, organize, and transform both the kind and the proportion of elements that make it up.[5] Not only does he posit for us the concept of an active composition—and hence an underlying if invisible set of rules and orders (primarily competition)—but sees the territory in question as composed of communities held together socially. What this concept of sociality gives us for the first time is an image of an overarching structure of directionality or evolution as well as the absolutely necessary correlate term— and as the great Ernst Mayr has tirelessly pointed out, a concept that has been almost routinely ignored, even by evolutionary biologists—of the "population."[6] For "population thinking" goes hand in hand with ecological thinking: according to the doctrine, every point and every element represents a potential that is different from every other; indeed, a population is seen as nothing but a field of differences, to be realized or not. What is ecological about this is that the differences in the field stabilize into approximate categories—the species— but the differences do not get extinguished and the stable forms are at best provisional and illusory. Once again, the true reality of what is going on in a landscape is not reducible to what is seen but to that in the embedded structure that holds it together, to the organization of forces and especially to the history and sequence of their appearance in the system.

The problems introduced by this Darwinian insight have not been widely understood. On one level, underlying instability is endemic and universal wherever there is information exchange. On another, the loose confederacies that make up a population represent unities in their own right, which interact with other populations even as they interact with the interactions between their own component elements. Hence the principle of "modularity" becomes very important both here and in ecological thinking in general, even if it has been largely ignored. The work of Herbert Simon represents one extraordinary application of ecological thinking—particularly around the concept of modularity (which he calls "nearly decomposable systems")—to fields and objects largely divorced from natural systems.[7] (Simon actually shows how ND systems are inherently and spontaneously evolutionary.) But the concept of modularity is widely applied today in genetics, neuroscience, and elsewhere and has shown an explanatory power greater than almost any other concept of recent times.

To return to the discussion of Darwin's square yard of turf and the principle of history and sequence: Ecological structure continues today to be the object of great mystery. In a series of experiments in the mid-1990s by the ecologists Stuart Pimm and James Drake on modeling the artificial assembly of ecological communities, it was determined that in such systems there is exhibited a "Humpty Dumpty effect"—in other words, the reassembly of an existing or found ecological community cannot be achieved even if one has exhaustive information of the species and relations that comprise it.[8][9] An ecological snapshot will not render the movements of a film. The sequence of introduction of species, even if many of the species later vanish from the system entirely, continues to structure the integrity of the system long after they have played their visible roles. In sum: Ecological structure is temporal structure.

There are many episodes of importance in the evolution of ecological think-ing between Darwin and Pimm and Drake, and many that are not widely acknowl-edged by practicing ecologists. It is worth enumerating a couple of these here, on the off chance that they will be of interest to both applied ecologists and theorists.

One case is that of Vladimir Vernadsky, a name relatively known today but almost entirely unknown to English-speaking scientists until the 1990s (although George Hutchinson refers to him in his 1970 *Scientific Monthly* article on the biosphere),[10] when his work from the 1920s was translated into English and came to the attention of Lynn Margulis, who saw in it a legitimate precursor of the Gaia hypothesis.[11][12] Vernadsky's work was known to philosophers long before; I learned of him in the 1970s through the writings of Georges Bataille, who evokes Vernadsky's concept of an adaptive, metabolic spherical system (the earth) driven by that of another (the sun). The conversion of energy into structure and into increasingly complex dispositions of matter as this drama unfolds on earth was seen by Bataille to lie at the foundations of wealth and of political economy. Vernadsky was the first, among many firsts, to understand geology (and later climate) as driven by chemical and biological activity, and is the inventor of the concept of the "biosphere."[13]

A second example is the work of theoretical biologist Jakob von Uexküll, who can be considered the father of the *modern* notion of ecology. Of preeminent interest is his concept of the *umwelt*, the practical world or physical environment that corresponds to the sensory and biological endowment of any given organism.[14] In a hilarious set of images from his book on "animal worlds" the point is made: the worlds of men, dogs, and flies overlap, but they do not correspond.[15] And yet each not only inhabits its particular *umwelt*, each organism is fully continuous and consubstantial with it. The figures in the world that represent assets for the organism—a small fraction of what can be said to be "out there"—correspond to a sensory system that is both possessed by and defines that animal. An animal is a segment of a circuit that connects triggers in the environment to responsive actions in another part: it is merely a more complex and layered part of the environment itself. This is what I will call the principle of "immanentism," a further central feature of "ecological thinking" according to which the distinction between organism and environment, inside and outside, is merely one of degree: a greater or lesser compression or dilation of information or life.

*　　　　　　*　　　　　　*

Nothing is more astounding than to watch a human (or an animal) reading its environment to harvest some order or energy or information from it. The ancient art of tracking is one of the most sophisticated disciplines of form reading. When a team of Oxford/Cambridge biologists put Bushman hunter-gatherers to the empirical, quantitative test, they found their readings of landscapes and events a full two days old to be 98.5 percent accurate.[16] This intimate, critical, fiercely scientific relationship to form and event is a unique and central aspect of animal being. It is the ceaseless creation of form; it is play, experiment, and science all in one. It is life. And it is the life of form to be animal.

I have been thinking about—and, in my way, studying—animals for thirteen years. The interest began in 1992 when National Geographic released the film *Eternal Enemies*, in which were depicted the most surprising filmed episodes of interspecies interaction, specifically between two distinct families of super-predator, lions and hyenas.[17] At the time of the film's release, I happened to be reading Bruce Chatwin's remarkable study of nomadism, *The Songlines*.[18] The film study by Beverly and Dereck Joubert and Chatwin's ruminative travelogue formed for me a decisive philosophical pair: they struck me as the most significant insights I had come across in years regarding the nature of space and human being. Chatwin's book included interviews with the founder of modern anthropology, Konrad Lorenz, meetings with African paleoanthropologists, and speculations on the predatory pressures that shaped the evolution of human consciousness and life forms. In both works, cats and hyenids were pitted together as the foundational forces and fields in which the human type emerged. Some years later, still in full thrall of these two documentary essays, I had occasion to travel to Africa to visit the specific sites in which they did their respective fieldwork, to see for myself if what they were proposing could possibly be true. Within hours of my arrival in the bush, I awoke from a nap that I was taking in a tree (having been been deposited there by guides who knew that I was safe, but had failed to fully assure me of this fact before leaving me) and experienced the most astounding two hours of my life.

The quiet, almost benign-seeming thorn-scrub landscape with its emptiness and almost infinite vistas had come to life as I slept, and I was awakened, as if by the bustle of a market in a Mediterranean city, by the sounds of a primordial commerce that I knew I had never heard before but still somehow "knew" as if preternaturally. The water hole next to my tree had become the site of what seemed a spontaneous generation of life: wave upon wave of organized animal herds descended in rhythmic turns to the cool pleasures of bath and drink: first the elephants, then the warthogs, the giraffes, the springbok, then elephants again, then larger antelopes and baboons, hornbills and egrets, then a few tentative mixtures of groups in decidedly nonrandom order and pairings. The incredible insouciance and playfulness of the elephants was strictly contrasted with the nervousness of the ungulates, the almost painful contortions of the giraffes (who must spread their legs far apart to allow for their mouths to reach the water's surface, making them susceptible to attack; they must also close the valves in the arteries of their necks so that the immense blood pressure levels needed to carry blood up their necks do not cause their bowed heads to explode). These were my first hours in the African bush, and I still knew nothing about how to read the landscape, but the presence of multiple pressures and dilations in the environment of behaviors was palpable to anyone with a nervous system. My eyes scanned the scene in something close to shock; certainly the procession of forms and fauna was astounding, but what amazed me most was the broad pattern, the deep, almost familiar rhythms of appearance, the immediate way in which my brain began to react by adopting a magical consciousness, taking on the sudden irrepressible *belief* that the animal patterns were actually being created before me and were not simply being revealed.

Some hours later the guides returned to retrieve me with a thermos of gin in tow (at this time I was paralyzed with fright from harassment by a merely curious but seemingly unhinged adolescent male elephant); the guides mounted the tree and began to identify the landscape's slower and subtler unfoldings and bass notes. Against the tawny Kalahari dust and at a distance of no more than 400 yards, they pointed to a dappled patch of stirring, ever so slightly greyer surfaces that were—to the knowing eye—the unmistakable collective pulsations of a pride of hunting lions.

The presence and proximity of these predators had been the metronome—or better, the conductor's baton—that had both regulated and charged the scene for the last few hours. Every emotion and startle that had passed through me in witness to the flow of life that amazing afternoon had been a product of sensations transmitted to me within a web of communicative actions and interactions of which, to my infinite surprise, I myself had played an integral part, just as did the pride of lions.

This, in sum, represented the dawning of a cascade of intuitions that overtook me in the weeks and years that followed that remarkable afternoon. I have never been able to see space or landscape in quite the same way. Yet I have not even begun to describe the insight I believe I stumbled upon that afternoon. For in the three weeks that followed, and on several subsequent trips, I spent each day during the hours around dawn and dusk in active submersion in the environment, actually cognitively hunting, as it were—searching for—animals. One quickly learns to search not so much for objects and things as for patterns, actions, disturbances—for a larger modulus of what one could call behaviors. One searches for so many emergences of concentrated intelligibility against the more dilute, or shall we say, more slowly unfolding and differentiating backdrop of geology and plants; it is in sum a search for differentials. The animal, to one who assumes the position of hunter—and we are all hunters when we dispose ourselves to discern pattern, meaning, and opportunity within the space we inhabit—is a literal byproduct of the environment, an expression of the environment, a literal synecdoche in which a "part" serves to represent or express the whole.

It is within the strange and, in today's world, idiosyncratic posture of hunting that we discover that we too are part of the whole—that we come to understand that our animal is continuous with those that we seek and find (the ones we humans primevally had been required in the name of survival to seek and find). The hunter seeks the animal, seeks to subdue and incorporate it, and in the hunting the animal is often said to migrate into the hunter itself, hence the universal lore in hunter-gatherer societies regarding "presentiment." The idea of presentiment, the phenomenon through which the hunter is said to feel the markings of the animal first as a tingling in the armpits, then as tattoos of sensation drawn on his own skin, was famously documented by Nobel anthropologist Elias Canetti in his remarkable and influential work *Crowds and Power*.[19]

Khoi and San Bushmen (and other hunter-gatherers) are renowned for their astonishing ability to track animals and to accurately deduce their actions, gender, age, level of fitness, maternal status, even intentions and mood, from disturbances or marks on plants or in sand or rock: indeed this systematic use of the senses to mine the environment has credibly been argued to represent the first appearance of a scientific attitude in human culture.[20] Consider the opening passage from a treatise on tracking by a contemporary American wilderness guide: "The first track is the end of a string. At the other end, a being is moving; a mystery, dropping a hint about itself every so many feet, telling you more about itself until you can almost see it, even before you come to it."[21]

A fundamental scientific insight was achieved in the nineteenth century by the French historian Jules Michelet in his book *The Bird,* in which he argued that the bird must not be considered separately from its nest, for only together did they form a single organism.[22] Similarly, what every animal teaches us— and I use the word animal here to refer to the capacity of any living process to mark or transform its environment—is that the animal is what makes space something rather than nothing; it is what determines the positivity of space even in the absence of concrete forms, what determines its capacity to organize, to affect, and to move.

The animal is this in two ways: first because it represents a condensation or contraction of the relationships in landscapes—climate, geology, vegetation, history, relational webs with other animal forms, etc.—and second because, endowed as it is with capacity to move and energy to expend, it represents a volatilization of space, an instigator around which space and being happen and unfold. This is precisely what the philosophical anthropologist Georges Bataille sought to express when, at the beginning of *The Accursed Share,* he declares, "The sex act is to time what the tiger is to space."[23] Both are forms of prodigal combustion.

Now when I say combustion, I mean precisely that, and in two ways: When one burns or combusts a log of wood, one harvests the potential chemical energy invested in it by the life of the tree that gave it form. In many ways this economic relationship is the same one Bataille spoke of when, following the work of Vladimir Vernadsky, he described the earth's system— and human civilization as a direct extension of earth's geochemistry—as one of managing and administrating the sun's energy, both trapping it in stores as well as expending it and letting it go free. The second way has to do with the harvesting of a different type of order, that which we call information. The landscape in its entirety is a dynamic material world and is a product of invisible algorithmic forces and logics that shape and direct it in accordance with, and in accommodation of, all other forces and logics present within it. When we study these relationships with reference to the forms that they produce, we call it evolutionary theory, but we also, and increasingly, call it "ecology." This connection is extremely profound, still incompletely acknowledged, and paramount. It is one that is necessary to grasp today.

Yet animals do not study evolutionary theory, nor do the human cultures whose livelihood depends on hunting and harvesting them. Rather, what animals and hunters do is enter into communicative webs with one another. Since they must either ingest or evade one another to survive, they must attune their nervous systems to one another's actions—and particularly to one another's actions on the environment. This ancient biological "tuning" too is a form of *tracking*, a form of knowledge practice, a form of combusting the legible organization in the environment. When two animals are locked in an evolutionary struggle—say through competition for the same food resources, or as a part of a predator/prey relationship—we say that an "arms race" occurs.[24]

For example, millions of years ago when the earth warmed and many climate systems dried up, grasslands replaced much of the forest cover. This gave rise to the first megaherbivores—huge animals like today's elephants that graze and concentrate huge portions of the landscape's flora and plant bounty into its body in the form of meat. As the rule goes, where there is prey, there are predators. Where there is energy, there will be combusters.

Thus saber-toothed cats evolved, specialists of a specific type of thrashing kill to which the megaherbivores were vulnerable, and the cats thrived. Then new species of hyena arrived on the evolutionary scene, with totally different behaviors, to scavenge the remains of these kills. When humans arrived sometime later, the megaherbivores were a prime and viable prey, and the famous cerebral and social efficiency of the humans ultimately denied the saber-toothed cats the only meal they were adapted to procure, and they soon died out.[25]

The hyenas, generalists that they are, were more versatile, and so began to evolve in a new direction toward accommodation of the new species imposing on their habitat: humans.[26] Here the webs of influence and communication are largely imperceptible, or shall we say embedded; they take place over great periods of time, are not available to perception or discernment within the attention or even life span of a single animal, yet the efficient transfer and circulation of information takes place regardless. The world and the species that make it transform.

This is one way in which the landscape is continually harvested or combusted by animal continuums. But it is not food, and the energy stored within it, that is in play here, but rather the economic information produced within, and distributed throughout, the broader ecology.

There are many forms of environmental combustion. I feel compelled to consider two others—the ecology of both teeth and brains. I remain uncertain as to whether teeth are not actually the greater determinant of an animal's life and culture, or better, of its *umwelt*. Teeth determine not only what an animal will look like, how it will socialize, how large it will be, with what other animals and forces in the landscape it will relate, and what types of behaviors it will evolve, but also what part of the landscape, and in what modality, the animal will seek to combust; in sum, teeth tell the whole evolutionary story, and nowhere more dramatically than in the ecological transition stories of ape to man. This is why paleoanthropologists so often find teeth when almost no other remains of an animal or its material civilization are present in the fossil record. But teeth tell a very important and very rich story. It is not only because teeth are frequently all that we have with which to cook up a story that they are so important; it is because they are *the* determinant features in an animal's life and culture. An animal's teeth determine what it can eat, and therefore to what elements in the landscape the rest of its being must direct itself and relate. And this in fact is all that any animal form is: the elements to which its forms relate.

Teeth tell the whole evolutionary story. From teeth one can determine all of the styles of an animal. This has been especially useful in studies of hominids. Changes in dentition reflected changes in social life, which reflected changes in food procurement, which reflected changes in landscape, which reflected changes in climate. This far the story is well known: ancient global warming and shifts in the rift valley plates decimated forests and produced savannahs. Primates were forced from shady treetops into the sunny plains. Diet was no longer principally fruit and seeds but now included meat. Hominid teeth record these transformations in minute detail. But teeth also incorporate (or combust) other environmental data. Procuring meat required great mental skill as well as social cooperation in the hunt. Surviving in the savannah required special adaptations such as bipedalism. All of these pressures together produced two related things: on one hand, encephalization—the rapid expansion of the brain case—and the emergence of language. The demands that these two pressures placed on the shape of the face were huge, and the teeth reflected these changes and combusted them nicely.

In the wilder animal world, an even more incredible story can be told regarding the evolution of what are known as "carnassial" teeth. These are teeth specialized for shearing and grinding. It may be said that the enormously evolutionary successful form of the hyena is a direct product of the emergence of carnassials into the wild. Originally primarily a scavenger, the hyena line developed an amazing adaptation with the appearance of its prodigious carnassials: it could now grind bones and live off of them when necessary for months at a time. The hyena, adept at challenging even lions for the spoils of their own kills, must often eat under severe harassment and for very uncertain periods. Its astoundingly powerful jaws and huge carnassials make it the most efficient eater on land: it can devour thirty-five pounds of flesh within its first minutes at a kill. The entire history of meat eating and the practice of one animal capturing another and ingesting it—in a word, predation—is the history of the evolution of the "carnassial shear," the function that allowed the most concentrated parts of the landscape—the animal—to harvest the bounties stored within other animals (and thus also make possible the evolutionary processes that require great amounts of energy to sustain, such as of course the mammalian brain). But the carnassial shear appeared first almost 65 million years ago in an ancient animal known as *Cimolestes* and was transmitted to a later group of terrifying prehistoric beasts known by the order name of Creodonta. Luckily for us, the creodonts had *only* great carnassials, and so, when the climate changed and they had to adapt to eating fruits and seeds and insects, they were out of luck, and they died. Next came the Miacids, who had molars behind their carnassials— the winning combination. Enter the omnivores who are able to eat anything, and who are able, more significantly, to adapt their behaviors without having to wait for an adaptation in the body plan.

Teeth also tell the broader story of the evolution of vertebrate predation and the general distribution and parcelling of resources in the environment:

there is no flower, for example, that has not incorporated these often violent stories and scenes. Let it be said then that the story of teeth, perhaps the most detailed lesson in adaptive form that we have—of which a single chapter is the emergence of the carnassial tooth that gave rise to the omnivorous combusters, or the generalists, whose lifestyle versatility created the ecological opening to allow evolution to bear no further on major body plan issues, but at last on brain development and cortical plasticity. Enter the large brain.

Large brains are clearly enjoyed by many of the animals that own them, but the fact remains, they are extremely expensive.[27] For not only are brains extremely expensive to run, requiring a great deal of high-quality food to power them, their high metabolic rate makes them prodigious producers of heat, and so they are also very expensive to keep cool. Brains are made up of exquisitely sensitive tissue, such that even a four-degree rise in its temperature is likely to result in death. You can't have a big brain without a very sophisticated cooling system. But as the newest stories about co-evolution of landscapes and organisms develop today, we are also learning that climate change—specifically the dramatic heating up of the environment 4 to 5 million years ago—was a prime cause (or was it a precondition?) of encephalization and hominization. As the environment got hotter, it also got dryer (at least in Africa where it mattered most in the late Pliocene and early Pleistocene), causing forest habitats to shrink and savannahs and grassy plains to flourish. Apes, as the story goes, needed to find food out in the open—a dangerous place fraught with seasoned predators—and so required an advantage of some type to protect them. What they got were several interconnected ones. The first problem was how to move quickly through the dangerous open spaces while carrying one's young. This problem was said to be solved by upright posture and the freeing of the hands for novel uses.[28] With a new set of ecological potentials for the hands (freed from locomotion) came new cultural possibilities (the central problem of hominoid and hominin ecology). Freed hands provided an opening—perhaps even a demand—for a new and enlarged brain to program them (the rise of tool industry, etc.). But the new environmental heat placed unprecedented stress on the animal to keep cool. A large, sensitive, heat-producing, and expensive brain represented a dangerous added burden, unless a highly innovative system of cooling could be found. Among the arguments that I find interesting today, and these are ones to which primatologist Richard Wrangham has recently supplied some highly provocative reinterpretations, have argued that the invention of a novel air-conditioning system constitutes the defining feature of, and even evolutionary impetus behind, the emergence of the human species.

Because humans have large brains, short faces, and special teeth—all effects of the environment-derived pressures to change diet and hence modalities of combustion—they do not possess snouts and therefore lack the hollow nasal chambers and the veinous adaptations in the head that most animals use to cool the blood that feeds the brain. If apes aspired to compete in savannah habitats, they were going to require innovative adaptations to manage the heat stress that came with this environment. All other savannah mammals use "selective cooling" based on the protruding face, the hollow snout, and a carotid rete in which blood is pooled in the sinus area or neck for cooling.[29] Humans cannot do this—their brain is proportionately too large, requiring a neck as wide as its thorax; they must use general (or full-body) cooling.

The first adaptation toward this end is said to be the achievement of upright posture, which has been calculated to cut heat load by more than 30 percent by exposing far less of the animal's body surface to the direct rays of the sun; it also moves the brain and organs away from the ground surface, where temperatures are significantly higher. The second is the shedding of the fur covering—the development of naked skin and the profuse sweating that permits ultra-efficient radiation of heat through evaporation.[30] But for this last adaptation, the animal would require regular access to considerable quantities of water; the increase in travel range and the size of hunting and scavenging habitat was an important result both of the entirely novel form of human bipedal locomotion and the cerebral cortex used in calculating interrelationships, navigational and otherwise.

What we encounter here is a whole "modulus" or network of relationships and especially forms, each changing in collaboration and communication with the others. But there were other more internal and less visible transformations that matter, ones involving feedback phenomena. Among the most important is how the emerging human form—and the human cultural type—managed not only its heat budget but its metabolic budget. If the brain is made up of expensive tissue that requires a great deal of extra calories and water to maintain, it is also true that no animal could pursue such a high-maintenance economic life if it did not have a very large brain. But more basic than this is the way the body sought to balance its books. It has been widely noted that the human gut is very short compared with that of other mammals of comparable size (indeed half the predicted length). In addition, physiological studies show that the intestines contribute as much or more to an animal's "basal metabolic rate"—the rate at which it combusts energy at rest—than does the brain. Intestines are also very expensive tissue. The massive increase in human brain size, according to a widely discussed theory of Leslie Aiello and Peter Wheeler, was thus balanced by a decrease in gut size, and this had definitive repercussions on every aspect of the human world. The first and most basic effect was to require a whole new approach to eating (Wrangham's most recent domain), the absolute requirement for very high quality nutritious foods that can be eaten in small quantities but at frequent and regular intervals.[31] This meant highly selective foraging and judicious identification particularly of reproductive elements, the most nutritionally dense parts of the environment: seeds, tubers, nuts, eggs. It also meant procuring protein and fat in the form of meat, an activity requiring immense adaptations for strategic hunting, which included the need to act in coordinated and cooperative social groups, and even, as Wrangham has stunningly suggested, to the rise of the family group and to the particularities of the age-old relations between the sexes.

The bottom line here is to affirm that the large brain is at once directly and indirectly a product and an expression of climate and ecology: it emerged as a response to an increasingly hot and dry environment and in tandem with the evolution of a novel and biologically unique cooling system. But once the movement toward encephalization began, a broad set of other regimes necessarily were triggered, based on the need to extract from the environment the resources to keep the brain running. Human life, the human physical form—including our beautiful faces, flat stomachs, dexterous hands, subtle humor, etc.—our complex behaviors, and our notable species achievements such as language, technology, and culture, may be little more than ecological responses to the broader and more mundane economics of satisfying the dietary and ethological demands of a large brain.

From this foundation, the entire human relationship to the environment was forever determined. Encephalization, one could argue, was not in itself driven by any need or desire to break off from the animal evolutionary tree in the direction of culture and language but occurred as a direct result of climate change and was triggered by the invention of a novel cooling system, followed by the requirements of food procurement (shall we now say "preparation") and the management of interspecies threats in a new ecological niche, and in a new landscape. These latter forces imposed on us the need for ever-more subtle ways of reading, remembering, and interacting with the environment, discovering ever-new opportunities within it. If we are human, it is because this Science of the Environment—empirical and intellectual combustion of our surrounding world—was forced upon us, and it is the source of our very human genius for formal and technical invention.

Notes

1_ Alexander Von Humboldt and Aimé Bonpland, *Essay on the Geography of Plants* (Chicago: University of Chicago Press, 2010).

2_ Ibid.

3_ Johann Wolfgang von Goethe, *The Metamorphosis of Plants*, translated by Douglas Miller, and with an introduction and photographs by Gordon L. Miller, Jr. (Cambridge, MA: MIT Press, 2009 [1790].

4_ Ernst Cassirer, *Rousseau, Kant, Goethe* (Rome: Donzelli Editore, 1999).

5_ Charles Darwin and Alfred Wallace, "On the Tendency of Species to Form Varieties; and on the Perpetuation of Varieties and Species by Natural Means of Selection," *Journal of the Proceedings of the Linnean Society of London. Zoology* 3.9 (1858): 45–62.

6_ Ernst Mayr, "Typological versus Population Thinking," *Conceptual Issues in Evolutionary Biology* (1994), 157–160.

7_ Herbert A. Simon, "The Architecture of Complexity," *Proceedings of the American Philosophical Society* 106.6 (1962): 467–482.

8_ J.A. Drake, "The Mechanics of Community Assembly and Succession," *Journal of Theoretical Biology* 147 (1990): 213–233.

9_ S.L. Pimm, *The Balance of Nature? Ecological Issues in the Conservation of Species and Communities* (Chicago: University of Chicago Press, 1991).

10_ George Evelyn Hutchinson, "On Living in the Biosphere," *The Scientific Monthly* 67 (1970): 393–397.

11_ Lynn Margulis, "A Pox Called Man," in Lynn Margulis and Dorion Sagan, *Slanted Truths: Essays on Gaia, Symbiosis, and Evolution* (New York: Springer, 1997), 247–261.

12_ L. Margulis and J.E. Lovelock, "Gaia and Geognosy," in *Global Ecology: Towards a Science of the Biosphere,* Mitchell B. Rambler, Lynn Margulis, and René Fester, eds. (San Diego, CA: Academic Press, 1989).

13_ Vladimir I. Vernadsky and Mark McMenamin, *La biosphere* (New York: Copernicus, 1998).

14_ Jakob von Uexküll, "An Introduction to *Umwelt*," *Semiotica* 134 (2001), 107–110.

15_ Jakob von Uexküll, "A Stroll through the Worlds of Animals and Men: A Picture Book of Invisible Worlds," *Semiotica* 89 (1992): 319–391.

16_ P.E. Stander et al., "Tracking and the Interpretation of Spoor: A Scientifically Sound Method in Ecology," *Journal of Zoology* 242.2 (1997), 329–341.

17_ Dereck Joubert and Beverly Joubert, *Eternal Enemies: Lions and Hyenas,* DVD, National Geographic, 2003.

18_ Bruce Chatwin, *The Songlines* (New York: Random House, 1998).

19_ Elias Canetti, *Crowds and Power* (New York: Macmillan, 1962).

20_ Louis Liebenberg, *The Art of Tracking: The Origin of Science* (Cape Town: Creda Press, 1990).

21_ Tom Brown, *Tom Brown's Field Guide to Wilderness Survival* (New York: Berkley, 1983).

22_ Jules Michelet, *The Bird* (London: Thomas Nelson, 1868).

23_ Georges Bataille, *The Accursed Share*, vol. 1, translated by Robert Hurley (New York: Zone Books, 1991).

24_ Edmund D. Brodie III and Edmund D. Brodie Jr., "Predator-Prey Arms Races," *Bioscience* 49.7 (1999), 557–568.

25_ Wolfgang Nentwig, "Human Environmental Impact in the Paleolithic and Neolithic," *Handbook of Paleoanthropology* (Berlin, Heidelberg: Springer, 2007), 1881–1900.

26_ Mary C. Stiner, "Comparative Ecology and Taphonomy of Spotted Hyenas, Humans, and Wolves in Pleistocene Italy," *Revue de Paléobiologie* 23.2 (2004), 771–785.

27_ Leslie C. Aiello and Peter Wheeler, "The Expensive-Tissue Hypothesis: The Brain and the Digestive System in Human and Primate Evolution," *Current Anthropology* 36.2 (1995): 199–221.

28_ B.A. Sigmon, "Bipedal Behavior and the Emergence of Erect Posture in Man," *American Journal of Physical Anthropology* 34.1 (1971): 55–60.

29_ Duncan Mitchell et al., "Adaptive Heterothermy and Selective Brain Cooling in Arid-Zone Mammals," *Comparative Biochemistry and Physiology Part B: Biochemistry and Molecular Biology* 131.4 (2002): 571–585.

30_ Peter E. Wheeler, "The Evolution of Bipedality and Loss of Functional Body Hair in Hominids," *Journal of Human Evolution* 13.1 (1984), 91–98.

31_ Richard Wrangham, *Catching Fire: How Cooking Made Us Human* (New York: Basic Books, 2009).

Adaptability is the capacity to adapt to ecosystem dynamics and the resulting changes that normally occur in any living system; the capacity for learning and transformation are fundamental attributes. For actors in a given system, it can also refer to their ability to manage that system's resilience, either by moving the system toward or away from change thresholds, or by altering the underlying features of the system within its current state.[1] NML

1. After Gunderson et al. (1995, 2002), Holling (1973, 1978, 1996), Lister (1998, 2008), and Folke et al. (2010).

ADAPTABILITY

Here, an ongoing set of prompts, interventions, and triggers renew or redirect processes-in-action; design has agency and intention in the act of redirecting, but it in no way is fully controllable—the mechanics at work are autonomous, independent. In this way, the designer becomes a producer or curator of effects, of dynamics, and of a whole range of social-environmental-urban conditions. Bee behavior in response to temperature, the careful and interactive staging of construction processes and growth mechanisms; training and management practices that spur new independent ecologies; the collusion of hydrologic and social agendas; emergent practice models; lifespan and project renewal processes; coordinated maintenance, operations, and administration regimens are all activated in the broader project of design thinking. CR

Bernd Heinrich. Thermoregulation of a Swarm Cluster of Bees. 1981.

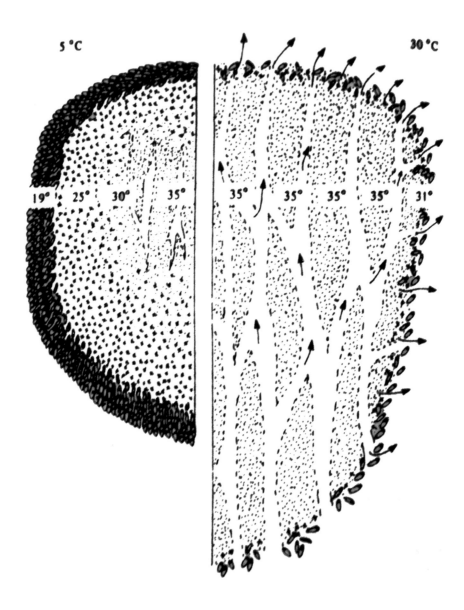

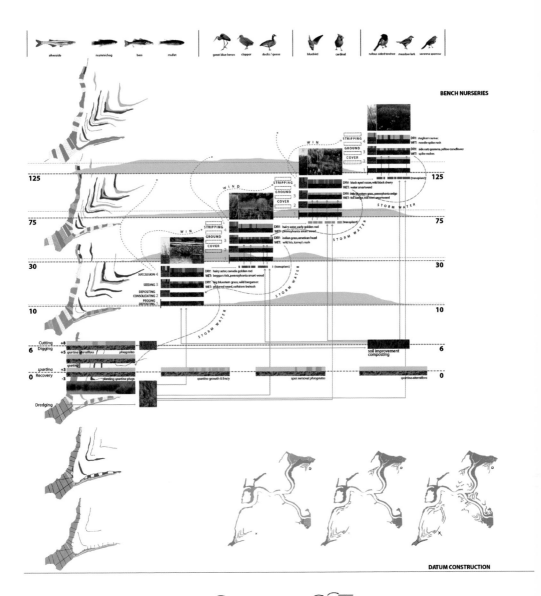

BENCH NURSERIES

DATUM CONSTRUCTION

DYNAMIC - 3

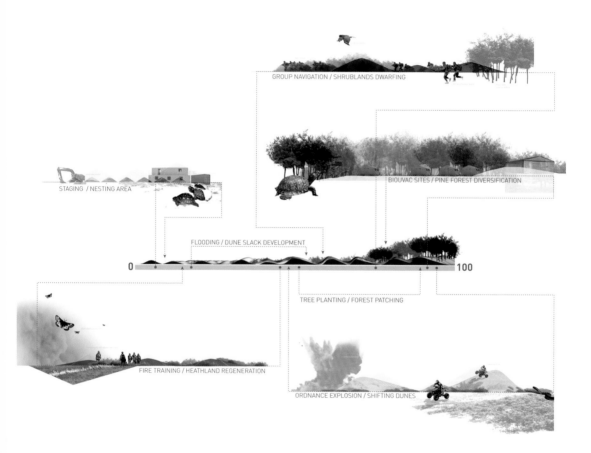

NON-LINEAR HABITAT MANAGEMENT
MASSACHUSETTS MILITARY RESERVATION

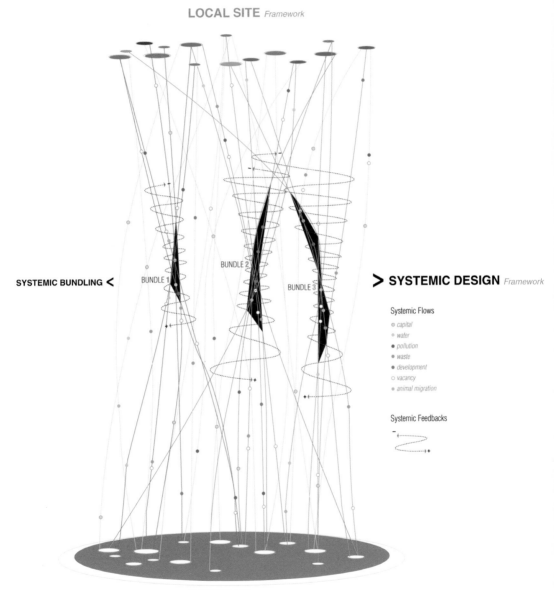

LOCAL SITE *Framework*

SYSTEMIC BUNDLING ‹

BUNDLE 1

BUNDLE 2

BUNDLE 3

› **SYSTEMIC DESIGN** *Framework*

Systemic Flows

- capital
- water
- pollution
- waste
- development
- vacancy
- animal migration

Systemic Feedbacks

REGIONAL *Framework*

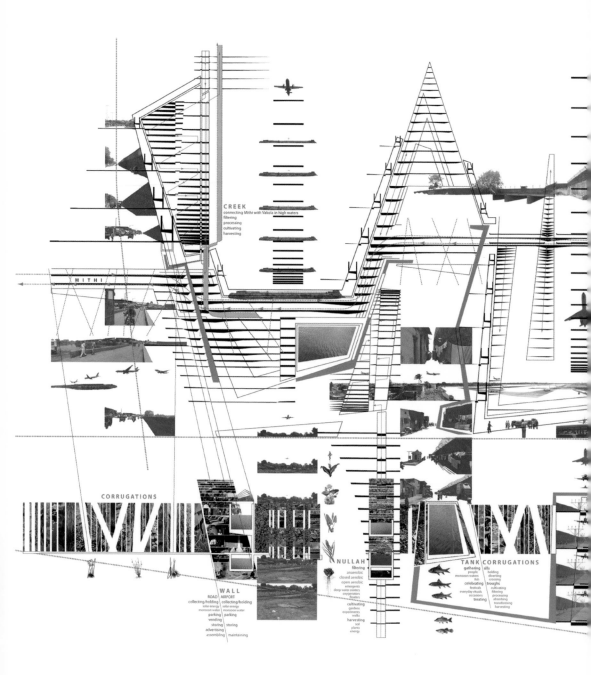

MITHI

NULLAH FIELD
filtering
treating
. anaerobic
. closed aerobic
. open aerobic
emergents
deep water zones
oxygenation
floaters
cultivating
gardens
experiments
walks
harvesting
soil
plants
energy
parking

CORRUGATIONS

NOV
DEC
JAN
FEB
MAR
APR
MAY
JUN
JUL
AUG
SEP
OCT

WALL
AIRPORT
collecting/holding
solar energy
monsoon water
parking

storing

maintaining

SETTLEMENT
collecting/holding
solar energy
monsoon water
parking
vending
storing
working
toileting
filtering
processing
cultivating

MAIDAN
playing
cultivating
celebrating
gathering
holding
fairs
games
rallies
water
parking

NULLAH
filtering
processing
cultivating
harvesting

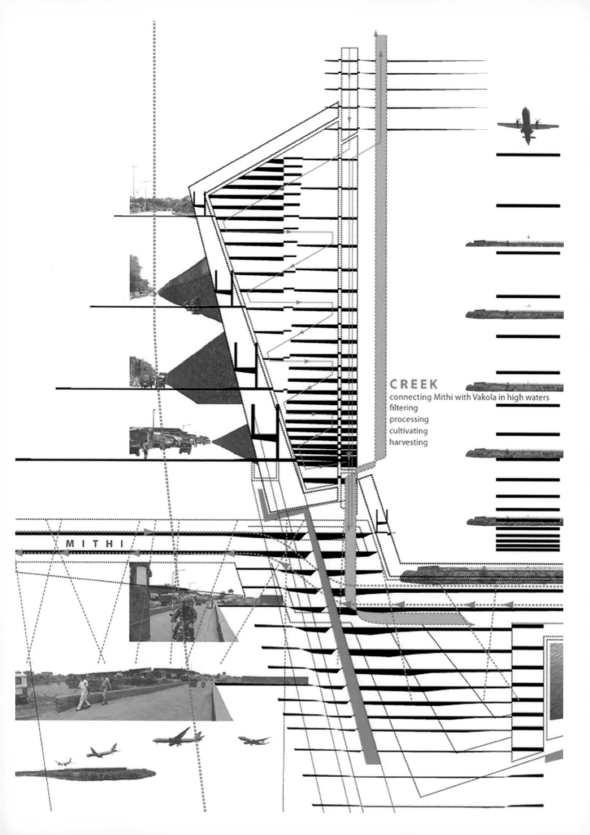

CREEK
connecting Mithi with Vakola in high waters
filtering
processing
cultivating
harvesting

MITHI

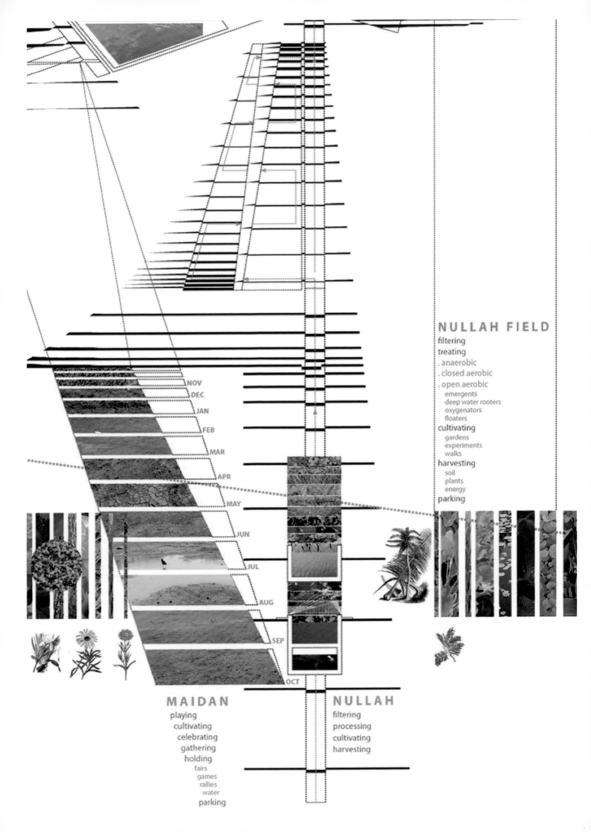

NULLAH FIELD
filtering
treating
. anaerobic
. closed aerobic
. open aerobic
    emergents
    deep water rooters
    oxygenators
    floaters
cultivating
    gardens
    experiments
    walks
harvesting
    soil
    plants
    energy
parking

NOV
DEC
JAN
FEB
MAR
APR
MAY
JUN
JUL
AUG
SEP
OCT

MAIDAN
playing
cultivating
celebrating
gathering
holding
    fairs
    games
    rallies
    water
parking

NULLAH
filtering
processing
cultivating
harvesting

Stoss/Chris Reed, Scott Bishop, Megan Studer. Lifecycles. Ephemeral Fields, Herinneringspark, Belgium. 2010.

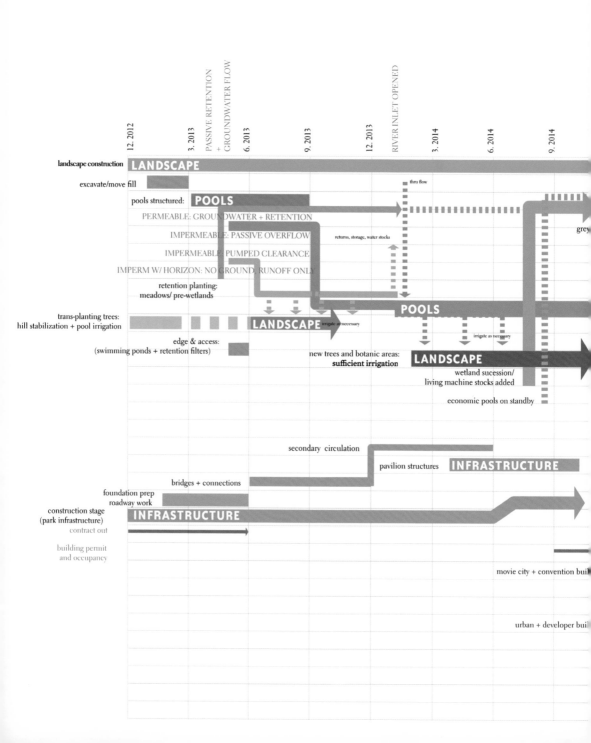

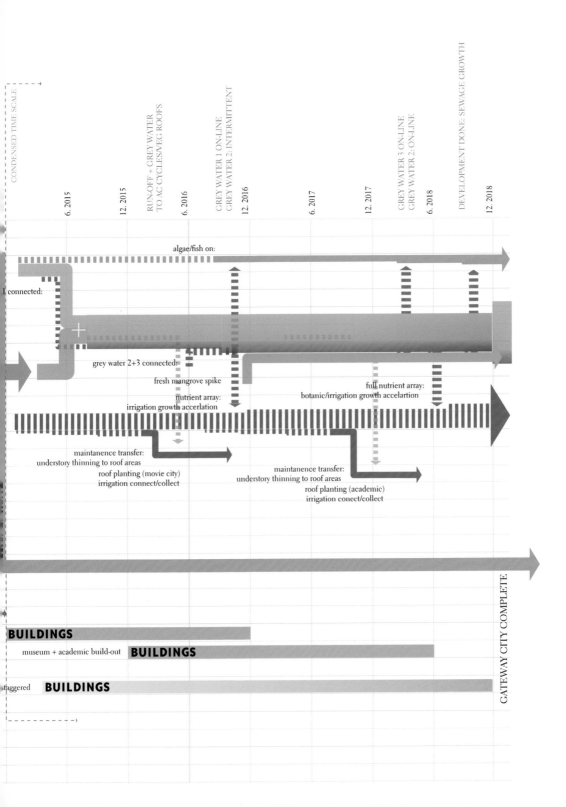

CONDENSED TIME SCALE

6. 2015

12. 2015

RUN-OFF + GREY WATER
TO AC CYCLES/VEG. ROOFS

6. 2016

GREY WATER 1 ON-LINE
GREY WATER 2: INTERMITTENT

12. 2016

6. 2017

12. 2017

GREY WATER 3 ON-LINE
GREY WATER 2: ON-LINE

6. 2018

DEVELOPMENT DONE: SEWAGE GROWTH

12. 2018

algae/fish on:

1 connected:

grey water 2+3 connected:

fresh mangrove spike

nutrient array:
irrigation growth accerlation

full nutrient array:
botanic/irrigation growth accelartion

maintanence transfer:
understory thinning to roof areas

roof planting (movie city)
irrigation connect/collect

maintanence transfer:
understory thinning to roof areas

roof planting (academic)
irrigation conect/collect

BUILDINGS

museum + academic build-out   BUILDINGS

staggered   BUILDINGS

GATEWAY CITY COMPLETE

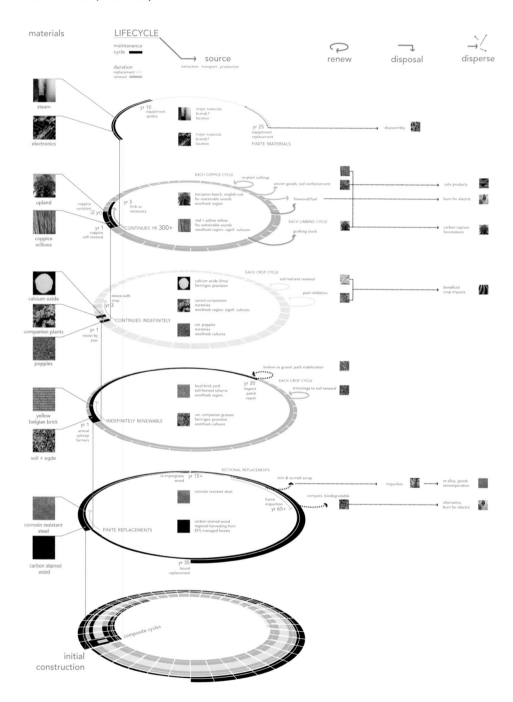

Stoss/Chris Reed, Megan Studer, Scott Bishop. Productive Landscape Ecologies. Detroit, USA. 2012. (SEE POSTER)

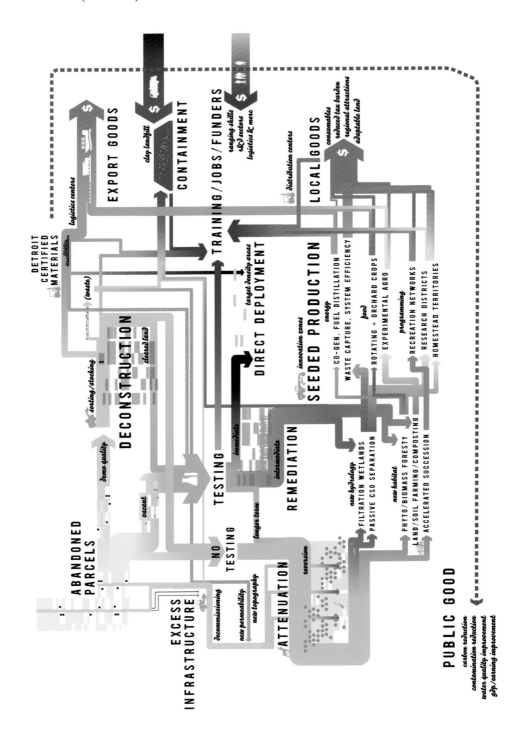

References for Drawings Commentary

Clements, Frederic E. *Plant Succession: An Analysis of the Development of Vegetation.* Washington, DC: Carnegie Institution of Washington, 1916.

Corning, Peter A. "The Re-Emergence of 'Emergence': A Venerable Concept in Search of a Theory." *Complexity* 7(6), 2002: 18–30.

Cowles, Henry C. "The Causes of Vegetational Cycles." *Annals of the Association of American Geographers* 1(1), 1911: 3-20.

Folke, C., S. Carpenter, B. Walker, M. Scheffer, T. Chapin, and J. Rockström. "Resilience Thinking: Integrating Resilience, Adaptability, and Transformability." *Ecology and Society* 15(4), 2010.

Gleason, Henry A. "The Individualistic Concept of the Plant Association." *Bulletin of the Torrey Botanical Club* 53, 1926: 7–26.

Gleason, Henry A. "Further Views on the Succession-Concept." *Ecology* 8(3), 1927: 299–326.

Gunderson, L., and C.S. Holling, eds. *Panarchy: Understanding Transformations in Human and Natural Systems.* Washington, DC: Island Press, 2002.

Gunderson, L., C.S. Holling, and S.S. Light, eds. *Barriers and Bridges to the Renewal of Regional Ecosystems.* New York: Columbia University Press, 1995.

Holling, C. S. "Resilience and Stability of Ecological Systems." *Annual Review of Ecology and Systematics* 4, 1973: 1–23.

Holling, C. S., ed. *Adaptive Environmental Assessment and Management.* London: John Wiley and Sons, 1978.

Holling, C.S. "Engineering Resilience versus Ecological Resilience." In P.C. Schulze, ed., *Engineering Within Ecological Constraints.* Washington, DC: National Academy Press, 1996, 51–66.

Lister, N-M. "A Systems Approach to Biodiversity Conservation Planning." *Environmental Monitoring and Assessment* 49 (2/3), 1998: 123–155.

Waltner-Toews, D., J.J. Kay, and N-M. Lister, eds. *The Ecosystem Approach: Complexity, Uncertainty, and Managing for Sustainability.* New York: Columbia University Press, 2008.

CONTRIBUTORS

Nina-Marie Lister is Associate Professor and Associate Director of Urban + Regional Planning at Ryerson University in Toronto. She is a Registered Professional Planner (MCIP, RPP) with a background in landscape ecology and environmental planning, and the founding principal of plandform, a creative studio practice exploring the relationship between landscape, ecology, and infrastructure.

Chris Reed is Principal of Stoss Landscape Urbanism in Boston and Associate Professor of Practice in Landscape Architecture at the Harvard Graduate School of Design. His work on landscapes and cities has been recognized internationally, including the National Design Award for Landscape Architecture from the Cooper-Hewitt National Design Museum and the Topos International Landscape Award.

Daniel Botkin is a scientist who studies life from a planetary perspective, a biologist who has helped solve major environmental issues, and a writer about nature. He is known for his scientific contributions in ecology and environment, and he has also worked as a professional journalist and has degrees in physics, biology, and literature. His latest books are *The Moon in the Nautilus Shell* (Oxford University Press, 2012) and *Powering the Future: A Scientist's Guide to Energy Independence* (FT Press, 2010).

James Corner is founder of James Corner Field Operations, based in New York City, and Professor at the University of Pennsylvania School of Design. His projects include the High Line and Qianhai City. Books include *The Landscape Imagination* (Princeton Architectural Press, 2014) and *Recovering Landscape* (Princeton Architectural Press, 1999). He received the National Design Award in 2010.

Robert E. Cook was formerly the director of the Arnold Arboretum. He is a biologist with a special interest in plant populations ecology. Previously he had been the director of Cornell Plantations and an Associate Professor of Ecology and Systematics at Cornell University. He retired in 2010.

Peter Del Tredici is Senior Research Scientist at the Arnold Arboretum of Harvard University and Associate Professor of Practice in Landscape Architecture at the Harvard Graduate School of Design. He is the author of *Wild Urban Plants of the Northeast*, published by Cornell University Press in 2010. In 2013 he was awarded the Veitch Gold Medal by The Royal Horticultural Society (England) "in recognition of services given in the advancement of the science and practice of horticulture."

Wenche E. Dramstad is Senior Research Scientist at the Norwegian Forest and Landscape Institute. Her studies have focused on natural resources management and landscape ecology. Previous work has included management of the Norwegian monitoring program for agricultural landscapes, and she continues work in linking ecologists and land-use planners.

Erle Ellis is Associate Professor of Geography and Environmental Systems at the University of Maryland, Baltimore County, and a Visiting Associate Professor of Landscape Architecture at the Harvard Graduate School of Design. His research investigates the ecology of anthropogenic landscapes and their changes at local to global scales toward informing sustainable stewardship of the biosphere in the Anthropocene.

David Fletcher is Associate Professor of Architecture at California College of the Arts. He is an urban designer, landscape architect, and writer. His work addresses process, urbanized watersheds, green infrastructure, and aesthetics. David is the founding principal of Fletcher Studio, an innovative and award-winning practice based in San Francisco.

Richard T. T. Forman is Research Professor of Advanced Environmental Studies in the Field of Landscape Ecology at Harvard University. His primary scholarly interest is linking science with spatial pattern to interweave nature and people on the land. Often considered to be a "father" of landscape ecology and of road ecology, he increasingly helps spearhead urban ecology.

M. A. Goldberg is trained as an economist. His work has included the development of the employment location models for the University of California's Bay Area Simulation Study. In addition, he has studied the interactions between land values, land rents, and transportation in urban areas, from both theoretical and empirical points of view.

Christopher Hight is an Associate Professor and Director of Undergraduate Studies at the Rice University School of Architecture. His first book, *Architectural Principles in the Age of Cybernetics* (Routledge, 2008), examined problems of architecture subjectivity and epistemology since the middle of the twentieth century. His current design research explores hybrid design strategies that mediate social, natural, and subjective ecologies. He is currently developing a book entitled *Spaces of Envelopment* that critically examines the genealogy of ecology within recent design discourse and practice.

C. S. Holling is a systems ecologist by training and has developed computer-simulation models of predator-prey interactions in ecological systems. He has extended many of these functional relationships to successfully simulate recreational land speculation in the Gulf Islands near Vancouver. He is a Fellow of the Royal Society of Canada and has been awarded the Austrian Cross of Honour for Arts and Science.

Sanford Kwinter is Professor of Architectural Theory and Criticism at the Harvard Graduate School of Design. He is a writer and editor who holds a PhD in Comparative Literature from Columbia University. He has written widely on philosophical issues of design, architecture and urbanism, and science and technology.

Sean Lally is the founder of Sean Lally/WEATHERS and an Assistant Professor at the University of Illinois at Chicago. He is the author of *The Air from Other Planets: A Brief History of Architecture to Come* (Lars Müller, 2013), and the recipient of the 2012 Prince Charitable Trusts Rome Prize from the American Academy in Rome in Landscape Architecture.

Katherine A. McGowan is Lead Researcher on the Social Prosperity Wood Buffalo project and former McConnell Post-Doctoral Fellow in Social Innovation at SiG@Waterloo. She has advanced work at the Waterloo Institute for Social Innovation and Resilience on developing social innovation theory based on historical case studies. With a doctorate in Canadian History, she focuses her research on studying the history of social innovations and broad system change, and on social enterprise and social change in Aboriginal communities in Canada.

James D. Olson is a contributing author of *Landscape Ecology Principles in Landscape Architecture and Land-Use Planning* and a specialist in ecologically based design and management projects. He earned a Masters in Landscape Architecture at the Harvard University Graduate School of Design and a Masters of Business Administration at the Columbia University Graduate Business School.

Charles Waldheim is the John E. Irving Professor and Chair of Landscape Architecture at Harvard's Graduate School of Design. His research examines the relationships between landscape and contemporary urbanism. Waldheim is recipient of the Rome Prize Fellowship from the American Academy in Rome; the Visiting Scholar Research Fellowship at the Study Centre of the Canadian Centre for Architecture; and the Sanders Fellowship at the University of Michigan.

Frances Westley is the J.W. McConnell Chair in Social Innovation at the University of Waterloo and a lead in the Canada-wide Social Innovation Generation (SiG) partnership. Co-author of *Getting to Maybe* (Vintage Canada, 2006), Westley is an internationally renowned scholar and consultant in social innovation, sustainable development, strategic change, visionary leadership, and interorganizational collaboration.

Jane Wolff is an Associate Professor at the Daniels Faculty of Architecture, Landscape, and Design at the University of Toronto.

IMAGE CREDITS

Front cover: Tomás Folch and Chris Reed, after Folch, Chaudry, McClure, and Newey. Harvard Graduate School of Design, 2011.

25, 70: Reprinted with permission from Howard T. Odum, *Environment, Power, and Society*, Figure C, p. 3. New York: Wiley-Interscience, 1970.

33: Richard T.T. Forman, *Land Mosaics: The Ecology of Landscapes and Regions*, Figure 11.7, p. 387. New York: Cambridge University Press, 1995.

34: "Bloedel Pool in Snow," Mary Randlett. 1996.

35: Courtesy of Hargreaves Associates.

36, 139: Michel Desvigne Paysagiste. Originally published in Desvigne & Dalnoky, *The Return of the Landscape*. New York: Whitney Library of Design, 1997.

68–69: Architectural Archives of the University of Pennsylvania.

71: Reprinted from William Whyte, *The Social Life of Small Urban Spaces*. New York: Project for Public Spaces, 1980.

72: Courtesy of West 8.

73: Courtesy of GROSS.MAX.

74–75: Courtesy of Andrea Hansen.

76–79, 142–147: Courtesy of Pierre Bélanger.

80–81: Courtesy of Aranda-Lasch.

82–83: Courtesy of Robert Pietrusko.

114–115: C.S. Holling and M.A. Goldberg. "Ecology and Planning," *Journal of the American Institute of Planners*, vol. 37:2, 1971. Published by Taylor and Francis.

136: Edward Lorenz, *The Essence of Chaos*. Seattle: University of Washington Press, 1993. Courtesy of the author's family.

137, 140–141, 214–215, 282: Courtesy of James Corner Field Operations.

138, 279: Courtesy of OMA.

148: Stephen Hubbell, *The Unified Neutral Theory of Biodiversity and Biogeography*. Princeton: Princeton University Press, 2001.

149: Brennan Baxley.

150–154: Michael Ezban.

170–171, 173, 176, 178: Erle C. Ellis.

186: **Figure 1**: National Oceanic and Atmospheric Administration. Site and date of access: http://www.katrina.noaa.gov/helicopter/images/katrina-new-orleans-flooding3-2005b.jpg, 1 May 2012.

188: **Figure 2**: Library of Congress, Geography and Map Division, Washington, D.C. Catalog Number 2003627055. Site and date of access: http://www.loc.gov/item/2003627055, 15 May 2013.

Figure 3: United States Geographic and Geodetic Survey, 1:24000 series, New Orleans East, New Orleans West, Spanish Fort, and Indian Beach quadrangles, 1998 and 1999 series.

190: **Figures 4a and 4b**: *Gutter to Gulf*, a research and teaching initiative at the University of Toronto and Washington University. Drawing authors: Jenny Bukovec, Annie Idris, Greg Warren, and Lu Zhang, University of Toronto, winter term 2010.

192: **Figure 5**: *Gutter to Gulf*, a research and teaching initiative at the University of Toronto and Washington University. Drawing authors: Tyler Bradt, Greg Bunker, Malgorzata Farun, Mengjie Han, Robin Heathcote, Jessica Wagner, and Yi Zhou, University of Toronto, winter term 2012.

196: **Figure 6**: *Gutter to Gulf*, a research and teaching initiative at the University of Toronto and Washington University. Drawings synthesized by Jonathan Dowse from the work of the Gutter to Gulf studios, winter term 2010.

198: **Figure 7**: Photograph by Jane Wolff.

200: **Figure 8**: *Gutter to Gulf* initiative.

206: Courtesy of Richard Forman. Wenche E. Dramstad, James D. Olson, and Richard T.T. Forman, *Landscape Ecology Principles in Landscape Architecture and Land-Use Planning*. Washington, D.C.: Island Press, 1996.

207: Stephen Hubbell, redrawn by Michael Ezban. *The Unified Neutral Theory of Biodiversity and Biogeography*. Princeton: Princeton University Press, 2001.

208–211: Dereck Revington Studio.

212: Anuradha Mathur and Dilip da Cunha, *Mississippi Floods: Designing a Shifting Landscape*. New Haven: Yale University Press, 2001.

213, 280, 288–289, 364–367: Courtesy Chris Reed/Stoss Landscape Urbanism, images copyright Stoss Inc.

216: Jing Zhang.

217: Sean Lally.

220, 225: Robert E. Cook.

241–255: Peter Del Tredici.

260, 261, 264, 266: Kazys Varnelis, Leah Meisterlin, David Fletcher.

272–273: David Fletcher.

278: Four Ecosystem Functions by C.S. Holling, redrawn from Lance Gunderson, *Resilience and the Behaviour of Large-Scale Systems*. Washington, D.C.: Island Press, 2002.

281: Christopher Tuccio.

283–284: Courtesy of Bradley Cantrell and Louisiana State University. Image by Christopher Hall.

285–287: Tomás Folch and Chris Reed.

305: Frances Westley and Katharine McGowan.

315, 321, 322, 324, 326, 329, 331: Sean Lally.

356: Reproduced with permission on the behalf of The Company of Biologists. Original source: Bernd Heinrich, "The Mechanisms and Energetics of Honeybee Swarm Temperature Regulation," p. 53, *Journal of Experimental Biology* (1981) 91:25–55.

357: Courtesy of Anuradha Mathur and Dilip da Cunha.

358: Geneva Wirth.

359: Alan Berger and Case Brown.

360–363: Anuradha Mathur and Dilip da Cunha, *Soak: Mumbai in an Estuary*. New Delhi: Rupa & Co., 2009.

Back cover: Robert Pietrusko.

POSTERS

PE1

Dynamics 1: Courtesy of Pierre Bélanger.
Dynamics 2: Courtesy of Robert Pietrusko.

Succession 1&2: Courtesy of James Corner Field Operations.

Adaptability 1: Anuradha Mathur and Dilip da Cunha with Tom Leader Studio.
Adaptability 2: Geneva Wirth.

Adaptability 3 & 4: Courtesy Chris Reed/Stoss Landscape Urbanism, images copyright Stoss Inc.

Resilience 1: Courtesy of James Corner Field Operations.
Resilience 2: Courtesy of Bradley Cantrell and Louisiana State University. Image by Christopher Hall.

Resilience 3: Four Ecosystem Functions by C.S. Holling, redrawn from Lance Gunderson, *Resilience and the Behaviour of Large-Scale Systems*. Washington, D.C., Island Press, 2002.
Resilience 4: Christopher Tuccio.

PE2

Dynamics 1: Lawrence Halprin Collection, The Architectural Archives, University of Pennsylvania.
Dynamics 2: Reprinted from William Whyte, *The Social Life of Small Urban Spaces*. New York: Project for Public Spaces, 1980.

Acknowledgments

Projective Ecologies grew out of a colloquium titled "Critical Ecologies" conceived and organized by Chris Reed in the spring of 2010; it was sponsored by the Harvard University Graduate School of Design and its Department of Landscape Architecture. Presentations by Richard Wrangham, Sanford Kwinter, Ann Dale, Peter Del Tredici, Alexander Felson, Steven Handel, Karen Kramer, Sune Lehmann, Nina-Marie Lister, Paul Moorcroft, Piet Oudolf, Steward Pickett, and Maximilian Schich—as well as conversations moderated by Charles Waldheim, Richard Forman, Anita Berrizbeitia, Christian Werthmann, and Michael Meredith—set a very broad table for taking stock of current thinking and practices across a range of disciplines relative to complex adaptive systems. The colloquium was instrumental in shaping the content and structure of this volume, and we very much appreciate the contributions of the colloquium participants, the contributors to this volume, and the authors of the drawings included here.

We would like to thank Mohsen Mostafavi and Patricia Roberts, Dean and Executive Dean, respectively, of the Harvard Graduate School of Design, and Charles Waldheim, Chair of the GSD Department of Landscape Architecture, for their steadfast support, resources, and contributions that have both informed the content of this work and allowed it to be presented in colloquium and book formats. In particular, we acknowledge the support of the GSD's John D. Scruggs Research Fund. We would also like to thank Assistant Dean of Communications Benjamin Prosky and Senior Editor Melissa Vaughn for their oversight and organizational and editorial contributions. Actar's Ramon Prat, Lluis Ortega, and Ricardo Devesa were fantastic in their efforts to organize and design this volume in a way that captures our full ambitions.

Thanks, too, to the phalanx of research assistants over a number of years who have helped to organize the publication and colloquium, and contributed to its content, including Christina Antiporda, Anne Clark Baker, Michael Ezban, Tomás Folch, Chris Alton, Marta Brocki, McKenna Cole, Kimberly Garza, and Difei Ma. Finally, we would like to recognize the various collective contributions of the incredibly insightful and interdisciplinary students in the research seminars we have taught at both the Harvard University Graduate School of Design and Ryerson University's Faculty of Community Services and the School of Urban and Regional Planning.

Chris Reed and Nina-Marie Lister

Imprint

Published by
Harvard University Graduate School of Design
www.gsd.harvard.edu
Actar Publishers, NY
www.actar.com

Edited by
Chris Reed
Nina-Marie Lister

Editorial supervision
Melissa Vaughn

Images supervision
Christina Antiporda

Graphic Design
Ramon Prat

Printing
Grafos, SA. Barcelona

Distributed by
Actar D
151, Grand Street, 5th Floor
New York, NY 10013 USA
Phone +1 212 966 2207
salesnewyork@actar-d.com
eurosales@actar-d.com
www.actar-d.com

ISBN 978-1-940291-12-3

A CIP catalogue record for this book is available from
the Library of Congress, Washington, D.C., USA

Harvard University
Graduate School of Design

www.gsd.harvard.edu

www.actar.com